Praise for Steve Larsen and

MY HEART HAS BEEN IN IT FROM THE START

"From the boardroom to the open road, Steve Larsen's memoir is a fascinating look at a life lived on the cutting edge of technology and adventure."
— Steven J. Snyder, Ph.D., Author of *Leadership and the Art of Struggle: How Great Leaders Grow through Challenge and Adversity*

"Steve's insights show that true mastery lies in simplifying the complex and lighting a path forward for everyone in the room."
— Tanaha Hairston, Impact Investor

"Steve Larsen takes us on the ride of a lifetime."
— Bill Dragoo, Dragoo Adventure Rider Training (DART)

"Steve Larsen turns setbacks into stepping stones, and transforms connections into lasting bonds."
— Ron Herem

"An unflinchingly honest story of faith, doubt and finding strength in the questions."
— The Rev. Dr. Kevin C. Brown, ordained minister (retired)

"From winding roads to boardroom battles, Steve Larsen takes us on an exhilarating ride."
— Chris Shipley, Author, *The Empathy Advantage*

"A heart-pounding journey through life's twists and turns. Larsen's passion for motorcycles leaps off the page, reminding us that life is meant to be lived at full throttle."
— Kazim Uzunoglu, Owner, *Kazoom Moto Adventures*

"Steve maps the complex path from sheltered faith to thoughtful questioning, articulating a journey many know but few can express. His path to agnosticism through 'honesty, respect and open inquiry' resonates across religious boundaries."
— Joseph Stickney, Catholic Church deacon

"Heart-stopping in more ways than one. From surviving multiple open-heart surgeries to navigating the digital revolution, Larsen's story is inspiring and captivating."
— Patrick DeValaria, MD and Cardiothoracic Surgeon

MY HEART HAS BEEN IN IT FROM THE START

MY HEART HAS BEEN IN IT FROM THE START

STEVE LARSEN

DIGITAL DYNAMICS, LLC | PHOENIX, ARIZONA

My Heart Has Been In It From The Start
© 2025 by Steve Larsen. All rights reserved.

Published in the United States of America by Digital Dynamics, LLC

ISBN 979-8-9915247-2-8 (hardcover)
ISBN 979-8-9915247-1-1 (paperback)
ISBN 979-8-9915247-0-4 (eBook)
Library of Congress Control Number: 2024925086

Steve Larsen is available for speaking engagements. Please email
steve@stevelarsen.net.

For bulk discounts, contact steve@stevelarsen.net.

Cover and interior design by AuthorImprints

Author photograph by Mark Trembley
Section illustrations by Margaret Larsen

Manufactured in the United States of America

To Maggie,

My wife, my partner and my secret weapon.

*This book, like so much of my life's work, owes its existence
to your brilliant mind and your magical way with words.*

*From dot matrix printer manuals to encyclopedia help systems,
from maintenance guides for classified aircraft to
capturing golfer Greg Norman's voice for a video game,
your words have touched countless lives, including mine.*

*You've made the complex simple and the technical accessible,
and working to live up to your standards has made me
look far smarter than I am.*

*Thank you for being my editor,
my teacher and my muse.*

CONTENTS

Acknowledgments   xi

INTRODUCTION   1

HEALTH: MATTERS OF THE HEART   9

  1 A Young Heart's Surgical Tale   11
  2 Time to Fix it Again   19
  3 Third Time's a Charm?   23
  4 Medicine and Science   26
  5 Amnesia and Other Recollections   32

CARS: A LIFE AMONG EXTRAORDINARY AUTOMOBILES   37

  6 The Genesis of a Car Enthusiast   39
  7 Hello Yellow: My 50-Year Love Affair with a Lotus Elan   43
  8 An Acura's Allure: The NSX that Stole My Heart   51
  9 Steve's Supercar Search: The Quest for the Ultimate Ride   59
10 Supercars and Automotive Humility   64
11 A Yellow Trilogy: Lotus, NSX and McLaren   67
12 Reflections on Precision Engineering   72

BUSINESS: A CAREER IN FAST FORWARD   75

13 Floating on Cigar Smoke and Martinis   78
14 Attics, Antiques and Airwaves   85
15 Amplifying My Career: The Schaak Electronics Experience   94

16 The Great Madeline Island Misadventure 110
17 The Digital Frontier: From Retail to Corporate Tech 116
18 Suits, Shake-ups and CDs 124
19 Goodbye AT&T—Hello Prodigy 134
20 Favorite Prodigy People and a Glass House 139
21 Rageboy and the Revolution: A Pivotal Moment in Tech 143
22 Prodigy's Potential and Payoff 150
23 Exit Strategy: Trading Stability for Startup Thrills 158
24 NETP and My Management Style 161
25 How Can You Tell I'm Not a Golfer? 170
26 Adventures in Venture: Making—and Following—My Own Path 174
27 The Google that Wasn't 182
28 Selling Inspiration: A Foray into Motivational Media 185
29 A Last Hurrah at PhoneTell 188
30 What Next? 191

FAMILY: THE TIES THAT BIND 195

31 The Oldest of the Youngest 197
32 Frozen Rivers and Bear Tales 202
33 Roots and Renovations: From Basements to Family Trees 208
34 Bums, Bullies and a Two-Finger Whistle 211
35 From Golden Gloves to Ghostly Encounters 218
36 Campaign Mischief: Adventures of Young Political Operatives 222
37 Summer Camp Chronicles 224
38 'Slow' to CEO: Unraveling Multiple Intelligences 226
39 New Horizons: Transformative Days at Fairmont High 232
40 Lost Letters and Found Family 236
41 Reinvention and Revelation: From Mayo High to Mankato 239
42 Fast-Track Learning: An Unconventional College Journey 244
43 Over this Laundry, I Thee Wed 249
44 Underwater Adventures: Close Calls in Pennekamp 252
45 Diapers, Dishes and Daddy's First Words 256
46 The Pirate Finger Payoff 261
47 Ski Slope Hubris: A Lesson in Humility 264
48 Ginger Takes Control 267
49 A Life Too Brief: A Tribute to Eric McKinley Larsen 272

50	A $183 Miracle: Twelve Kids Restore Faith	290
51	From Speed Demon to Barbie Boat	293
52	Sheep, Steak and Single Malts	297
53	A Father-Daughter Stage Legacy	305
54	A Father's Support: From Fish Tanks to Lab Rats	309
55	Dad Woke Up Dead	311
56	Unexpected Connections: A Daughter Discovered	315

MOTORCYCLES: TWO WHEELS, ENDLESS HORIZONS

327

57	Riding a Leif Original	329
58	Youthful Bravado and a Face Plant	331
59	Riding Camaraderie	336
60	Marin's Faithful Flyers	339
61	Scenic Overload in Kiwi-Land	342
62	Epic Dakar	346
63	Speed Is Relative: Adventures in a Polaris RZR	361
64	Batman Meets Santa	365
65	Between the Earth and the Sky	368
66	Purple Rider in Death Valley	374
67	Climbing Trees on Two Wheels	381
68	Road Rules in Brazil	386
69	Admiring the Adriatic	389
70	Fast Track to Humility	396
71	Wheelies: Between Physics and Fear	403
72	Behind the Badge: Making a Motor Officer	407
73	The "Just Turn Left" Riding Plan	422
74	A Safety-Obsessed Outlaw's Confession	427
75	Design, Dedication, Ducati	432
76	The Quest for the Perfect Motorcycle	436
77	Tales from the Road: Writers Who Ride	443

RELIGION: FROM FAITH TO REASON

447

| 78 | When it All Ended | 449 |
| 79 | A Debate Champion's Guide to Not Being Fooled | 457 |

80 Getting a Grip on God   463
81 My Life with the Jesus Freaks   467
82 Playing the Long Game: A Father's Important Lesson   471
83 Going to Hell in a Handbasket   475
84 From Genesis to Genetics   480
85 Politics   485
86 When, Exactly, Is the End of the World?   490
87 Balancing Religion's Pros and Cons   496
88 Saints and Scholars: Three Men of Faith   501
89 The Price of Belonging   505
90 We're All Believers—Just in Different Things   507
91 Ethics Beyond the Pulpit   509
92 Navigating Life Beyond Belief   512
93 Morality Beyond Religion's Influence   518

EPILOGUE   523

Index   525

ACKNOWLEDGMENTS

THIS BOOK HAS BEEN A long time coming. The desire to share my life's journey with my oldest daughter, Christie—who came into my life as an incredibly pleasant surprise when she was 39 years old—provided the incentive.

But completing it relied on finding the best in my collected writing from prior published magazines and newspaper articles, my public newsletter and all the personal papers and notebooks where I'd recorded my thoughts and feelings, with no expectation they'd see the light of day. I've never been so happy about being a pack rat.

Throughout this project, more than a year in the making, I received the greatest support from my wife and life partner, Maggie. Her way with words has always made me look good, and she never hesitated when I asked for her help in crafting this book.

After reviewing early drafts, other family members and friends also provided valuable feedback that improved many of the chapters. Kevin Brown and Rob Kost, who intelligently questioned some of my ethical positions, are in this illustrious group. Chuk Batko and Corky Hall set me on the right path to the title, for which I'm most grateful. With his vast knowledge of fonts and typography, Chuk also weighed in when it came time to design the book for publication. Photographer extraordinaire Mark Trembly lent his considerable expertise.

I also want to thank Ed Sweet, a professional writer and editor, who saw the story with fresh eyes and gave me a lot of positive feedback. Besides spotting needless sentences and paragraphs (and chapters), as well as some questionable grammatical choices, he moved things around to improve the flow and make the narrative more cohesive.

Design and production duties fell to David Wogahn and his creative team at AuthorImprints. Against impossible odds, they made an end-of-year delivery date possible. For anyone interested in doing a book like mine, I highly recommend David's informative guide, *Before the Launch*.

My list of dear friends who have helped bring this book to fruition is too long to include here, but many more are acknowledged in my mind and heart. Thank you, all—from the bottom of my heart.

INTRODUCTION

WILL THE REAL STEVE LARSEN PLEASE STAND UP?

EARLY IN 2012, I RECEIVED an email from Steve Larsen.

"My momma went to heaven on Sunday," it began. "I thought you might like to read about her."

This man from Idaho—who shares my name—provided a link to her obituary. She was indeed a remarkable woman.

Twenty-five years before receiving this email, when the Internet was just heating up and people were clamoring to get URLs in their own name, I discovered that Steve Larsen from Idaho had already snapped up the URL I wanted, stevelarsen.com. Frustrated, I had to settle for stevelarsen.net, the web address I still use today.

I knew little of this other Steve Larsen, except that he stole my URL and ran a consulting business. His website had a contact form on it, so I reached out to see if he'd be willing to sell me his domain name. He wasn't. But he seemed like a nice guy and we began a dialog that grew into an unexpected friendship.

He even said he'd help me out by directing people to me if they happened to stumble upon his website by mistake. A week or two later, he asked me to check his website and take a look. There it was, right on the home page:

IF YOU'RE LOOKING FOR THE REAL STEVE LARSEN, CLICK HERE

True to his word, the link went to my website. He's kept that message on his home page ever since, cementing Steve Larsen's place in my heart as one of the more generous and gracious people on the planet.

Over the years, Steve and I have shared Christmas newsletters and fishing stories. My wife Maggie and I have been invited to the weddings of Steve's many children: We never went, but we always sent a gift. We even met Steve face-to-face in Phoenix a few years ago, and I found him to be as tall as I am short. He's a wonderfully warm human being and it was fun to spend some real time together.

To add to the Steve Larsen confusion, a professional road racer and triathlete with the same name came on the scene in the mid-1990s. Not only did I have to deal with Steve Larsen the consultant, but here was another Steve Larsen who was an actual, genuine celebrity.

This famous Steve Larsen died in 2009 at age 39, leading to an outpouring of condolences on my website. I did my best to respond to everyone and direct them to the Steve Larsen they were really looking for.

I'm not a consultant from Idaho or a professional athlete, but I am Steve Larsen. I'm the Steve Larsen who survived three open-heart surgeries. I'm the Steve Larsen who fell in love with British sports cars and rides motorcycles across breathtaking landscapes all over the world. I'm the Steve Larsen who navigated the wild days of the Internet boom.

Why should you care about this Steve Larsen? Well, you might be interested in my story if you know me in some capacity. But my story isn't just about me. It's about the unexpected turns life can take, the resilience of the human spirit and the connections we make along the way. I find connecting with other humans one of the most meaningful parts of my life, and some of the most random meetings—like the one between me and Idaho Steve Larsen—have been among the most rewarding.

* * * * *

In January 2019, when I was 68, I found out that I had a 39-year-old daughter from a previous relationship. It was a shocking revelation, but one that I—along with Maggie and our daughter Ginger—enthusiastically embraced.

As I got to know Christie Will and her family, including my two amazing granddaughters, I realized there was a lot they didn't know about me. With the sands of time slipping through the hourglass, I felt an urgency to share stories with Christie of the father she never knew. But whenever we were together, those memories were pushed aside by more immediate concerns and contemporary issues, such as places we'd like to visit, books we've read, movies we've seen and the kids' school progress.

So the idea came to mind to write it all down as a book. It would be a nice legacy for both my daughters, a record of things about me and my life they might want to know or look back on.

But then the idea grew.

I thought of motorcycle buddies and readers of motorcycle magazines who only knew me as a fellow rider or "that motorcycle writer." I thought of business associates who only knew me as a tech entrepreneur or "a marketing guy." I thought of car enthusiast friends who shared my passion for fine cars, especially ones made in the UK. And I thought of family members who only thought of me as their cousin, brother or uncle. What would they think if they knew the whole person—the broader story?

The tapestry of my life has been woven from six threads: Health, Cars, Business, Family, Motorcycles and Religion/Ethics. Within each, I've experienced great joys and intense traumas, incredible successes and indelible failures. I've experienced heart-stopping moments of pure joy—the birth of my children, the thrill of a perfect ride, the rush of a successful business deal. But I've also faced heart-stopping moments of fear and grief—lying on an operating table, losing a young son and watching a business crumble.

Through moments of profound connection and periods of deep uncertainty, my heart has indeed been in it from the start. Perhaps it's because I've always felt things more deeply than most, somehow more attuned to life's subtle melodies and discordant notes alike. This sensitivity has been a blessing and a curse, allowing me to fully embrace life's highs while also feeling its lows with acute intensity. It's made me who I am—a man whose heart, quite literally and figuratively, has been the center of his story.

Health concerns have been a persistent companion in my journey. I hold the dubious honor of being one of a rare few who've survived three open-heart surgeries. The first was in my teens and the other two occurred in my early 60s. They can't do another one because of all the scar tissue around my heart, so I'm on a daily dose of antibiotics to keep life-threatening infections at bay. Each day is a gift, a reminder of life's fragility and the importance of making the most out of every moment.

Despite the shadow cast by my heart condition, I've always been determined to live life to its fullest, pursuing passions that make my pulse race—in a good way. Cars, in particular, have been a lifelong fascination. It all began with a 1969 Lotus Elan, a car that captured my imagination and set me on a path of automotive enthusiasm.

Whether I was behind the wheel of that nimble Lotus or, years later, a high-powered Supercar, the sensation was always the same: the perfect fusion of man and machine, a symphony of engineering resonating with the rhythm of my heart. The thrill of acceleration, the precision of a well-executed turn, the freedom of the open road— these experiences have been a driving force in my life, shaping my outlook and relationships in unexpected ways. Cars have taught me about persistence, the beauty of fine-tuning and the joy of pushing limits.

Business provided me with another thrilling ride, from the twilight of the analog age into the dawn of the digital era. I started as a sales associate in a stereo retail store, worked my way up to management, and helped open one of the first computer stores in the country.

That experience catapulted me into the corporate technology world, where I rode the rapidly rising wave of personal computers at companies like CDC, Prodigy, IBM and AT&T, and parlayed the experience into several startups in the dot.com era. While never reaching the stratospheric heights of a Gates or Bezos, I was in the right place at the right time on a few occasions, as a witness to, participant in and influencer of a revolution that changed the world.

Through it all, family has been the bedrock of my existence. I was blessed with an extended family and parents who loved me. My childhood was idyllic, filled with freedom and adventure. I have cousins I love like brothers, and I treasure my wife and two daughters.

But life isn't always kind. Losing my son before he was two years old was the most traumatic experience I've ever endured. Eric's brief life taught me a great deal about the depths of grief and the unfairness and randomness of existence. He showed me how joys and sorrows can come when least expected, shaping us in profound ways.

My son's death also triggered a crisis of faith that I'm not sure I've ever fully resolved. It forced me to confront questions I had long avoided, and to reexamine beliefs I had taken for granted. Religion has been a complex and evolving theme in my life, and I've gone through periods of fervent belief, crushing doubt, angry rejection and quiet searching.

Raised in a religious household, I've found myself caught in a tug-of-war between faith and reason. On the one hand, I'm awestruck by the unfathomable beauty and complexity of nature. The magnitude and mystery of the universe often leave me breathless, hinting at something greater than ourselves. On the other hand, I'm equally amazed by human ingenuity—the precision of a finely tuned engine, the elegance of computer code, the artistry in a well-designed car, advances in medicine and our understanding of the body. These marvels of human ingenuity speak to our own ability to use science and intellect to shape and understand our world. The tension between the divine and the human, the natural and the artificial, has been at the core of my spiritual struggle.

For decades, I yearned for the religious epiphany I saw many others experience, but it remained elusive. I attended services, read scriptures and debated with believers and non-believers alike, always hoping for that moment of clarity or divine touch. Yet, the more I searched, the more complex the questions became. I've witnessed the power of faith to inspire incredible acts of kindness and compassion. But I've also seen its shadow side—a zealous hypocrisy that can twist belief into a weapon.

In the end, I've come to appreciate the journey itself. My struggles with faith have made me more empathetic, more curious and more open to the myriad ways people find meaning in their lives. While I may not have found the answers I initially sought, I've discovered that the search itself has profound value, continually challenging me to grow, to question and to engage deeply with the world around me.

My best escapes have always been on two wheels. There's something indescribable about riding a motorcycle through breathtaking landscapes. A responsive engine, finely tuned suspension, the wind rushing past, the vastness of the Earth in its natural beauty surrounding you—it's a visceral experience that touches the soul. I've felt genuine awe, even a sense of the sublime, speeding along coastal highways, winding through mountain passes and crossing vast deserts.

* * * * *

This autobiography is a chronicle of a life fully lived, with all its twists and turns. It's for Christie, the daughter I'm still getting to know. It's for Ginger, the daughter I've watched grow from a baby into a remarkable woman. It's for Maggie, my wife and partner in all of life's adventures. It's for all the family members, friends, medical professionals, business associates and fellow gearheads who've helped shape the particular version of Steve Larsen I am today. And it's for anyone who has ever grappled with life's big questions, faced unexpected challenges or simply wondered what it means to live a life with heart, passion and purpose.

So, if you're ready, let's embark on this journey together. From the operating table to the driver's seat, from boardrooms to distant highways, from family gatherings to struggles of faith, this is my story. It's a tale of resilience, passion, love, loss and the continuous search for meaning in a complex world.

Will the real Steve Larsen please stand up? Well, here I am.

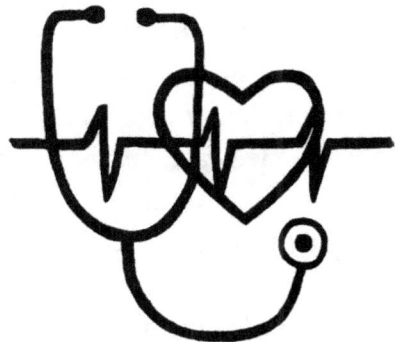

HEALTH

MATTERS OF THE HEART

IN 1966, AT AGE 15, I faced my first major health crisis. What started out as a routine physical turned into a life-altering diagnosis: a coarctation of the aorta. This condition would lead me to become a pioneer of sorts in the world of open-heart surgery, a field that was still in relative infancy.

Over the years, I would undergo not one, not two, but three open-heart surgeries, each more complex than the last. My experiences mirror the evolution of cardiac care itself, from the early days of experimental procedures to the cutting-edge techniques of the 21st century. As a beneficiary of these scientific advancements, I've become a living testament to the courage and innovation of the medical pioneers who paved the way, pushing the boundaries of what was possible in cardiac surgery.

While I explore the broader implications of medical marvels in this section, I also delve into some of the more personal aspects of living with a serious heart condition. You'll find unexpected moments of levity, like how comedy albums became an unconventional form of therapy—and how I got to thank one of those famous comedians years later. You'll meet the dedicated medical professionals who've been my guides and guardians, as well as the loved ones who've stood by my side. You'll witness the rollercoaster of emotions coming with each diagnosis, procedure and recovery.

This section also serves as a bridge to later discussions on faith and science. My experiences within the healthcare system have informed my perspective on these topics, offering a unique lens through which to view the interplay between scientific advancement and personal belief.

But beyond the medical details and philosophical musings, this section is a story about living. It's a tale of facing mortality head-on and choosing to embrace life fully, even when the body doesn't cooperate. It's about recognizing limitations—like an unfinished hike in New Zealand that served as a wake-up call—and celebrating monumental victories.

As you read through these chapters, I hope you'll gain a new appreciation for the incredible machine that is the human body and the indomitable spirit that drives it. Take a deep breath, feel your heart beating and let's get right to the heart of the matter.

1

A YOUNG HEART'S SURGICAL TALE

THE FIRST THING I NOTICED was the beeping. Steady, rhythmic, almost hypnotic. Then came the pain, a dull ache that seemed to radiate from my chest to every corner of my body. I tried to open my eyes, but they felt heavier than lead. When I finally managed to pry them open, the world was a blur of white and silver.

"Welcome back, Steve," a voice said from somewhere to my left. "The surgery was a success."

Surgery. Right. That's why I was here, in this strange, sterile room that smelled of antiseptic and something else I couldn't quite place. I was 15 years old, and I had just undergone open-heart surgery. The year was 1966.

As I lay there, trying to make sense of my new reality, I couldn't have known that this was just the beginning of my experiences with medical science. I couldn't possibly have imagined that I would have to undergo two more open-heart surgeries in the decades to come, not to mention five additional debridement surgeries, which opened my chest but not my heart.

* * * * *

It all started with a routine physical so I could sign up to play junior high football. Dr. Kramer, our local physician in Fairmont, Minnesota, worked near the school and I walked over to his office after class. After flipping through old copies of *Family Circle* and *Life Magazine*, I entered the exam room and stripped to my underwear.

Dr. Kramer couldn't seem to get a normal blood pressure reading. "Steve, did you run over here from school to get here on time?" he asked me.

"No, doctor." I replied. "I didn't have to rush."

He had me get dressed and asked me to sit in the waiting room for a few minutes. Back to the old magazines! About a half an hour later, he called me back into the exam room and tried to get a blood pressure reading that made sense to him. He couldn't do it.

While I sat in his office, Dr. Kramer picked up the phone and called my mom, who was a nurse at the local hospital. He told her about my blood pressure readings, extremely high in my arms but almost impossible to detect in my legs. He wanted me to see a colleague of his who specialized in heart issues.

A couple of weeks later, my parents came with me to see the heart specialist. That was my first clue that something might be amiss. After an exam that included lots of listening with a stethoscope, blood pressure measurements on my arms and legs and questions about which activities came easily and which ones I found difficult, he announced that I had a coarctation of the aorta.

In layman's terms, this meant that my aorta—the large blood vessel that branches off from the top of the heart and delivers oxygen-rich blood to various parts of the body—at one point had a constriction, a narrowing hour-glass shaped section that was limiting blood flow. My heart had to work overtime, causing it—and my chest—to get bigger than normal. My blood pressure was high in my upper body but barely detectable in my legs. In addition, some murmurs indicated that tiny holes could be allowing blood leakage between the chambers of my heart.

Just one month shy of my 16th birthday, I was wheeled into an operating room at the University of Minnesota Heart Hospital. It was the end of August, and I was glad that I been able to spend most of the summer having fun with my friends like a normal kid.

On that fateful day, the surgeons were about to carve a 17-inch incision across my body that began on my back, continued under my left arm and ended at the left side of my chest. While I was hooked up to a heart-lung bypass machine, they cut out the restricted portion of my aorta, sewed the ends back together and patched up two holes between my heart's ventricles. All in a day's work, right?

I recall being hospitalized for about a week, then returning home for a longer convalescence. And when I got back to school, gym class got a lot more interesting. Whenever I removed my shirt, my scar got a lot of attention. A few kids were brave enough to ask questions: "Hey, what happened to you?"

My first response was always, "Not much. You should see the other guy," before revealing the scar's true source. It was easier to deflect with humor than to explain the complexities of congenital heart defects to my fellow teens, who were more interested in football scores than medical procedures.

I went back to the doctors for a couple of years and was finally told that my heart problem was fixed. The surgical repair was successful, and no further appointments would be necessary. My doctors told me to "have a long and happy life," and I've tried my hardest to take their advice.

Pioneers of the Heart

My timing couldn't have been better when I had my first open-heart surgery, as a massive amount of progress had been made in the field. Until the 1950s, most pediatric heart operations were performed on or around a closed, beating heart. The elusive goal back then was to find a way to stop and restart the heart safely so surgeons could actually operate inside it.

Early on, hypothermia (dramatic chilling) was the preferred method to interrupt blood flow during intra-cardiac operations, but it had to be fast and there were complications. But then they began testing various sorts of cardiopulmonary bypass techniques with a roughly 25% survival rate. Early bypass approaches were done on children with a parent serving as an oxygenator, cross-circulating their arterial blood into the patient. This led to the belief that a temporary cardiopulmonary bypass might be feasible, and research found a suitable pump and mechanical oxygenator to replace the living and breathing ones.

Dr. John Lewis performed the world's first successful open-heart procedure at the University of Minnesota Heart Hospital in 1952, just 13 years before my surgery. Using hypothermia and inflow occlusion, he managed to repair atrial septal defects without severe complications in about 20 different patients between 1952 and 1953. This groundbreaking work paved the way for my successful operation.

Fortunately for me, the University of Minnesota Heart Hospital was at the forefront of cardiovascular surgery between 1950 and 1967. This was due in large part to Owen Wangensteen, MD, a leader whose commitment to creating an environment for achievement earned him recognition as the "mentor of a thousand surgeons." My surgeon, Dr. Aldo R. Castaneda, was one of Wangensteen's protégés and went on to become president of The American Association for Thoracic Surgery.

Laughing My Way to Health

Recovery from open-heart surgery is no walk in the park, especially for a teenager more interested in sports and girls than scar tissue. But my parents, in their infinite wisdom, had brought me an unexpected ally: a small, portable record player and a collection of comedy albums.

Bill Cosby's *Wonderfulness* and *Why Is There Air?* always came through with some big belly laughs, but the Smothers Brothers were my favorite recovery room companions. Their albums *Aesop's Fables* and *Mom Always Liked You Best!* had me cracking up, despite the pain in my chest. I would listen over and over, laughing at the same bits.

Little did I know that those fits of laughter were doing more than just lifting my spirits. The deep inhalations as I guffawed were exactly what my body needed to rebuild. My nurses were amazed at my rapid progress, unknowingly witnessing the healing power of humor firsthand.

Years later, I had the chance to thank one of the Smothers Brothers in person. While living in San Francisco in 2003, I spent a weekend with my friend Philip Richter at the Sonoma County estate of his friend, Fred Furth, a prominent Bay Area attorney, winemaker and philanthropist.

Arriving at Fred's Chalk Hill winery and estate, we unpacked in a plush guest house. In the evening, Fred picked us up in a new yellow Rolls Royce convertible and we drove to a charity auction attended by a Who's Who of the Northern California wine elite.

After an extensive happy hour, with area vintners pouring their most expensive and notable wines, my friend Philip and I were seated on either side of Fred at one of the most prestigiously placed tables with some of the largest donors. At the other end of the table was Francis Ford Coppola and Jess Jackson of Kendall-Jackson fame, with other renowned vintners in between. These rich and powerful men were friends but also competitors, and they delighted at goading each other.

Furth's Chalk Hill chardonnay was widely recognized as one of the finest and best-selling white wines ever produced. One of the vintners at our table directed a question to Furth, but loud enough for Coppola to hear. "Fred, have you tried Francis' new chardonnay?" he asked. It was a loaded question: while Coppola enjoyed a solid reputation for his red cabernet sauvignon, his whites were a work in process.

Fred, briefly glancing down the table to be sure Coppola was listening, considered the question. After a long pause, he looked at the questioner and replied, "I've always considered Francis Ford Coppola to be one of the best movie directors in the world." He then smiled wryly, lifting his glass toward Coppola in a toast.

"Well, thank you ever so much, Fred," Coppola said in response, raising his glass in acknowledgement along with his middle finger in an obvious "FU Salute." The table rolled in laughter.

Later, during the auction part of the evening, a white puppy came up for bid and Fred decided he wanted this dog. Perhaps he needed a replacement for the dog he recently lost, a Great Dane that had accompanied him on an eight-day, round-the-world trip in his Cessna Citation jet. Furth was an avid and skilled pilot, and perhaps one of the few with a canine for a co-pilot.

As the bidding began for the dog, Fred walked between the tables, roaring that he was going to win the bid for this dog no matter what and daring anyone to outbid him. When the bidding stalled around $4,000, Fred doubled the bid to $8,000.

As the hammer was about to come down, Fred stood in front of a table urging anyone to bid $9,000. "I promise, the second you do, I'll bid $10,000. It won't cost you a dime and we'll do more for the charity, right?"

He got the $9,000 bid and, true to his word, immediately topped it. He repeated this at several more tables, pushing bids to over $25,000 before finally sitting down. We took the dog home with us later in the evening.

But the most memorable part of that whole event was seeing Tommy Smothers, who was there in his capacity as owner of the Smothers-Remick Ridge Vineyards. Going against my personal rule of never approaching or fawning over a celebrity, I couldn't stop myself. I briefly told him of my lifelong love for his work with his brother and the unlikely role he played in my recovery from heart surgery as a teenager.

He smiled, nodded and thanked me, but I could tell he wanted to get away. As he left, I kicked myself for my amateur behavior. Oh well, we all make mistakes.

During the auction, as I was sitting on a riser with a curtain separating the area from the traffic below, I saw Tommy Smothers approaching a man who appeared to be his business manager. They couldn't see me, but I could hear everything they said.

"You'll never believe what happened," Tommy told him. "This guy came up to me and told me that our records helped him recover from heart surgery as a kid."

I couldn't believe what I was hearing. "It was amazing," Tommy continued. "I didn't know what to say. I was so touched, I almost cried."

*At 15 years old, posing with my Bill Cosby and
Smothers Brothers record collection.*

The Beat Goes On

As I grew older, my early brush with heart surgery faded into the background of my life. The doctors had declared me fixed, and I was all too happy to believe them. But medical science, much like the human heart, doesn't stand still.

In 1995, at the age of 44, I received a call from the University of Minnesota Heart Hospital. They were conducting a follow-up study on patients who had aorta repairs between 1950 and 1970. Would I be willing to participate?

Their retrospective studies showed that individuals who had surgeries like mine also had greater incidences of hypertension, premature coronary artery disease, stroke, aortic valve abnormalities and dilatation of the aorta and bicuspid valves later in life.

Those two days of exams and tests brought me face to face with the long-term realities of my condition. I had three out of four problems common among study participants with a similar medical history. The doctors put me on mild heart medication and delivered news that would echo in my mind for years to come: I'd need a "valve job," most likely when I reached my 60s.

2

TIME TO FIX IT AGAIN

THE REALIZATION HIT ME LIKE a freight train when I was walking on a serene New Zealand hiking trail. It was January 2016 and I found myself on a motorcycle trip, taking a break from the road to enjoy a two-mile hike up to an overlook. But something was terribly wrong. I couldn't keep up.

For someone who had always prided himself on keeping pace with my fellow travelers, even in questionable physical shape, this was a shock to the system. Half a mile into the hike, I found myself gasping for air.

Fortunately, I was able to seek refuge on a nearby bench. As I sat there, watching my companions disappear up the trail, a cold realization settled in my chest: my heart wasn't just skipping a beat; it was falling behind.

Back in the States, I paid a visit to my cardiologist. His words were cautious but clear: it might be time to visit a surgeon. "Don't make the appointment if you're not prepared to have surgery," he warned. "They're surgeons and they'll want to cut. It's what they do."

The following month, I sat across from Dr. Patrick DeValeria at the Mayo Clinic in Phoenix. And true to my cardiologist's prediction, Dr. DeValeria did indeed want to cut me up. So on April 13, 2016 I was once again wheeled into an operating room, a feeling both familiar and foreign after so many years.

This procedure was more complex than my teenage surgery. This time, my heart would be stopped just 10 minutes shy of two full hours. Dr. DeValeria replaced my bicuspid aortic valve with a bovine/carbon fiber model, a high-tech upgrade. He also swapped out my ascending aorta for an artificial one, something that looked disconcertingly like a small vacuum cleaner hose. It was guaranteed never to break or stretch.

The day after surgery I was up and about, making laps around the nurse's station like a man on a mission. Five days later I was heading home, feeling pretty good and eager to start my cardiac rehabilitation. Life was looking up, and Maggie and I even made plans for a 37-day cruise around South America to celebrate my recovery.

But then the weirdness began.

It started with a cough: persistent, nagging, seemingly innocuous. We sought help from respiratory specialists at Scripps Memorial Hospital in San Diego before embarking on our extended cruise, but they couldn't identify the cause. Back at Mayo in Phoenix, I got a diagnosis of throat damage during surgery. A speech therapist armed me with exercises and lidocaine to relax my throat muscles.

The cough improved, but something still felt off. A strange bubble was forming near my surgery site. The folks at Mayo said it was a keloid, a common post-surgery occurrence. But on September 4, during a lunch meeting at BJ's Brewhouse, that bubble burst—literally.

It was unpleasant but not painful, so I drove to my surgeon's office—just a few blocks away—to show him what happened. His reaction was immediate and alarming: I was admitted to the hospital on the spot.

What followed was a whirlwind of emergency surgeries and massive doses of antibiotics. On the Saturday of Labor Day weekend, Dr. DeValeria assembled an entire surgical team, interrupting their off time to operate. Two days later, before they could discharge me, they decided they hadn't quite removed all the infected tissue so they brought me back to the surgical suite.

These two debridement surgeries left me with a rather large hole in my chest. After a two-week stay in the hospital with massive IV antibiotic drips, I went home with a wound vac and a twice-daily regimen of antibiotics delivered via IV. Nurses showed up at the house in the morning and again at dinner time to deliver the drips, each lasting about two hours.

Because my doctors wanted the surgical wound to heal from the bottom up, they left the hole in my chest open, covered with a breathable bandage. Daily dressing changes became a painful routine, and even after several weeks I looked like a modern-day Frankenstein's monster.

No sooner had the wound healed than another abscess appeared, a process that repeated itself again and again. The outbreaks didn't make me sick, so I started carrying a wound kit whenever I left the house for very long. I resumed riding my motorcycle, including off-road trips to Moab, Utah and the Copper Canyon in Mexico. "Have wound kit, will travel," became my motto.

After three more debridement surgeries, (making a total of five), the doctors concluded there was likely something far worse going on very deep down, so deep that the surface surgery couldn't fix it. Upon further investigation, the doctors deduced that the problem stemmed from the artificial valve and my new aorta. These non-human body parts were perfect hiding spots for infections, unreachable by even the most powerful antibiotics. Blood is the delivery system for antibiotics and other infection-fighting molecules, and if it can't get to the foreign objects, those objects don't get cleaned.

As the gravity of the situation sank in, my wife Maggie and I found ourselves on a medical tour, visiting the Cleveland Clinic in Ohio and the Mayo Clinic in Rochester, Minnesota. Both came to the same unpleasant and feared conclusion: a dangerous and determined infectious bug had attached itself to the prosthetic parts in my heart. If we couldn't find it and eliminate it, it would kill me. And given its resilience in the face of multiple surgeries and antibiotic regimens, it was likely to do so sooner than later—and suddenly.

The doctors didn't mince words about how it would happen. First a fever, then chills and rapid breathing, followed by mental confusion and death—all within 24 to 48 hours. The alternative? Another major open-heart surgery—incredibly complex and risky, but really the only option if I wanted to live longer than a few months.

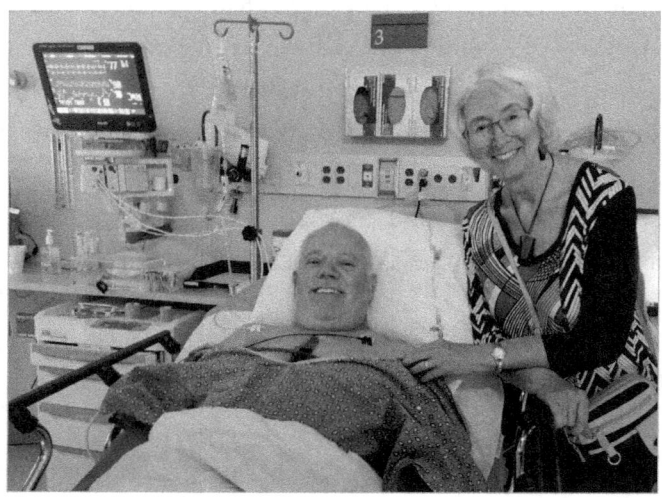

Maggie and me after one of my five debridement surgeries, done to remove the infection from around my heart. They all failed.

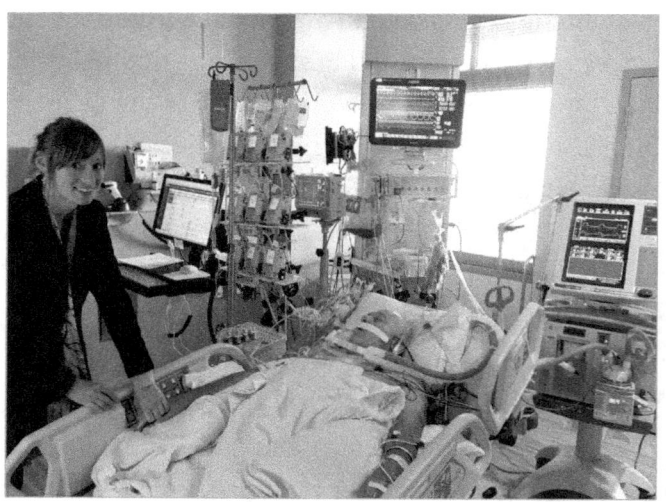

Ginger visits me while I'm still connected to wires and monitors after open-heart surgery.

3

THIRD TIME'S A CHARM?

APRIL 23, 2018, TWO YEARS after my previous operation, was a date that would be etched into my memory—and my chest—forever. As I was wheeled into the operating room at the Mayo Clinic in Rochester, I couldn't help but reflect on the journey that led me there. This would be my third open-heart surgery, a medical hat-trick no one ever wants to achieve.

The gravity of the situation wasn't lost on me. Fatalities in second surgeries are 10 times greater than in initial open-heart procedures, and this was my third. If I survived, I'd be one of only a few people ever to successfully undergo three open-heart surgeries. It was a club I never aspired to join. To give myself the best shot at success possible, I embraced a regimen of fasting and a vegan diet, and I continued the "no alcohol" stance I adopted for my 2016 surgery.

In consultation with Dr. DeValeria in Phoenix, we chose a surgical team at Mayo in Rochester—that specialized in risky, do-over surgeries like mine—to perform the complex, 11-hour operation. They were very familiar and experienced with all the intricacies involved: cutting away the bad stuff; finding healthy, uninfected tissue; sewing in clean parts; and irrigating the area post-surgery to stop any infection in its tracks.

As Dr. Pochettino and his team began working on me at 8:00 a.m., I drifted off into anesthesia-induced unconsciousness. During the operation, my heart was stopped for a total of 260 minutes, just 40 minutes shy of five hours. That was more than twice as long as my heart was stopped for my 2016 surgery, which, at 110 minutes, was pushing the boundaries of what's safe.

Stopping the heart is risky business. It doesn't always restart, and the duration of the stoppage is a key factor. Typical open-heart surgeries stop the heart between 30 and 90 minutes. Under 60 minutes is considered quite safe, while anything beyond 90 minutes increases risk significantly.

Eleven hours after they wheeled me into the OR, my surgical team met with my family—Maggie, my daughter Ginger, my sister Naomi and my cousin Ron Herem and his wife Gwen. The news was cautiously optimistic: they had accomplished everything they set out to do, and I had survived. "There was a pool of something that looked like dirty dishwater right around the valve," Dr. Pochettino told them. "It's good we got in there and removed it."

An hour later, as my family gathered around me, the care team brought me out of anesthesia for a couple of minutes. It was a critical moment—a test of my brain function to see if I recognized everyone. I passed the test, much to everyone's relief, before being put back under until the next morning.

My recovery from this third open-heart surgery was a grueling process. I spent 10 days at the Mayo Clinic's Hospital in Rochester, followed by another seven days at the nearby Charter House with twice-daily trips back to the Clinic for antibiotic infusions. The IV drips entered through a port under my left arm, delivering medicine to what one nurse colorfully described as "the Niagara Falls of the circulatory system"—a vessel just above my heart.

On May 5, in a carefully coordinated move, I had my morning IV drip at Rochester Mayo, flew to Phoenix and immediately transferred to the Mayo Emergency Room there for another pre-arranged IV drip. This marked the beginning of eight more weeks of twice-daily infusions at Mayo, but at least I got to sleep in my own bed.

After the first few weeks, during which Maggie or our next-door neighbor, Francine Buchhalter, would drive me to the hospital for my infusions, I regained my driving privileges and could make the trips to Mayo myself. Every morning, I arrived at the infusion center, got hooked up to an IV with a cocktail of three different drugs and spent the next two and a half hours reading or chatting with the nurses. I'd be out by mid-morning, ready to start my day.

At 6:00 p.m., I was back at the infusion center for my evening dose, typically just under two hours. I didn't miss a day for 60 days and was on a first-name basis with the infusion center staff. Once the IVs were no longer necessary, the doctor prescribed a twice-daily oral antibiotic to take for the rest of my life. It was a small price to pay for being alive.

Today, as I write this, I'm doing well. My daily routine includes taking my antibiotics and Warfarin, and a weekly pin prick to measure my International Normalized Ratio (INR)—the time it takes for my blood to clot.

The infection hasn't recurred, which is perhaps the best news of all. My doctors have made it clear they can't do another open-heart surgery on me. I've reached the maximum number that can be done, given all the scarring from prior surgeries. It's a sobering thought, but also a motivating one. Each day is a gift, one that I don't take for granted.

My remaining issues are no longer life-threatening. I'm doing everything I need to do from a medical standpoint, and I'm enjoying all the fun things I had to postpone while we got this sorted out.

After several years of strict adherence to my vegan diet, I'll admit I got a bit bored. A conversation with my brilliant primary care physician, Dr. Rajal Mehta, led to some welcome changes. Her advice was simple but liberating: avoid meat from four-legged creatures, enjoy two-legged chicken and turkey on occasion and feel free to eat fish and other things with no legs anytime. This adjustment has provided all the flavor variety I need while still keeping me healthy.

Life is good.

4

MEDICINE AND SCIENCE

THESE DAYS, CONVERSATIONS WITH MY "old guy" friends often center around our health concerns and various ailments—topics that used to drive me nuts when I was in my youth. I once swore I'd never indulge in such behavior, but that was before I had health issues to trump nearly everyone else's. It's become my personal Crocodile Dundee moment: "That's not a health issue . . . THIS is a health issue!"

Each scar on my chest tells a story of close calls and second chances, of medical successes and human resilience. They're a roadmap of my life and a constant reminder of the fragility and preciousness of existence.

As someone who's been under the knife more than most, I've developed a unique perspective on the world of medical science. It's a world of miracles and missteps, of life-saving breakthroughs and humbling setbacks. It's not just a body of knowledge, but a process—a never-ending quest for understanding that can sometimes feel like a high-stakes game of trial and error.

Let's start with an acknowledgement: I'm alive today because my parents chose science over faith healing when it came to fixing my faulty ticker. Given what we heard in church, our path should have been to pray and trust God to heal me, and perhaps schedule a visit with a preacher or minister said to heal through the laying on of hands, such as Oral Roberts, Peter Popoff or Pat Robertson.

Fortunately, my parents, when the life of their child was on the line, chose science and the medical establishment to find a solution to a heart defect that otherwise would have sent me to an early grave. A very similar defect had, indeed, killed my mother's oldest sister's child, Charles "Chucky" Gravley, in 1952 before his first birthday because the condition went undiagnosed.

Similar heart issues played a role in my son living only until he was two years old. Eric's death wasn't a failure of science, however. It came about because one doctor decided his opinion was superior to the specific written and verbal instructions by more qualified experts. His "gut feel" and "faith" decision killed my son.

When it comes to matters of the heart, I'm a staunch believer in the scientific method and its inherent humility. Science knows what it knows, and more importantly, it knows what it doesn't know. It's constantly testing, retesting, updating and upgrading its conclusions. It doesn't get offended when new facts come along—in fact, one sure way to get ahead in the scientific field is to challenge and disprove previously held assumptions.

Take my three open-heart surgeries, for instance. Each one was a testament to the progress of medical science. From the pioneering work of Dr. John Lewis at the University of Minnesota in 1952 to the complex procedures that kept me ticking in 2016 and 2018, every cut was guided by years of rigorous research, experimentation and peer review.

For those interested in diving deeper into the history and development of open-heart surgery, I highly recommend two books: *The Sublime Engine* by Stephen and Thomas Amidon, and *King of Hearts: The True Story of the Maverick Who Pioneered Open Heart Surgery* by G. Wayne Miller. These works provide fascinating insights into how we've arrived at our current state of cardiac care.

When Science Gets Personal

We live in one of the most productive eras of science in history, and cardiovascular science has shared in and benefited from this growth. Yet, despite the vast body of knowledge available, conceptual gaps remain in the understanding of heart disease. Several large-scale clinical trials, initially believed to be logical approaches to therapy, haven't worked out as planned.

I know because I participated in one from August 2020 until January 2023, which allowed me to swap my daily dose of Warfarin (and those pesky weekly pin pricks) for a new wonder drug called Eliquis (apixaban). Originally developed to prevent blood clots, Eliquis was also used successfully to treat several heart issues with very few side effects. The trial I participated in was an attempt to expand the market by getting Eliquis approved for use with people like me who had artificial heart valves.

For two glorious years, I enjoyed freedom from my previous medical routines. No more weekly needle jabs. No more sending results to Mayo. It was like a medical vacation.

But then researchers noticed more people were dying in the Eliquis group than the Warfarin control group. The moment the statistical scales tipped to show that perhaps Eliquis was not as good as Warfarin and the risks were too high, they immediately ended the trial and switched everyone, including me, back to Warfarin.

As disappointing as it was to go back to the weekly pin pricks and the routine I thought I'd left behind, that's science in action. Truth beats convenience every time.

The Humbling Power of "I Don't Know"

The Eliquis experience taught me a valuable lesson about the nature of scientific inquiry. In science, saying "I don't know" isn't a sign of weakness, it's a starting point for discovery. When the study was halted, the researchers didn't try to fudge the results or stick to their original hypothesis. They admitted that their initial assumptions might have been wrong and went back to the drawing board.

This willingness to admit ignorance and change course in the face of new evidence is what sets science apart from dogma. It's a contrast to the world of faith and belief, where unchanging certainty is often valued above all else.

Take, for example, the ongoing debate between evolution and creationism. Charles Darwin's breakthrough hypothesis on the origin of species has been put through the scientific wringer more times than I've had my chest cracked open (and that's saying something). Every attempt to disprove Darwin's ideas has only served to refine and strengthen them. The enduring power of evolutionary theory lies in its ability to withstand and even grow stronger from these challenges. Like a seasoned boxer who's faced countless contenders, Darwin's ideas have weathered every punch thrown their way, emerging not just intact, but more robust.

When I was growing up, I often saw religious people defying or working to undermine science, particularly the theories of Darwin. Evangelical Christian leaders spoke out against Darwinism as a threat to biblical truth. Preachers like Dwight L. Moody and Billy Sunday denounced evolution in their sermons. The famous Scopes "Monkey Trial" in 1925 challenged the Butler Law passed in Tennessee, which banned the teaching of evolution in schools.

While church people imprisoned Galileo for life because he said the Earth goes around the sun, now practically everyone believes that Galileo was right—even people of faith. Some flat-earthers still point to where the Bible talks about Earth's four corners in Revelation 7:1, showing that when your life is ruled by faith over facts, two millennia of scientific consensus means nothing.

Unlike the rigorous testing process used to determine the efficacy and safety of drugs like Eliquis, religion often relies on faith to support its truth statements. In science, faith without evidence is a vice, while in religion it's often seen as a virtue. I remember listening to sermons highlighting how Jesus reportedly said to "doubting Thomas," "Thomas, because you have seen me, you have believed: blessed are those who have not seen and yet have believed."

This fundamental difference in approaching the unknown has real-world implications, especially in medicine. When faced with a life-threatening condition, do we put our faith in prayer and miracles, or do we trust in the ever-evolving, sometimes-uncertain world of medical science?

My own journey through multiple heart surgeries and experimental treatments has convinced me of the value of scientific uncertainty. Every "I don't know" in my medical history has been followed by research, experimentation and eventual breakthroughs. It's this constant questioning that's kept me alive.

I recognize that for many, faith provides comfort in the face of life's uncertainties. The challenge, as I see it, is to appreciate the role of faith in providing meaning and comfort, while relying on science to solve real-world problems and make progress.

In the end, my scars are a testament not just to medical science, but to the power of "I don't know," the driving force behind every medical breakthrough that has extended and improved my life.

The Human Element in the Scientific Equation

Let's not forget that behind every scientific advance, every clinical trial, every new treatment, there are human beings. Researchers, doctors, nurses and patients like me all play our parts in the grand experiment of medical progress.

I've seen firsthand how the scientific process can save lives. But I've also experienced its limitations and the very real risks that come with being on the cutting edge of medical research. It's a reminder that while science is a powerful tool, it's not infallible. It's a human endeavor, subject to human error and human limitations.

When setting up an experiment, humans tend to try and prove what they want to be true. The scientific process expects and anticipates this frailty and compensates first in how tests must be set up, such as double-blind testing, and also in requiring strict and exhaustive peer reviews. Many scientists make it their cause to repeat experiments with greater thoroughness than the original work to deeply test the conclusions of the initial researchers. In science, this isn't bad manners, it's a highly respected and important part of the process leading to the truth.

My experience in debate competitions has given me a unique perspective on this process as well. During these competitions, my partner and I rarely knew which side of a proposition we would argue until just minutes before the competition began. Learning to be equally persuasive on both sides of a resolution sharpened and deepened our understanding of the issues we debated. This experience taught me the value of considering multiple perspectives, a skill that's necessary for effective scientific inquiry.

5
AMNESIA AND OTHER RECOLLECTIONS

IMAGINE GRADUALLY BECOMING AWARE THAT you're in a strange place, surrounded by familiar faces but having no idea where you are, how you got there or even what day it is. Now imagine this happening not once, but several times. It's happened to me on four occasions since 2016. Welcome to the world of Transient Global Amnesia (TGA).

During these episodes, I apparently start acting very strange. I can't recall the city, state or country I'm in. The date? A complete mystery. My current activity? Your guess is as good as mine. This peculiar state lasts about 30 to 45 minutes, during which my companions usually whisk me off to the nearest ER.

By the time a doctor is ready to see me, I'm typically back to full awareness, with no memory of my "lost time." It's as if someone hit pause on my life, then fast-forwarded through a chunk of it.

The first time it happened, I was convinced my friends were pulling an elaborate prank. "Nice try, guys," I remember thinking, "but you're not that creative."

The diagnosis of TGA is mildly amusing, in a frustrating sort of way. In medical terms, Transient Global Amnesia means, "we've identified nothing that can be attributed to the symptom you just had." It's a diagnosis of exclusion, arrived at after ruling out all potential causes for the symptom being reported: no stroke, dehydration, epileptic seizure, head injury, psychiatric disorder, encephalitis, meningitis or even Wernicke-Korsakoff syndrome (alcoholic blackout). Since it's none of these things, it must be TGA. Of that, they are certain. The diagnosis becomes circular. What is TGA? None of these things, so TGA.

Living with the possibility of suddenly losing chunks of time is disconcerting, to say the least. But it's taught me to appreciate the present moment more fully. After all, you never know when your brain might decide to take an impromptu vacation without informing the rest of you.

TGA is just one more performance in the grand variety show that is my medical history. Let me take you on a tour of some of the other curiosities that have graced my body over the years.

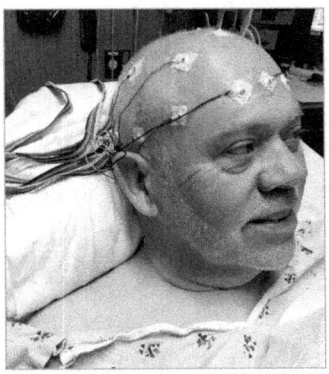

Attempting to track down the causes of TGA.

The Great Bleed-Out

At age 69, I had a brush with mortality that had nothing to do with my heart. Due to a Warfarin dosage issue combined with an ulcer, I lost over four pints of blood. To put that in perspective, the human body typically contains about 10 pints. I had lost close to half.

I spent several days in the hospital, feeling like a vampire's all-you-can-eat buffet. The months spent rebuilding my blood count were a stark reminder of how delicate the balance of life can be.

The Lingering Loop Recorder

In 2014, complaining of lightheadedness, I was diagnosed with a right bundle branch block. This is a fancy way of saying that the electrical signals in my heart were taking the scenic route instead of the express lane.

To monitor this, doctors implanted a loop recorder in my chest. This little device was supposed to detect any arrhythmias and help pinpoint the cause of my dizziness, but it never found anything of interest.

Even after the battery died and I underwent countless surgeries, the defunct loop recorder remains in my chest. I have no idea why it's still there.

The Great Mint Rebellion

In my early 40s, I was single-handedly keeping the antacid industry afloat. I consumed at least one roll of Tums a day, sometimes more. We had jars of Tums scattered around the house.

One day, a doctor asked if I used breath mints. Of course I did! Working in an office, one always wants to avoid offending anyone with bad breath. Little did I know, my minty fresh breath was the culprit behind my digestive woes.

The doctor suggested I try eliminating all mint from my diet. The result was nothing short of miraculous. I stopped eating mint and haven't had a single stomach or digestive issue since. And, by the way, cinnamon breath fresheners work just as well as the mint ones do.

A Tale of Two Eyes

Tired of constantly misplacing my eyeglasses (they were always in the last place I looked, funny how that works), I decided to take the plunge and get LASIK eye surgery in 1999. Dr. Richard Lindstrom, the LASIK surgeon for the Minnesota Twins baseball team, corrected one of my eyes for distance vision.

After 26 days of uncomfortable dizziness and weird vision, something snapped into place in my brain and I could once again see perfectly. My brain uses one eye for distance and the other for reading up close.

The Sum of My Parts

From heart surgeries to blood loss, from bifocal vision to bouts of forgetfulness, my body has been through quite a journey. Each health challenge has left its mark, not just physically, but on my perspective on life.

These experiences have taught me resilience, patience and the importance of finding humor in even the most dire situations. They've shown me the marvels of modern medicine and the mysteries that still puzzle our best minds. Most importantly, they've reminded me to never take my health for granted.

So here I am, a walking, talking medical textbook, with a heart that's been remodeled, eyes that don't match and a strict no-mint policy. But I'm still here, laughing and making new memories—even if I might forget where I put them from time to time.

CARS

A LIFE AMONG EXTRAORDINARY AUTOMOBILES

THE FIRST TIME I HEARD Jim Roller's hopped-up Dodge Charger at the Lutheran Brethren Bible Camp near Alexandria, Minnesota, its rumble awakened something in me. That sound spoke of possibilities beyond the quiet streets of Fairmont, Minnesota. It ignited an image of speed and engineering wonders, bursting with power and precision.

But it wasn't American muscle cars like the Charger that really captured my heart. It was a used Jaguar XK120, sitting in a small dealership just past the Fairmont high school on Highway 15. Its curves were poetry in metal, a stark contrast to the boxy sedans populating our town's driveways. Next to it stood a Studebaker Avanti, all sleek lines and promises of 150 mph speeds. These weren't just cars to me; they were portals to another world.

Minnesota's icy winters became my personal driving training ground. While others saw treacherous roads, I saw opportunities to perfect the art of drifting, to understand the balance between traction and slide. Every empty parking lot was a potential racetrack, every ice-covered lake a chance to push the limits of car and driver alike.

The chapters in this section map out a journey that spans decades and continents, from rural Minnesota to the winding roads of Europe, from classic British roadsters to groundbreaking Supercars. It's a tale of three yellow beauties: a 1969 Lotus Elan that taught me the true meaning of handling, an Acura NSX that redefined my understanding of what a car could be and a McLaren MP4-12C that brought Formula One technology to my garage.

These are stories of restoration and revelation, of heart-pounding track days and serene Sunday drives. You'll learn of the connections between my carefully selected machines, from their shared obsession with reducing weight to the influence of racing legend Ayrton Senna.

This section is a celebration of automotive excellence. It's also an exploration of how cars have shaped my life, challenged my skills and brought me immeasurable joy.

6

THE GENESIS OF A CAR ENTHUSIAST

WHILE THE EXACT MOMENT WHEN cars and driving became a defining passion in my life eludes me, I recall several events in my youth that contributed in major ways. The thunderous rumble of Jim Roller's Charger, which I heard many times at the Lutheran Brethren Bible Camp, was one of the first. That car had me and every other young boy sprinting to the parking lot to see what it was. Roller was a friendly fixture at this church camp, although I never quite understood his role or what his position was.

As a kid, I always lent a keen ear as my older cousins talked about cars. Cousins Dennis or Donny Larsen occasionally gave me an old car magazine. And Tom Felber, my uncle Bub and aunt Effie's only son, even built a hot rod once. I read junior fiction stories that featured hot rods, but they never captured my imagination and I found my automotive interests veering in a different direction.

While appreciating the ubiquitous and popular American-made cars of the 1950s, I was more drawn to the exotic and the unique. At a small dealership on Highway 15, just past the high school in Fairmont, I remember being entranced by a used Jaguar XK120. Its curvy lines enthralled me, and I rode my bike a few miles just to look at it almost every week. Alongside the Jaguar stood a Studebaker Avanti, which, while made in America, looked nothing like other American cars. It had a design focused on speed and performance, enabling it to reach over 150 mph.

I enjoyed looking at cars, but I liked driving them even more. Getting behind the wheel, going fast around corners and squealing tires was always a thrill for me. I was lucky, because the icy Minnesota winters offered countless opportunities to perfect my drifting skills. And if the roads were cleared of snow and slush too quickly, I could always drive out onto an ice-covered lake with my buddies and practice racing there.

Oddly enough, my genuine passion for cars was triggered by an unexpected quirk of history. In the aftermath of World War II, the British government was strapped for hard currency and pressured its domestic automakers to export 70% of their production to the United States. This mandate, combined with the enthusiasm of returning U.S. soldiers who had been exposed to these cars in Europe, explains the surprising availability of British sports cars to car-crazy American teenagers like me.

When my cousin John Gravley rolled into Fairmont in an Austin-Healey 100-6—a green, two-seat British racing drophead with a six-cylinder engine and overdrive—I fell in love. Despite being a year younger, I managed to convince (or perhaps bully) John into letting me drive it all over town the week he stayed with us.

I knew little about the car, but its impact on me was profound. The purr of the engine, the rich scent of leather, the perfectly positioned seats and its uncanny ability to hug corners were all revelations. That brief encounter with a small British convertible sparked what would become a lifelong love affair with British sports cars.

John Gravley in his Austin Healy on the farm.

The next car to tug not only at my heartstrings but also my wallet was a white, rusting 1965 Triumph Spitfire convertible. It belonged to Jerry Russell, a controversial fixture among the Jesus Freaks I lived with in Iowa City, Iowa during my college years. The Spitfire sat forlornly in a snowbank outside Jerry's double-wide mobile home, and where others saw a lost cause, I saw potential. In my mind's eye, I was already cruising down the highway to the beach with the top down and a bikini-clad beauty by my side.

Once again, my cousin John became my enabler. He gave Jerry his 1964 Ford Fairlane, I put in some cash and the Spitfire was ours. John drove it through the fall and winter, often braving snowstorms to visit his girlfriend Linda Gambil in Mount Vernon. Eventually, John got another car and the Triumph and I ended up in Rochester, Minnesota.

For nearly two years, the plucky little Spitfire was my primary mode of transportation. My high school friend Randy Larson had the newer and more popular Triumph TR6, and we took great pleasure in parking our British sports cars side by side in the parking lot of KNXR radio, where we both worked.

Triumph had introduced the Spitfire to compete with the Austin-Healey Sprite, but it wasn't quite in the same league as John Gravley's Austin-Healey. With its single Zenith Stromberg carburetor, the small, 1147 cc four-cylinder engine was underpowered, generating just 63 horsepower and 67 lbs. of torque at 3,500 rpm. It had a top speed of 90 miles per hour and managed 30 miles to the gallon. While these specs weren't impressive, the real challenge was its body, which seemed powerless against the corrosive assault of Minnesota's salted winter roads.

Plus, the car had its share of charming idiosyncrasies. To access the engine compartment, you had to flip two locks low down on both sides of the front of the car. The entire front hood and fenders would then lift, exposing the engine completely. While complex, the design actually made it easy to work on the engine by sitting on either front tire—it was a level of accessibility I've never encountered since.

In the summer of 1972, determined to breathe new life into the Spitfire, I took matters into my own hands. I struck a deal with a local auto body shop, working part-time to finance a new paint job. At night, I used their space and tools to work on the Triumph. After repainting the car and letting it cure, I pushed it over to Munger Imports, just a block away.

Jeff Munger, the service manager, was a friend and a regular customer at Schaak Electronics, where I also worked. His father and grandfather owned the foreign car dealership that bore his last name. Jeff agreed to do the engine work on my Triumph at a steep discount, as long as I wasn't in a hurry and understood that his mechanics would work on it between other jobs. The deal was sweetened by my promise of a good discount on some new speakers for Jeff.

On a fateful Saturday morning in the summer of 1972, Jeff called to tell me that my 1965 Triumph Spitfire repairs were complete, and that the car was ready for pickup. As I arrived at the shop, my eyes were drawn to a yellow sports car being pushed toward the open showroom door. Before the afternoon was over, I had become the proud owner of that little yellow car—a 1969 Lotus Elan that I refused to part with for the next 50 years.

The white 1965 Triumph Spitfire John Gravley and I bought in Iowa City.

7

HELLO YELLOW: MY 50-YEAR LOVE AFFAIR WITH A LOTUS ELAN

A SHORT TEST DRIVE OF the barely-used Lotus left me utterly stunned. I had never experienced anything like it. Rounding the curves at the end of 4th Street, the car seemed to hug the road, but it felt like I was being launched from a slingshot when accelerating out of each corner. I was instantly, irrevocably smitten—or, as we might say today, "gobsmacked."

Without hesitation, I made an offer on the car, which only had 3,112 miles on it. They eventually agreed to my price, but I had to pay cash and they refused to take my Triumph on trade.

To finance this impulsive purchase, I sold my Triumph to Rick Husband, a part-time employee at Schaak Electronics. Unfortunately, Rick totaled the car before he could pay me or get it insured. His debt was slowly repaid with items from his father's furniture store, which came in handy for the new house I had recently purchased in Kasson, Minnesota.

My decision to buy the Lotus Elan was purely visceral, based on two factors: its stunning beauty (it was the first yellow car I'd ever seen and the most gorgeous), and its unparalleled handling, which I experienced during that initial, three-mile test ride. I had no idea what a Lotus was or even who made it. I recall asking Jeff, "So, who manufactures Lotus?"

During my first few weeks of Elan ownership, I would wake up at night and look out the window to make sure it was still in the driveway. While I was on my shift at Schaak Electronics, I took breaks just to go to the parking lot and stare at this superb machine. Infatuation led to deep affection, and finally, the realization that I was hopelessly, head-over-heels in love.

I took the longest possible route to work each day. And after parking the Elan, I'd walk slowly backward to the mall's entrance, watching the car the whole time. I couldn't wait for the day to end so I could get back in the Lotus and drive. I dreamed about the car, literally not believing my good fortune. I kept thinking that I would wake up to find the car completely gone.

Embarrassed by how little I knew about this fantastic vehicle, I began a quest to find out everything I could about it. This was way before the Internet, so I had to scour back issues of car magazines at the library. I visited foreign car dealerships, showing them the car and asking what they knew. Slowly, I began to understand that my Elan was unique and, while not widely acclaimed, had caught the imagination of some of the most discerning moto-journalists and more than a few hobby racers.

My thirst for knowledge led me on an adventure that would cement my love for the Elan and deepen my appreciation of its origins. In September 1973, I decided to track down the Elan's birthplace. I traveled to the UK to visit the Lotus factory, armed with nothing but an address and a hefty dose of youthful enthusiasm.

After a two-hour train ride from London to Hethel, near Wymondham in Norfolk, a taxi dropped me at the factory door. I had no appointment, just an earnest desire to see where my beloved car was made. Showing up an hour before lunch, I announced to the bewildered receptionist that I was from the United States, owned a Lotus Elan and wanted to see where it was made.

After a 20-minute wait in the lobby and frantic phone calls by the receptionist, I was greeted by the head of Lotus PR. To my relief and delight, he seemed to find my surprise visit a lot more interesting than whatever else he had planned for the day.

He gave me a tour of the entire factory and introduced me to all sorts of people. "This bloke owns a Lotus Elan in the United States and he came to visit its birthplace," he'd say. I shook a lot of hands and soaked in every detail.

At one point, the PR guy pointed toward a group of men walking into an office. "That's Colin Chapman," he said. "He runs the place." What a thrill to catch a glimpse of the genius behind the Elan.

My guide took me to lunch in a new prototype vehicle, and loaded me up with brochures, review reprints, T-shirts, pens and a cigarette lighter when we got back to Lotus headquarters. He even gave me the Lotus Annual Report for 1971, which I still have along with most of the other memorabilia.

Later that night, back in London, I was as high as a kite. It was September 30, my birthday, and this trip was the best present I'd ever given myself. The next day, I capped off my UK adventure by seeing a revival of Noel Coward's *Private Lives* at the Queen's Theater in the West End, directed by John Gielgud and starring Jill Bennett, John Standing, Geoffrey Palmer and Pinkie Johnstone.

Learning to get the most from my Elan meant track days with expert instructors.

For the first several years, the Elan was my daily driver. Although I was told it would be unreliable, it wasn't. I drove it through the Minnesota winters, although careful not to take it out when there was snow on the road.

Eager to explore the Elan's capabilities and show off a little bit, I entered club-sponsored Autocross and Gymkhana competitions. The car's impressive handling earned me several trophies, including a couple of first-place victories. To help me go faster, I found a driving instructor at a slalom training day who was familiar with leveraging the Elan's tendency for twitchiness.

As life progressed, the Elan moved with me to Milwaukee and then back to Minneapolis. Its tiny size, limited storage, poor heater and lack of air conditioning eventually relegated it from primary transportation to a weekend warrior and special occasion car. I drove it to automobile races, car shows and camping trips, including a memorable journey to upper Wisconsin and another to Colorado.

Older car enthusiasts would often approach me, drawn by the Elan's classic lines. They'd share stories of their first English sports cars and how, after marriage and children, they had reluctantly sold them. They'd look wistfully at my Elan and say, "Selling my (Triumph, MG, Morgan, Jaguar, etc.) was the dumbest thing I ever did. I'd do anything to have that car back again. Never sell this car, son. You'll regret it the rest of your life."

In early 1980, as I changed companies and started a new career, I also met a new love—Maggie. At our wedding reception, my dear aunt Effie (my dad's sister) approached my new bride and whispered, "Now that Steve's married, will he be getting rid of that little yellow girl-catcher of his?"

Maggie thought a moment, looked up at Effie, and delivered a line that would set the tone for our relationship with the Elan for decades to come: "If my husband is going to have a mistress, I'd prefer her to be in the garage so I can keep an eye on her."

True to her word, Maggie never once complained about how the Lotus had taken up precious garage space, or about the cost of moving it on trucks across the country multiple times, first to Los Angeles, then to New York, back to Minnesota and finally to Phoenix.

* * * * *

I shielded the Elan from the Phoenix desert climate as much as possible, but I didn't do it any favors by not driving it regularly. Early in 2013, inspired by Jay Leno's Elan purchase and 14 extensive videos on its restoration, I decided to rebuild the car I loved so much. I finally had the three things I needed most: Space, time and funds. Any restoration attempted without these three critical elements is doomed.

The restoration was pushed to the fore by a minor rodent issue. Stored outside our house temporarily for several months, the Lotus had become home to something that was eating the electrical wires. I promptly moved the car into the garage, but the mice came with it. I put my best exterminator on the job—our little cat, Gilda.

Before this assignment, Gilda's biggest catch was a bird that was killed when it flew into a window. She'd picked it up after it was dead and trotted around like a royal huntress for a day. I had faith that she could hunt live game, so I put her in the garage and closed the door for the night.

Gilda had never been forced to sleep in the garage, so for a half an hour she howled at the door to be let in. Then things were quiet. An hour later, she was howling again and I let her in this time. As I opened the door to the garage, I couldn't miss it. There, lined up carefully on the rug leading into the house, were three dead mice. Good girl, Gilda!

With the car now rodent-free, I could start the rebuilding process with expert support from my friends in the local Lotus club. I also found Brian Buckland in the UK, the undisputed authority on the Lotus Elan. His book on rebuilding the Elan is the bible for Lotus enthusiasts undertaking any significant work on their cars. Buckland made an early trip to Phoenix to see my car, along with some of the Arizona sights, as part of his guest appearance at an annual Lotus-owner event in New York.

On his first trip to see me, Buckland examined every inch of the car and helped chart the direction for the rebuild. He provided invaluable guidance on what steps to take and in what order, and he advised me on where we might have pitfalls. Buckland made two additional trips to the States during the 30-month rebuild process, to supervise specific aspects of the work and personally undertake some of the trickier bits.

When the restoration was complete, I showed off the Elan at various car shows and events. At the Annual Lotus Owners Gathering in Colorado in August 2015, the judges selected it as "Best Elan."

* * * * *

As proud as I was about my Elan's restored glory, I began to realize that my garage was becoming increasingly crowded. The Elan had to share attention with a 2002 Acura NSX, a 2014 McLaren 12C and a couple of Polaris products, the 3-wheel Slingshot and the big off-road RZR—not to mention all my motorcycles. Eventually, I had to face the difficult truth that the Elan might need a new home where it could receive the dedicated attention it deserved.

This realization led me to reflect on my half-century of bonding with this remarkable machine. While not unique, owning one car for 50 years is rare. It says a lot about the car and a thing or two about the owner. Over the years, I chronicled the Elan's story and its coveted place in automotive history on my website, recording what car aficionados like Jay Leno, Gordon Murray, Peter Egan and Philip Richter have said about it. I even wrote a book about my 30-month rebuild of the Elan. But I've written very little about why I kept the car for so long. As I contemplated parting ways with it, however, I could finally articulate the reasons behind this enduring relationship.

From the first day I owned the Elan, I knew it was special. It was impossible to drive without a sense of wonder at how everything fit together so perfectly. Seeing the various engineering choices when working on the car, my friends and I would frequently pause, scratch our heads and mutter, "That is just friggin' brilliant." This didn't just happen once, but time and time again.

Colin Chapman, the man behind the Elan who I got a glimpse of when I visited his factory all those years ago, is today recognized as one of the greatest automotive designers to ever live. While perhaps not the best automotive businessperson, Chapman's creativity and innovation are lauded by every significant and respected critic. Chapman was at the zenith of his powers with the Elan, and my S4 may be its best incarnation.

That absolute magic, the unmistakable sense of awe at least once in every ride, delivered a driving experience like nothing else. Those moments were pure ecstasy, bringing me unmatched feelings of joy and exhilaration.

* * * * *

In late 2021, I received a phone call that transported me back through five decades of Lotus memories. Gary Turner, the new owner of my Elan (VIN: 459764 for any historic car lovers among my readers), was on the line. He had purchased the car from a dealer in California, who acquired it at the Gooding Auction earlier that year. Now, my old four-wheeled friend was embarking on its final journey—back to its spiritual home in the UK where it would join a small but elite collection of cars.

The Elan's new garage mates are a 1959 Porsche 356A, a 1986 Ferrari 328 GTS and a 1972 Porsche 911, all with low mileage and in concours condition. I couldn't have been more pleased. The Elan was returning to the land where it was made, into the hands of someone who truly appreciated cars of this vintage and style.

Mr. Turner's automotive pedigree was impressive. He had been involved in the industry since his youth, working for Rover, Jaguar and Ford before moving into consulting with firms like PwC and KPMG. He purchased my Elan while living in Toronto, Canada. Even more serendipitous was the fact that Brian Buckland, who played a crucial role in my 2013–2014 rebuild, now finds it more convenient to visit my old Elan in Bristol, England than to make the trip to Phoenix.

As I hung up the phone, I couldn't help but reflect on the incredible journey this car and I had shared. From that first encounter in Rochester to its new home across the Atlantic, the Elan had been more than just a car, it had been a constant companion, a catalyst for adventures and a thread woven through the fabric of my life story.

While it was bittersweet to see it go, I took comfort in knowing that it would continue to be loved and cherished, just as I had done for half a century.

My Lotus Elan, in the middle of its epic, two-and-a-half-year rebuild.

8

AN ACURA'S ALLURE: THE NSX THAT STOLE MY HEART

IN 2020, MY COUSIN KATHY Magee posted an old photo of me on Facebook. I was in my late 20s, standing in front of her parents' farm and sporting a permed head of curly hair. My cousin Margaret's husband, Dave Murra, was in the background. But the star of the photo was my copper-colored Mazda RX-7, gleaming in the sun.

I can still vividly recall explaining the RX-7's unusual features to my uncles and cousins. "It's got a rotary engine," I'd say with barely contained excitement. "The RPMs go to over 10,000. It's like piloting a boat on a lake with no wind, in total calm—like glass."

By this point in my life, it was becoming clear that my attraction to unique automobiles was more than just a passing phase.

My copper Mazda RX-7 with a two-rotor Wankel motor.

While the RX-7 was a lot of fun, the vehicle that had the biggest impact on me, besides my 1969 Lotus Elan, was Acura's NSX. Every self-respecting "car nerd" has experienced that moment when a particular automobile seems to reach out and speak to them. And it's not always an iconic, out-of-reach pinup gracing the cover of a glossy magazine. More often, it's a chance encounter—a sleek silhouette gliding past on the highway, or a quiet masterpiece sitting in a parking lot. Something strikes us, a combination of color and lines, and says, "I'm special—You see, don't you?" Those moments are often recounted and shared with others in this same club of people smitten by inspired, rolling, automotive art.

Occasionally we fall for some four-wheeled beauty and nothing comes of it. The car may be too impractical or out of our price range. We placate our desire by looking at pictures, reading about it in magazines or ogling it at car shows. But other times, if we're lucky, we manage to acquire the "dream car" and relive the magic of our first encounter every time we slide behind the wheel.

Not all cars that capture our imagination go on to become legends. The Edsel, Saturn and Pacer all had their fervent admirers, but you don't hear much about them these days. My Rochester friend, David Parkin, would buy a new Cadillac Eldorado convertible every year, storing the low mileage car it replaced carefully in a barn. David was convinced their value would skyrocket one day. They never did.

On the flip side, those with a keen eye for automotive potential sometimes spot future classics before the rest of the world catches on. Who among us doesn't wish we recognized the timeless appeal of a 1960s Aston Martin DB5, a 1970s Lotus Esprit or an AC Cobra when they first appeared?

In my case, two cars spoke to me louder than any others: the Lotus Elan and the Acura NSX. I was fortunate enough to acquire both near the beginning of their production runs. Over time, each has been recognized as an extraordinary machine, unique in automotive history and only appreciating in value as the years passed. In my opinion, only the 2014 McLaren MP4-12C comes close to matching the Elan and NSX in terms of impact and significance.

I saw my first Acura NSX on a parking garage roof in White Plains, New York. As I was walking toward my Nissan 300ZX (a decent, but not iconic car) I saw an amazing looking machine parked at the far end of the lot. It was set apart from the other vehicles—aloof, lean and sleek. I had no idea what it was.

Drawn like a magnet, I set my briefcase down and circled the car several times. At first, I couldn't discern the logo and thought it might be Italian, but closer inspection revealed its Japanese origins. I would have loaded my phone with pictures if smartphones were around back then. Everything about the NSX was so fresh, crisp and precise.

I was utterly smitten, wishing desperately for a camera to capture the moment. Although it would be years before I saw another NSX in person, that brief encounter left an indelible mark on my psyche.

*　*　*　*　*

Fast forward to 1997. I had just returned to the Twin Cities after a stint in Los Angeles at CitySearch, a promising tech startup backed by legendary investor and company creator, Bill Gross. After a year there, I agreed to join a Minneapolis-based startup called Net Perceptions, which was funded by the brilliant venture capitalist Ann Winblad. As the company's fortunes rose, I decided it was time for a new car.

The BMW M5 (E28 series) caught my eye. It had been dubbed "the Beast" by the automotive press. With 400 HP and 398 lbs. of torque, it promised to be a rocket ship disguised as a family sedan. Automotive writers were going ga-ga. With a zero-to-sixty time faster than a Corvette and a top speed of 180 mph (with the limiter removed), it was the ultimate wolf in sheep's clothing.

Here was a "family car" that was quicker in a quarter mile than an Aston Martin DB7. It beat the Ferrari F355 Spider in cornering (measured on a 300-foot skid pad). It was faster through the slalom than a Lamborghini Diablo. Throw in a manual gearbox and brilliant handling, and what's not to love?

I had to have one.

One afternoon, I stopped at Motorwerks BMW in Bloomington and began the ordering process. Within 30 minutes, I had "configured" my car: Titanium Silver with a red leather interior and a host of options. With the selected extras, the car priced out at around $80,000, a staggering amount of money then and now. But it was 2000, a year full of economic optimism, and I was riding high on the dot-com wave. What could go wrong?

My excitement quickly turned to frustration when they told me I had to wait 14 months for the car. Threatening to cancel the deal didn't help. They told me this would only move me further down the list for one of the most coveted icons in automotive history, a car for which BMW had pledged to limit production.

I finally agreed to their terms. But what would I drive in the meantime? The new car manager introduced me to his used car expert Paul Kline, who put me together with Troy Chamberlain. A talented and experienced driver who was piloting a race-prepared BMW, with sponsors, at tracks throughout the Midwest, Troy was thrilled to learn I owned a Lotus Elan, which he had once raced. We spent hours discussing different vehicles, how they handled and the best ones for the road.

My last question to him was, "What's the best handling, most amazing street car—not race car—you've ever driven?" He quickly replied, "Simple question and simple answer: That would be an Acura NSX." He owned one for a year while living and racing in Germany, and he and his wife had fallen in love with it. His biggest regret was not bringing it back to the States. He showed me some photos of his NSX, and I remembered the car I'd seen on the roof of the parking lot in White Plains.

By the end of our conversation, I wanted one—bad. The dealership didn't have any on the lot, but they promised to find me a used one at the dealer auctions. They proposed buying it for me, and I'd pay them exactly what they spent on it. Then they'd take it back in trade for my BMW M5 when it arrived, with zero mark-up and no extra charge for miles added.

Before my next visit with Paul Kline, I'd done enough research to know exactly what I wanted: a red car with a black interior and removable Targa top (NSX-T), manual transmission, low miles and a 1995 model year or newer.

Two weeks later, I was pulled out of a work meeting to talk to a breathless Kline. He had just inspected "the perfect" car, which met everything on my wish list and more. This model had a carbon fiber interior kit and a Comptech factory exhaust upgrade.

Paul thought it might be bid over the price we agreed on, and he asked me if I could go higher. When I hesitated, he said, "Steve, I'll tell you what: I'm convinced you'll love this car. If you don't want it for what we pay for it, I'll buy it myself."

A few days later, back at the BMW dealership, I saw this freshly detailed 1995, one-owner, red Acura NSX-T (VIN: JH4NA1186ST000274) for the first time. It was gorgeous. And then I drove it. Sublime! It's handling reminded me of my Lotus Elan, but it was much, much faster—and it had air conditioning, a working radio, cruise control and lots of other creature comforts. If you put the windows up, the car was as quiet as, well, a Honda. If you rolled them down, the engine's exhaust notes were symphonic. I was in love.

The timing was perfect, as I was celebrating my 50th birthday a few days after I drove the NSX home. Maggie and I hosted a fun riverboat party on the Mississippi River. I parked the NSX in the parking area leading to the boat dock, and Maggie put an enormous red bow on it.

As time passed, I became more and more attached to the NSX. Even Maggie learned to love it. My daughter, Ginger, learned how to drive a stick shift in the NSX after failing to learn on our Toyota 4Runner. Like many girls her age, she was oblivious to car brands, not caring what was in our garage. One day, however, after I dropped her off at her high school in the red NSX for the first time, her interest was suddenly piqued.

When I got home from work that night, she asked several uncharacteristic questions: "Dad, what kind of car is the red car? How many 'horsepowers' does it have? How fast can it go?" Some boys at her high school had been asking her all about the NSX.

The months went by, and eventually BMW called to say that my new M5 (VIN: WBSNB93598CX10660) was ready to be picked up. At the dealership after work the next day, I spent an hour on paperwork, got briefed on the new car and turned over the keys to my NSX.

I drove home in my brand-new BMW M5, less than a dozen miles. The first drive in the car was amazing, and even though it was in its break-in period it was scary fast. Plus, it had the new car smell! I entered the kitchen, tossed the keys on the counter and told Maggie, "I think I may have just made a mistake."

Don't get me wrong, the M5 was, and still is, a fantastic car. It holds four adults in total comfort. It's blindingly fast and solid as a tank. You could cruise at 80–90 mph and feel like you're only going 40. The sound system is incredible. The list of positive attributes goes on and on.

But the car scared Maggie to death, and its low gas mileage and thirst for oil really ticked me off. "It goes 40 mph in neutral," Maggie said as she vowed never to drive it again. "I just look somewhere and before I know it, the car is there."

As I drove the car less and less, I realized that the whole "wolf in sheep's clothing" concept that echoed in the heads of many car nuts was also a major bust. Sure, you can pull up in an M5 at a stoplight next to a new Corvette or just about any other hot car and smoke them, but who cares? How many times is this fun? Who were these people in the other car, and did they even know you were racing them? They probably just think you're being a jerk.

As it turns out, the experience of approaching a stoplight in an NSX—and having other drivers occasionally lower their windows in recognition, smile and stick out their arms with raised thumbs—gave me a far greater kick. Sure, the NSX would draw the occasional driver who'd want to race, but pulling away casually felt so much classier.

When we moved to Arizona in 2003, the M5 made the trip in the back of a moving van. Having that car made even less sense in Arizona, and we no longer needed two cars with a backseat. It was about this time that an alluring NSX siren song began floating in from the desert.

On a lovely January day, it occurred to me that Acura dealerships in the northern part of the country might have an unsold NSX or two. "How many people up there were walking into Acura dealerships asking if snow chains would fit on an NSX?" I thought.

So I started calling around. On my third or fourth try, I found an Acura dealership with a brand-new NSX in Libertyville, Illinois. The car was a 2002 model, so they were willing to deal. And it was yellow—the same color as my Lotus Elan. My knees went weak.

I told them about my BMW M5 with just 9,000 miles on it. I suggested that we make an even trade, reasoning that the M5 was something they could easily sell in the winter. After some negotiation, we agreed to trade cars but they squeezed $10,000 out of me, arguing that the M5 was "used."

The new, yellow NSX proved to be more than just a car; it was a driving experience like no other. I owned that incredible vehicle for more than 20 years and accumulated more than 40,000 happy miles in it. When we parted company in 2023, it looked as new as the day I bought it. Even Maggie misses it to some extent: young men driving Asian tuner cars occasionally followed her and stopped her in grocery store parking lots to ask if she had a boyfriend.

Over the years, I've become more secure in my personal assessment of cars. Educated friends like Clayton Saffell and Brett Engel have been superb teachers, and I stand by my belief that the NSX is something special. Hundreds of journalists have written about the NSX since its inception. Gordon Murray, the South African designer of Formula One racing cars and, according to Jay Leno, the greatest car designer that ever lived, loved the NSX, too. Murray, renowned for creating the McLaren F1 among other remarkable cars, has publicly stated how much the NSX influenced his vision for what the McLaren F1 should be.

The NSX's perfect balance of performance and practicality, plus its reliability coupled with exotic car looks and handling, made it a true standout in automotive history. From that first sighting in a New York parking garage to the countless miles we shared together, the NSX has left an indelible mark on my life as a car enthusiast. It remains, to this day, one of the finest cars I've ever had the privilege to own and drive.

Where does one go after an NSX?

From one NSX to another, with an M5 detour in between.
My first NSX (red), the BMW M5 and yellow '02 NSX—the keeper.

9

STEVE'S SUPERCAR SEARCH: THE QUEST FOR THE ULTIMATE RIDE

AFTER COMPLETING THE REBUILD OF my Lotus Elan in 2014, I found myself at a crossroads. The project had consumed two and a half years and over $65,000, including some select outside labor. While I hadn't done all the work myself, it was my car, my project and my fingers were in every part. Everyone who touched the vehicle was the very best in their field, and the result was nothing short of perfection.

The Elan emerged better than it had left the factory; a superb driver's car that honored Colin Chapman's vision while adding a few minor, modern safety features to improve reliability. Yet, for all its charm, it still wasn't a car for casual, everyday use. It had no air conditioning, the soft top wasn't automatic and climbing in and out wasn't as much fun as it was when I was younger.

Two thoughts crystallized in my mind: first, I could now afford a Supercar, and second, my heart health was putting an expiration date on my days. "Supercar now, die later" became my mantra. The idea of leaving this world without having owned an over-the-top Supercar seemed like a regret I'd carry into eternity.

As a car show and Cars & Coffee junkie, I'd often drive my Lotus or NSX to events, park and immediately start wandering around, admiring the array of exotic machinery and talking with the owners of various makes and models. Over the years, I'd flirted with various Supercars at these events. The Ariel Atom, while not technically a Supercar, fascinated me with its performance when equipped with a 350 HP Honda VTEC engine. But frankly, it was purely a race car with zero creature comforts (such as doors, luggage compartments, windows, a windshield or a glove box). But I sure had fun with one at an Ariel Atom track day. The Audi R8 caught my eye, too, and I almost put a deposit down on one but a test drive revealed it lacked the magical handling of my Lotus or NSX.

Through countless conversations, I developed a somewhat unscientific profile of different Supercar owners:

- Ferrari owners formed an exclusive club, emphasizing style, sound and history over performance. Most had never considered taking their cars to a track day. Several Ferrari owners bought the same car repeatedly, every other year. And many Ferrari dealers won't sell a new one to someone who hasn't purchased a used one.
- Lamborghini owners were an eclectic lot, former racers and entrepreneurs with a keen interest in performance and a penchant for self-deprecating humor. They also changed cars more frequently, switching among brands and models.
- Audi R8, Aston Martin, Bugatti Veyron and Ford GT owners were a mixed bag, ranging from pretentious to down-to-earth. They tended to be non-joiners.
- McLaren owners stood out. They drove their cars more, taking them on long trips and to the track. They were welcoming and eager to discuss their cars' virtues. While a friendly and welcoming group, they were not particularly well organized.

Interestingly, owners of classic, aka vintage, Supercars were a different breed entirely—a far smarter and more entertaining species. Many had found and gained their vehicles when they were at a low-value point and then held onto them. They had far-ranging, and often conflicting, opinions, and I took it all in.

My discussions with all these Supercar owners pushed me into the McLaren camp. It also helped that I had genuinely expert friends: Philip Richter wrote for *Sports Car Market* (SCM) magazine and was the proprietor of the highly regarded Turtle Garage website, and Keith Martin published SCM. Harry Mathews in Colorado, the McLaren race team owner and the man who knew more about McLarens than anyone in the United States, was another tremendous asset, and we became good friends.

But it was a chance conversation with a Lamborghini Aventador owner that truly swayed me toward McLaren. After I helped guide him into a parking spot at the Gainey Ranch Cars & Coffee in Scottsdale, Arizona, I asked him about his current ride. He admitted he'd only put about 700 miles on it since trading in his McLaren, so his opinions were still forming.

But then he flooded me with information about his 25 years of owning more than 15 Supercars, including many Ferraris, Aston Martins, other Lamborghinis and a Veyron. "I call my new Aventador 'my Audi' as it's so unlike my previous Lambos," he said, giving a nod to Audi's purchase of Lamborghini. "It's an amazing car, but it's become so civilized it's now less of an adventure to drive. The McLaren was the Supercar I drove the most."

He described how his McLaren outperformed every car he ever owned, and how it was a delight to drive with outstanding visibility and comfort. "While 'my Audi' is a splendid car, it's not a McLaren," he told me. "My wife and I thought nothing of throwing a couple of bags in the McLaren and driving to our condo in San Diego. I would never do that in one of the others. The McLaren is all about the driver."

Intrigued, I dove into researching what McLaren had to offer. They were relatively new to producing cars for sale to the public, as their experience was in building Formula One race cars. The only vehicle they ever made for "real people" was the highly regarded F1, built from 1992 to 1998.

Each F1, designed by Gordon Murray, took three and a half months to build. In six years, they only made 106 of them, each costing $1 million. One of those F1s won the 24 Hours of Le Mans race in 1995. Used ones today sell for north of $15 million. Comic actor Rowan Atkinson sold his F1 for $12.2 million in 2015. It had accumulated 41,000 miles in the 17 years he owned it, and had also been involved in two serious accidents. In 1999 it was rear ended, and in 2011 Atkinson lost control of it on a slippery road, hitting a tree and a road sign before catching fire. The car was rebuilt by McLaren each time.

The new production-level McLaren, the MP4-12C, first made it to the United States late in 2012. It looked nice and ticked all my "high performance" hot buttons. Plus, McLaren had found a way to produce the carbon fiber in one tenth of the time it took for the F1, resulting in McLaren being able to drop the cost by 75%.

The 12C was the first entirely gear-driven Supercar, with no belts, pulleys or anything else to wear out or break under high stress—just like an F1 car. Most McLaren owners find their cars go tens of thousands of miles with no more service requirements than changing the fluids. Jay Leno owns several McLarens, including an F1, and says all he ever does on any of them is change the fluids.

In a conversation a few years back with Aristeo Izguerra (Izzy), the brilliantly competent service manager at my local McLaren dealer, I asked how they could keep a repair shop operating given McLaren's history of reliability. He smiled and said, "That's why we have track days."

I saw my first McLaren 12C in person at a car show, and I was captivated. The owner allowed me to crawl all over it and sit in it while answering my hundreds of questions. I loved the designers' commitment to lightweight, carbon-fiber construction and so much more. When rumors of a new McLaren model, the 650S, began circulating I panicked. The new design just didn't appeal to me. I liked the MP4-12C better with its rounder curves.

Afraid that I'd never get a chance to buy a 12C before they stopped making them, I decided to see if I could find one. Adding a McLaren to my NSX and Lotus would almost make up a "collection." The three cars would have fundamental similarities—a focus on low weight, putting driver needs at the center of things and a willingness to try alternative materials to achieve performance goals. The Elan used glass-reinforced plastic (fiberglass), the NSX used aluminum and the McLaren used carbon fiber.

As luck would have it, McLaren was just wrapping up production of the MP4-12C as I began my earnest search for one to call my own. With the new 650S model on the horizon, many early adopters were trading in their 12Cs, creating a wealth of options on the market.

While I had a lot of great inventory to choose from, there were no McLaren dealers in Phoenix at that time. I began calling dealers nationwide and was happily surprised to find many exciting cars at discounted prices. With the stars so well-aligned, I found the McLaren I wanted—a new Spider model with volcano yellow paint, sport exhaust, upgraded wheels and a total carbon fiber interior package.

I flew to Dallas and headed straight to Park Place McLaren, picked up my new car and drove it the 1,100 miles back home. For those two days and 16 hours, I experienced intense nervousness, acute anxiety, pure adrenaline and absolute fun.

The McLaren draws attention wherever it goes,
especially with the license plate MCLAREN.

10

SUPERCARS AND AUTOMOTIVE HUMILITY

AUTOMOBILE MANUFACTURERS DISCOVERED early on that success on the racetrack translated to sales in dealer showrooms—"Win on Sunday, Sell on Monday!" While most modern cars have little in common with their racing counterparts, Supercars and near-Supercars are a different breed altogether. Manufacturers like Aston Martin, Ferrari, McLaren, Porsche, Lamborghini and Pagani sell cars to the public that boast substantial performance and, in many cases, track-like capabilities.

But therein lies the rub: how much of a car's capability can the average driver actually use on the street? My journey through various high-performance machines has been a humbling lesson in this regard. Let me walk you through my experiences with three very different cars.

The Lotus Elan: A Deceptive Teacher

From the moment I first drove my Lotus Elan, I knew it was out of the ordinary. Its twin overhead cam engine made it exceptionally fast and its lightweight design gave it an edge in handling. At amateur SCCA and Gymkhana races, first-place trophies became almost routine.

Feeling confident, I took it to a genuine track school. After classroom instruction, timed practices and coaching from professional drivers, I thought I was extracting 90–95% of the Elan's capabilities. I was shaving hundredths of seconds off each lap, feeling like a pro.

Then came the reality check. The instructor took the wheel of my Elan and, with me as a passenger, knocked two to three full seconds off my best time. And remember, he was carrying my extra weight! Humbled, I revised my estimate: on my absolute best day, I might be using 80–85% of the Elan's potential. And that was being generous.

The Acura NSX: An Eye-Opening Video

While I never tracked my 2002 yellow NSX, I did take its predecessor—the red 1995 model—to the track. The NSX is a dream to drive at speed; its predictability and precision can make even a moderately skilled driver feel like an expert.

At an open track day, I was passing most of the other cars with ease. With nearly 300 HP in a 3,000-lb. aluminum body, the NSX's near-perfect balance had me feeling invincible. By day's end, I estimated I was using 75–80% of the car's capabilities.

Then I saw a video that shattered my illusions. It showed the legendary Brazilian F1 driver Ayrton Senna piloting an NSX around a racetrack in Japan. The grace and skill on display were otherworldly. His hands were a blur between the shifter and steering wheel, his footwork on the pedals a masterclass in precision. It's no wonder, really. Senna was deeply involved in fine-tuning the NSX chassis and played a critical role in evolving the car's performance.

Suddenly, my estimate plummeted. Once again being generous to myself, I'd say that on my very best day, with extensive practice and coaching, I might—might—approach 60% of the NSX's true potential. And I won't argue with anyone who thinks that's delusional. The NSX is capable of 179 mph, but I've never taken it above 155. And I've never driven it faster than 110 mph through a turn on a track.

The McLaren: A Glimpse into Another World

My yellow McLaren Spider represents a huge leap in performance from either of the other two cars. Embarrassingly, it's never seen a racetrack, and I've never even tried its launch control feature. I had to replace the original tires because their date codes had expired, not because they were worn out. That's how little I've pushed this car.

I did rent a McLaren for some high-speed laps on a track once, however, and it was absolutely mind-blowing. With a good coach beside me, I saw my speeds increase and my lap times fall. The car's F1-derived features shine when you push this 640 HP, sub-3,000-lb. beast to its limits.

After some spirited driving on curvy roads between Phoenix and Prescott, I thought I might be using close to 40% or even 50% of the McLaren's capability. Then came another reality check. At a McLaren owner's event, I rode with Chris Goodwin, McLaren's Chief Test Driver. A highly regarded former racer, Goodwin seemed to meld with the car. After just a few miles on city streets, I realized how far off my estimate had been. I revised it down to 30–35%—at best.

The Humbling Truth

Here's the irony: the more capable the car, the less of its potential the average driver can access. It's a humbling realization. While I may never come close to the performance limits of these machines, the precision and joy they offer, even at a fraction of their capability, is unmatched.

It's easy for someone like me, who has been fortunate enough to own several of these automotive phenomena, to admit that owning them is, in some ways, a waste of their true potential.

But hey, we can all dream.

11

A YELLOW TRILOGY: LOTUS, NSX AND MCLAREN

WHEN MY THREE "COLLECTOR" CARS were lined up in my garage, their associations were impossible to miss. Their shared yellow color is more than a coincidence—it's a reflection of my personal taste and, interestingly, a nod to racing history. The "Volcano Yellow" of the McLaren MP4-12C, according to designer Frank Stephenson, was inspired by Ayrton Senna's racing helmet.

While the yellow hue is the most obvious link among my three favorite cars, even casual observers could sense deeper associations. Some are apparent, others more subtle, but most go far beyond mere color. Here are the most significant:

Weight: The Pursuit of Lightness

The first common attribute begins with Colin Chapman of Lotus and his dedication to weight reduction. He's famous for saying, "Simplify, then add lightness." Chapman is to lightweight cars what Houdini is to magic. He believed that while adding power made a car faster on the straights, subtracting weight made it faster everywhere.

Chapman's obsession with weight reduction was legendary. He once quipped that any car that holds together for an entire race is too heavy. There's even a story about him complaining, upon returning to the factory after a few days away, that all his cars had gained weight in his absence. This philosophy is evident in all three cars.

- **The Lotus Elan:** When I rebuilt my Elan, I discovered its steel frame weighed just 76 lbs. The fiberglass body added only 210 lbs. Fully assembled and with fluids, the entire car weighed just under 1,500 lbs.

- **The McLaren MP4-12C:** Its frame, made entirely of carbon fiber, weighs 275 lbs. The whole car, without fluids, tips the scales at just 2,868 lbs. The BBC documentary on the creation of the MP4-12C highlights Ron Dennis and his team's fierce commitment to weight reduction. Frank Stephenson, the 12C designer, declared, "Weight is the enemy." Their efforts sometimes bordered on the obsessive—the McLaren has no gas cap or glove box because they "add weight."

- **The Acura NSX:** The designers focused heavily on creating a lightweight vehicle. The car is all aluminum, from the engine to the chassis to the body, weighing just 3,000 lbs.

*L to R: My 2014 McLaren MP4-12C, my 2002
Acura NSX and my 1969 Lotus Elan SE.*

Ayrton Senna: The Human Connection

The next common thread running through all three cars is Ayrton Senna, one of the greatest Formula One drivers of all time. Senna drove for Lotus between 1985 and 1987 before moving to McLaren in 1988, winning 41 Formula One races in his career.

Beyond his driving prowess, Senna was renowned for his ability to provide detailed technical feedback about car performance—long before computerized telemetry sensors became commonplace. His sense of a car under racing conditions was unparalleled, as was his ability to communicate that to engineers.

Remarkably, Senna played a vital role in testing all three cars:

- For Lotus, he provided valuable feedback during his time as their F1 driver.
- With the NSX, his input led to a 50% increase in chassis stiffness. Later, at the first dedicated Japanese NSX tests at the Nürburgring, he provided further input to help Honda's (the NSX is only branded Acura in the U.S.) engineers tweak the NSX. Senna's perfectionism helped create a masterpiece, and Senna ended up owning several NSXs personally.
- At McLaren, Senna's feedback was instrumental in developing their road and race cars. He also convinced Ron Dennis and Gordon Murray to look at the NSX, which significantly influenced the McLaren F1's development.

Gordon Murray: The Design Genius

Murray, who was just beginning his design work for the McLaren F1 when Senna directed his attention to the NSX, once said, "From the moment I drove the little NSX, all the benchmark cars we'd been using as references for the F1—Ferrari, Porsche and Lamborghini—just vanished from my mind."

Perhaps more importantly, at least for me, when Murray was asked about his dream car, he said: "I've actually got my dream car, a Lotus Elan. I've never driven a better sports car. It's just what I like in a car, and it has the best steering feedback ever. The F1 was close, but the Elan nails it. It looks pretty, too, and makes a pleasant noise. I had one in 1970 when I first got married, and I've had two since."

Jay Leno: The Enthusiast's Perspective

The final connection among my three cars comes through Jay Leno, a genuine car enthusiast who appreciates all three vehicles. Leno owns a McLaren F1 and several Elans, including a 1969 model like mine.

He even credits Gordon Murray's praise of the Elan as the reason he bought one, citing an interview where Murray is asked to name the car and the road he would drive if it was his last day on Earth. "That's easy," he said. "It would be a Lotus Elan on the Scottish Highlands." Leno has documented the extensive rebuilds of two of his Elans on his YouTube channel, sharing his passion with the world.

Differences Amidst the Similarities

While these cars share many connections, they also have distinct characteristics. The Elan is about half the weight of the other two, with its fiberglass body. The NSX is aluminum, and the McLaren is carbon fiber. In the end, the NSX and McLaren were daily drivers, offering incredible performance on demand, while the Elan provided a pure sports car experience.

And, of course, they're all from different eras. As much as I love older cars and the ability to work on them, the handling, performance, reliability and comfort of newer cars are all incredibly appealing to me.

The Elan delivered an exhilarating, attention-demanding drive with its precise steering. The NSX added modern comforts like air conditioning, more room and worry-free reliability for long trips, handling like a docile Honda Accord until pushed to its limits. The McLaren, while comfortable, offered performance so intense and unlike a normal car that it's hard to describe—it's like being strapped to a hungry cheetah chasing an antelope.

* * * * *

There's no getting around the fact that 70+-year-old guys shouldn't be driving around in McLarens. I think I look good driving a Lotus Elan (we're closer in age), but they're too hard to get in and out of for me now.

Supercars like the McLaren are expensive to buy and insure, and they depreciate at an astounding rate. My McLaren, which has been driven less than 15,000 miles, is much like the day I drove it off the showroom floor. In some ways, it's better. I've added paint protection and carefully returned it to the dealer for factory-mandated updates. And yet, if I sold it now, I'd be lucky to get half what I paid for it.

Depreciation is the biggest downside to Supercars, and they all do it. If you have the patience to wait for 25 years and you've picked a classic, like I did with the Elan and the NSX, you'll get all your money back and then some.

However, I'd never recommend buying any car as an investment. The real payoff is the intangible joy of ownership and the exhilaration of driving. Pure, unadulterated fun is an experience that can't be measured in dollars and cents.

12
REFLECTIONS ON PRECISION ENGINEERING

DURING A RECENT DRIVE TO the Mayo Clinic in Scottsdale, I had an epiphany about my McLaren. As I navigated the streets, I was struck anew by the car's precision in a way I'd previously overlooked. When pondering why a car like this commands double the price of others with similar performance numbers, I realized: it's the precision.

This revelation brought to mind Simon Winchester's book, *The Perfectionists: How Precision Engineers Created the Modern World*. Winchester, a master storyteller, examines history through the lens of precision, from the Industrial Age to modern times. The book's structure itself is a testament to increasing precision, with chapter titles progressing from "Tolerance: 0.1" to "Tolerance: 0.000 000 000 000000 000 000 000 000 000 000 01."

As I drove northbound on State Route 51 in Phoenix, the McLaren's precise steering became unmistakable. This car goes exactly where you point it—absolutely straight, with no appreciable deviation. It doesn't move a single degree off center.

This level of precision stands in stark contrast to my friend David Barnett's 1948 MG-TC, which I once had the pleasure of driving. With David's coaching, I learned to turn the wheel in the general direction I wanted to go, then wait to see where the car actually headed before making further adjustments. That was an acceptable level of precision in 1948, and while nearly all modern cars have vastly improved steering, the McLaren takes it to another level.

The McLaren's precision surpasses even that of the Acura NSX, and I suspect it outperforms many other high-end automobiles from Ferrari, Aston Martin and Lamborghini. But how did McLaren achieve this?

Two factors come to mind:

1. The McLaren MP4-12C was designed and built by engineers fresh from their work on Formula One racing cars, where precision requirements are far stricter than for road cars.

2. McLaren's price point—around a quarter-million dollars for a base model in 2014—allowed for this level of precision. As Winchester notes in his book, exactitude comes at a price. Until a new level of precision can be amortized over many units, it remains extremely expensive.

With the 12C, McLaren's engineers had both the budget and the know-how to introduce a level of precision that even someone like me can appreciate. That says a lot. What struck me on that drive to the doctor's office was this: without consciously thinking about "precision," I noticed the exact responsiveness of the steering wheel, not just on straightaways but in corners, too. The accelerator and brakes conveyed the same precise, highly accurate response to every input. And no, I wasn't on any mind-altering drugs at the time!

My friend Clayton Saffell, a brilliant engineer, understands this innate sense of precision. Precision—or the lack thereof—is everywhere once you start looking for it.

Yet, even amidst this celebration of the McLaren's attention to every detail, it's worth remembering Gordon Murray's humble admission about the F1: "It's pretty good; we got most things right, but we never could get the steering as good as the Lotus Elan."

BUSINESS

A CAREER IN FAST FORWARD

MY CAREER HAS BEEN THE ultimate long-distance ride, with unexpected detours, thrilling straightaways and challenging terrain. From my early days in retail to the high-speed lanes of the dot-com boom and beyond, this section chronicles routes I've taken in entrepreneurship, corporate America and the world of venture capital.

The story begins in the attic of a mansion in Rochester, Minnesota, where I lived while attending Rochester State Junior College. It was here that I first glimpsed the world of business beyond my small-town upbringing. Working at Schaak Electronics, I learned the fundamentals of sales and customer service, skills that would serve me well throughout my career.

I also learned valuable lessons about networking, laying the groundwork for my future success in building and maintaining professional contacts.

As my career progressed, I was drawn to cutting-edge technology. Managing Digital Den, one of the first computer stores in Minnesota, marked my transition from traditional retail to the rapidly evolving world of personal computing. This experience was pivotal to my career trajectory. My background in consumer electronics merged with the digital revolution and gave me a view of how technology would reshape the world.

My time at Control Data Corporation marked my entry into the world of big tech. It was here that I met my future wife, Maggie, in a serendipitous "terminal affair" that blossomed over the company's internal messaging systems.

The 1980s and 1990s saw me navigate the corporate ladders of giants like AT&T and IBM/Prodigy. These experiences taught me the intricacies of large business operations and the challenges of innovation within mature corporate structures. They also stirred a desire for something more.

This desire led me to the world of startups, where I found my true calling. From CitySearch to Net Perceptions to BigFix, I dove headfirst into each technology adventure. At Net Perceptions, I learned the highs and lows of starting a company and taking it public. CitySearch taught me about the power of local digital communities, while BigFix showed me the complexities of government and large enterprise software sales.

In the latter part of my career, I found myself on the other side of the table as a venture partner at St. Paul Venture Capital and later at Emergence Capital. This experience gave me a new appreciation for the funding side of startups and allowed me to mentor and guide a new generation of entrepreneurs.

In retirement, I found new ways to contribute to the business world, from teaching at the Thunderbird School of Global

Management to judging startup competitions for the Arizona Commerce Authority. These roles have allowed me to pass on the knowledge and wisdom I've accumulated over the years to the next generation of business leaders.

Whether you're a budding entrepreneur, a seasoned business professional, or simply curious about the inner workings of the business world, you'll find something of value in these pages. Welcome to my business journey—a tale of innovation, perseverance and the ever-present pursuit of the next big idea.

13

FLOATING ON CIGAR SMOKE AND MARTINIS

SOMETIMES A SINGLE ENCOUNTER CAN change the entire trajectory of your career. For me, that moment came on a snowy evening in Rochester, Minnesota in the late 1970s. I was in my mid-20s, managing a Schaak Electronics store and feeling pretty good about my prospects in retail. I had gotten serious about the woman I was dating, a court sketch artist for the local television station. Her name was Tami Redman and she had two young children, Jamie and Jolie, from a previous marriage.

Some of my store's best customers worked at the Mayo Clinic or IBM, the two largest employers in town. These men (nearly all buyers in our store were male) were everything I wasn't—wealthy, worldly and deeply connected in circles I could only dream about.

One customer was Dr. Ed Banner, a highly regarded physician at the Mayo Clinic who moved to Rochester from "the big city"—Chicago. He let me glance into a part of the world that was foreign to me, making me feel like there was nothing I couldn't accomplish if I set my mind to it. We were vastly different in age and lightyears apart in economic and social status. Still, he treated me as an equal and a friend.

He heard me coughing in the store one Sunday and told me to call his office at Mayo the following day. Even then, I knew people waited months for an appointment at the Mayo Clinic. When I called, his assistant told me she'd been expecting to hear from me and to come right down. After a quick stop in his office, I was soon examined by the head of Mayo's ENT department. As the head of the Gynecology

Department, Dr. Banner wouldn't be treating me himself. I was prescribed a few pills and was on my way.

Dr. Banner drove a Ferrari and sported a shock of red hair. His coming into our store always felt more like a "grand entrance" than someone casually strolling in to browse the aisles. He purchased stereo systems for his living room, office and other spots in his house, and frequently bought expensive gifts for his family and friends.

Anyone spending even a short time in Rochester heard stories about Dr. Ed Banner. His exuberance, confidence and style made him the center of attention everywhere he went. He lived large and possessed a bigger-than-life presence. He was hard not to notice and impossible to forget.

One Saturday morning, a few weeks before Christmas, Dr. Banner finished making his seasonal purchases and we were chatting at the counter. He asked about my plans for the evening. Typically, my life was pretty dull, but this time it occurred to me that I could impress the good doctor. "Well, Doc, tonight I'm having dinner with my girlfriend at the Country Club," I said.

Rochester's Golf and Country Club was private and far too expensive for me—I had never even set foot inside it. The 18-hole golf course, designed by A.W. Tillinghast in 1916, was considered the finest of its kind. The club had all the amenities, including the requisite pro shop, bar & grill and swimming pool.

It also featured the Shawnee Dining Room, an upscale spot known for great food and elegant dining. That evening, the club was hosting KROC Television's (later KTTC) annual holiday party. My girlfriend worked at the station and invited me as her date. I was excited about going to "the country club" and proud of it.

No sooner had I revealed my plans when Banner said, "Ah, yes, Alice and I will be dining at the club this evening as well." He paused, thought for a moment, stroked his chin and asked, "Steve, do you like martinis?"

I never had one in my life but I instantly replied, "Yes, I do." I had only seen the odd-shaped martini glasses on television.

"And do you by any chance also enjoy a good cigar?" he asked.

Again, despite my inexperience, I heard myself saying, "Of course, Doc." The only cigars I had ever tried were those horrible Swisher Sweets in college.

What followed was an invitation that would change my life: "Steve, why don't you come over to the house about an hour before you're set to pick up your date. We'll have a martini and a cigar. I think you'll like that."

That evening, I arrived at the Banner residence just as snow flurries—the big, puffy, slow-moving ones you can see clearly as they lazily float past—started. Dr. Banner's wife greeted me warmly, saying, "You must be Steve. Ed is waiting for you in his library." She guided me past windows overlooking downtown Rochester and toward the rear of the house.

Dr. Banner stood up from his desk in a large, comfortable office that was, indeed, full of books. Classical music played at a low volume from bookshelf speakers I recognized as ones from our store. Mrs. Banner closed the double doors and Dr. Banner and I shook hands in greeting. After some preliminaries he said, "Now, let me make you one of my famous martinis."

Moving to a bar in the corner of the room, he pulled out a large bottle of gin and a smaller bottle of vermouth, carefully pouring out just the right amounts of the spirits into a stainless-steel shaker filled with ice. Spinning the liquid around, he told me it's essential not to be too vigorous, as one could "bruise the gin." After a minute, he left the room and returned with two large martini glasses.

From their frosted appearance, I knew they'd been chilled. He filled each glass with the crystal-clear liquid from the shaker and said, "Do you know what the ladies say about my martinis, Steve?"

I said nothing.

His eyes twinkled as he continued, "Well, they say, 'Doc, I'll have just one, two at the most, because three I'm under the table and four I'm under the host.'"

Before I could even sample my drink, he suggested that we "leave these here to rest just a bit while we find something to smoke."

We left the room and entered his garage, where he opened a refrigerator-turned-humidor filled with boxes and boxes of cigars from Cuba and South America. "Many of my patients are the wives of South American politicians and business executives," he said. "And when they wish to show their appreciation they send me boxes of cigars."

He pulled out two boxes and opened them, saying, "Here are my two current favorites. While the fillings are virtually the same, you'll see one is wrapped in a green leaf and the other a brown leaf. Which wrapper might you prefer, the green or the brown?"

I looked at them briefly and said, "I'll try the brown one."

He pulled one of the enormous brown cigars from the top of the box and handed it to me. Then, he selected one of the green ones for himself. But before we left, he took another large green cigar from the box and slipped it into my inside suit jacket pocket, saying, "Why don't you take one of these for later?" Then he took one of the brown ones and put it inside his jacket.

Back in his office, Dr. Banner patiently took me through the ceremony of circumcising a cigar and showed me the right way to light one. Apparently, you never use a lighter—only large stick matches— for cigars of this caliber. Obviously, he knew I was a novice and unfamiliar with all of this, but he never once treated me like we were anything other than equals performing a ritual we'd done hundreds of times together.

As we sat across from each other in classic Eames chairs, I'll never forget the smoke and its deep, rich fragrance wafting slowly around our heads and filling the room. I recall sipping the super-chilled martini and hearing quiet music in the background. We clinked our glasses in a toast or two. It was like being in a deep and relaxing dream, while simultaneously being fully awake and hyperaware of every sensation.

Before I knew it, Dr. Banner was rushing me out the door, insisting I mustn't be late for my date. I drove to Tami's apartment in a dreamlike state. As I walked up to her door, I felt as though I was floating rather than walking. I looked back toward my car and saw no footprints in the snow.

We got to the country club on time and soon found the party in a semi-private area at the rear of the large dining room. No doubt because of Tami's model-like appearance, we were seated at the head table with the owners of the television station from Quincy, Illinois, the local station's general manager, the evening news anchorman and his wife. Dinner progressed easily and comfortably, although as soon as people learned I wasn't involved in the television business they ignored me, and I was fine with that.

After dinner, while desserts were being served, there was a commotion behind me. I watched the eyes of the people across the table from me as they stared, transfixed. Someone special had obviously entered the room and was heading for our table, stopping here and there on the way toward us.

The voice soon became recognizable as I heard, "Good evening, I'm Dr. Banner. So pleased to meet you."

"Yes, hello Bob," he said at another table. "I'm happy you could be here tonight. And Cynthia, you look lovely. Is that a new necklace?"

I watched over my shoulder as Dr. Banner slowly worked his way in our direction, moving along as if he was running for office and everyone there was a potential vote. Talk about a grand entrance!

With a big brown cigar clenched in his teeth, he shook hands and finally arrived at our table. The local station manager stood and introduced this local celebrity to the out-of-town visitors. Dr. Banner exchanged pleasantries with them while resting his hand on my shoulder.

Then he looked down at me, as if noticing my presence for the first time. "Now, everyone knows I like these Cuban cigars with the brown wrappers," he said with a twinkle in his eye as he held up the large cigar to admire it. "But every once in a while, I come across a discerning gentleman who's been lucky enough to find one with a green wrapper."

Pausing, he looked down at me and quizzically asked, "Might you be him?"

At that moment, I suddenly remembered the green-wrapped cigar Dr. Banner had slipped into my breast pocket several hours earlier. I slowly reached in and pulled out the cigar. I held it in front of my face, slowly moving it under my nose like I'd seen Banner do in his garage. I looked at it thoughtfully, then turned to Dr. Banner and asked, "Yes, but how did you know?"

Dr. Banner's response was perfect. He looked down at me, smiled and said conspiratorially, "I can smell them! Here, let me light that for you." And he did.

This memorable night was likely just one of thousands for the incredible Dr. Banner, but for me it was transformative. It offered a glimpse into a world of sophistication and influence I'd never known, and planted seeds of ambition that would shape my future career. As I left the country club that night, my head spinning with new ideas and possibilities, I knew that my path in life had somehow shifted. The world of business suddenly seemed much larger and more exciting than I had ever imagined. I didn't know exactly where this new perspective would lead me, but I knew I wanted more.

* * * * *

Dr. Banner passed away at age 80 in Vail, Colorado, on November 5, 1992. After getting his medical degree in 1939, he began a fellowship in obstetrics and gynecology at the Mayo Graduate School of Medicine in 1942. In 1947, he was appointed a consultant in obstetrics and gynecology at Mayo. In 1969, he became a professor at the Mayo Medical School.

While he never mentioned it to me, Dr. Banner was on the board of directors of the Rochester Country Club. His son, Dr. Ed Banner, Jr., graduated from Mayo High School in 1969, as did I. Young Ed Banner, who did his undergraduate studies at Harvard and attended medical school at the University of Minnesota, is a highly regarded physician and anesthesiologist practicing medicine in Houston, Texas.

14

ATTICS, ANTIQUES AND AIRWAVES

ROCHESTER, MINNESOTA WAS AN EXCELLENT backdrop for me during the development of my early career. After graduating from high school there, I left to attend Minnesota State University in Mankato. I also spent an interesting summer in Iowa City, Iowa, under the pretense of wanting to enroll in the University of Iowa's renowned writers' workshops. In reality, I made the move to live in a commune with a group of self-named "Jesus Freaks." I was trying to make sense of my confusion about religion, and I thought that living with these people would help me figure out what God was all about and how He wanted me to behave.

My cousin John Gravley and our friend Kirby Walton joined me on this adventure. John worked at a fast-food place and brought home hamburger patties and large blocks of cheese slices, which, in his judgment, were slightly too old to serve to customers. I did various temp jobs, from repossessing pianos to assembling pre-manufactured homes. After six months, I returned to Rochester with the Triumph Spitfire that John and I bought together in Iowa. It was good to be back home again.

In this May 1971 photo, my hair was still pretty long.

Enrolling at Rochester State Junior College (RSJC) in 1971, I gravitated to the Drama Department under the direction of Bob Clausen. I got the lead in the fall production of *Tango*, an avant-garde play about counter-conformity written by Polish dramatist Slawomir Mrozek. *Tango* tells the story of the generation gap in contemporary society, presenting a world that defies logic. Its unconventional narrative structure and non-linear plot confused our audience—and even a few of the cast members.

Our drama teacher, Mr. Mikesh, who spent 20 years as a professional actor in hundreds of productions in New York while only making a living and never getting his "big break," questioned why we chose that particular play. The best thing about it for me was the two full-page spreads that appeared in the RSJC yearbook, featuring me in many of the photos.

While attending RSJC, I lived in the attic of the lower mansion at Mayowood, part of the estate built by Dr. Charles H. Mayo, co-founder of the Mayo Clinic, and his wife Edith in 1911. Three generations of Mayos lived in the opulent, five-story upper mansion, surrounded by more than 3,000 acres that include a terrace overlooking the Zumbro River, beautiful botanical gardens and a charming Oriental Tea House. No one lived in the upper mansion by the time I got there, but it was open for tours.

The lower mansion, located directly across from the old livery stables, was owned by Dr. Myron Wilson of the Constance Bultman Wilson Center, a controversial adolescent psychiatric center in Faribault that accepted teens with significant problems. My roommate, David Dolliff, had been a patient there. Dr. Wilson hired David to care for his lower mansion apartment when he wasn't there, which was most of the time.

David was quite the character. At one point, he stole a canoe from the Sears store at Apache Mall because he wanted to go canoeing on the overflowing Zumbro River. He got away with the canoe and somehow got it home, but he'd forgotten paddles and got caught shoplifting when he returned to the store to get them.

The attic apartment, where David and I lived, had an outside exit, two bedrooms, a small kitchen, a living room and a single bath. It was an exotic place for me, large and stunning. My drama teacher, Mr. Mikesh, also lived in the lower mansion with his wife. They occupied half of the lower level.

The route to Mayowood along Bamber Valley Road was otherworldly, with large, mature trees and low stone fences. It reminded me of a country lane in England. These miles of stone fences had been a project of the Works Progress Administration (WPA) in the late 1930s and 1940s.

Across the road from us were the Mayowood Galleries run by Rita Mayo, who became a close friend. Rita, recently divorced from Edward (Ned) Mayo, often worked events in the evening at her downtown antique gallery while I babysat her three children (Lilli, William and Ian). Even though she was 16 years older than me, I adored Rita and was actually infatuated with her. She was intelligent, classy as hell and smoked a pipe.

Born in England in 1934, she was a champion swimmer. She was going to represent England in the Olympics, but missed out on the opportunity when she contracted the mumps. She began working at a hospital and training as a nurse when she was just 16, eventually becoming an Emergency Room (ER) nurse in East London. After reading a flyer advertising jobs for English-speaking nurses at the Mayo Clinic in Rochester, Minnesota in 1958, she packed her trunk and took a ship to America.

After I put her kids to bed and she returned from her events, Rita and I would watch TV and talk for hours. She smoked her pipe and we drank red wine. From May through November 1973, we couldn't turn away from the extensive coverage of the Watergate hearings.

Rita passed away in February 2024 at age 89. The last time I saw her was with my brother-in-law, John Woychick, in 2001. It must have been tough for John to listen to the two of us laugh and talk for hours. He had to drag me away!

Another Mayo contact who influenced my life was Joanne Mayo, the mother of Joseph "Joe" Mayo III. Joe, Charles H. Mayo's great-grandson, graduated from Mayo High School the same year I did. Although we didn't hang out much in school, we were friendly and often ran into each other when he was home from college during the summers.

I occasionally had coffee with Joanne while I waited for him. A superbly accomplished businesswoman, she was the Vice President of Olmsted County Bank when I met her. She was also President of the Business and Professional Women's Club. She took an interest in me as one of her son's friends and gave me financial advice that has paid enormous dividends.

Explaining my desire to buy a new car, I told her I'd never borrowed money before and she laid out a precise plan for me to follow. I was to visit the local Olmsted County Bank branch and ask to borrow a thousand dollars. "Oh, tell them you're going on a trip or something," she said. "What it's for doesn't matter. Ask them to set it up so you can pay it back over a year. You've got a good job, so that won't be a problem."

"Once you have the money, deposit it in your bank account," she continued. "And when you get the loan repayment book, drop off the payment or mail it in a week before it's due. Do this for three months. Then, in the fourth month, go into the bank and pay off the full balance."

That sounded easy to me. I thought the lesson was over, but it was only just beginning.

"Wait three months, return to the bank and ask to borrow $5,000," she went on. "Repeat the same process of paying on the loan for a few months, then coming in and paying off the entire balance. Within a year, you'll be so well thought of that when you go to buy a new car, you'll have no problem."

I followed her advice to the letter and even expanded on it, always borrowing increasing amounts of money and paying it back far before the agreed-upon date. I've never had an issue borrowing money my entire life, although I did screw up once when I lived in Los Angeles. I won't go into details, but had it not been for the intervention of my cousin, Roger Larsen, a guy with some clout in LA banking circles, I could have been labeled a real scofflaw.

My buddy Joe Mayo went into medicine and became an orthopedic surgeon. We speak on occasion and he keeps me up to date on his mom.

* * * * *

Like many college students in Rochester, I got a summer job at Libby Foods, the local canning factory that sat below the famous water tower built and painted to look like a giant ear of corn. The last time I was in Rochester the tower still stood, but the factory was demolished in 2019.

For income support, I also worked for a local school bus company that recruited college students as drivers. The bus barn was on the edge of Rochester, close to Mayowood. I picked the kids up early before my own classes started, and I also picked up a few afternoon routes. It was a fun job, and I learned you could drift a bus around a snowy country road—never with any students inside, of course. One high school girl slipped me love notes as she left the bus at her stop, which I dutifully turned over to the bus company after reading them.

Once, the bus company asked fellow driver Dan Painter and me to take the college ski club on a trip to Colorado. Dan and I loved this idea, as we'd get to drive the big tour bus, a genuine motor coach. The bus company manager made us both promise not to go skiing under any circumstances, which we didn't. Well, not on the first day. Technically, not the first half of the first day.

Once we got the "I won't tell if you won't tell" formalities out of the way, we hit the slopes. This was so cool; we were getting paid to stay in a dorm-like setting with college kids who loved to party. Meals and drinks were free and we were making money. We only had to pay for lift tickets and ski rentals. What a gig!

Bus driver Steve, hitting the slopes on my first trip to Colorado. Minnesota skiing would never again be as appealing.

My best job in those days, however, was at KNXR-FM Radio. I already had my third-class radio operator's permit, and that was all I needed.

My first role at KNXR was as the morning engineer for Harley Flathers, the area's most famous and popular announcer. KNXR owner Tom Jones had lured Flathers away from KROC to launch his new FM radio station. KNXR was one of the first FM radio stations in the state, and getting Flathers to join was a big deal. He was a remarkably talented on-air personality, and he dragged a legion of listeners to the new station. Many people bought FM radios just to hear him. Flathers, a polio victim who used a wheelchair to get around, had a 63-year career in radio. Once, during a massive flood in Rochester in 1978, he stayed on the air for 24 hours straight. He passed away in January 2016 at the age of 84.

Running the control board at KMSU in Mankato, Minnesota.

When I first started at KNXR, the station broadcast from a small studio beneath the 1,000-foot radio tower on Highway 14 at the north end of Rochester. During the day shift, we undertook the often painstaking, manual process of editing recorded interviews. Flathers would interview anyone pushing a local event or new advertisers. It was no small feat to take 15–20 minutes of rambling, disorganized answers and turn it into two or three minutes suitable for broadcast.

To remove all the "ahs" and "ums," we had to manually cut them out of the reel-to-reel tape and splice the ends back together. We had to "rock" the reels repeatedly until we found the exact point we wanted to make the edit and mark the spot with a grease pen. Then we had to pull the latch holding the tape in the transport, stretch the tape down to the cutting block and make a cut with a razor blade at a 45-degree angle. After that, we had to latch the transport and hit play while the section we were editing out spooled into a pile.

When we got to the spot where we wanted the splice to stop, we rocked the reel again to find the precise place, marked it with the grease pencil, unlatched the tape transport and then cut and taped the two ends together with splicing tape. Then we had to play it back to see if it sounded right, knowing it could always be better. Making a decent interview took hours.

Once, at an event at the Kahler Hotel, I overheard a man telling his friend that he'd heard him interviewed on the radio by Harley Flathers. "You sounded good!" the man exclaimed.

"Yes, I did, didn't I?" the guy replied. "My wife heard it, too. She thinks I should get into broadcasting."

I laughed to myself because I was the one who edited that interview. It was challenging to find a few coherent sentences, and I eliminated tons of his "ums" and "ahs." I even had to boost the bass to add resonance to his reedy voice.

Once the station had moved its studios to downtown Rochester, I began engineering the legendary John Doremus Show at night. The station had years and years of old shows from the famous Chicago radio personality on seven-inch reel-to-reel tapes, along with the rights to broadcast them. The recordings had all the vocal breaks, music introductions and folksy stories, and we supplied the music from our record library. The pre-recorded Doremus did the song intros and the in-between song breaks, queued the "news" and station ID, and we did the rest.

"Songs about the Moon, will man ever reach there?" Doremus quipped during one show. "Who knows, we can dream. Maybe someday..." We broadcast this episode well AFTER the July 1969 Apollo 11 moon landing. While we worked hard to ensure all the material was "evergreen," sometimes a slip like this would occur. Even though John Doremus passed away in 1995, you can still catch his show on YouTube.

After spending three hours a night making it sound like John Doremus was live in our studios via the magic of radio, I'd stick around to engineer for Dave Frogner, a co-owner of the station who played a late-night mix of entertaining and sophisticated jazz standards. He was my favorite announcer to engineer for, and he turned me into a real jazz fan.

When KNXR studios moved to the lower level of the large Holiday Inn Hotel (now the Hilton) downtown, the spacious new digs meant owner Tom Jones had turned the tables on every other radio station and broadcast studio. Broadcast radio stations are generally small and ridiculously cramped, but the new space was large, comfortable and had floor-to-ceiling windows all along the front, offering passersby views into the radio production process.

I loved radio work, and most of my friends were jocks, announcers and engineers. Randy Trom, aka "Randy Dynamite Dean," was a friend who worked at KWEB and was Rochester's #1 rock and roll jock. We always conspired to use our industry status to get free stuff, dates and invitations to parties. We never made much money, and the on-air guys always had better luck getting girls.

15

AMPLIFYING MY CAREER: THE SCHAAK ELECTRONICS EXPERIENCE

ONE OF MY RESPONSIBILITIES AT KNXR was to handle remote broadcasts from the Schaak Electronics store at Apache Mall. Tom Jones, KNXR's owner and chief engineer, pioneered a way to broadcast in four channels and it was the rage back then.

As I got to know the Schaak team, I was drawn to the energy of assistant manager Gary Eiesland. During one of their frequent sales events, I volunteered to help. What started out as ferrying gear to customers' cars on a two-wheeler soon blossomed into a part-time position with a decent hourly wage, commissions and special payment incentives for fast sales, called "spiffs." These spiffs were a revelation. I marveled at pocketing $60–$150 in cash after a six- or eight-hour shift, just for selling the company's private-label speakers (Omega I–Omega III), the high-end DLK line or high-margin phono cartridges.

DLK loudspeakers, the brainchild of noted engineer and acoustician Donald L. Kliewer, were marvels of sound engineering manufactured for Schaak by D. Michael Shields. They produced a vibrant sound, built to exacting standards, at an attractive price point. Even today, fervent collectors seek them out with enthusiasm.

One of the things that impressed me the most at Schaak were the company's sales training classes, designed and taught by Towru Nagano, a Japanese American wunderkind from Los Angeles. They left an indelible mark on me. Towru, who joined Dick Schaak in the 1960s as VP of corporate development and expansion, became highly influential in my life. His classes weren't just about selling; they were life lessons on purpose, responsibility and passionate dedication. Towru's wisdom echoed in my mind throughout my career. He passed away in December 2016 at age 91, leaving behind a legacy of inspired salespeople.

Towru told the story of his father, who had a landscaping business in Los Angeles. He and his older brother had to finish all their school activities by 4:00 p.m., when his father's landscaping truck would roll up at the school door. One day, his brother was competing in a close tennis match against another school and walked off the court right in the middle of it when he saw his father's truck. It was a matter of discipline and priorities.

I loved working at Schaak, and when Gary Eiesland took the reins as store manager I was even happier. Gary's tenure felt like a breath of fresh air after the often bizarre and ill-conceived projects led by the previous store manager, Carl Este. One time, Carl began a store remodeling project two weeks before Christmas. No store manager in their right mind does that!

Gary proved to be a brilliant manager, giving me and my friend Jim Skiff free rein to be the best sales associates we could be. We often outsold the rest of the staff combined, and dominated nearly every sales contest Schaak threw our way. Gary became something of a father figure for us, as he was the only married man with kids in our crew of young bucks. His innovative ideas for sales, store layouts and promotions ignited our enthusiasm, driving us to make him proud.

When Carl Este left town, Jim Skiff snagged Carl's mobile home in a small park near downtown Rochester and I moved in with him to split the rent. As is common in mobile neighborhoods, the homes sat barely ten feet apart. Carl had been the ideal neighbor with his quiet ham radio hobby, but Jim and I upset our older neighbors with our penchant for cranking up our powerful stereo systems late at night.

Within months, Jim was asked to move amid a flurry of complaints. He found a more spacious mobile home park past the Rochester Airport on Highway 63, near Stewartville, which was happy to take his mobile home. On moving day, disaster struck when Jim's shed, which was attached to the back of the trailer, slid off and onto Highway 63. The next day, the *Rochester Post Bulletin*'s front page featured Jim's wayward shed in the middle of the Interstate, cars swerving around it.

With more breathing room in the new location, the noise complaints ceased but a new source of neighborly consternation arose. Jim brought down his C-modified dragster from storage in the Twin Cities. This beast, built to race in the gap between Super Stock and Gas classes, could tear up the quarter mile in under nine seconds at speeds up to 175 mph.

While not quite as earth-shaking as a Top Fuel dragster, Jim's C-modified monster could still be heard counties away. Hosting parties where alcohol may have clouded his judgment, Jim would often decide that someone needed a wake-up call. He'd clamber into the trailer-bound car, fire it up with a deafening roar, rev it for a minute or two, then dash back inside to await the inevitable visit from the Stewartville police, usually 15 or 20 minutes later.

When the cops knocked, Jim would turn down the music, feign innocence and ask how he could help. They'd report complaints of a loud car disturbing the peace. Jim would always plead ignorance, backed up by our corroborating stories about loud music masking any outside noise. After a stern lecture and warnings not to repeat the offense, they'd leave until the next time Jim felt the urge to shake the neighborhood foundations.

In the fall of 1973, after several years at Schaak's Apache Mall location in Rochester, I was transferred to Milwaukee, Wisconsin to manage Schaak's Allied Radio Store on North Port Washington Road. It was my first shot at running my own store.

Jim Skiff and I were best friends and the top sales guys at Schaak.

The prior manager, George Klauser, became my assistant manager, and Jack Carrow, the manager of a competing Radio Shack in Rochester, agreed to work for me, too. I'd known Jack for about a year, and he was ready to make the move: He lived in a camper mounted on his pickup truck in the parking lot behind the store.

Things did not go well for me during my first couple of months in charge. I was inexperienced and it showed. Somehow, I believed that having a badge on my shirt that said, "Store Manager" would automatically generate the kind of respect we gave Gary Eiesland back in Rochester. It didn't. I got angry and frustrated and we missed our sales quotas.

Finally, George and Jack came to me and said I needed to change. I felt lost and ready to give up. Being a top sales guy didn't provide me with the skill set required to manage a store. Both George and Jack had managed stores and said if I'd just calm down and back off, we could fix everything. And we did.

First, I stopped trying to act like a boss. We slowly became a team, with George taking over what he excelled at (and where I failed) and Jack doing the same. We fully turned it around within three months, and the store hummed like a top. The hands-on lessons I learned back then on how to work as a team and manage people were as impactful, if not more, than the dozens of management books I read later in my career.

During my time in Milwaukee, one of my duties was checking in on the Allied Stores Schaak had purchased in Chicago. I also stopped in at Schaak stores in large regional malls, like the Woodfield Mall in Schaumburg, Illinois. When it opened, it was the largest shopping mall in the United States.

But my memory has nothing to do with the mall's size. What I remember most was the cold. Late one afternoon, I searched desperately for my car in the mall's massive parking lot. It was a painfully bitter winter afternoon, with the light rapidly fading. The frigid wind from Lake Michigan blew in, and I was freezing. This lake air was so cold it would have cut through any parka I would have been wearing, if I was lucky enough to have one. In the 15 or 20 minutes it took to find my car, I got colder than I've ever been in my life—and this is from a Minnesota kid who grew up in Canada. The car heater didn't even warm me up on my 90-minute drive back to Milwaukee. After crawling under my blankets with the thermostat set as high as it would go, I still shook for nearly an hour.

The Milwaukee store performed great and I learned to love the city. I adapted to the cold and experienced the magic of a genuinely multicultural environment for the first time. The ethnic and cultural diversity changed my world, and not just from all the fantastic food I learned to love from Italian restaurants, Jewish delis, Mexican establishments and German beer gardens. Events like Summer Fest, Beer Lovers Festival, Taste of Korea, Polish Fest, Kraken the Firkin Ale Day and many car and bike shows all contributed to the amazing, multicultural milieu.

Seeing people of different races and backgrounds opened my eyes to a world I hadn't known existed. But Schaak decided they

needed me back in Minnesota before a year passed, so, in 1975, I returned to manage the Rochester store in Apache Mall.

*Early work in radio made remote radio broadcasts from the
Schaak store in Rochester easy for me (on left) and they
were an effective way to bring customers into the store.*

As manager of the Rochester store I did everything I could to promote it, from wrestling a bear to joining the Lion's Club, a business
services organization dedicated to helping people with blindness
and other sight issues.

As a younger member of the club, I benefited from the networking opportunities that came my way at fundraisers and other social
events. I met local attorney Bob Suk, banker David Parkin, barber
John Dube and builder and liquor store owner Stan Mohn. These
business owners accepted me as an equal. David Parkin and church
deacon and musical director Ernie Giles became my closest friends.

David was an impeccably dressed, large man with an excellent
job at a local savings and loan. He owned two dozen rental properties
and employed his sister and brother to collect rent and maintain, ad-
vertise and show the units. He laughed quickly and loved big front-
wheel-drive Cadillac Eldorados—he was the guy I told you about in

the Cars section, who bought a new one every year and stored the old ones in a barn, hoping they'd increase in value.

David invited me to parties at his home, where I met many professional men of the "lavender persuasion," as David called them. David had me tag along on trips to gay bars in the Twin Cities as his designated driver. And he may have enjoyed having me by his side because I was cute in those days.

His favorite haunt was the Gay 90s bar on Hennepin Avenue in Minneapolis. It's still going strong today and has become a haven for the entire LGBTQ+ world. Here, David and his friends could let their hair down, meet friends, dance with other men, flirt and have fun without constantly being on their guard like they had to be in Rochester.

The bar was a safe, loud, boisterous and fun place, even for a straight guy. There were plenty of women at the club, but they weren't interested in the men. Everyone got along great. Several years later, Paul Hagen planned and organized my bachelor party at the Gay 90s, right before my wedding. Unlike more traditional bachelor parties, all my strippers were male.

These initial associations and friendships with gay people were a significant discovery for me. While feeling honored to be a trusted member of the club, I was angry at the fear and prejudice that made their secrecy necessary. Unlike in Minneapolis, gay men in Rochester were all deeply closeted and had to be. The term "out" hadn't even been invented yet. Enough examples existed of men who lost their jobs and careers when someone "discovered" their secret and began talking about them. These men had to be careful, even paranoid.

I recall one professional businessperson who played the organ at his church. A parishioner had seen him put his arm around another man while walking into a local restaurant and reported it to the church pastor. The organist spent months in limbo, not knowing if his musical gig, something he loved, would end. Attitudes have changed, thankfully, but it's important to remember what a horrid and unfair time this was for so many people.

Rumors circulated about a gay person working in the marketing department at Schaak Electronics in the Twin Cities. Most of my fellow managers assumed it was Chuk Batko, a tall, slender, athletic guy who could adopt effeminate postures and sometimes affected what might be called a gay lisp or accent as a punch line to a story. But it wasn't Chuk, it was Paul Hagen. Paul was the first non-closeted gay person I met, and he was an exception. While Paul didn't broadcast his sexual preferences, he did little to hide or disguise them, either.

Wrestling a bear for publicity. The bear won.

During my tenure as manager of the Rochester store, I got my first speeding ticket in my Lotus Elan. As the only Lotus owner in Rochester I was used to getting pulled over by the police, mostly to answer questions like, "What kind of car is this?" or "Who makes Lotus?" However, when I tried to outrun one of those cops, things changed. Have you ever wondered if you can get out of a speeding ticket written for 120+ mph?

I was returning home from a sales meeting at Schaak HQ in Minneapolis. It was a warm, cloudless summer night as I headed south on Highway 52, a four-lane divided highway. Just south of Cannon Falls, I somehow attracted the attention of a car full of guys, perhaps high schoolers. They made the classic male, testosterone-fueled, aggressive automotive gesture—pulling level with my driver's window and moving parallel with me for a bit while revving their engine. Then they floored their accelerator and sped off.

After a few hundred feet, they slowed down again, allowed me to catch and pass them, and then repeated the process while I kept my speed consistent at 60–65 mph and attempted to ignore them.

By the fourth time they were yelling obscenities at me, and I had enough. I dropped the gearbox from 4th to 3rd and floored the accelerator. If you know nothing about cars, let me briefly explain the concept of weight-to-horsepower ratio (PWR). You divide the power output of a vehicle by its weight. For example, in a car that weighs 2,000 pounds and has 250 HP, the PWR will be 250/2000 = 0.125 HP for every pound of the vehicle.

My memory says they were driving an older, four-door Impala. Those cars weighed in at 3,600 lbs. dry. Add fluids and four average-sized farm guys and you're looking at 4,500 lbs. easy. A 235 cubic-inch, 135 HP engine powered the 1960 Chevy Impala four-door sedan.

On its best day, the Elan had only 115 HP so the Impala outpowered it by 20 HP. However, the Elan weighed only 1,550 lbs. and I just added 150 lbs. to the total. With horsepower that close and weight that much different, the term "leaving them in the dust" came to mind as I rapidly pulled away. I got up to about 90 mph when I shifted into 4th and again pushed my foot to the floor, keeping it there until the car wasn't speeding up anymore.

Years later, my friend Brett Engel, who owns a racing version of the Lotus Elan, explained it as not much of a contest. "Even without the radical difference in weight, your Elan had far better suspension, weight distribution, lower polar inertia and aerodynamics," he said. Watching their headlights disappear behind me, I gradually slowed down. But the guys in the Chevy were soon back, apparently wanting to make another run at it.

At this point I saw the sign near Hader, where Highway 57 would take me directly south to Kasson in Dodge County, where I had recently bought a house. As they raced their motor and rapidly pulled ahead of me, only to quickly return level with me once again, I waited and then braked rapidly to take the exit onto Highway 57 South. You'd be correct if you think a light car, like an Elan, accelerates quickly. But it's nothing compared to how quickly it will slow down and stop.

The Elan's four-wheel disc brakes slowed me to an easy turn-off speed, while the Impala had no chance of making the turn. Although they tried to stop, their car continued straight on Highway 52, where the next exit was at least a mile down the road. Even they knew enough not to try backing up on an interstate highway at night.

As I drove south on Highway 57, I gradually relaxed and saw nothing for the next 10 or 15 miles. No sooner had I concluded they were history than I saw headlights rapidly approaching me. Now I was worried. This was no longer a large, wide forgiving Interstate but a rural, two-lane blacktop. As the headlights approached, I sped up but kept watching behind through my rearview mirror. Sure enough, as my speed increased so did the car behind me.

Guessing that perhaps alcohol may be involved in the car I saw behind me, I decided to get out of there fast. I knew I had a long straightaway ahead that dropped gradually down to a bridge before hitting an uphill stretch, also straight. I decided that if I was going to lose them, now was the time. As I hit the downhill stretch and their lights dropped out of sight, I dropped a gear to 3rd and felt the rush of acceleration for a few seconds.

I floored it and then shifted back up to 4th. The Elan's little twin-cam engine howled with delight as I sped up the hill. I felt I was closer to flat out than I'd ever been. At this speed, the Elan feels almost like an airplane wanting to lift off the ground. I kept my eyes focused straight ahead as I threaded the slight narrowing of the road and flew across the bridge.

With my foot still buried to the floor, and halfway up the hill on the other side, I risked a glance behind me. That was when I saw the rack of lights on top of the police cruiser pursuing me. "Aw, shit," I thought, "I'm in for it now."

Cresting the top of the hill, I immediately used the Elan's stopping prowess and pulled off to the side of the road. I knew what would happen next and it did. The police car crested the hill at high speed, saw me as he raced past, and frantically applied his brakes.

It still took at least 100 feet before he could stop. He backed up slowly, and I watched him pull his car in front of mine and get out. By this time, I'd exited the Elan and leaned against the driver's door.

The first words out of his mouth were, "What the hell kind of car is that?" He followed up with, "Why the hell were you driving so fast?" Failing to come up with any better excuse, I related my I-52 experience as calmly as I could, letting him know that I thought he was "one of those guys, coming back to run me off the road."

I may have left out the part about me blowing them off on the Interstate. I explained that I feared for my life and was in a panic, attempting to get to the police station in Mantorville to seek refuge.

I'll say this. He listened to my tale although I'm not sure he believed it. He finally wrote me a ticket for 120+ mph, and said, "I don't know how fast you were going, but my car's odometer (a Ford Police cruiser) only goes to 120 mph and you were pulling away from me, so I'm saying 120+.

I took the ticket and drove carefully the rest of the way home. God, I was in trouble. The next day, I called Bob Suk, my Lion's Club buddy and the attorney who'd helped me with some real estate deals. I asked him to represent me on this ticket as I was pretty sure they would throw the book at me and stick me with a hefty fine or maybe even jail time. I had no reference for this. What could happen? Could they take my car away?

Have you ever heard the adage that sometimes it's better to be lucky than smart—and always to tell the truth? When I called the

Dodge County courthouse to plead not guilty and get my court date, I was told they'd need to call me back. A week went by and I heard nothing. Then, Bob called and said he'd set up a meeting with the judge. He gave me the date and time I needed to attend.

On the scheduled day, I met Bob in the courthouse parking lot and he explained a few things. It turns out that Dodge County couldn't afford to have its own prosecuting attorney. As a result, they contract with Rochester's legal community for this service. Rochester attorneys take on this typically light workload as an adjunct to their regular practice, rotating the responsibility every year to someone different so no one person was burdened with the task all the time. Well, guess whose turn it was to be Dodge County's prosecutor that year? Ah, yes, you're correct. It was my attorney and friend, Bob Suk.

He'd called the judge and explained that one of his clients faced a serious moving violation charge. He said he had to recuse himself on this case, as he would be defending me and couldn't act as prosecutor. Dodge County would have to find an interim prosecutor and pay that person to prosecute me.

This prospect was a tremendous headache and a paperwork nightmare, so the judge asked if we could meet. In the parking lot, Bob told me that when we got inside the judge's office I was only to answer the precise questions directed at me and nothing more. "Steve, I know you like to talk, but you need to shut up and only answer the questions this time," he coached.

As we entered the judge's office, I saw the police officer sitting in his uniform who'd written the ticket. I thought, "Well, this can't be good."

After introductions, the judge asked the officer to recount what had happened that night that led to him writing me a ticket for 120+ mph. After describing the circumstances, the judge asked the officer if the defendant (me) had offered any explanation for my driving behavior. The officer recounted what I'd told him about my encounter with the rowdy guys in an Impala and wanting to find a police officer in Mantorville.

The judge looked at me and asked, "Is this what you told the officer?" I replied in the affirmative. He then asked me if it was true, and again I said yes. He looked around the room for a bit, then said, "Well, Mr. Larsen, we've decided to let you off with a warning this time but we never want to see any more driving behavior like this again. Is that clear?"

"Yes, Sir," I said, and a few minutes later we left.

Before I could congratulate Bob on the result, he asked me, "Do you know why that just happened?"

"No, what do you mean?" I replied.

Bob explained, "Last week, when I spoke to the judge I relayed the story you told me about your being pulled over. That officer just told the judge the same thing. When that happens, judges feel they're getting the truth and you get points for that with some."

I smiled.

"But I'd still watch your speed around here," he added. "They're going to be keeping an eye on you."

The Lotus Elan in Kasson, soon after its experience with "the law."

Running the Rochester store, being part of the community and no longer totally sucking as a manager was a thrilling time for me, professionally and personally. Our tight knit team dined together, partied at bars and hung out at each other's homes when we weren't working. We also had each other's backs, regularly lending money if someone needed it and taking on designated driver duties whenever the occasion warranted. We even tackled a few home remodeling projects together, although the results were questionable.

Our close relationships helped maintain our ranking as one of the top stores in the Schaak Electronics chain, as did our reputation for superior marketing and promotion. The business community saw me as a responsible professional, and I was gaining a great deal of experience and confidence.

The crew of the Rochester, MN Schaak Store that made it all work. L to R: Mike Tieden, Bill Cordell, Mark Freeborn, me, Greg Donovan and Dan Knappe.

A home builder from Kasson, Minnesota (a small town 16 miles west of Rochester) began casing Apache Mall, talking with store managers and offering to build new homes for us, at payments less than we were paying for rent. Within a month, a half dozen people signed up, including me and my store colleague, Mark Freeborn.

I had gotten serious about Tami Redman, my girlfriend who was with me when Dr. Ed Banner made me a hero at his country club. She had two young children, Jamie and Jolie, from a prior marriage and we had become engaged. It would be good to have a house, I thought.

But while the house moved smoothly toward completion, our relationship did not. The closer the wedding date came on the calendar, the more panic I felt. I began having nightmares, and eventually we called off our engagement and split up.

The new house I built in Kasson, Minnesota.

In December of 1978, Schaak asked me to leave Rochester again and manage its store at the Ridgedale Center in Wayzata, on the west side of Minneapolis. It had been one of the company's top-producing stores for years, but it was now underperforming. The salespeople had grown mistrustful of each other, and they didn't feel heard or respected by their manager.

Soon after I arrived, I identified a problem employee and let him go. Like lancing a boil, the problems immediately went away. Everyone instantly got happy. Using the same approaches I had perfected in Rochester, the Wayzata location once again competed for the top spot every month.

My move to the Twin Cities put me closer to the home office and my heroes in the advertising department, Judy Zehnenter, Chuk Batko, Paul Hagen and their boss, Paul Ginther, who I viewed as a god. Judy Z led the department, while Batko was her art director and Hagen a copywriter. She also had a photographer, Kevin Gordon, who, years later, would photograph my wedding. This group created all the company's newspaper ads and radio commercials, and I idolized the lot of them.

Marketing VP Paul Ginther had a beautiful and cloyingly flirtatious secretary, Ellen Cote. He drove a Jaguar XJ-S, and I wanted to be Paul Ginther when I grew up. It would be years before I understood and acknowledged the degree to which I'd modeled myself on this man.

I also had great respect and admiration for Michael Shields, who ran the company's private label speaker company, DLK. Shields introduced me to Russ Borud and his partner, Tom Fletcher. After only a few live recording sessions with them, I received more of an education about live music recording than I did during all my years working at KNXR's recording studio.

But it was with the advertising folks that I really clicked. Paul Hagen wowed me with his skill at putting words together. Chuk became a very close friend and was my best man when Maggie and I married some years later. Judy Z and I dated for a year: She came to my wedding reception in a sexy black dress, dragging "Big Mary" and another friend of hers along with her, all clad the same way. My uncles couldn't take their eyes off them.

Living in the Twin Cities and working for Schaak was a ball. Rochester had been a big step up from Fairmont, and the Twin Cities delivered a similar upgrade from Rochester in terms of size, diversity and things to do.

16

THE GREAT MADELINE ISLAND MISADVENTURE

MY TIME AT SCHAAK ELECTRONICS introduced me to the world of retail and consumer electronics. But as I was beginning to learn, success in business wasn't just about what happened inside the store or the office. It was also about how you approached challenges, adapted to new situations and learned from your experiences, even when they didn't go as planned.

While I was honing my skills in sales and management, I was also developing in other ways. My curiosity and eagerness to try new things weren't limited to the business world. In fact, one of my most memorable adventures during this time had nothing to do with work, but it taught me lessons that would prove valuable throughout my career.

It was the spring of 1973, I was confident in my sales skills and the long Minnesota winter was finally loosening its grip. As the snow melted and the days grew longer, my colleague, friend, manager and mentor Gary Eiesland and I found ourselves within reach of an adventure goal that occupied our thoughts the entire winter.

One January day, Gary had asked if I liked hiking and camping. Given his Svengali-like influence on me, I could only say, "Of course." Soon, Gary brought in outdoor magazines filled with exciting stories and ads for camping and hiking equipment. A store selling adventure gear, a precursor to present-day REI, had opened at the other end of the mall and Gary and I would head in their direction whenever business was slow. We wandered the aisles in awe, fantasizing about all the places we'd go and the top-end gear we'd buy.

It must have been February when we made our first big purchase: authentic, expensive genuine hiking boots. These boots were the precise ones you'd buy if you were heading off to hike the 2,000-mile Appalachian Trail. We had watched the salesperson pitch these boots many times before, and we carefully examined the cut-in-half version of the boot to gain insights into its advanced features and superiority. To ensure a proper break-in for our as-yet-to-be-determined epic hike, we wore the boots to work daily, along with our three-piece suits. We were oblivious to the fact that we may have looked ridiculous.

The boots were just the beginning of our gear acquisition phase. We needed a tent, sleeping bags, gas lanterns, portable cooking pans, foldable plates, canteens, a compass and specialty glasses with yellow lenses to better illuminate game trails as we traversed through the woods. And, of course, we loaded up on survival food, strategically placed near the cash register to maximize impulse buying during our visits.

Boy, did they have us pegged! We bought bars so full of concentrated protein and vitamins that a single square would keep a grown man alive for days. We bought dozens of oatmeal-type roll-ups, with the promise that each one would keep a lost hiker from starving for a week. After all, you never know what might happen in the bush and we wanted to be prepared.

Our decision about which backpack to purchase involved studying various reviews, followed by months of arguments and discussion. Buying the wrong backpack could be a disaster. So, we borrowed one backpack after another from the gear store, took them out behind the mall to the banks of the Zumbro River and loaded them up with smooth river rocks. Then we'd walk back and forth around the mall parking lot, making thoughtful assessments about weight distribution.

Finding the right sleeping bag generated at least as much animated activity as the backpacks. The perfect bag would need to be light and supportive enough to safely suspend us on the side of El Capitan in Yosemite National Park, yet be warm enough to keep us alive on Mt. Kilimanjaro where we'd heard the temperatures got to -20 degrees Fahrenheit (-29 degrees Celsius). And what about the wind chill? If there's one thing two Minnesota boys understood, it was wind chill.

The long winter contributed a bit more shopping time than might have been optimal. Although we may have been able to get along without every single item, it never occurred to us that we might have extras.

One weekend, when the weather warmed, we pitched our tent in Gary's backyard and set up camp to practice. It hadn't been too long after we'd unrolled and crawled into our sleeping bags when Gary's wife strolled into the backyard with Gary's young daughters. "Do you have any idea what I can tell our neighbors about why my husband is sleeping in a tent in our backyard with a guy from work?" she asked.

Morning eventually came. We took the tent down and carefully packed it as outlined in the instructions. We meticulously rolled up our sleeping bags and mats and stowed our gear in Gary's garage. The day when we might head out and use it all on a real trip filled our brains like the smell of roasting turkey in a house on Thanksgiving Day.

Eventually, the snow melted and we seriously began planning our epic trip. We decided that before spending the big bucks and traveling to a distant, international locale, we'd do a hike in our own region. However, it had to be appropriately devoid of civilization to give us a genuine sense of roughing it. This meant no "easy outs" if things went wrong. We needed to test our newly acquired gear— and our outdoor problem-solving abilities. So we settled on a trip to northern Wisconsin.

Gary had heard of the unpronounceable Chequamegon-Nicolet National Forest in the most northern reaches of the state. He said there was nothing but wilderness and wild beasts like deer and bears. It was settled. The very next Friday morning, we would head north.

Since all this happened before the Internet, our ability to research and plan every detail was limited. But spiritually, our goal was simple—drive into Wisconsin, a state known to be wilder and less populated than Minnesota, and take every road going north until civilization ran out. At which point, we'd be in the deepest, darkest forest where we would hike, camp and forage. Yippee!

We decided to drive my Lotus. One great feature of all the gear we bought was that it was compact and fit into the Elan's trunk. Plus, the car was pretty new and the idea of a long road trip was exciting.

Our first hint of not-quite-perfect planning was making far better time than we expected. Six hours after starting our trip, we pulled into Bayfield, Wisconsin—gateway to Madeline Island. We caught the last ferry of the day and were told that if we went out there we'd be trapped overnight at least, maybe longer if the weather got bad. Perfect!

We arrived on Madeline Island less than an hour later as a light mist was falling. We drove past a large old hotel with neon lights advertising beers in the windows—and we looked away. Following the only road heading north, we took it out of town.

In about half an hour, the road gave out and turned into a logging trail. We kept going. Finally, we were in the backwoods and had to pull over, bravely unpacking our gear and pushing ahead on foot into the dark, wet forest.

Noting the compass and sighting in on a distant tree, Gary indicated our direction of travel. We hiked through the thick terrain. When we reached the tree, we sighted another and pushed forward, our pant legs soaked from the wet brush. Soon, the water worked its way into our hiking boots. Somehow, the promise of being waterproof had not covered the effects of a relentless mist.

After an hour, suitably deep in the north woods and with our feet getting colder and colder, Gary said, "We need to find a clearing, start a fire and camp for the night." Just then, we crashed through some bushes and saw a nice red cabin in front of us.

Shoot! Nothing smacks more of civilization than a cabin. We had to distance ourselves, and fast.

Gary pointed to his left and off we went. Our cold feet—and the realization that we were close to some damn cabin—made us more and more miserable with every step.

Approaching a clearing, Gary pointed to a grassy spot and asked, "How about here?"

I looked around and noticed something odd. I pointed further to Gary's left and said, "Let's try over that way a bit."

We pushed in that direction about 50 feet, came around a massive oak tree, and there it was—my lovely bright yellow Lotus Elan. I thought that tree looked familiar!

We'd read about stupid hikers getting lost in the woods and their tendency to walk in circles, but had never assumed it could happen to us. It felt like we were walking in perfectly straight lines the whole time.

But at this point, we were tired and our feet were soaked and freezing. We just wanted to get warm, so we unpacked and pitched the tent a few feet from the car. Before undressing and crawling into our sleeping bags we tried to light a fire, but the wood we gathered from the forest floor was wet and we couldn't get it to start.

Then Gary recalled the stack of wood covered with a tarp along the driveway of the red cabin we'd passed. He talked me into hiking back and stealing a few sticks of dry wood. We got a small fire going, but the rain kept putting it out. Nothing we did would keep a flame long enough to roast the wieners we brought along. In fact, it would barely light the joints of prize weed Gary had purchased for our trip.

But all was not lost: Besides a bag of Cheetos, we had boxes and boxes of emergency, super-high-protein, "keep you alive for a week" candy bars, a perfect chaser to the cold hot dogs. With the sound of rain on the tent's roof, we dealt with an artificially induced case of the munchies. We consumed every single fruit/oatmeal roll-up and all the contents of our backpack pockets, where the emergency rations were hidden.

In the morning, as soon as there was light, we crawled out of our sleeping bags and rolled up the tent and other gear the way most men fold fitted sheets—but faster. We stuffed these gear wads into the Elan trunk and headed back to the ferry dock. We got the first ferry to Bayfield and, from there, headed home to Rochester in the rain with the windows down, allowing some of the most rancid farts ever produced to drift out of the car and pollute the road behind us.

This experience was life changing. Since then, unlike my riding buddy and avid outdoorsman, Bruce Rauner, I've never felt a serious temptation to go on an overnight hiking trip with a tent. Been there. Done that. Thank you!

17

THE DIGITAL FRONTIER: FROM RETAIL TO CORPORATE TECH

AS THE 1970S DREW TO a close, the world stood on the brink of a digital revolution. Personal computers were about to transform the way we lived and worked, and I found myself at the forefront of this exciting new frontier.

In 1978, Dick Schaak tapped me to manage his first Digital Den store in the massive Burnsville Center Mall. Dick had seen the future and knew he had to broaden the company's appeal beyond stereo equipment.

Unsure then what a computer store would stock and sell, we had a broad inventory mix. Besides computers and accessories like printers, memory and disk drives, we also carried VCRs, large-screen TVs, telephones and phone recorders—six categories in all. It was a giant experiment, led by me and the most nerdy and geeky salespeople we could find. At the end of the first year, the numbers didn't lie. While computers represented 50% of our sales, they accounted for nearly 90% of our profits.

Working in a store with a lot of smart people had its advantages. In 1978, the revolution in Iran caused global oil production to fall to record lows, and stores in the mall were required to keep their thermostats at or above 78 degrees in the summer to aid the conservation efforts. This made the store hot and uncomfortable. But one of my geeky guys figured out a workaround.

He mounted a spotlight on a riser and pointed it at the thermostat. With a remote-control switch at the counter, we could turn the spotlight on or off. Turning the light on heated the thermostat, making it think it was hotter in the store than it really was. The AC would kick on and soon we'd all be comfortable.

We kept a keen eye out for the mall cops, who were in charge of enforcing the 78-degree rule. Whenever we saw them approach, we switched the spotlight off. Feeling the cool air wafting from our store, they'd stroll in, confident they'd be able to hit us with a $75 fine. But when they arrived to inspect our thermostat, it was always set to 78 degrees and we were never penalized.

In the fall, on Sundays, our line of televisions attracted a wandering horde of men, sometimes two or three deep, who'd rather watch football in our store than shop in the mall with their wives and kids. It got so crowded in the store that we couldn't run the business effectively.

We tried every nice way to get rid of them, but nothing worked. Finally, one night I set up a video cassette recorder (VCR) and began taping nothing but commercials.

In the end, I had a two-hour VCR tape containing one commercial after another. When the store got too clogged with guys watching the game, I'd switch the feed from the live broadcast to this VCR tape. I was always surprised by how long it would take some men to figure out that the game was never coming back on.

To promote the store and this new "computer age," I spoke at local computer clubs, went to the first COMDEX show in 1979 and was often interviewed on local radio and TV shows about these strange new devices you could buy for your home.

When we became the authorized Apple Computer dealership for Minnesota, the company had me travel to Cupertino for training so we'd have a "factory-authorized" repair person on staff. For about a year in the late 1970s, if you owned an Apple Computer in Minnesota and it required warranty work, I was the one who fixed it. Fortunately, they rarely broke, and when they did they were easy to fix with a simple diagnostic disk. It was gratifying to be recognized for my Apple computer mastery, when it was nothing more than a computer disk and a simple, well-documented repair process.

Demonstrating a Commodore Pet computer to a potential buyer. Yes, it's a perm.

In July 1979, the *Minneapolis Star & Tribune* wrote a story about Digital Den and someone at Control Data Corporation (CDC) saw it. In August, a recruiter reached out to me and within a few weeks I left Schaak Electronics to help CDC get into the computer retail business. Ending my eight-year career with Schaak was bittersweet, but CDC doubled my income and I knew it was a good move.

Dick Schaak inadvertently helped me in this new adventure more than he could have ever imagined, when he fired off an angry letter to Bill Norris, the CEO of Control Data. Schaak complained about CDC "recruiting his best people" while promoting how they supported small businesses. The letter reached my boss, who read Schaak's anger as a sign he'd hired top talent.

The contrast between a small, Midwest-based chain of retail stores and a $3 billion, 65,000-person, global mainframe and super-computer manufacturer was striking. At Schaak, we sold complete hi-fi systems to consumers starting at $299. CDC sold computers for a million dollars each to universities, big companies and governments.

Not only was my salary more than generous, but the employee benefits also included insurance, annual bonuses, an expense account, a secretary and more resources than I could ever take advantage of. But CDC was also bureaucratic and complex, much less like a family than Schaak was.

CDC put me in charge of marketing for this new division and made John Bonte from Team Electronics head of operations. Stuart ("Stu") Baker was our general manager.

Baker, a Harvard graduate (class of 1960) and former Boston Consulting Group (BCG) consultant, was the perfect boss. He had little to no idea what we were doing, yet he supported John and me in everything and never failed to get us the resources we requested.

Baker loved the interplay of senior manager meetings, after which he always emerged with the money to get the job done. He also enjoyed large bird-bath martinis at the nearby Decathlon Club, where we often went for lunch. After joining him one time for his double martinis, Bonte and I vowed never to do it again: We could barely work when we got back to the office.

Baker told us a story once about how, after a late Saturday night of carousing and dining in downtown Minneapolis, he surprised himself by waking up before 7:00 a.m. the next day. He went out on his deck and looked out at the joggers bouncing along the path circling Lake of the Isles. He had an almost irresistible urge to go down to the garage, find an old sweatshirt and running sneakers and join them. "But then, I went back to bed," he said. "And by 11 o'clock I was fine."

* * * * *

CDC sent Bonte and me to visit nearly every Control Data Institute learning center in the United States, to see if the locations would fit our requirements for retail space. Few of them did. The Control Data Institute, created in the late 1970s, featured the PLATO System (Programmed Logic for Automatic Teaching Operations), the first computer-assisted instruction platform ever offered.

The system supported several thousand graphics terminals distributed worldwide. Many modern concepts we take for granted, such as multi-user computing and social media, were developed around PLATO. The team that designed and ran the system created message boards, online testing, e-mail, chat rooms, private chat, image processing, instant messaging, remote screen sharing and real-time multiplayer games, decades before they became popular on other platforms.

Another reason for our visits was to assess the people working in these centers, to determine if we could hire them to work at our new CDC Business Centers. On a trip to St. Louis, I would meet yet another person who would change my life forever.

When Margaret Kirven (Collins) walked into the room, my heart flip-flopped and stopped briefly as our eyes met. I was totally captivated. Maggie was cute, witty, wickedly smart and utterly unimpressed with the "bigshots" from corporate headquarters who'd invaded her offices. When she left, telling us she wasn't interested in any of the positions in our new enterprise, I said to Bonte, "I just met the woman I'm going to marry."

Control Data was an early adopter in online education, just one of many new windows into electronic communications that seemed to open every month. We had an Intranet for management reports and information and, as I would soon discover, a separate underground version of it.

The underground intranet was like a private club. Someone had to know and vouch for you before you could get the secret ID and password. The best I could tell was that sci-fi fans had started the group, as most of the members took names of characters from their favorite sci-fi novels to remain anonymous. Soon after our meeting, Maggie "sponsored" me. Her online name was Fiona, after a character in one of poet and sci-fi writer Roger Zelazny's books.

Our public notes and written repartee led to private e-mails, "term-talk" (a form of live, one-to-one chat) and an ever-increasing number of phone calls. We supplemented our electronic relationship with snail mail and actual visits in the "real world." Within a year, I convinced her to leave St. Louis and join me in Minneapolis, a fortunate turn of events that improved my life significantly.

* * * * *

Our team began building out CDC's plan for retail computer stores, which included selling small business computers built by Wang, Ohio Scientific and others, along with our own brand. While CDC finally managed to cobble together something based on a PLATO terminal after locating a 6502 chip on the disk controller, it was a kludge that only barely worked, performed poorly and cost a mint. Ultimately, we scrapped it and decided to hire someone else to build a private-label, CDC-branded computer for us.

After investigating several potential partners, I selected Altos Computer in Palo Alto. The decision had less to do with the company's founder, Dave Jackson, than it did with Ron Conway, their brilliant and highly-effective business development guy. In the year we negotiated the contract, Ron and I, nearly the same age, developed a friendship that lasted for many years.

Maggie and I even babysat his kids when we stayed with him in California. Maggie, Ron's wife Gale and I once met Ron in the baggage claim area of San Francisco's airport to pick him up from an overseas trip. We carried crudely made signs, dressed outlandishly and, upon seeing Ron, began boisterously shouting to the point that Ron pretended not to know us. Alcohol may have been involved.

Ron Conway would evolve into the most significant angel investor who ever lived. He was the early money behind Google, Ask Jeeves, Napster and PayPal. *Forbes* has Ron on its list of *Midas Touch* deal makers. As of this writing, Ron's been an early investor in more than 650 companies, including Reddit, Airbnb and Facebook.

* * * * *

Control Data relished the attention its new Business Centers were gaining for the company, and the higher ups encouraged my involvement at various conferences. Future Computing, a market analysis group led by Portia Isaacson, held many events where I spoke. At a well-attended seminar on February 2, 1983 in San Diego, "IBM PC Compatibles—A Software/Hardware Market Forum," I gave a talk and stayed in one of the nicest rooms at the Hotel Del Coronado.

The most significant events, however, were the annual PC Forums that ran through the mid-1990s. They were founded in 1977 and led by Stewart Alsop. He later proposed investing in one of my startups, PhoneTell, but not on terms my co-founder Wendell Brown and I wished to take. PC Forums were invite-only, attracting very senior people who were always at the center of what was happening in tech. I made a host of contacts and friends there.

The West Coast Computer Faire was another early PC industry event. Ben Rosen's *Research* newsletter was an enormous influence, and soon I met Ester Dyson who founded Edventure Holdings. Her *Release 1.0* newsletter had a notable impact on my thinking. Jerry Michalski, one of her writers/editors, would become a dear friend.

Sheldon Adelson founded the COMDEX Show, which, by 1984, came to dominate every other technology trade show until 2001. It filled the Las Vegas Convention Center, with displays spilling out of the exhibit hall. At its peak, the show had 225,000 attendees and more than 2,337 exhibitors displaying more than 10,000 products. Being a speaker there secured the best rooms, free admission and raised one's industry profile significantly.

The first COMDEX show I attended was in November 1980. I'll never forget it because I woke up in my room on the third day to sirens. Opening my curtains, I saw that the MGM Grand across the street from me had smoke pouring from every window and door. Eighty-five people died in the deadliest disaster in Nevada's history. The fire began in a restaurant and thousands of people were evacuated. New fire safety guidelines were written and fire codes were changed in many states.

* * * * *

As a major public company, Control Data had an annual performance appraisal and review process. After my first positive review (from Stu Baker in June 1981), I was hooked and saved nearly all of them. The positive comments from my managers spurred my promotions at the company. In 1981, CEO Robert M. Price named me to the eight-member, long-range strategic planning task force, the only non-VP in the group.

Control Data provided me with many opportunities to understand how large corporations, and business in general, worked. What I didn't know was that the company was stumbling. As 1984 began, CDC executives realized they'd never be a contender in the retail computer space and disbanded our group. I lobbied hard for a high-level management role but lost to an internal candidate with 15 more years at the company. While not letting me go or reducing my salary, they moved me to a part of the business they knew would be unsatisfying, given my drive and need to contribute at a high level. They were right and I was soon gone.

18

SUITS, SHAKE-UPS AND CDS

FRUSTRATED AND READY FOR A change, I found myself pouring my energy into preparing for a new chapter in my personal life: Maggie was pregnant with our daughter, Virginia Ruth Larsen, who arrived on March 14, 1984. Chuk Batko, the best man at our wedding, painted a fabulous mural in the baby's room. We had baby showers and I began collecting everything ever sold to new parents.

Later in the summer, during a short-lived Mr. Mom period where I was a stay-at-home dad, Ann Winblad called me to schedule a lunch. We'd met when CDC private-labeled her company's accounting software, Open Systems. I negotiated the contract on behalf of CDC and I always enjoyed my interactions with Ann, who was far more intelligent and better able to see the big picture than most of the people I worked with.

Over lunch, Ann asked me to join her at Open Systems and take over the marketing department. She and her co-founders had decided to sell the company and wished to replace the current founders with credentialed, seasoned and well-respected professionals in all the critical roles of CEO, CFO, VP of Marketing and VP of Product. Along with me as VP of Marketing, they brought in Peter Davis, an experienced CEO in the software space.

The timing couldn't have been better. With a new family to support and a desire to make my mark in the business world, I jumped at the chance. Suddenly, I found myself as the VP of Marketing at a cool company, with health insurance allowing Maggie to leave CDC and focus on our newborn daughter and our home.

It was during this time that I had a moment of realization. After washing and waxing my 10-year-old silver Jaguar XJ6 one Saturday,

I looked out my driveway and suddenly understood that I'd achieved something significant. I finally gained the job title and the same model car (even down to the color) of the businessperson I had most admired in my early career—Paul Ginther of Schaak Electronics. While emulating him hadn't been a conscious ambition, it had likely been a subconscious goal motivating me for years.

Now that I had "achieved Paul Ginther," it was time to set a new goal. And perhaps I could do it at Open Systems.

Our Jaguar XJ6 with red leather seats, parked here
in my parents driveway in Rochester.

My time at Open Systems, while relatively brief, was filled with valuable experiences. One day, I walked past a small alcove outside Ann's office and noticed a familiar-looking person reading a book. He didn't look up, so I continued along my way and went into Denny Shield's office. Denny was our COO and happened to be married to Ann Winblad's sister. I asked him if the man reading the book was who I thought it was.

"Yes, that's Bill Gates," he replied. "A friend of Ann's. He and Ann are going somewhere later."

Ann thought nothing of leaving Bill waiting an hour or more as she finished what she needed to do before they headed out. Years later, when Ann started a venture capital firm with John Hummer called Hummer Winblad Venture Partners, Microsoft became one of their limited partners.

I've known and worked with a lot of brilliant people over the years, but Ann Winblad may be the smartest individual I've met in the business world. She has a staggering intellect, which seems to give her the ability to see into the future. Few people match her impressive track record of picking winning companies.

Not only did Ann and her firm invest in one company I co-founded, but she would also speak at the Personalization Summit conferences I created years later at a company called Net Perceptions. This brought us even closer together and we become good friends. We're close to the same age, although Ann insists that I'm two years older. I certainly look older—Ann still looks like a 20-something.

Occasionally, during the go-go late 1980s, our travel schedules co-incided and Ann would offer me rides on the corporate jet she used. Once, as we took off from San Francisco, she looked at me and said, "Steve, this is the last time you're hitching a ride like this with me."

Confused about what she was getting at, I had no idea what to say.

"Well, you know, it can become habit-forming!" she joked.

By the fall of 1985, it became clear that Peter Davis and I weren't seeing eye-to-eye on things at Open Systems. With Ann having been gone for almost six months, the excitement had faded and it was time for me to move on.

* * * * *

Soon after leaving Open Systems, AT&T offered me a management position. The Area VP in the Twin Cities, Gil Rainier, had called Robert Price, Control Data's CEO, to see if he knew anyone with a particular set of skills. Price gave him my name and I received a job offer after our first meeting.

My entry into AT&T was nothing short of dramatic. On my first day, I arrived early, grabbed a newspaper and was greeted by a screaming headline: "AT&T announces 24,000-person layoff in Information Systems Division."

Hmm, I thought, "That doesn't sound good—that's the area that just hired me."

Scanning the story, I noted the layoffs would affect 6% of AT&T's total workforce, directly hitting the 117,000-person Information Systems division. Perhaps my first day will be my last, I thought, setting a "shortest tenure ever" personal record.

Entering Gil Rainier's office suite on the top floor of the AT&T building, I held up the newspaper and said, "What's going on with this?"

Not expecting this greeting, he hesitated and said, "Well, it's one of the reasons you're here."

He explained that he was in charge of five regional branch offices, each with 100 to 120 employees. His orders were to downsize each branch office to 25 or 30 people and reduce his area staff from nearly 40 to 25 or less.

"I know most of these people personally," Gil said. "We're friends. I can't do this objectively, so I was hoping you could help us make these painful reductions along with your other responsibilities."

As it was my first day on the job, it was impossible to say no.

Amazingly, before we implemented these reductions I had time and budget to hire one of my most effective lieutenants from Control Data—Bill Shell—a native Oklahoman who never lost his accent. Bill was one of the most organized, hardest working and effective managers I ever met.

Once Bill was on board, we constructed a plan to exceed the Midwest Area's annual quota for selling AT&T computers and equipment. As we moved into full execution mode on our sales plans, the layoffs began. My team continued with the plan, while I put the cloak of doom over my shoulders and headed to the branch offices.

AT&T was not heartless. It cushioned the layoffs with generous "separation packages" that gave each laid-off employee close to a month's salary for every year they'd been with the company, provided they signed the "I won't sue" paperwork. Plus, AT&T covered health insurance for two additional years, or until people found other employment that offered coverage.

A softened blow is still a blow, however, and many of the meetings I had were filled with tears and anger. Several employees told me AT&T was the only place they'd ever worked, and after 20-plus years they couldn't imagine what else they would do. Lots of the employees I met with felt that a significant part of their lives was over.

Sometimes, they yelled and screamed at me. AT&T wasn't just a workplace, it was also a social outlet where people met some of their closest friends. I felt ill-equipped to deal with the despair, frustration and hopelessness they expressed.

* * * * *

For years after I left AT&T, I couldn't attend an industry conference, trade show or event without running into at least one of these former AT&T colleagues. Approaching me, they'd ask if I remembered firing them. Then they told me how much they hated me and the company for doing that.

But here was the surprise. In only slightly different words, everyone said, "That was the best thing that ever happen to me. My life changed for the better that day and I've never been happier."

Everyone told me, in retrospect, how much they'd been stagnating at AT&T. They'd lost themselves in this behemoth company where their efforts were unseen, unappreciated and disconnected from what made a company successful.

They told me how they were now working at places where the impact of their contributions was evident. They knew the value they were adding, and so did those around them. This was a feeling they hadn't had before. They were thrilled. And, of course, it made me feel better, too.

I'm sure not everyone managed through their layoffs with such positive results, but I learned that being forced to wake up and change things doesn't have to be entirely negative. Being let go is never fun, and everyone fears the unknown. But venturing out can sometimes turn your life around, whether you take the step voluntarily or not.

* * * * *

Before my time with AT&T ended, they promoted me to General Manager and transferred me to Los Angeles, where I would make one of the most boneheaded business mistakes I've ever made.

To prepare for the move to LA, we sold our home on Stewart Drive in Eden Prairie for a loss. However, we would have faced an almost impossible situation if my cousin, John Gravley, hadn't stepped up to help. We had funded building this twin home with a construction loan during the real estate boom, urged on by my "smarter" Control Data buddies as homes doubled in value between 1979 and 1980. Suddenly, home values reversed when loan interest rates rose to 18%.

We never planned to live in this house, we just wanted to build it, sell it and reap a profit. But when real estate buyers evaporated, we had no choice but to move into one side of the home and rent out the other half. When the opportunity came to move to Los Angeles, we bit the bullet and sold the side we lived in at a tremendous loss.

Since he had the GI bill, John Gravley could take advantage of a once-in-a-lifetime benefit of having the government underwrite a mortgage. He bought the other side of our twin home, saving our bacon. To this day, Maggie and I don't know what we would have done without John's help. This is a favor I can't imagine how to ever repay.

During our first week in LA, we lived on our friend Zach Bovinette's sailboat in the Long Beach marina. Trying to keep a rambunctious two-year-old from jumping overboard kept Maggie and me on our toes. Early house-hunting excursions were disappointing, so we rented a townhome in Arcadia, right off Huntington Drive and south of Santa Anita Park.

In transitioning to the GM slot in Los Angeles, I inadvertently made a business blunder from which no recovery was possible. It led to some valuable advice for anyone switching jobs or taking on a new assignment in a different division or geography. I know precisely how it should NOT be done.

The right approach, for at least the first two weeks, is to listen, watch, listen, ask questions, listen and keep your mouth shut. If asked a direct question, resist the urge to give an answer and say instead, "That's an excellent question. What would you say to that?" I didn't do this, so the next three or four years of my professional career were a living hell.

Before explaining, it may be helpful to understand how IBM, AT&T and other large company field organizations operated. The United States was broken into regions, such as the Midwest, West, Northeast and Southeast, with each region managed by a regional VP or SVP.

Branch offices were established within a specific area—or country in the case of Europe—to manage all the company's business and sell its products and services in that area. For instance, in the Midwest AT&T had branch offices in Minneapolis, Chicago/Milwaukee, St. Louis, Kansas City and Oklahoma City. Branches were composed of roughly 100 employees, half or more in sales and customer relationship positions. Branch managers were the ultimate authority: It was a key position that paid well and offered vast autonomy. Once arriving in this role, many were reluctant to ever leave.

An old story illustrates the attitude of many of these branch managers: A golf foursome of talented players is playing at Pebble Beach. One player's game is off, and she's falling behind the rest. After a particularly frustrating hole, the player lines up her next drive and hits the ball with a great deal of force into a tree, where it falls onto a cement footpath and bounces high into the air, where a passing eagle catches it. The eagle flies away with the ball toward the green and drops the ball, where it rolls into the cup for a hole-in-one. One of the foursome remarks to the others, "Who does she think she is, God?" Another player says, "Well, no, she actually is God—but she thinks she's an AT&T branch manager."

Walt Elser, the SVP of the Southern California region, recruited me to California with a promotion and generous pay package. He asked me to come out, visit his branches and assess each of the 10-person data sales teams' ability to meet that year's quota of data products.

I did as Elser asked, spending a week visiting each branch manager, the data sales teams and the managers who would report to me. These meetings were informative, and it was easy to identify a host of problems, weak personnel and missed opportunities.

Back in Minneapolis, preparing for our move to LA, the phone rang in my home office. I was working on a report to Mr. Elser, outlining what I'd learned during my week in LA and a series of recommended next steps. I took the call and discovered I was on speakerphone in Mr. Elser's weekly staff meeting with all his branch managers. He asked me to review what I'd found, branch by branch, and without a second thought I did just that. After all, my notes happened to be right in front of me, so why waste time?

Perhaps if I'd been in the room and able to observe the devastated looks on the branch managers' faces as I outlined each misstep and shortcoming, I would have known to "Shut the F up!" But no such luck. Within 20 minutes, I single-handedly destroyed any chance of having a working relationship with these branch manager peers, who had a lot of power to make or break my career. I was so stupid and naïve.

When I finally got to Los Angeles and began doing my job, it took me forever to figure out why it was so hard to meet with and gain cooperation from these branch managers. And in fact, I never did. Elser's branches didn't make their data quota that year, or even the next one. My only saving grace was that other regions across the country were doing even worse.

As AT&T's top strategy folks realized that a full-out assault on Wang, Digital Equipment Corporation (DEC), IBM, Data General and Honeywell would cost more in dollars and time than their appetites would allow, I was moved to a low visibility, out-of-the-way position. Assigned to an office in Orange County, staffed entirely by a group of wonderful Filipino nationals, I had a ball overseeing a steady but unexciting part of AT&T's empire. It required only about half my time, and I soon began planning and implementing my first startup on the side.

* * * * *

In the mid-1980s, most music aficionados, me included, spent an hour or two each week checking out new releases at our favorite record stores. In LA, Tower Records dominated. Music Plus was closer to me, but Licorice Pizza had titles the others didn't.

I bought one of the brand-new CD players, and although they were expensive and finding CDs was difficult, I saw an opportunity. I knew retail and thought that starting a compact disc-only store could be a winner. And so I opened one, naming it Compact Disc Warehouse (CDW).

Like many California startups that would follow, it began in my garage. We took out a second mortgage on the house, found a suitable location at the corner of Rosemead and Colorado Blvd. in Pasadena, built out the space, ordered inventory and cash registers, set up a point-of-sale system and were off to the races in about nine months.

Key to making this happen was learning the business and hiring a team. So I signed on as a part-time employee at Music Plus, working nights after leaving my office at AT&T. I made the small section in the store where they carried CDs my focus, talking with as many customers who looked through our limited CD inventory as I could. Sometimes, I probed their interest in shopping at a store that only carried CDs and they all loved the idea.

Since I was doing this part-time, I needed a full-time manager. I found one in Philip Hockwald. He was the manager of a Music Plus in nearby Glendale, and after a few lunches with him he was ready to jump ship.

Employees at Siechert & Wood, a technical documentation company in Pasadena where Maggie worked, had become good friends of ours. We drafted them to wait on customers, demonstrate how to use our demo stations and ring up sales. My cousin John Gravley flew out to LA and also spent a few weeks pitching in.

Our grand opening weekend was truly a thrill. My heart nearly stopped in anticipation as we turned the key and opened the store on the first day. We were ahead of our time, and the store was nearly always busy. I loved spending my weekends working there.

Over the next three years, we opened two additional stores. We learned that the formula for one successful store doesn't always translate to different locations, especially without the resources to hire someone to oversee our managers. Instead, Philip managed our flagship location while attempting to supervise the managers of the two other stores as well.

I signed the business over to Philip when I left AT&T and moved out of Los Angeles. He eventually retracted to just one location, which provided him with a good living for the next five years. But by then nearly all other music retailers had abandoned LPs and switched to CDs, taking away our edge. The big chains could negotiate better prices, carry more products and out-promote Compact Disc Warehouse.

Early days at CDW: John Gravley is behind me on the left, ringing up a sale and Carl Siechert is on the right, greeting a customer coming in.

19

GOODBYE AT&T—
HELLO PRODIGY

I LEFT AT&T FOR A new startup, The Prodigy Services Company. The venture was funded by IBM, Sears and CBS, and I felt it was a perfect fit. Within several months of joining the company, my mojo and confidence returned: I was part of an exciting team that would launch Prodigy's new online service.

The way I got the job at Prodigy wasn't unusual, but it taught me a useful lesson about truth. In 1989, Stu Fishler, a corporate headhunter in Los Angeles, called me to discuss the opportunity. He was looking for a local LA branch manager, but my interviews with six department heads would take place at Prodigy's headquarters in New York.

I understood that the most critical interview would be with Ross Glatzer, a former Sears executive who would go on to lead Prodigy as CEO. At the time he was the company's COO, working for CEO Ted Papes, who came out of IBM and was in his last role before retiring. Glatzer ran the show and was to be my final interview of the day.

Fishler had prepared me well, and the early interviews went smoothly. Sometimes, I wondered why I was meeting with certain people as they had nothing to do with my prospective role at the company. Finally, the interview with Ross Glatzer, the big boss, arrived. I was tired from all the scrutiny and questions, but at least I had well-practiced answers.

After a few typical interview questions, Glatzer asked me something no one else had. "Steve, I've been looking at your resume and see you've never spent over five years with any company," he began.

"While it appears you initiated many of your job changes, I'm concerned. If you join us, will you only last five years and leave for greener pastures?"

My first instinct was to fabricate a small lie and say, "Of course not, Mr. Glatzer. I would never do that."

But then, at the point where I almost didn't care if they offered me the job or not, I thought to myself, "What the hell?"

"You're right, it's a risk," I said out loud. "I get bored. I suspect if I'm no longer involved in new and interesting things, I'll probably quit. But if I'm engaged and challenged, I'll stay as long as you like."

I could tell from his face this wasn't the answer he was expecting, but I think he also knew it was the truth.

* * * * *

My first role at Prodigy was to take on management of the LA branch office in Sherman Oaks. It had gotten off the ground with Jim O'Connell (alias, "Jimbo, Billy-Bob, Bubba, O'Connell"), a tall, gregarious, outgoing Irishman who I grew to love. He'd been the "advance man" manager and was now off to open more branches in less critical cities, leaving me in charge of LA.

Jim had hired a terrific team and we created some of the most exciting and unique sales promotions and events in the company's history. Office manager Lori Colombano was the heart and life of the group. Of our two salespeople, Don Janke was terrific and he worked along side a hard-charging blonde woman named Bev. She had more drive and determination than anyone I've ever met and rounded out the team.

As the branch manager, I handled sales and market planning, distribution, and subscriber acquisition and retention in Los Angeles and, eventually, Orange County. We launched the Prodigy Service in Los Angeles late in 1989, which allowed me to be involved in the historic precursor to the Internet where many innovative and breakthrough technologies were unveiled. Back then, the idea of shopping, playing games, doing banking and chatting with friends on a computer was brand new and seemed weird to many.

My years running the Prodigy branch in Los Angeles were a blast. My small team was tasked to introduce technically interested members of the public to Prodigy, one of the world's first online services. We presented at computer user groups, visited computer retail stores like Egghead and set up displays at other dealers. We also decided, in LA, that we would attempt to meet with as many actual users of the service as we could.

Our team created eye-catching Prodigy promotions on the windows of our retailers, in this case, Egghead Software.

My team gained a reputation for punching far above our weight when it came to promotional prowess. After setting up KMPC morning radio announcer Robert W. Morgan as a Prodigy member, for example, I became a semi-regular visitor on his morning radio program. He used the service to take questions from listeners and often corresponded with them on the air.

The legendary actor Gene Autry owned the radio station, and had his friend and cowboy movie sidekick, Pat Buttrum, sit in a couple of days a week and tell jokes and stories on Robert's show. Being in the studio with these guys was thoroughly entertaining.

Buttram was a brilliant character actor, best known now for playing Mr. Haney in the TV series *Green Acres*. He was also the voice of many of Disney's animated characters. Buttram would arrive in the studio and, after a few pleasantries, sit down with a briefcase full of 3X5 cards that contained hand-written jokes, notes and ideas for bits. As he listened to the news and Morgan's patter, Buttram would eventually look in his briefcase, pull out a card, make some notes and give Robert a sign. Within seconds, Morgan would activate Buttram's mic and he'd go into his bit, often pulling Robert—and even me if I was there—into the conversation before delivering a usually corny but sometimes hilarious punch line.

Being on the radio in Los Angeles helped connect me to my cousin, Roger Larsen, a bank Vice President in Orange County. He loved Robert W. Morgan's show and got a kick out of the fact that I was on it from time to time. He also used Morgan's sports betting tips for upcoming games.

Maggie and I made several trips to see Roger and his wife Joy, and we met his kids, Lori and Scott. Roger bailed me out of a knuckle-headed credit mess I'd gotten into, and to reward him for his effort I sent my brother Leif to his bank when he was in town for a visit. Roger hadn't seen Leif in many years, and Leif dressed in shorts and a t-shirt to see if Roger would give him a loan to buy a surfboard. It took a few minutes for Roger to piece things together, and Leif could only keep the charade going so long. Leif finally confessed his identity, they hugged and the encounter has become a favorite family story. Roger's daughter Lori would play an important role in my life years later.

* * * * *

Many of our sales promotion schemes at Prodigy worked so well because, however wild an idea was, our brilliant and energetic office manager Lori Colombano would figure out how to make it work. Another reason things worked well was my habit of executing first and asking questions later.

I remember being on a call with a fellow branch manager when the company was months overdue with our budgets for the coming year. It was late January, and his branch had done nothing because he still hadn't gotten his budget. "I'm stuck," he said. "I don't know what we can afford to do and what we can't, so we're just sort of twiddling our thumbs until we know."

Staring out my office window at the traffic stranded on the 405, I told him I looked at it differently. For me, not having a budget was an opportunity to commit and pre-pay for a good amount of advertising and to quickly start a series of promotional contests and events. I figured once we got our budgets and learned we'd overspent, I'd just plead mea culpa and say I didn't know it would push us over.

That's precisely how it worked, and we were fine. This is a relatively common example of the way I made many business decisions when managing in large companies, and many personal decisions such as planning a vacation or buying a house. I think through the upsides and potential downsides and usually aim for the upsides.

* * * * *

When I look back at the number and variety of sales promotions and events we did at Prodigy in Los Angeles, even I shake my head at all we accomplished. We had a weekend cruise for Prodigy members on a real cruise ship, which sold out. We had events at hundreds of retail stores. We spoke or gave Prodigy demos at countless high schools and colleges.

My star rose rapidly in the Prodigy sales arm, and after a few years they asked me to move to the New York headquarters. I was a young executive, and this was a big deal. My young son Eric was thriving after battling a serious heart condition and we were all going to move to the business capital of the world.

Quite unexpectedly, Eric died before we left California. The tragic event turned all our lives upside down, but we were still going ahead with the cross-country journey.

Looking back, I sometimes think, "How did we survive everything that life threw at us?"

20

FAVORITE PRODIGY PEOPLE AND A GLASS HOUSE

I OCCASIONALLY CROSSED PATHS WITH Prodigy CEO Ross Glatzer in New York, although I never reported directly to him. Other than my direct boss, Bill Young, Glatzer was the only person to approach me about the death of my son, caring enough to seek me out and ask me how I was doing. Long after I left Prodigy and became part of the founding teams of various early-stage companies, I never forgot the care and attention Ross Glatzer and his team at Prodigy put into every person hired, myself included.

When I moved to Prodigy headquarters, I joined a team led by Dave Waks to investigate taking Prodigy to business customers. The brilliant but eccentric Bill Young soon replaced Waks as the leader of our team, which also included Rob Kost, Sam Meo, Marty Evancoe and a sales guy we never saw because he was always out of the office selling something, somewhere, to someone and we never knew to who or what.

Another thing we didn't know, but our boss did, was that Bill Young was dying. He'd gotten a terminal diagnosis with not a lot of runway—a year, maybe two. He told no one, and we had no idea what was motivating our brilliantly supportive boss. He married his girl-friend (Mary) and legally adopted her children from a previous mar-riage. He lobbied to advance the careers of each of his direct reports.

Bill was the only one from Prodigy to fly across the country from New York to attend my son's memorial service in California. He was a noble and good person with an overwhelming sense of decency. Whenever I'm tempted to take shortcuts or not bother with the extra step I think of Bill, which often gives me the energy to do the right thing.

Toward the end, when most of my team lost faith in Prodigy's new CEO and management, Bill left Prodigy and went to IBM. Within a month, he tried to recruit all of us to come and work there, with good jobs and excellent salaries. But by then I was already headed for the door and had other ideas. When Bill passed I was in California and didn't get the news until weeks later. Rob Kost and Sam Meo let me know that Bill had provided for his family financially and perhaps, most importantly, with his life example.

* * * * *

I treasure my time at Prodigy because of the wonderful people I met there. I instantly hit it off with Rob Kost and we've been friends ever since. We often rode to work together, spending our 30- to 40-minute commute debating religion, philosophy and ethics. Not only was Rob a brilliant business strategist, but he also majored in philosophy in college before getting his law degree and passing the bar in Washington, D.C.

Our mutual friend, Sam Meo, was another integral part of our group but, tragically, we lost him in 2010. Sam spent a terrible year sick with AIDS, and Maggie would go into the city to his apartment every week to care for him.

We were also fortunate enough to meet Josh Kopelman. I marveled at his intense focus and clarity of vision, even though he looked like a 14-year-old kid. Josh, a Wharton School graduate, would found First Round Capital, but not before creating Infonautics and Half.com, which he sold to eBay. Josh would later invest in one of my companies. Sometime later I would become a limited partner in one of his funds. Dollar for dollar, that investment paid off more than any other investment I've ever made—perhaps more than all the others combined.

* * * * *

Another nice thing about our move to New York was the house we found at 120 Truesdale Drive in the idyllic town of Croton-on-Hudson. The house was beautiful, high on a cliff above a river, with a wall of windows. This new home was vacant and had never been lived in. Three doctors had built it as an investment and completed it several years earlier. When the real estate market collapsed after the recession in 1990, the owners let the home sit empty, hoping for a market turnaround. They finally grew tired of waiting and put it back on the market with an asking price less than the construction cost.

Walking in for the first time and seeing the breathtaking views of the Croton River through large panes of glass that were the hallmark of this one-of-a-kind residence, I pulled Maggie aside and whispered, "You can't let our realtor know how much we love this house."

Maggie nodded. She'd had the same instant attraction I did. It was stunning.

In the weeks after first moving in, we learned about the local merchants and found doctors' offices and car repair places. We were often asked where we lived. Everyone could tell we were newcomers because we "sounded funny."

When we told them our address, they all knew the house. Since it had been vacant for over a year, at least half the people in town had wandered through it. It was spectacular, although we later learned that the builders had taken many shortcuts. The foundation was as solid as a rock, but they skimped on some of the interior finish components, the windows and the roof.

The house had other peculiarities, including 13 skylights, about 40 windows and a tile floor that allowed Maggie to practice roller-blading indoors. There was a sunken formal living room, a sunken family room, a home theater on the lower level and our shared offices on a level below that. All the bedrooms were on the second floor, so the house technically had six levels. Most houses we've purchased since have been on a single level—we've paid our dues with stairs.

As we settled in deeper and things got better for us as a family, every once in a while on a Sunday morning I'd get interesting, innovative people to come by and eat, drink wine and talk. There were glimmers of million-dollar ideas and lively voices at these parties, which became known as the "Larsen Sunday Salons." Lots of the New York new media folks would come up and engage with others who either lived in or around our town, or were just passing through.

Chuck Martin of *The Digital Estate* would often be there, IBM-casual gadgets and all. Jack Rickard, editor of *Boardwatch Magazine*, made regular appearances with his fishing vest stuffed with pens, keys, notebooks and cigars. Chris Locke, who founded the *Internet Business Report*, drove over from Stamford, Connecticut. Dread-locked Jonathan Steuer from *HotWired* was another regular. One time he brought Justin Hall, who ran a website called Justin's Links from the Underground, an expansive, hypertext rendering of his life and mind—everything from his father's suicide when he was eight years old to his dating life. Justin's site finally influenced me to create my own website and deal more openly with the death of my son.

The crowd shifted and blended and shifted again, making each semi-random gathering its own unique adventure. In that spirit I was looking forward to the retreat planned by Jerry Michalski and Esther Dyson in Philadelphia in June of 1996.

21

RAGEBOY AND THE REVOLUTION: A PIVOTAL MOMENT IN TECH

AS PRODIGY'S FATE HUNG IN the balance, a group of us had been meeting regularly, acutely aware of the looming opportunities the Internet offered. We were desperately trying to chart a course through the rapidly changing digital ecosystem. It was an exhilarating, if uncertain, time.

On a sunny June afternoon in 1996, I found myself driving back to New York from Philadelphia in my 1991 Nissan 300ZX. The car's responsive acceleration, grippy tires and finely tuned suspension gave me an almost visceral connection to the road. There's something magical about the interplay between foot, pedal and asphalt that even the most advanced technology struggles to replicate.

Beside me sat the inimitable Christopher Locke, his stream of consciousness narration as relentless as the chain of menthol lights dangling from his lips. Locke, an analyst, journalist, author and speaker, had an uncanny ability to see the future of tech. His raspy, boyish voice, which sounded like a brick through a window, had earned him the fitting moniker "Rageboy".

We were both riding an intellectual high, having just left a conference that felt more like a glimpse into the future than a typical industry gathering. For a few wonderfully unstructured days, more than 50 of the brightest minds in tech had come together to throw paper airplanes, engage in free-wheeling discussions and plan our next moves.

The event's open, organic nature made it feel like we were explorers, discovering a new world brimming with possibilities. It was much like the salons I held at my home in Croton-on-Hudson—but on a much larger scale.

* * * * *

The atmosphere at Eagle Lodge, where the conference was held, pulsed with a sense of freedom and possibility. Jerry Michalski and Esther Dyson had brought together this diverse group of thinkers, each miles apart in their disciplines but united by a shared sense that something big was on the horizon. Esther had been running PC Forum successfully for decades, and Jerry convinced her it was time to put a new bunch of people together.

All 54 of the people who were invited to this special retreat had said something to Jerry in the past year that made him think, "Aha."

We became known as his "Aha people," though since then we've more often referred to ourselves as "Jerry's Kids." Whether an individual's interests had been commercial or social or political or spiritual, there had been something there—a sense of things shifting and moving smoothly, like tumblers in a great lock.

The unstructured nature of the event allowed for a level of candor rarely seen in professional settings. If the consensus was that IBM could kiss our collective asses, well, there was no reason not to say so. It was explicitly stated that each individual there would speak for themselves, regardless of where they worked.

The conference's physical setting matched its intellectual openness. Eagle Lodge, with its tall green trees and stone paths, was personally selected by Jerry and Daphne Kis, Esther's partner at Edventure Holdings, and provided the perfect backdrop for our discussions. The amphitheater, in particular, fostered an intimacy that allowed everyone to see and hear each other clearly.

Just northwest of Philadelphia, Eagle Lodge isn't far from the site of the first Quaker meeting in Pennsylvania. This was oddly important to Jerry, who'd attended a lot of Quaker sittings and had some notion of a similar structure for the conference: One could only break an open silence if they were certain the silence could be improved. It was a nice idea, although not everybody grasped it.

I knew what Jerry was thinking. A few months earlier he invited me on a cold, clear, sunny winter Sunday to a Friends meeting in Connecticut, at a church in Wilton. The structure was beautiful, as only New England churches can be, white with a modest steeple and at the edge of a wood with trees all around.

There was a sanctuary area, a semi-circle of pews facing an enormous fireplace, and as the Friends moved into it they became quiet. No opening hymn, no reading from the Bible. We just sat in the unbelievably peaceful stillness and I felt myself cocooned by a cascade of images and words—some thought, some felt and some that came from another place entirely.

About 40 minutes into the silence, one woman spoke and briefly shared how she'd suddenly seen God's hand in something she'd never noticed before. Everyone took it in, but no one added anything. "Speaking only when you can improve the silence" is a high bar.

At the end of an hour, a church elder rose and read a short list of announcements—a food shelter needed contributions and help, some church members were ill and needed prayers. And with that, we filed out.

Eagle Lodge certainly wasn't as pure or as quiet as the church that hosted the Friends meeting, but the sense of freedom was exhilarating. Anyone who needed to speak could do so. And speak we did, the words and thoughts moving back and forth like a well-played basketball game. Some attendees disappeared, only to return with impromptu presentations, while others spoke off the cuff.

This conference was clearly Jerry's baby, and he chose to give it back to the attendees—Don Norman, Doc Searls, Arthur Einstein, David Isenberg, Emily Davidow, Jack Henry, Malcolm CasSelle, Omar Wasow, Udi Shapiro, Yossi Vardi, Judi Clark, Howard Greenstein, Kyle Shannon, Eric Hughes, Nick Givotovsky and many other technology luminaries.

From the moment Chris and I arrived, we knew this wasn't your typical conference. We were handed white t-shirts to decorate and colorful paddles for expressing agreement, curiosity or dissent during sessions. The childlike atmosphere was further enhanced by an assortment of toys scattered around—miniature Slinkys, puzzles and lots of Silly Putty.

The conversations were incredible, and for the first time in my life I participated in a real dialogue with 50-plus people. Jerry led the group in determining what we wanted to talk about and took on the role of moderator.

The group was chaotic, and initially it seemed like Jerry's task was as challenging as trying to control a group of unruly cats. However, over time, he resembled famed basketball coach Pat Riley, who led the highly successful Los Angeles Lakers team.

At one point, Chris Locke stood up and yelled, "What the fuck!"

It wasn't a question, it was a statement of fact that got everyone's attention.

"I've been stuck at IBM for a year with my thumb up my ass, waiting for someone to figure out what the fuck is going on with this Internet thing," he continued, "They've got plans I give them all the time and they file them and say 'Yeah, Chris, that's great.' Then they take me into some fucking egg carton room and tell me what I've got to work with, which is nothing—no money, no equipment, no staff— and then they give me a check and I fucking go home and sit there."

No one moved.

"They want me to do all the Internet thinking and get them into it," he went on. "But they tell me I've got no resources and say, 'Oh, by the way, don't talk to anyone about this stuff without clearing it through channels.' And I sit here and some of what I'm hearing today is all about how to work in the system. Well, I say fuck the system— it's dead, it's stupid, it's non-responsive, it's counterproductive, it's fucking socially evil and if we put any more of our goddamn time into propping up these dead-ass morons, we deserve what we fucking get!"

The veins were standing out in his neck.

"Go Rageboy, go!" Esther yelled out.

And he did just that. "THEY DO NOT WANT US, AND THEY'RE CRIMINALS BY INSTINCT ANYWAY, AND IF WE PUT ONE MORE YEAR INTO FUCKING AROUND WITH THESE DEAD-FROM-THE-FUCKING-TOP-DOWN PIECES OF MANUAL-BOUND SHIT, WE'RE GOING TO MISS THE GODDAMN TRAIN!"

Whistles and cheers came from the crowd. People were standing, one guy on top of his table. Paper airplanes and erasers filled the air as Chris kept going. "Let me tell you—I'm Program Director for Online Community Development at IBM and they're paying me to do nothing," he said. "And when I say, 'Hey, I'm getting paid for doing nothing,' they say, 'As long as you understand the situation.'"

The crowd was with my friend, cheering him on at every word.

"Brave new fucking world, huh?" he asked. "These guys are the Emperor's guys. These are fucking Entropy Brigades and the closer we get to them, the more the heat drains out of our systems. If that's what you want, fine, go for it, but don't expect me to sit here and nod my head about how you're gonna use these guys, because THERE IS NO USE FOR THESE GUYS unless you want to hollow them out and use them for fucking floor lamps."

His rant achieved eloquence, as rants occasionally do. Later, speeding toward home on the loathsome New Jersey Turnpike, peering red-eyed through the cloud of smoke from Locke's interminable cigarettes, we turned over a lot of information, twisting and bending it as we shot into the twilight and the greasy salmon-smear around Newark, just like always.

Much like his public rant, our private conversation on the trip home was a mix of hard information, coffee dregs, healthy contempt, real-world pragmatism, mashed toxic cigarette butts, visionary eloquence, trailing-off-in-the-haze 1960s enthusiasms, pure rage, a sense of mission, Thirteen Ways of Saying Fuck It, a highly tuned bullshit detector with wires and lights and everything, democratic zeal, arcane rock and roll, a dollop of Howl, a cloud of menthol smoke and a driver with his head in and out of the window, trying to breathe, at 90 mph, bearing down on the Hanging Gardens of Newark.

"We absolutely have to fucking burn the Fortune 500 down to the waterline," he said to me. "This is a moral obligation, an absolute fucking obligation."

Chris waved his left hand in the air as he talked, the smoke from his cigarette eddying around in search of some free air to poison.

* * * * *

A lot of things happened after that event in Philly. Don Norman, author of *The Design of Everyday Things*, left his day job and started his own consulting group. In 1998, he published *The Invisible Computer*, which predicted that the complexity of the PC will kill it and give way to information appliances.

Doc Searls went on to co-author *The Clue Train Manifesto* with Chris Locke and edit the *Linux Journal*, both vital to the growth of the open-source initiative.

David Isenberg published an essay called *Rise of the Stupid Network*. In 1998 it was a bombshell inside AT&T, but it found its way to *The Wall Street Journal* ("fascinating, scathing") because he also released it to the Internet. Shortly thereafter, David quit to do his own thing.

Israeli entrepreneur Yossi Vardi's company, Mirabilis, later gathered over 40 million users and got AOL to acquire it for $400 million. ICQ introduced the term "viral marketing." Malcolm CasSelle would become a player in Bitcoin and never reach his 51st birthday.

You know what it's like when you wake up as a kid on Saturday and there are no chores and there's nobody in the house and the sun is shining and everything is possible? Well, surprisingly, in a fast, smoke-filled car full of waving arms outside Newark, that's what it felt like—that things could be that way, at last.

Chris was working for IBM, a mismatch of epic proportions. I was still working for Prodigy—God help me. The Internet world was our oyster, and we nearly cracked it open on that drive.

22

PRODIGY'S POTENTIAL AND PAYOFF

MY FINAL FEW YEARS AT Prodigy involved managing its Bulletin Board system and communications products. Jenny Ambrozek was the real expert and did all the heavy lifting, while I was charged with looking at the bigger picture. One thing Ambrozek instilled and reinforced in me was the value and promise of "Online Community," and it's something I've never forgotten.

Community used to be a simple concept when everyone who lived in a place knew everyone else. In Fairmont, Minnesota where I grew up, the adults knew all the kids and any mischief I might have gotten into always found its way to my parents. Small towns often had only a few churches, so your religious community was frequently the same as your secular community. And your secular community was so small that everybody recognized a stranger in town.

Today, it's different. Society has become more mobile and fragmented. Many old rules related to geography and neighborhoods no longer apply. Cities are far too large for us to know every person living in them; houses of worship are far too many for us to claim membership in the religious community; and frequently, we can't tell a stranger from a resident on our block or even in our apartment building.

Communities are essential to us, however, and they rise up because people need other people. We like to belong. We want to identify with something important to us. But what is a community, anyway?

Saturn Motor Company talked about a "community of Saturn owners." Harley Davidson owners meet up at events all around the country, including an annual gathering in Sturgis, South Dakota, which, like a pilgrimage to Mecca, is a "rite of passage" among Harley riders.

Churches still consider themselves communities, as do Boy Scout troops, the American Legion and unions. There are hundreds of communities identified by specialty magazines covering hunting, fitness, food, quilting, home design, computer programming and photography.

Leaving Prodigy, I sensed that the future might lie in online communities, or at least in the content users created and shared with each other. I vowed to be on the cutting edge, and I felt I had the experience and understanding to pull it off.

My online community experiences happened first at Digital Den, with an acoustic modem connecting to the Usenet and various bulletin board systems. The WELL and Control Data's PLATO system were next.

Then I spent five years with the PRODIGY Service, which was really an eye opener. In LA, I met one of our members, Barb, who took part in the food board and organized a face-to-face meet-up of her group at the Red Dragon Café downtown. Members would travel from all over California and she wanted to know if I would join them. I showed up with trinkets, Prodigy T-shirts, mugs and pens. While instantly popular, I soon realized the star attractions at this event were the online friends everyone was meeting in person for the first time. My presence was quickly forgotten.

It was amazing what we learned from observing and managing these online communities. While Facebook (now Meta), Twitter (now X), Snapchat and TikTok would make these concepts commercially successful years later, they still wrestle with the same issues we faced then: How much free speech is permitted? Is any speech prohibited? What are the taboo topics?

If all speech is permitted and no topics are taboo, how do you handle illegal or libelous messages? What responsibilities do system operators have for user-created content? Who determines whether content is allowed? Do you allow people to post their intention to commit suicide? To threaten to kill someone? Does the system operator have a responsibility to act if they see such a posting? What action should they take? How does this scale from one or two suicide threats per night to thousands?

The list goes on and on: To what extent can or should participants be self-governing and self-regulating? Do you allow anonymity for participants? What's the process for resolving disputes? The physical world has established methods for working through many of these issues, but the electronic world is still figuring it out.

* * * * *

As my days at Prodigy in New York were winding down, I experimented with some of my own theories around building online communities. These were pre-Web days, so Prodigy business analyst and former attorney Rob Kost and I bought a reasonably powerful desktop computer, ordered several phone lines, bought some bulletin board (BBS) software from Tim Stryker's Galacticomm, Inc. and created "HOGWILD!"—the nation's first BBS for Harley-Davidson owners—in my Croton basement.

As an avid rider myself, I knew that the guys who loved Harleys were anything but the group of wild, unwashed ex-cons riding the countryside, terrorizing small villages and towns they're depicted as being. They have actual jobs, children on the honor roll and big houses with nice garages to store their bikes.

Despite sporting patches that say "Born to Ride," they typically log fewer than 5,000 miles a year in the saddle. What they like to do, though, is talk to each other about their bikes.

The board was an immediate hit, and news of its existence—augmented by small ads in a couple of biker magazines—spread rapidly.

Soon, hundreds of Harley owners were logging on, uploading photographs of their bikes, trading favorite riding routes, creating chat rooms and helping each other with maintenance advice. My role was that of an Inn Keeper: I gave them a place to gather and stayed out of the way.

The audience contributed the editorial material that was most valuable to other users. Our own content, such as a database of Harley models and recordings of Harley exhaust notes and photos, was just window dressing, a facade defining the conversational areas where strangers introduced themselves and became friends. The reason people kept coming back again and again was to share a mutual passion with like-minded people.

When people help create a community and contribute to its ongoing well-being, they become extremely loyal. They feel part of something larger than themselves. That's why, when a commerce function is introduced into an existing community it typically establishes high-value, lifetime customers among members of the community. This is true online as well as offline.

HOGWILD! had been operating about a year when Harley-Davidson's legal department notified us that they owned the rights to any use of the word HOG. To make a long story very short, Rob and I shut the board down to avoid getting sued for all we owned.

To this day, despite many attempts, Harley-Davidson has been unable to stimulate the level of participation or the spirit of camaraderie that Rob and I achieved in my basement with one PC and some phone lines. When I left Prodigy and began a period of independent consulting, I fantasized about where this could all go. My draft business plan for a national network of local online services got some good feedback, although no one was excited enough to throw money at building it.

* * * * *

As Rob Kost, Larry Smith and others puzzled about where the Internet was going and attempted to sort through the impacts on people and business, I'd heard about Bill Gross' efforts in Pasadena with a company he named CitySearch. Bill and I had crossed paths several times at LA-based computer user groups during my Prodigy years. Bill promoted Magellan, and later a natural language interface called HAL, to Lotus 1-2-3 while I demonstrated Prodigy. Lotus 1-2-3 would acquire Bill's company.

Magellan was a computer indexing program for searching and finding things on your own computer. I still miss that product and wish I had it. Magellan scanned every directory and file on your system, creating a control index. It allowed you to see your file contents without having to launch the programs that created them. Its search algorithms were powerful, connecting keywords and related information no matter where it existed on your system.

I knew Bill to be technically brilliant and incredibly innovative. He sold solar energy products through the mail as a kid. While attending Caltech, he invented a loudspeaker called GNP that I thought sounded exceptional and, as he explained to me, was "full of profit."

Gross had run with the idea, conjured up by Jeff Brewer and Caskey Dickson, to create CitySearch out of his IdeaLab offices and brought in Charles Conn to get it up and running. When I first heard about it, I knew it was right up my alley and a perfect fit with my experience. It even mirrored the business plan I was just beginning to shop with investors in New York City and I knew I could help them. A lot.

I traveled to Pasadena from New York and pitched Bill and the founders of CitySearch to hire me as a consultant. Charles, recently the managing partner at McKinsey's office in Australia, explained they were all ex-consultants and CitySearch didn't use consultants. However, they needed a Vice President of Business Development. Would I come aboard?

I said yes almost immediately, receiving a modest salary and my first-ever equity stake and early-stage co-founder role. The aversion to consultants was telling, given that Charles was the only individual to make partner at McKinsey before turning 30 besides Lou Gerstner, who would later become the CEO of IBM.

Unsure about how Maggie, Ginger and I all felt about moving back to Pasadena given our mixed memories from there, we went slowly. Richard Wood, the father of our friend Chris who was Maggie's former employer in Pasadena, offered me a room in his home. His wife, Marny, had passed away some years earlier and his children all thought he might value my company.

It turned out to be a perfect arrangement. I worked all day at CitySearch and came home with food around 7:00 p.m. Richard and I would eat if he hadn't already had something, and we'd watch old WWII programs on television. On weekends, when I wasn't working or traveling, we'd walk the dog.

One day, Richard asked me if I'd ever heard of a GMC Typhoon, a limited-edition, high-performance SUV that resembled a pickup truck. I had not. Produced in 1991–1993, fewer than 2,500 were ever made.

Like the BMW M-5, it was a classic wolf in sheep's clothing. Its engine, like the Corvette, was a 5.7-liter V-8 modified with lower-compression pistons, custom-made exhaust manifolds and a Mitsubishi Turbocharger and Garrett intercooler. Its performance compared favorably to the Chevy Corvette, Ferrari 348TS and Nissan 300ZX turbo—but it really did look like a pickup truck.

Richard found one he wanted to buy, so I went with him to check it out and take it for a test ride. Man, it was fast! He bought it, landing us both in hot water with his kids when they learned he'd been using it to drag race up and down Colorado Boulevard.

* * * * *

As I approached a year with CitySearch and the company investigated an IPO in the summer of 1998, we leveraged many of the partnerships Charles Conn and I had created. One of my contacts put me in touch with Barry Diller, who then operated from his base in Hollywood. At the time he was running USA Network, which he had recently purchased.

After some discussion, Diller pitched the idea to combine Ticketmaster and CitySearch and take them public. While I'd been doing business development for years, it was never in this league.

Diller, who one year was the highest-paid executive in the United States, had a reputation for shrewd deal-making. Lucky for me, Charles Conn, who had spearheaded the largest oil and gas merger in Australia's history, was every bit up for the challenge. Thomas Layton, another CitySearch co-founder, was with us and also no slouch.

I'll never forget that first meeting with Diller in the cabana by his pool in the backyard of his home. As the one who'd arranged the meeting, I began by telling him what we were all about. When Diller began asking questions, Charles quickly took over, answering them all. This was an immense relief to me. For a few minutes I kept up but I was soon lost in a world of acronyms and shortcuts. Diller would ask a question, Charles would respond and Diller would interrupt with another question.

Soon Charles was asking questions and interrupting Diller. They conducted their negotiations in a language and manner of deal-making that only true masters of the game could understand. The meeting didn't last long, maybe 30 minutes, but I sensed they had reached the outline of a deal.

I have many Charles Conn and Thomas Layton stories. After I left CitySearch, I once rode my yellow Honda Goldwing from the Bay Area to visit Charles and his family in Sun Valley, Idaho. At 973 miles, it was my longest single-day (24-hour) motorcycle ride. And don't get me started on Thomas Layton's wine collection or his passion for the outdoors!

* * * * *

CitySearch embodied many of the lessons I learned about communities. It was a hybrid mix of a strong online effort, focused 100% on a single local physical community. All CitySearch cities were built from within the community, using local resources and working with local governments, Chambers of Commerce and local media outlets. Each one depended economically on firm support from locally viable businesses.

Throughout these experiences, I learned several key lessons:

1. Online communities can support and enhance real-world relationships.
2. Meaningful connections don't require sophisticated tech.
3. Online interactions reveal different aspects of people with few physical or social cues.
4. The most valuable content comes from users.
5. Managing online communities involves complex issues of free speech, content moderation and user responsibility, all full of political and legal ramifications.
6. Successful online communities grow organically; they can't be manufactured.
7. When people contribute to a community's creation they become loyal.

These lessons remain relevant today as companies work to navigate evolving and chaotic social media platforms. The challenges and opportunities presented by online communities continue to shape our digital interactions and influence how we connect with others in virtual and physical spaces.

CitySearch would go public and its mission would change, but it was an honor to be involved in getting it built and moving it as far along as we did.

23

EXIT STRATEGY: TRADING STABILITY FOR STARTUP THRILLS

MY DEPARTURE FROM PRODIGY WAS made financially possible by years of conservative and diligent saving, a habit that began when our daughter Ginger was born. After the wake-up call in my early 40s about the expensive future medical procedures I'd likely need, I specifically sought employers like AT&T and IBM/Prodigy, whose size ensured extensive health care benefits without pre-insurance physicals.

From then on, 10 percent of every paycheck went directly to savings, along with every bonus, tax refund or other random income. We carefully lived within our means.

Right after leaving Prodigy, I spent six months with the World Merchandise Exchange (WOMEX). This startup was the vision of Ron Nyman, who'd grown up in the world of international trading. His father and grandfather were some of the first to open trade with China in the 1950s.

I accomplished everything Ron asked me to do, but decided not to join the team full-time. They were in Connecticut, and the cross-Westchester commute from our house in Croton was a bear. Plus, while WOMEX had promise, it wasn't where I saw the future.

Instead, I gravitated toward New York City, spending time with Rob Kost, his partners Larry Smith and Rich Masterson, and industry visionaries like Esther Dyson and Jerry Michalski. With our nest egg intact and Ginger healthy and approaching her teens, I felt we could take some calculated risks with my career. I became far more vigilant about my health, allowing me to cast a wider net for opportunities.

The Internet was the new frontier, and everyone was scrambling to monetize it. With our online experience, Rob and I were viewed as experts, presenting me with the chance to become an independent entrepreneur.

To bridge the income gap, we counted on Maggie's writing and documentation skills to supplement my consulting gig income. One of Maggie's projects during this period was writing Grolier's 26-volume *Encyclopedia Americana*. Well, she wrote the help system and user guide for the first electronic version of this product, but I always love saying she wrote *the Encyclopedia* and correcting myself afterward.

Another project kept her on the phone for hours, often in the middle of the night, with Australian golfer Greg Norman. A game publisher had partnered with him to create *Greg Norman Ultimate Challenge Golf*, a CD-ROM-based game that, for the first time, included sophisticated algorithms to accurately reflect the effect of wind and green terrain on a golf ball's trajectory. Maggie learned a lot about golf and made sure it was Greg Norman's voice that was transferred to the official Player's Guide.

I always marveled at Maggie's ability to rapidly comprehend complex technical concepts and skillfully make them understandable. As we sat at back-to-back desks with the Croton River rapids raging below us, she wrote a series of articles outlining IBM's position on Asynchronous Transfer Mode (ATM), an emerging standard for a packet-oriented, digital communications protocol. The proposed standard called for efficient, small fixed-size packets called cells to transmit various data types, including voice and video. She lived and breathed this emerging world of "packets" in virtual switching networks in the home office we shared. It was glorious. I had no idea what she was talking about.

Some weeks after she had submitted her last article on this topic, we invited a group of techie friends and colleagues to our home. Ever the conscientious host, when I overheard a group of engineers talking about asynchronous transfer modes, I naturally went and found

Maggie, brought her to the group, and said, "Meet my wife, Maggie. She knows all about ATMs." They looked at her, she looked at them, and then she looked back at me with a puzzled look on her face. "Automated Teller Machines?" she asked. They finally got on the same page, but it took a while. "I'm sorry honey, but once a project is over I clear everything from my mind," she told me later. "Everything I know about something is usually gone before the check clears the bank."

I was writing too, working on a book called *Competing in Cyberspace: Guidelines for Market-Driven Web Site Planning and Design* for Find/SVP, a marketing research firm. The $20,000 advance was welcome, and the recognition was valuable, too. Drawing heavily on work being done by Larry Smith, my friend Barry Golson who became editor of *Yahoo! Internet Life* after a long career at *Playboy*, and Steve Reynolds, a top analyst at Find/SVP, the book introduced the SNAP framework (Substance, Navigation, Activity and Presentation) that Smith had first presented at a New York New Media Association conference in 1996.

Rereading the book recently I was struck by how prescient it was, outlining website design strategies still relevant today. Its $1,795 price tag limited its commercial appeal, but that wasn't the point—it was intended as a resource for Find/SVP clients.

Being unemployed but successfully earning money as a consultant was both exhilarating and nerve-wracking. To save money, Maggie reminded me that she often set the thermostat to 60 degrees in the winter while Ginger was at school to help save money. She wore gloves at her keyboard and a beanie on her head.

24

NETP AND MY MANAGEMENT STYLE

AFTER LIVING THE BACHELOR LIFESTYLE with Richard Wood in Pasadena for a while, Maggie and I decided we'd lived apart long enough and began house hunting in Los Angeles.

Just as we were getting started, Ann Winblad called me out of the blue. As you might recall, she was the one who hired me as VP of Marketing for Open Systems, a computerized accounting software company. Soon after I joined Open Systems, Ann moved to the Bay Area and founded Hummer-Winblad, one of the most successful Venture Capital firms ever. Ann and I remain good friends.

On the phone, Ann explained that she was planning to invest in a startup in the Twin Cities. Although not yet named (it would become Net Perceptions), she wanted me to join as a co-founder with her friend from Microsoft Steven Snyder as CEO and John Reidl, a University of Minnesota Ph.D. who was managing a project there called GroupLens. Was I game?

I told Ann that getting someone to move to Minneapolis who knew the place and had also lived in New York and LA would be a tough sell.

"Oh no, it won't," she countered. "It's always easy to get people who've grown up in Minnesota to come back."

She was right, of course, and after meeting Steven, John and others on the team I gave Charles Conn the news. Sensing the future of CitySearch post-IPO, he encouraged me to make the jump. He also graciously accelerated the vesting of my CitySearch stock options, which he technically didn't have to do as I was a month shy of the required 12 months. When CitySearch went public, it was a pleasant bonus.

* * * * *

Net Perceptions quickly found funding from Winblad's firm and St. Paul Venture Capital, a local Minnesota venture firm. Co-founding a company at this stage, although familiar territory, was a bit different with this many smart collaborators and solid financial backing. Steven Snyder and I rapidly found and fell into our respective strengths, which complemented each other remarkably well.

Snyder had been around Microsoft long enough to observe the way Bill Gates and Steve Ballmer worked together, and while neither of us had aspirations of being Ballmer or Gates we adopted a similar model of divided duties in running Net Perceptions. Marketing strategy, public relations, business development and strategic partnerships were my areas.

Software development, engineering, finance, operations and nearly all the other heavy lifting fell to Steven, with both of us having a hand in fundraising. Of course, strong, professional and accomplished executives aided us, such as Tom Donnelly, our CFO; John Riedl, co-founder and CTO; Brad Miller who led our software development efforts and George Moser, our top sales executive.

Lessons from former companies and close relationships with CEOs like Charles Conn and Ann Winblad left me with sound ideas on how to create a brand and culture, which became one of my most important focus areas at Net Perceptions. In every new employee's first month, for example, they'd have a lunch or breakfast meeting with me—no exceptions. In these meetings I got to know them a bit, what their role was and what they planned to bring to the job.

Perhaps the most important dictate I gave every employee was this:

"In this job, you're probably going to screw up at some point. Just about everyone does. Your first instinct will be to cover it up and

hope that no one finds out. Don't do that. If you do and I ever find out, I will fire you in a New York minute. However, if you immediately go to your manager and report your mess, you're off the hook. At least for the first one, and probably the second. If it becomes a habit, maybe we'll have to have a conversation about whether you're in the right place. But if you ever try to cover up a mess, just once, the consequences are non-debatable—you're out."

Years later, I've had Net Perceptions employees come to me and say this was the most important bit of advice they've ever gotten.

During one of these lunch sessions, I met with a software engineer working for Brad Miller, our VP of Engineering. In my prep for the meeting, I learned that this engineer also played first chair trombone for the Grammy Award-winning Minnesota Orchestra. In the course of our conversation, I told him I thought it was great the way he balanced a tight, disciplined and highly analytical programming job with such a marvelous creative outlet.

He looked at me for a moment, confused, then smiled and said, "Actually, Steve, you've got it completely reversed."

Then I gave him a perplexed look.

"In the orchestra, I'm following a musical score under the direction of a ridiculously demanding conductor," he explained. "I have to hit every note perfectly, at exactly the right time and at precisely the right volume—not too loud, not too soft. And I have to do this for every note in the score, perfectly, for every performance. There is absolutely zero creativity. Now, programming is entirely different. Every single programming problem or challenge can be solved in hundreds of different ways. You can be fast, elegant or complex as you create and structure the code. Did you know our boss, Brad, can tell who wrote each bit of code without our names being on it? He knows because who we are and how we code is so expressive."

Learning to view software developers in this new way, not as analytical robotic machines, but creative and innovative designers, served me well in every subsequent company I led.

* * * * *

Net Perceptions created and patented something called collaborative filtering algorithms. If we knew five or six of your favorite movies, books or songs, we could accurately predict others you would like. This core technology would go on to power Google page rankings, Facebook ads and thousands of other applications. But we were the first.

Our initial and most noteworthy customer was a company that was billing itself as "The World's Largest Bookstore"—Amazon.com. Our algorithms would find users who liked or loved a certain set of books. By comparing those with others who'd purchased or expressed similar feelings for those books, we could recommend other books to customers they'd almost certainly enjoy—and more importantly, buy. And just as Amazon.com expanded way beyond books, our algorithms could predict preferences for lots of other things—tires, vacation destinations, you name it.

Early on, our approach required "explicit" ratings. Users had to tell us their favorite books or movies before we could make a recommendation. Later, our engineers figured out how to make recommendations based on "implicit" preferences. Internal debate suggested that while recommendations based on implicit factors would be faster, they wouldn't be as accurate. I disagreed, believing they would actually be more accurate.

While this was mostly an academic discussion because we already committed to the implicit approach, it turned out that I was 100% correct. My reasoning had been, "No one is going to say they watch the Jerry Springer show, but we all know what the ratings say." Believe what people do, not what they say.

Predictions made on actual behavior versus what people say they do are far more precise. That's why the predictive algorithms we developed are in use today in hundreds of different companies and applications.

* * * * *

As a marketing specialist, arguments about the value of advertising expenditures and the importance and power of a good PR effort always appealed to me. At Prodigy, I watched us and our biggest rival, AOL, spend millions of dollars on advertising that I felt was unnecessary. We (and AOL) mailed people hundreds of millions of startup disks, many of which were simply thrown away.

Believing that constraints breed creativity, I refused to allow a single dime to be spent on advertising at Net Perceptions—ever. We put all that money into PR, hiring the best agency we could find, Alexander/Ogilvy. We also got lucky and brought on consultant Dottie Hall, a graduate of MIT's Sloan School of Management, who was married to Vern Rayburn.

Rayburn had opened one of the first computer stores, the Byte Shop, about the time I launched Digital Den for Schaak Electronics. When he joined Microsoft early on as employee #18, he worked closely with Gates and Ballmer. As EVP, Rayburn took the lead in getting Microsoft products into the consumer market.

After leaving Microsoft, he continued to have a strong impact in technology. He served as EVP of Lotus, CEO of Symantec, CEO of Slate and finally as president of the Paul Allen Group. Paul Allen would invest in Net Perceptions and Rayburn joined our board. He would later found Eclipse Aviation in Phoenix, with Bill Gates as a major stockholder.

While I got credit for much of the marketing that propelled Net Perceptions to a highly successful IPO, it was Dottie who guided me in those early months and Ann Winblad was the catalyst who made it all happen.

So, instead of advertising we went to computer shows, creating a big trade show booth to disguise our small size. One time, one of my team members came to me and said we were finally going to do some advertising because it was going to be "free." As part of our booth space purchase, we would also get a full-page ad, every day of the show, in the trade show daily paper.

"Wait a minute," I said. "How much is it going to cost to create the ad? We don't have any ads. Call them back and find out what else we can get for the same amount."

It turned out we could exchange the ads for 40 3 ft. X 12 ft. banners with our name on them. I'll never forget walking into New York's Jacob Javits Convention Center and seeing Net Perceptions banners plastered everywhere. It looked like it was a Net Perceptions show.

Alexander/Ogilvy pulled some strings and got me a speaking slot at the TED8 conference in Monterey, California on February 19, 1998. I was never so nervous before a speech, although Ann was there coaching me. Alexander/Ogilvy had also hired Phil Proctor of *Firesign Theater* fame to coach several of their clients, me included.

All I recall of his coaching was him telling me to stand on my toes, but I was doing that anyway because I was so excited to be meeting one of my heroes. My roommate back in the Schaak Electronics days, Jim Skiff, had introduced me to the weird, wacky and hilarious *Firesign Theater* albums. My favorite was *I Think We're All Bozos On This Bus*.

My strongest memory from the TED8 talk was being relieved that I spoke before the person who followed me—Julie Taymor, the woman who brought *The Lion King* to Broadway. She brought the house down with her presentation, and no one after her had anywhere near the effect she had. Find and watch her TED8 Talk on YouTube and you'll know what I mean.

* * * * *

One of our most effective marketing initiatives at Net Perceptions was creating what we called the Personalization Summit trade conference. We held the first one at the Fairmont Hotel in San Francisco on November 15 and 16, 1999, attracting top executives from some of the most innovative global companies. More than 600 attended the inaugural event. More than 1,000 came later that year to our Boston Summit. And we attracted 300 people to the first international Summit in London. The second summit in San Francisco, in November 2000, brought together 1,500 people.

By then, attendees were responding with quotes like "Best conference I've attended in 20 years!" and "I can't believe I saw John Hagel, Don Peppers, Malcolm Gladwell, Mary Modahl, Thomas Stewart, Christopher Locke and Robert Krulwich all on the same bill."

None of this would have happened without Layne Gray and her company, LKE Productions. A friend of both Dottie Hall and Ann Winblad, Layne and her team helped cement our industry-leading reputation and fill our coffers. The revenue we generated from these shows covered our entire marketing budget.

Malcolm Gladwell spoke at our conference in 2000, just after he published *The Tipping Point*, the book that made him famous. During the summer of 1999, our PR firm Alexander/Ogilvy had pitched *The New Yorker* with an angle on a potential article. The magazine liked it and assigned a young English-Canadian staff writer named Malcolm Gladwell to the project.

Malcolm and I began having phone conversations, sometimes late into the night. And in October 1999, he published his article, *The Science of the Sleeper*. When he sent me a copy of *The Tipping Point* the following year, he included a handwritten note: "Thanks, Steve. You'll see yourself." If you've read the book and wonder what he meant, he used me and my experiences, and those of several others, to create the character he referred to as "The Connector."

As master of ceremonies for all the Personalization Summits, it was my job to introduce each speaker. One year, I decided to do the introductions in a different way. Instead of recounting each person's professional accomplishments, I was going to tell a story from their childhood. But it could only work if the stories came as a surprise to everyone in the room, including the speakers themselves.

Working with our agency, we obtained home phone numbers for each speaker's parents. Sometimes we had to get them from the speakers, but we never told them exactly why, and they always went along without asking questions.

As I made my phone calls, I explained my introduction plan and asked for a story about their son or daughter from childhood. These fun and unique introductions were a tremendous hit with the audience, and the speakers were thrilled with them, too.

One of the speakers I introduced that year was my friend Ann Winblad. I'd contacted Ann's mother, who told me a wonderful and illustrative story about ten-year-old Ann's Art Gallery Weekend. The future venture capitalist cordoned off a good portion of their home and hung artwork she'd collected from her neighborhood friends. And then she charged everyone to go through her gallery, including the contributing artists and their parents.

* * * * *

In March 2000, Net Perceptions went public as the leading firm in the nascent personalization space. Proceeds of the IPO to our 400-person company were $84.8 million. The *Minneapolis Star Tribune* reported that I owned 420,000 shares of stock, valued at the prior day's closing price of $29.81 per share—or $12.5 million ($21 million in today's money) in total. Later, the stock rose to $61 a share. Whoo-hoo—I was a rich man!

Or was I?

An important factor for founders and executives in this position is something called lock-up agreements. These legal restrictions kept me and other Net Perceptions founders from selling any of our shares until twelve months after the IPO. By the time it was legal for me to sell, my Net Perceptions stock was trading at less than $3 a share. Still, $1.26 million was nothing to sneeze at.

But before I could spend a dime, the IRS came knocking. They had a problem, and I had a bigger one. Soon after our IPO, as the stock price climbed, our senior team's financial advisors advised us to "lock in" the value of our stock at $34 per share. This meant I had a tax liability on a $14 million gain, an amount I wouldn't come close to covering as I had sold all my shares at $3 each.

My heart stopped as the reality sank in. I couldn't pay my taxes. Would I go to jail? After two years with lawyers and the IRS, it finally came down to one question: The IRS asked, "How much money do the Larsens have—all in?" When our accountants told them, they said, "Okay, we'll settle for that amount."

While Net Perceptions was a fun ride and I learned a lot, I ended up losing the nest egg that had helped get me there in the first place.

25

HOW CAN YOU TELL I'M NOT A GOLFER?

MY CURRENT HOME IN ARIZONA overlooks a golf course, as do 84.4% of all homes in Phoenix (just kidding). But neither Maggie nor I play. In fact, if any of my golfing friends were asked, "Does Steve play golf?" they would likely say, "Not so much."

When I was with Net Perceptions we had another home on a golf course in Eden Prairie, Minnesota, and I loved the rolling green lawn that stretched from my backyard, seemingly forever. Best of all, I didn't have to lift a finger to keep it looking spectacular.

Our deck overlooked the green of the first hole, a 520-yard Par 5, from which we enjoyed hours of entertainment. Being the first of 18 holes, the last players of the day passed our home early in the afternoon. With no golfers on the course, I could take a bucket of balls and chip them from my backyard onto the green if I wanted to, and then step onto the green and putt them all into the hole.

While I never played the course, I got along well with the club management, pros and groundskeepers. Once they needed to use our lawn for sand trap repairs and I made it easy for them. I knew most of the groundskeepers and waved every morning as they made their rounds. But one day I noticed an older guy I didn't recognize operating one of the riding mowers.

Compared to the rest of the crew, who appeared to be college-age and in pretty good shape, this guy stuck out like a sore thumb. Curious, I asked about him at the club's golf shop one day. After describing him, a look of acknowledgment came across the course manager's face. "Oh, he's not a groundskeeper, he's one of our members," the manager said with a wry smile. "Due to all his DWI arrests, he lost his driver's license but he misses driving. So his wife brings him over here and we let him drive the mowers around."

While I'm not a true golfer, I became more familiar with the game during my five-year stint at AT&T, where golf was part of the culture. Not only did people make deals on the course, but AT&T also sponsored numerous golf events like the Pebble Beach Pro-Am. The sponsorships enabled AT&T executives to invite high-value clients and arrange for them to play with genuine professionals and other AT&T leaders. Like it or not, I was expected to attend and play.

While I didn't need to be a stellar golfer, embarrassing the company by shooting a poor game was also unacceptable. After several lessons and lots of practice, my game settled into one where I could hit the ball straight, even if it didn't go very far. It turns out this often resulted in a half-decent score, especially when playing with those who plastered the ball a great distance but not always in the right direction.

* * * * *

I bought my golf clubs used for $15 at a garage sale in the early 1990s. I never thought much about them, I just threw them into my trunk and onto a cart whenever I was called upon to play. For at least 10 years of playing at a good number of prestige events, these were my only clubs.

After Net Perception's successful IPO, and before the Internet bubble burst in 2001–2002, it appeared on paper that I may have had a good deal of money. And while all the money was tied up in lock-up agreements and not in my bank account, I still felt very rich.

One downside of suddenly gaining large amounts of instant money is the mistaken belief that you've also gained more brains. This leads to thinking you must have the magic touch when it comes to picking investments.

And of course, those opportunities are being thrown at you right and left by people whose business it is to follow newly rich people around and snatch up some of the loot. This is how I was exposed to, and made, a $25,000 investment in a company that manufactured custom golf clubs.

Here's how the scam—I mean "business model"—worked.

It began with a desperate-to-improve golfer in a golf shop talking to the local pro about improving his game. Everyone knows buying something, like special long-range balls, or the "super driver of the decade" or the "magic putter which makes all putts roll accurate and true" is much simpler than taking lessons and practicing.

So at some point, the pro suggested that the stock, off-the-shelf clubs the player is using may be holding him back. What might help is a set of custom-made clubs, with grips tailored to his hands, the shaft lengths cut to fit his exact height and the club heads all angled for his particular sweet spot.

"Expensive?" he'd ask.

"Oh no, not really, and think about consistently shaving off half a dozen strokes from each game," the pro would reply.

A full set of top-brand clubs typically ran about a thousand dollars back then, and the fully customized set with fitted shafts and grips was about $2,500. The pros would arrange a "fitting," using the computer software, camera and other goodies provided by the company I invested in.

Once the company got the specifics for a golfer, they tweaked their stock shafts, clubs and grips to match the order sheet, applied the logo of whichever brand was specified (Callaway, Ping, Wilson, etc.), and packed them up to look like high-value works of art.

Part of my $25,000 investment was the promise of a "free" set of these custom clubs. All I had to do was go to the local factory for a fitting. I knew the wholesale cost was only around $220, but I couldn't resist "free" and was on time for my appointment the following week.

After arriving at the company's warehouse-like facility on a Saturday morning, I removed my clubs from the trunk of my car.

They'd asked me to bring the set I currently played with, perhaps as some baseline—I wasn't sure. I dutifully hefted them onto my shoulder and strolled through the wide-open double garages of the warehouse space, where I was welcomed by the investment guy and one of the measuring pros.

The pro grabbed my bag and looked at it. "Oh, Mr. Larsen, you must have grabbed the wrong bag," he said. "These are ladies' clubs. Did you pick up your wife's by mistake?"

When I looked at him quizzically, he said, "I'm serious. These are Mickey Wright signature clubs." Apparently, this Mickey Wright logo I'd been seeing for the past decade wasn't some renowned male golf pro but a famous female golfer. Oh god!

Do you recall the scene at the end of *The Sixth Sense* when Bruce Willis' character flashes back on a series of prior scenes, realizing he wasn't in them and redefining the entire film? My mind flashed over years of strange looks from other golfers and caddies as they saw my clubs and did a double-take.

Duh! I finally realized what all those funny looks were about.

* * * * *

Since then I've realized that having money doesn't make you any smarter than you were the month before, the year before or any other time before. And unfortunately, the market crash and subsequent IRS issues wiped out any semblance of my "being rich," which, in the long run, was probably all for the good.

The custom-club experience certainly changed the way I thought about investing. I stopped looking for home runs and returned to the long-established approach of saving at least 10% of any money that came my way. While perhaps not the "smartest" play one can make financially, it's consistent with my values of hard work, persistence and determination. In the end, that's always served me best.

As for golf, I gave it up for good and gave my manly set of $2,500 custom clubs to my cousin.

26

ADVENTURES IN VENTURE: MAKING—AND FOLLOWING— MY OWN PATH

MANY PEOPLE (ESPECIALLY YOUNG ONES) struggle with making choices about their lives and careers and say things like: "I don't know what I want," or "I don't know where I'll be in three years (or five years, etc.)" or "What if I decide to do this and then I want to get married and move away?"

My advice is to pick something and try it. Anything. It's okay to change your mind later. Nothing will be lost by doing that and you'll be forming the person you become in the future. Sometimes we're a leaf floating on the river of life and sometimes we're in a canoe, steering our way through it. Every choice makes a difference.

Here's an example of how I steered my course through the years 2000 to 2004. After the dot.com bubble burst and Net Perceptions became a public company, my early-stage company building skills were less needed. Professionally, 2000–2001 was a transition year. I consulted, joined the board of a Boston-based startup that my friend Bruce Katz had invested in and hung around with the guys at St. Paul Venture Capital (SPVC). They were early investors in Net Perceptions.

While many VCs distribute stock to their limited partners after an IPO, SPVC had a policy not to hold investments in public companies. So, soon after Net Perceptions went public, SPVC liquidated its investment and disbursed the cash to its limited partners. This was before the stock shot up to over $60 a share, but perhaps more importantly, before it dropped to $2. Brian Jacobs, one of SPVC's general partners, remembers that they made about $80 million on the deal.

In September 2001, I officially joined SPVC as a partner. They sent out a press release about me that got picked up by PRNewswire on March 27. It read:

St. Paul Venture Capital Adds Steve Larsen as Venture Partner

MINNEAPOLIS, March 27 /PRNewswire/ -- St. Paul Venture Capital today announced that Steve Larsen has joined the firm as a venture partner. He will split his time between the firm's Silicon Valley and Minneapolis offices. Larsen is an addition to the firm's Software and Services team and he will focus on supporting and building St. Paul's portfolio of companies. He is currently serving as the acting vice president of business development for Visage Mobile, an early-stage company in St. Paul's portfolio.

Prior to joining St. Paul, Larsen, 51, held founding executive roles at four start-up companies: Net Perceptions, Ticketmaster Online-CitySearch, Unicast and World Merchandise Exchange. As senior vice president of marketing and business development at Net Perceptions, Larsen helped commercialize collaborative filtering and advanced analytics software -- technologies that fundamentally changed the way business is done on the Internet. He also helped lead the company through a successful initial public offering. St. Paul Venture Capital was an early investor in Net Perceptions.

"As we worked with the management team at Net Perceptions, we developed great respect for Steve. He's an expert in high-tech business development and marketing," said Brian Jacobs, general partner, St. Paul Venture Capital. "His management experience and his extensive contact network make

Steve an invaluable resource for our portfolio companies."

As head of business development at CitySearch, Larsen negotiated key partnerships for the company with the *Los Angeles Times* and *The Washington Post*. Before 1995, Larsen held senior management positions at the Prodigy Services Company, AT&T, Open Systems and Control Data Corporation. He currently sits on the board of School Extra and is a founding board member of the U.S. Internet Association. He also was founder and president of The Personalization Summit, an executive-level Customer Relationship Management conference, and serves as program chair for Pop!Tech, the Camden Technology Conference.

A frequent speaker at industry conferences, Larsen is the author of *Competing in CyberSpace: Guidelines for Market-Driven Web Site Planning and Design*. He has been an instructor and guest lecturer at the Carlson School of Management at the University of Minnesota, Duke University's Fuqua School of Business and Darden's Graduate School of Business at the University of Virginia.

About St. Paul Venture Capital

St. Paul Venture Capital is one of the largest early-stage venture capital firms in the United States with $3.0 billion in committed capital and offices in Minneapolis, Boston and Silicon Valley. The firm, founded in 1988, invests primarily in the areas of Communications Technology; Software and Services; and Health Care. Additional information can be found at the firm's website at http://www.spvc.com

In my first year with the firm, I tried on different hats within the Software and Services and Wireless teams. Among other things, I:

- Helped portfolio companies get moving more quickly by ensuring they were doing the right things to increase their odds of success.
- Assisted the firm in getting better deal flow, by meeting and vetting entrepreneurs with ideas that needed funding.
- Attended board meetings of portfolio companies and helped with recruiting, consulting, guidance and hands-on support.

I worked with all the SPVC general partners, but Brian Jacobs and I got along particularly well. And as the firm opened an office in Silicon Valley, I went with him to California. Just as in Minneapolis, I attended board meetings and watched for opportunities to add value by helping our portfolio companies achieve greater success.

Eventually, Brian decided to leave SPVC and form a new venture capital firm, Emergence Capital, with a set of top general partners. Everyone was pleased with the name until a call came in the first week from someone asking, "Is this Emergency Capital?" That wasn't the image they wanted.

My work continued with Emergence, at pretty much the same terms I had with SPVC. Since my niche at the firm had become one of working with portfolio companies, I suspected it wouldn't be long before I'd be back in a full-time operating role. So I paid close attention to how company founders and startup CEOs behaved in board meetings. I observed how they answered questions, conducted the meetings and the areas they focused on most. Before long, I'd accumulated quite a list of dos and don'ts.

Here's one example of a "don't." At a board meeting for a portfolio company one day, the founder and CEO arrived without his Chief Financial Officer (CFO). When asked where the missing officer was, the CEO told the board that he fired him the previous day. I quickly learned that boards of directors and CFOs often have a special relationship, and that a CEO should never fire a CFO without talking with the board of directors first.

While occasionally taking operating roles within portfolio companies, my first loyalty was to the VC firm where I was a partner. At the same time, I could collect for services and receive stock options at the companies I worked with, as if I were an employee. Each time this happened, I took care to exercise (pay for) those options.

In one case, I got options for 10,000 shares of a company named Visage Mobile, an Emergence Capital investment. I put the paperwork into a file folder at home and soon forgot all about it. Years later, I received a registered letter from a company that the original entity had eventually become. With countless additional capital raises and at least one merger, they were trying to clean up their books. My ownership position of 10,000 shares was messing with their count.

They said to expect a check and asked that I be sure to sign the paperwork and return it to them as soon as possible. I could hardly wait—found money! A few days later, a FedEx envelope arrived with documents requiring my signature. Opening the envelope, I immediately dug for the check and there it was. Large and official, made out to me for $1.15. The cost of the FedEx was 20X the amount of the check. But hey, clean books are important and so are cautionary tales about the risks of early-stage investing.

My experience in the venture capital world was like being on the top of a mountain after a long hike and deeply inhaling the fresh air. I loved the variety and the massively flexible schedule, which allowed me to become extraordinarily productive. My natural style was to work in spurts and then take time off. I made the majority of my overseas motorcycle riding and writing trips during this period. No one seemed to care about my odd schedule, or even be aware of it.

* * * * *

In December 2002, I was asked to step in as the interim CEO of BigFix, a portfolio company in Emeryville. This was the company where the CEO had lost the board's confidence after showing up without his CFO. Within a week of that incident, I was asked to take over the

CEO position and was delighted to be back in the saddle, even if it meant ending all fiduciary ties to my venture capital firm.

I loved BigFix and found an apartment in Sausalito, just on the north side of the Golden Gate Bridge from San Francisco. My friend Jerry Michalski had rented a room in the lower half of a duplex there, but he got a gig in Japan and sublet his place to me. He also asked me to babysit his brand-new, red Ducati Monster. He'd barely ridden it. I happily agreed to take care of it for him, and I accumulated enough miles on it for its first service at Munroe Motors in downtown San Francisco.

The landlord was Rita Burgett, a world-class, traveling software implementation consultant. She was brilliant at her job, which often involved staying months at a time in other cities. She needed someone to watch her Sausalito place, collect the mail, monitor things and occasionally take her vintage Mercedes 450S convertible for a spin to make sure the fluids kept moving. We got along well, so I volunteered and the arrangement worked out for both of us. Rita would come back to San Francisco every few months and we'd have dinner. Occasionally, she'd have me clear out of the apartment for a day or two when she was entertaining.

What made the Sausalito apartment so ideal, besides its views of Angel Island and Alcatraz, was the reverse commute to Emeryville. I'd leave the apartment in the morning and head north on a near-empty Highway 101 at 90 mph, looking across at cars crawling in the other direction, backed up to cross the GG Bridge into San Francisco. Zipping past San Quentin prison, I'd cross the Richmond Bridge, cruise through Berkeley and exit in Emeryville, just as things were jamming up for cars heading into Oakland or San Francisco on I-80.

The board and I looked for a permanent CEO for BigFix, but we had trouble finding a suitable candidate. With no other option, I was made permanent CEO in May 2003. BigFix presented some unique challenges, not the least of which was the founder's son, Orion

Hindawi. He, with some justification, blamed me and the board for ousting his father from his own company.

While some on the board advised me to let Orion go, it was clear that he was integral to what made BigFix work. He was incredibly smart and the lynchpin for keeping the company's development team on track.

I had some clear wins at BigFix. For example, I recruited a top VP of marketing and a talented product manager, Greg Toto, who stayed with the company long after it was acquired in July 2010. He brought clear thinking and discipline to that side of the business.

Since I didn't have a deep understanding of this part of the software industry, I also recruited an advisory board, something the company had never had since its 1997 founding. Advisors included Glenn Ricard, the founder of CenterBeam and former CTO of Novel; Phil Dunkelburger of Pretty Good Privacy (PGP); and John Hagel, an ex-McKinsey consultant and business strategist. I also recruited Peter Watkins, the former president and COO of Network Associates Inc. (NAI), to our board of directors.

Sales had been an issue for some time, but with a new team in place we soon landed a three-year/$9 million deal with a major government reseller with a large advance payment. And when I left the company, a three-year, $15 million term sheet was being negotiated.

While the new advisors helped shore up my lack of industry knowledge, the board still felt the need for a buffer between me and Orion Hindawi. We looked for and found a solid COO, Dave Robbins. Within a few months, everyone realized (well, maybe everyone except me) that Robbins was more than qualified to run the whole company. He was, in fact, the CEO we'd been searching for earlier and had been unable to find. So, in November 2003, I was encouraged to bow out and let Robbins take over.

Without the baggage of being the one who fired Orion's dad, Robbins quickly got things on the right track. While the company's eventual profitable exit wasn't quick (seven years), it was a good one.

The company was sold to IBM for $400 million, making it one of my most successful financial startup experiences—a welcome relief after earning less than zero from Net Perceptions.

I once again found myself at Emergence before returning to Arizona, spending most of 2004 on non-business-related pursuits. These included finding a new house in Phoenix, selling our Eden Prairie home, and riding my motorcycle on adventures that filled the pages of *Motorcycle Consumer News*, *Rider Magazine* and *Overland Journal*.

Does it appear that I was a leaf on the river of life or more like steering my canoe? Way back in my 20s I set my sights on becoming a store manager, then a district manager for Schaak Electronics, which was a springboard to the much larger world of Control Data Corporation. I deliberately stayed with big companies for a lot of years because they provided health benefits that were critical to me and my family, given some of my health concerns.

Throughout those years, however, I consciously aimed for a time when I could be more independent. First, I saved money. Maggie and I worked hard to accumulate at least two years' worth of my salary as a cushion. Also, I gave myself a second, part-time job—freelance writer—to make money and to build my personal "brand." And the third major effort was meeting lots of people, making friends and keeping in touch.

With these three building blocks, I've always been able to reach out and find another door to open. I don't feel like I've ever been "stuck."

To everyone reading this, but especially my nieces, nephews and grandchildren: Keep trying new things.

27

THE GOOGLE THAT WASN'T

TWO YEARS AFTER LEAVING BIGFIX, I received a call from Brian Jacobs, my former partner at SPVC and Emergence Capital. He had an opportunity he wanted me to consider. A fraternity brother of his from MIT, Ken Krugler, was starting a code search company after a long stint at Apple Computer. If I would come in as CEO and partner with Ken as co-founder and CTO, Brian and Emergence Capital would provide the first round of funding.

Ken and I spent a week doing due diligence on each other, agreed it could work and were off to the races. We formed the company, Krugle. Yes, "Krugle" was pronounced the same as "Google." We expected that once we emerged from stealth mode, Google might reach out to us since we were a search engine and our names did sound alike. But they didn't. Not for a while. Then the letter about our name finally came from Google's legal department. It wasn't at all what I expected.

To better understand the letter Google's legal department fired across our bow, let's dip back in time to 1994, when Rob Kost and I concocted and launched our online motorcycle bulletin board. No other motorcycle-oriented bulletin boards existed, so we started "HOGWILD!" for Harley Davidson riders. We thought the folks at Harley Davidson might be concerned, but we were so small we figured they wouldn't even bother with us. Why would they?

After a little more than a year of successful operations, however, Harley Davidson shut us down with heavy legal threats. Their letter used words like "immediately cease and desist," and warned of massive penalties that could wipe out our personal assets.

Google's letter to us at Krugle was worded much differently. It said something like this:

> *"Good afternoon, this is Google's legal department. Hey, we see you have a company named 'Krugle,' which sounds a lot like 'Google,' and since you're a search company, there may be some confusion in the marketplace. We're willing to wait and see but wanted you to know we were aware of you."*

It was signed by an attorney at Google, with full contact information if we had any questions. We read it as having their blessing to move forward, leaving our name as it was. They reserved the right to change their position, should confusion arise in the market, but it never did.

* * * * *

Krugle met and exceeded every milestone we set. After the initial $1 million seed round, we raised a $9 million Series A in 2006. Our product team, under Ken's direction, did a stellar job creating a search engine that could crawl and index software code repositories. They built interpreters for nearly every programming language, indexing massive open-source libraries and making it easy for developers to find precisely the exact bit of source code needed for their projects.

Imagine you're a game developer and you want a sky with a bunch of fluffy clouds floating around in the background. You know you could take a few days to write the code for it, but it would be easier to just grab someone else's. But where? And which "sky-cloud code" is in the language you need? We allowed software developers to search for and find bits of code as easily as they could use Google to find a new pair of tennis shoes.

Although critically acclaimed for its value and usefulness to software developers searching across open-source code repositories, we struggled to find a viable business model. Krugle was a wonderful idea with an extraordinary product/search engine for programmers, but how do we charge for it? The whole idea behind open source is "free."

Eventually, we realized that big companies with large code assets and repositories could benefit from using our product behind their firewalls. And, unlike open-source developers, they had money. Given the high security requirements these companies placed on their code assets, they'd only allow these scans to run if we re-created Krugle on a server and installed that server behind their firewall with strict security controls.

After about a year of adapting to this new idea, we knew we could make it work. By that time, however, we were in a race. Our funding was running low, and while we had numerous customers lined up who'd given us deposits, we needed a full-on, enterprise-level sales team. Hiring an experienced enterprise sales force required money we didn't have.

Soon after we launched our enterprise product, we had 10 signed corporate partners and were on our way. We hired a sales VP and team and were making progress. Everything was looking up. Even the building in Menlo Park where we were located, always about to be condemned, was being refurbished.

And then the market for software development tools crashed—right when we needed another $1 million to keep going. By early 2009, we sold the assets of Krugle and shut it down, never knowing what Google might have done to us.

Looking back, I suspect Krugle could have been a highly successful and profitable company if the timing had been different.

28

SELLING INSPIRATION: A FORAY INTO MOTIVATIONAL MEDIA

IN EARLY 2008, I GOT a call from Pat Hopf, who was the managing partner at St. Paul Venture Capital, the firm I had joined after leaving Net Perceptions. After years of funding early-stage companies, Pat had decided he wanted to get actively involved in creating one.

He backed Eric Worre's idea of developing a media company around motivational speakers and personalities, such as Stephen Covey, Tom Peters, John Gray and Ken Blanchard. Worre was an up-and-comer in the positive thinking marketplace.

These high-powered authors marketed themselves individually as speakers, business consultants, management gurus and leadership experts, and Hopf wanted to form an organization that would pool their efforts and capabilities. His promise was to cut the costs associated with creating, marketing and running events, and to get better publishing deals and richer royalties.

I flew to Minnesota and arranged to stay with my cousin Ron Herem while I worked with Pat and Eric to see if we could bring the idea to life. After a few months, however, I lost confidence in Eric's business judgment. Pat, acting as chairman and sensing my concern, agreed, and while he kept Eric on as CEO he had everyone in the company report to me. Although technically a consultant with no equity stake, my title was COO of Better Life Media.

It was at our "National Leadership Summit" in June at the Minneapolis Convention Center where I finally learned Eric Worre's value. The camera loved him. In the studio with our producer, editing a set of videos from the conference that would become our first product line, my jaw dropped watching what happened when Eric began talking directly to the camera.

He delivered what appeared to be ad-libbed, impromptu introductions of each speaker flawlessly. He was totally charismatic, authoritative, knowledgeable and in command. I would have followed him anywhere.

* * * * *

During my short tenure with Better Life I recruited Sam Tutterow, who I first hired at Net Perceptions. Pat brought Carrie Massine in from SPVC. I asked friends and top branding consultants, Corky Hall and Chuk Batko, to help us, along with marketing genius, Chuck Kushell. Hall, Batko and Kushell had all worked with me at Net Perceptions. In one of our early meetings, I heard one of them remark, "Looks like Larsen is getting the band back together."

Two things stand out in my time working with Pat and Eric. The first involved Lori Nelson, our brilliant and beautiful receptionist. One Saturday, while diligently working alone in my office, she stepped in unexpectedly. Naturally, I asked what she was doing there.

She explained that to make ends meet, she'd taken over for the company that cleaned our offices. Pat was paying her the same as what he paid for the outside cleaning service. This, along with her other job as a bartender at nights, made it just possible for her to support herself and her children after her ex-husband left them high and dry.

The following week, Corky and Chuk were at the office for a working session. After they left, Lori came into my office and asked who the shorter of the two was. She said he seemed nice when they checked in at her reception desk. Then she let on that she thought he was "kind of cute," and did I know if he was married or not?

I was well aware of Corky's divorce a year before and actually had several beer-fueled consoling and counseling sessions with him. But I didn't know if it would be safe to tell her all of that, so I just said, "Let me check."

A few days later, Chuk, Corky and I met outside the office for a working lunch. Near the end, out of the blue, Corky asked me to tell him the name of our receptionist. So I told him. He asked if she was married. When I said no, he asked if she was dating anyone.

"I don't think so," I replied. "Why don't I see what I can find out?"

Long story short, they began dating and got married the following year. I've never met a happier pair of people. Corky worships Lori and she's head over heels in love with him. Every time I call their home they remind me of how grateful they are for the tiny role I played in getting them together.

My second noteworthy experience at Better Life Media was a fundraising meeting we had in Rapid City, South Dakota. Pat and I were pitching two brothers who made a several hundred million dollars when they sold the drugstore chain they built over 50 years. Both were in their late 80s. One brother was in a home, so we met with the other one at the office he still maintained in a bank building downtown. Pat had our pitch deck on his PC and was projecting it on a screen at the front of the room.

When we were just on the second slide, our prospective investor asked, "Sorry to interrupt, Pat, but may I ask before we go too deep, how long before you expect this investment will pay out?"

Pat explained our plans, which would take the next three to four years, then another year to groom the company and target potential acquirers.

Our prospect threw back his head and laughed. "Pat, you need to know at my age I don't even buy green bananas!"

Pat chuckled at the joke for a few seconds, then moved on to slide three. Our prospect looked over at me with a quizzical look.

"Pat, I think we're done," I said. "Let's go to lunch."

"What? No. We've only just started," Pat replied.

Our prospect pointed at me and said, "Pat, I think you should listen to your young friend here."

29

A LAST HURRAH AT PHONETELL

IN 2009, WHILE ATTENDING CHRIS Shipley's DEMO Conference in San Diego, my last startup opportunity presented itself. Over the years, I launched several companies at this annual event, which was held in Palm Desert, Phoenix and other glorious locations.

Shipley is a smart and accomplished woman, thoughtful and kind. Over time, she and I became good friends. She built the DEMO Conference into one of the best places to start a new firm, helping founders launch hundreds of companies. Everyone wanted to be named one of each year's "DEMOgods," and try as I might, I never won that award. Until I did, which was for the final company I presented at DEMO, PhoneTell.

At one of the startup tables in San Diego, Wendell Brown and Adrian Vanzyl were hyping an idea for a company named CallSpark. It was just the two of them, but the idea was big and intriguing. After Brown explained it to me, I couldn't get it out of my head. He and Vanzyl immediately began working on me to join them, as neither one had my operational experience.

Brown had been a computer prodigy in high school. He grew up in West Virginia and graduated from Cornell University. He's a brilliant inventor, responsible for innovative tape editing systems used by top recording artists like Peter Gabriel, Fleetwood Mac, the Pointer Sisters and Motley Crue, among others. His interests had always been in the entertainment side of technology, but he spent time at National Semiconductor as a cryptography expert and created Walk Softly—the first mass market software cybersecurity program—with Mark Klein in Palo Alto.

Over the next three years, we worked to get CallSpark off the ground under its new name, PhoneTell. For tax reasons, Brown was careful to not be in California more than a certain number of days each year so he made his home in Las Vegas.

PhoneTell was the first startup I'd done with only angel investors, no institutions. At the GSMA World Congress in Barcelona in February 2010, we got close to several deals but couldn't get acceptable terms signed. We paid ourselves nothing, putting every dime into getting the product live and setting up agreements with carriers and telephone manufacturers. My living situation went from couch surfing at friends' homes and apartments in San Francisco to finally locating the company in Palo Alto and living in the same apartment I had when we built Krugle. It felt like home.

In April 2010, Apple had scheduled a big event for a new product launch. Carefully leaked bits of information had journalists spilling what they knew about the new device. Seeing the write-ups, I explained to Brown why this product, a cross between a phone and a computer, would be a bigger dud for Apple than the Newton or the Lisa. It was too big to carry as a phone, and too small to work as a computer.

The hole that Apple saw for a product like this was totally delusional. Brown went to the launch event for the iPad and bought two of them. Back at the office, he gave me one before I left to spend the weekend in Phoenix, telling me I should play with it, decide what I thought and let him know the following week. Of course, I refused to give it back. I was hooked! The device was brilliant and I was, once again, so wrong.

As we struggled to raise money, we brought in more investors who leveraged our weaker negotiating position to gain more control. One morning, one of our more recent investors, Ted West, showed up at the office. He was there to fire me, but we were friends so the meeting was short, efficient and friendly.

While remaining a significant shareholder, I turned my CEO role over to him at the close of business that day. During our conversation, the most top-of-mind thought going through my head was, "Don't grin, don't smile, don't laugh with joy, don't throw up your hands and scream 'Thank you, thank you!'" And I didn't, keeping it together until I finally asked if I could go outside and break the news to my wife.

Ted, always a gentleman, said, "Of course."

Once I had Maggie on the phone and was well out of earshot, I could tell her what happened. I was genuinely relieved that this overwhelming weight of stress would soon end. I think I know how people feel when they win the lottery. The next day, I loaded my belongings into my car and drove to Phoenix. It had been a brutal three years, but one that put me in an ideal position for my next move.

30

WHAT NEXT?

AFTER SOME MUCH-NEEDED R&R IN Phoenix, and with calls from contacts and recruiters who heard of my leaving PhoneTell gradually tapering off, I finally decided I didn't want to go back to work. But I was only 61. Could I actually be done working at age 61?

It turns out, yes I could, but major transitions like this are best when they're not abrupt. Now was the time to give back. My international travels over the years had brought me into contact with graduates of the Thunderbird School of Global Management in Phoenix. They were always smart people, often holding significantly responsible positions in their companies. As I researched some more, I realized why international companies prized graduates of this school. And here it was, right where I was retiring.

While now owned and operated by Arizona State University, back then it was independent. After meeting several staff members, Dr. Robert Hisrich recruited me to teach in his entrepreneur classes. Dr. Hisrich, who passed away in 2023, was the most academically accomplished entrepreneur I ever met. He authored or co-authored more than 35 books on entrepreneurship, international business management and marketing. In December 2021, Stanford University named him one of the top 2% of researchers worldwide. When he wasn't writing or teaching, he started and ran more companies than I could count.

The school is called Thunderbird because it was founded on a decommissioned World War II Air Force base of the same name. Its most highly sought-after degree was an MBA in Global Management. It also offered undergraduate degrees in international trade, leadership and global affairs. Notable alumni include Walid Chammah, the former chairperson of Morgan Stanley; Joaquin Duato, CEO of Johnson & Johnson; the CEO of British Petroleum (BP) and a host of other prominent business personalities. Don Novello, the comedian best known for playing Father Guido Sarducci on *Saturday Night Live*, is also an esteemed alumnus.

I loved teaching at Thunderbird and was especially proud of creating the Thunderbird Angel Network. Hisrich conceived of the idea and asked me to take it on. Charged with its implementation, I roped in a young teaching assistant and Thunderbird alumna, Tanaha Hairston, who did all the work. It succeeded more due to her efforts than anything I did.

* * * * *

After its acquisition by Arizona State University, I left my position as Entrepreneur-in-Residence at Thunderbird and joined the Arizona Commerce Authority (ACA). My first and continuing role there for the past 10 years has been as a judge for the annual Arizona Innovation Challenge, which uses an evaluation matrix I helped create. My job is to review applications from a dozen early-stage startups, who compete for $1.5 million annually in non-dilutive financial support from the state.

At a recent ACA mentor breakfast, our leader Joseph Bianchi asked participants to introduce themselves with a two-to-three-minute summary of their career and their motivation for mentoring at the ACA.

I never know what to say in these circumstances. So I just blurted out that I was Tom Blondi's dad and he invited me. Tom Blondi is a high-energy entrepreneur and investor who's given a great deal of time and effort into making the ACA what it is today. His personality also lends itself to frequent kidding.

What would I say about my career if I was being honest? What have I really done that has my fingerprints all over it? What did I do when a business opportunity passionately consumed me and took all my efforts? That's certainly a lot more interesting than any of the many jobs I've had.

Through my founding roles at eight startups, I've distilled the following principles:

- Understand the problem you're solving and who has the problem, not just your product
- Focus on paying customers—the more the better
- Build a team of people who share your vision, complement each other's skills and excel in their disciplines
- Identify and consistently monitor the key data points that define success.
- Pivot sooner than later
- Cultivate a small group of two or three trusted advisors and pay attention to them
- Be ethical, honest and transparent in all your dealings

These lessons, hard-won through successes and failures, form the core of my entrepreneurial philosophy and remain relevant today. They're more than just lessons from my past, they're guideposts for the future of entrepreneurship.

In the end, the true measure of an entrepreneur's success isn't just in the companies they build or the profits they generate. It's in the problems they solve, the innovations they spark, the joy and goodwill they create and the wisdom they pass on to the next generation of visionaries.

This is the legacy I want to leave, and I hope you'll take it on. The world is waiting for your ideas, your passion and your willingness to learn and adapt. So go forth, innovate and remember: the next great startup could be yours.

FAMILY

THE TIES THAT BIND

FOR BETTER OR FOR WORSE, our family shapes who we are and influences the paths we take. As I reflect on my life, I'm struck by how deeply my family experiences have molded me, from my earliest childhood memories to the unexpected joys and heartaches of adulthood. This collection of stories is a tribute to those family bonds, exploring the web of relationships that have defined my world.

I was born in 1950 in Fairmont, Minnesota, the firstborn child of Paul and Ruth Larsen. Dad, with his carpentry skills and pastoral calling, instilled in me a strong work ethic and sense of purpose. Mom, a registered nurse, showed me the power of perseverance and unconditional love, especially during tumultuous school years when others gave up on me.

My siblings, Leif, Naomi and Jurene, each brought their own personality and talents to our family dynamic. Leif, my brother and closest playmate, shared my mischievous streak. Our sisters added new dimensions, teaching me about protectiveness and the different ways love can be expressed.

My own journey into fatherhood began with the birth of my daughter, Ginger, in 1984. Watching her grow into the remarkable woman she is today has been one of life's greatest joys. But parenthood also brought unimaginable pain. The loss of my son, Eric, when he was just two years old, was a tragedy shaking the very foundations of our family. It forever altered how we approached life and love, deepening our appreciation for each other and the time we have together.

Life, however, had another surprise in store. Decades later, I discovered I had another daughter, Christie, born before I met my wife, Maggie. This revelation brought a new chapter of joy and connection to our lives. Watching Ginger and Christie form a sisterly bond, seeing my grandchildren Emmy and Parker grow and integrating the Will family into our lives has been a heartwarming journey of redefinition and expansion that I never expected but now treasure deeply.

Maggie has been my partner in all things for more than four decades. Together, we've navigated the highs and lows of life, from exciting career moves across the country to the depths of grief and back. Her steadfast support and love have been an anchor through it all.

As I grow older, I find myself increasingly drawn to preserving and chronicling our family history as a legacy for my children and grandchildren. The stories and anecdotes I've included in this section are one attempt to capture the essence of our collective experience—tales of enduring love, bonds strengthened through adversity and the beautiful, messy, wonderful details of family life. It's a tribute to what binds us—the laughter, the tears, the triumphs and the challenges that have shaped our family.

31

THE OLDEST OF THE YOUNGEST

GROWING UP, MY FAMILY'S ORIGINS were impossible to ignore. All my aunts, uncles and cousins had Norwegian or Danish heritage—Norway on Mom's side and Denmark on Dad's. Both my parents were the youngest children in their families. We had relatives across the ocean, still living in the "old countries," often on the same property as their ancestors from centuries before.

My mother, Ruth Janett Herem, was born in Rake, Iowa in 1923, the youngest of five. She followed brothers Knut (1915) and Oscar (1918), and sisters Bertha (1917) and Alma (1921). Her mother, Ragnhild Bakka Herem, was born in Sauda in 1882 and died just 42 years later in July 1924, when my mother was only 14 months old. Mom's upbringing was left mostly to her siblings. Her father, Jacob Olaus Knutson Herem, was born in Rogaland, Norway, near Sauda, in 1867.

My cousin, Ron Herem, has documented our family history on my mother's side all the way back to King Harald III Bluetooth (916–988) and beyond. Ron's book on the Herem/Bakka family, *Descended from Kings*, is well-researched and filled with fascinating stories. He discusses how King Harald's dead front tooth, which had turned a blue/gray color, earned him the nickname "Bluetooth." Jaap Haartsen, a Dutch electrical engineer trained at the Royal Institute of Technology in Sweden, named the Bluetooth wireless communications protocol he invented after my ancestor, King Harald III. Historians credit Harald with introducing Christianity to Denmark and unifying much of ancient Jutland and Zealand, encompassing a significant portion of modern Denmark and parts of Sweden.

In 2023, after visiting family on my mother's side with our cousin John Gravley, Ron and I spent a couple of days in Denmark. There, we met relatives on the Larsen side and uncovered a treasure trove of documents and a wonderful group of people.

My father, Paul Townley Larsen, was born in 1917, the youngest of six. He followed brothers Wilmer Carroll (1915), Gordon Leonard (1913) and Elvin Walter (1911), and sisters Effie Eleanor (1909) and Alma Katherine (1907). His father, John Walter Larsen (1875), was born in Tibirke, Denmark.

March, 1962. My dad with his sisters, brothers and mother. L to R: Elvin, Alma, Paul, Gordon, Grandma Carrie Larsen, Effie and Wilmer.

My grandfather and his brother, Carl Gustav Larsen (1878), were both master carpenters. With Denmark's economy under stress, John Walter moved to the United States in 1893, settling in Martin County, Minnesota and marrying Kari "Carrie" Thorson 10 years later in 1903.

My uncle Elvin, the oldest boy, was compact, serious, ambitious and hard-working. He succeeded in business and family life. At the urging of Hubert Humphrey (who later became Vice President of the United States), Elvin ran for the Minnesota State Senate from Martin County in 1958. Running as a Democrat, he lost in this heavily Republican district. He married Gladys Vogen of Harlen, Iowa and had three boys, my cousins Donny, Roger and Dennis. Before I

---

*Roger Larsen passed away in his home in Beaumont, California on November 11, 2024.

was born, Elvin and Gladys owned the Prairie Avenue grocery store, which Gladys managed.

When I was in junior high school, long after the grocery store had closed, I often stopped to see Gladys at Hilstead's drugstore, where she worked. One time, made up and in costume for a school play, I went into the store to fool Gladys into thinking I was actually a feeble old man. She bought it for perhaps six seconds. Elvin died in 1999 at age 88, but Gladys would live to be 97. They passed away in California, where they'd moved to be closer to their sons and grandchildren.

Uncle Gordon was serious and soft-spoken. His military service from April 1942 to November 1945 may have contributed to his quiet nature. My uncle Wilmer was rejected for service because of a heart murmur, and my dad was rejected for unknown reasons.

Wilmer, like Gordon, was tall—well over six feet. Unlike Elvin and Gordon, Wilmer always intrigued me and my cousins. He had a lab and knew how to make things, like toys and puzzles to amuse us kids. He also made jewelry and even dentures for people who needed new teeth. Wilmer always engaged us kids in conversation, while my other uncles spent most of their time talking among themselves.

L to R: Gordon, Elvin, Paul and Wilmer Larsen.

Uncle Elvin seemed to be the most industrious, starting and running a small grocery store, buying land, building homes and working in construction with my dad. There were few things they couldn't build together. When I was born, Elvin had moved an old schoolhouse to a property he owned at the end of Lucia Street in Fairmont. He rented it to my parents, and I spent the first year of my life there.

My Dad's sisters, Alma and Effie, were mysteries to me growing up. I didn't understand how they fit into the family, and no one explained it to me. Their husbands didn't look or sound like my Larsen uncles. Who were those guys and where did they come from? I often wondered, "How are we related?" They even had different last names.

Much of this confusion stemmed from the fact that my dad wasn't that close to his sisters. When he was 15, Alma was 25 and already married, while Effie was 23 and married a year later.

At 31, my dad married my mother on September 30, 1949. They welcomed me into the world exactly one year later, on September 30, 1950. I remember telling people, within my mother's earshot, that I'd been born on their wedding day—pausing long enough to hear her shout out, "A year later ... You have to say one year later!"

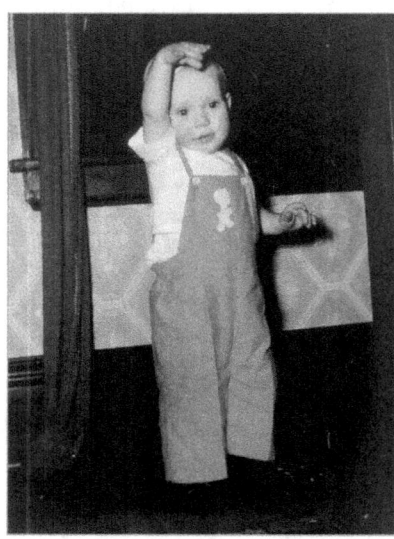

Me at about a year old.

Leif Nathan came along two years after that in 1952, followed by sisters Naomi Ruth (1954) and Jurene Lois (1958). While I'm not convinced that birth order affects our path in life, I enjoy speculating about it. My life seems more like my uncle Elvin's, who was also the oldest. Academic papers on the subject of birth order's impact on personality, however, offer little to support the idea that where you fall in order of your siblings has any effect on how you turn out.

My brother and sisters have told me that their approach to navigating life smoothly was to observe me. If and when I got in trouble with our parents, all they had to do was the opposite of what I did or do what I did and avoid getting caught. It seemed to work for them, but for me, not so much.

Minnesota residence requires new fathers to take their sons fishing.

32

FROZEN RIVERS
AND BEAR TALES

WHEN I WAS TWO YEARS old, just a few weeks after my brother Leif was born, our family moved to Rainy River, Ontario, Canada. Rev. Roland White had recruited my father to pastor the Evangelical Covenant Church there from 1952 to 1954. My sister Naomi, born in Rainy River, gained dual U.S. and Canadian citizenship. She recalls hearing stories of Dad's early seminary days at St. Paul Bible Institute in the late 1940s. This institution, founded in 1916, evolved over the years, eventually moving to St. Bonifacius, Minnesota in the 1970s. Its enduring motto: "Called to Serve. Prepared to Lead."

My mom and dad holding me in September, 1952, as the Rainy River church welcomed my father as their new Pastor. Photo courtesy of Rev. Mark Mast.

Life in Rainy River brought many unique experiences. We often crossed the frozen river by car in winter to shop in Baudette, Minnesota, avoiding tolls and customs delays. I remember crossing with the car doors open, supposedly to protect us in case we broke through the ice. The Evangelical Covenant Church's current pastor, Mark Mast, who grew up in the area and remembered my mom and dad, shared more about these crossings when I connected with him in 2024. He told me that, in the summer, people would use the railroad bridge to avoid paying tolls, timing their crossings to avoid the trains. "The cost back then was $2.00 per vehicle and 10¢ per person," Pastor Mast recalled. "While it doesn't sound like much now, back then it was enough of an incentive for us to cross the railroad bridge on our bicycles. It was also fun to jump from the railroad bridge into the river!"

Mom holding newly born Leif and Dad holding me, in Rainy River.

After a few years, safety concerns forced the Canadian National Railway to prohibit all traffic by foot or bicycle. But of course, in the winter, crossing the frozen river was easy, and the authorities made it even easier by frequently plowing it. My mother, after she retired to Arizona, wrote a story about this called *Natural Bridges,* a book that many members of our family hold dear.

* * * * *

After serving the church in Rainy River for two years, Dad became pastor of the Bergen Church in nearby North Branch, Ontario. We lived in a small, two-story parsonage built into to the rear of the church, with a tiny kitchen and sitting room downstairs and a narrow, steep stairway leading to two bedrooms above. An unattached garage stood next to the church, along with an outbuilding that the church ladies occasionally used for sewing projects. I recall playing on the church grounds and in the surrounding woods.

North Branch, Ontario, Canada wasn't a town, but rather the intersection of two gravel roads, Bang and Brannon. Our church stood on a corner across the road from a one-room schoolhouse for grades one through 13. The other two corners stood empty. In 2024, Pastor Mast told me that the church burned down years ago after lying in a state of disrepair for quite some time. Per Google Earth photos, the school across the road remains.

My first year of school was in that one-room schoolhouse, with plank wooden floors and desks bolted to them in straight lines. One teacher taught all the grades and every subject. Fortunately for her, some grades had no students. Rambunctious kids would occasionally escape through the tall, narrow windows on both sides of the room when the teacher was distracted, which I thought was kind of funny. I remember liking school back then, experiencing none of the problems I'd have when I returned to the U.S.

Heading off to my first day of school in North Branch, Canada.

Dad's church, where we lived in the back. I remember lots of snow.

As young, curious, energetic and mischievous boys, Leif and I were always on the lookout for new things to try, testing our abilities. One day, I found a way to climb up to the roof of the garage. Leif was too small, so it took some careful calculations and help for him to reach the roof with me. Getting down proved to be far more challenging, especially for Leif. His short legs couldn't come close to the first support, and I couldn't assist him, so he ended up stranded.

From the house steps, I watched Dad arrive to find his younger son waving excitedly from a very unexpected place. Leif's relief turned to fear upon seeing Dad's angry face and hearing him yell, "What in the world are you doing up there?"

Sure enough, once safely down with my father's help, Leif received the typical and most favored discipline delivered in those days—a spanking. I watched, feeling a good bit of guilt, but not enough to cough up the details on how my brother had gotten up there.

Long periods of below-zero temperatures in the winter strained the supply of wood we stacked in the fall to last us until spring. Some days the pump over the well froze solid. We have a photo of my dad working to free it by heating it with a blowtorch.

In winter, after the plows went through, snow was often several feet over the roofline of our car. Homes were on farms spread miles apart. Woods peppered the landscape, home to deer, moose, black bears and countless smaller wild animals, like wolves, squirrels, red fox, mice and bats.

Without indoor plumbing, we used an outhouse. Small, covered pots by our beds spared us any nighttime outdoor trips, which were dangerous due to bears and large cats on the prowl. During the day, we played in the woods near the house but rarely strayed too far from view.

Residents set hefty traps for any bears that developed a habit of getting too close to barns, farm animals and houses. One day, Dad put Leif and me into the car, and we drove to a farm about two miles south of us. The farmer had trapped a large black bear that had gotten too close and killed it, then hung it from a large tree to be dressed.

After all the bear stories we'd been hearing, being this close to a real (and large) bear terrified Leif and me, even though it was dead. We both had nightmares for days and wouldn't go deep into the woods for months. Even after we moved back to Fairmont, we initially refused to play with friends outside after dark for fear of bears.

Once, when playing near the edge of the woods in North Branch, I heard a twig snap near us. I turned, yelled "Bear!" as loud as I could and began running toward the house. Leif was hot on my heels. Crossing the driveway, I looked back to see that my longer legs had left my brother a good way behind me, but with no bear giving chase. I relaxed a bit, but still clambered into the house.

Through the screen door I watched my approaching brother, panic in his face as he imagined the large black bear gaining ground behind him, its mouth full of large, sharp teeth. As he got close to the door, something evil momentarily took over inside me and I slipped the lock on the door. While I let him in after a few seconds, Leif remembers it to this day. He swears he was out there pounding on the door and screaming to be let in for an hour, with a large bear nipping at his heels.

* * * * *

When I was five or six years old, we returned to Fairmont, Minnesota, the town of my birth. Dad took up where he left off as a carpenter, working with his oldest brother Elvin.

My father was always a frustrated preacher. I suspect he wanted to support his family through ministry work, but it just wasn't financially viable. The churches that resonated with him were often small, with minimal funding.

Back in the U.S., my dad made sure our family had a solid grounding in church life. Sundays were the biggest days, with Sunday School before the morning service and prayer meetings or slide presentations from visiting missionaries in the evening. Tuesdays were reserved for choir practice, Wednesdays brought prayer meetings or catechism classes and Friday night was youth night. It seemed like I was always in church.

Early on, I developed a desire to perform in front of crowds. While my dad was nervous addressing groups larger than a few dozen people, I thrived on it. The bigger the audience, the better. I don't know if there's a gene for this, but if so both my daughters inherited it, I'm delighted to say.

My parents dressed me to look like a carpenter: This is about as close as I ever came to being one.

33

ROOTS AND RENOVATIONS: FROM BASEMENTS TO FAMILY TREES

BACK IN FAIRMONT, WE BEGAN reconnecting with uncles, aunts and cousins. It was impossible for me to keep straight who was who. My parents had nine siblings between them, and, when you totaled them up with spouses, I had 18 aunts and uncles. Each couple averaged four kids each, which added up to 36 cousins of various ages and genders. No one ever took the time to explain who everyone was and how they all fit together.

One day, my aunt Gladys (who was married to Dad's brother Elvin), sat me down in her living room with a scrapbook where she kept her sons' sports achievements. I suspected that she noticed my lack of sports participation and wanted to inspire me with some photos of my older cousins Donny, Roger and Dennis. Their exploits spread across the sports pages of the *Fairmont Sentinel* newspaper, and Gladys had kept every clipping.

After many failed attempts at organized sports (Little League, gymnastics and football) we finally found out I had a heart defect. A coarctation of my aorta caused my heart to funnel most of my blood supply to my head and upper extremities, to the detriment of my legs. So, even though I looked like a "mini bodybuilder" and all the coaches wanted me on their teams, it was always me and Fat Albert trailing far behind all the other kids at every practice. The coaches thought I was just lazy and assigned me extra laps. It could've killed me, but we didn't know it then.

* * * * *

Before my father left for Canada, he helped his brothers build homes for themselves in Fairmont. My dad and Elvin, with the help of their brothers and brother-in-law, Erve Huvden, built the 1409 Lucia Avenue basement that we moved into upon returning to the States. Elvin, Gladys and their three boys lived next door to us. It's hard to imagine it now, but five of us were living in one small basement apartment until just before my youngest sister Jurene was born. By the time she came along, Elvin and Dad had completed a two-story top for the 1409 house, and we were finally able to move upstairs. My brother and I had one bedroom, as did my sisters, and Dad rented out the basement for extra income.

Our house at 1409 Lucia Ave. in Fairmont, circa 1955. That's me standing with my mom on the step and my brother Leif in the baby carrier.

When Dad came home from Canada and gave up on the ministry, he got his union carpenter card and relied on it to get construction jobs here and there with my uncle Elvin. Because the lifestyle was unpredictable, Elvin began developing lots and building homes with my dad's help. Eventually, the two would travel to Mankato, Minnesota, about an hour north of Fairmont, to work on the college being built there. They'd often drive up and spend the week, only coming home on the weekends.

This affinity for building seems to be part of our family DNA, tracing back to our roots in Denmark. While my grandfather, John Walter (Johan Valdemar) Larsen, immigrated from Tibirke, landed in Fairmont and became a farmer, his brother, Carl Gustav, became a prominent builder in Denmark. In 1950, the year I was born, the two brothers reunited in Fairmont after being separated for 57 years. John Walter was 75 years old, and his younger brother Carl Gustav was 72.

In 1956, Elvin visited Carl Gustav in Denmark and had his photograph taken in front of the building where he had his large workshop. Years later, it would become the home of family relatives, Jens Serup and his wife, Lise Westphal. In a touching connection to our family history, when I visited in 2023 with my cousin Ron Herem, we slept in the very room my grandfather's brother used to do his work.

The room with the two windows on the left was my grandfather's brother's workshop. My cousin Ron and I slept there during our 2023 visit.

34

BUMS, BULLIES AND A TWO-FINGER WHISTLE

FOR MY BROTHER LEIF AND me, our grade school years in Fairmont were all about exploring the groves across the field behind our house and the shores of George Lake, fishing, catching turtles, building rafts, attempting to build boats and getting into as much mischief as possible.

We met Jay and Ray, two old guys our parents referred to as "bums," who built shacks near the George Lake dam. We loved sliding down the mossy sluiceway in the summer, a super slippery slide with pools of water at the bottom. Jay and Ray lived near the dam during the warmer months. Whenever it got so cold that their pot-bellied stoves couldn't keep up (or they'd run out of wood to burn), Jay would check himself into the VA hospital and Ray would move into his sister's house. Then the pair waited for spring so they could return to their life of fishing and schooling the young boys who came to visit them.

George Lake Dam: Jay and Ray had shacks just under the trees.

Jay and Ray constructed their tiny, well-maintained shacks about a mile across the fields from where we lived. The only road coming close to them was Fairlakes Ave., on the other side of the lake. That dirt road was over the railroad tracks and past Lake Cemetery, where many of my relatives are buried.

Leif and I never approached the dam via the road. We always trekked across the fields along George Lake, walking its northern edge to get to the dam. Water from the dam fed Center Creek, which meanders for miles. One branch eventually joins the Blue Earth River, and eventually, the Mississippi.

Jay and Ray had cleared the brush around their shacks and built an outhouse and a fire pit under enormous trees, which provided lots of shade. They tended a large garden. Jay's shack had room for a single bed, always carefully made, a small counter and two orange crates fashioned into a bookshelf. The lower shelf contained piles of old *True Detective* magazines, whose covers were festooned with scantily clad women in lurid poses.

Jay had an old .22 rifle he used to shoot rabbits, which he made into a stew with vegetables from the garden. Unlike our father and uncles, who were always busy, Jay and Ray always made time for us. We loved listening to their stories and learning how to clean fish and make stew. Years later, I learned from my cousin Roger that he and his pals had steered clear of those "crazy ol' bums" who they had heard were "mean sumbitches."

* * * * *

While I learned a great deal from Jay and Ray, my formal education was a different story. I was failing catastrophically at the public school in Fairmont. At the end of third grade, my teachers concluded that I couldn't advance. They suspected I had not yet learned to read, and had somehow been faking the tests.

SKILLS AND KNOWLEDGE

Quarter - | 1 | 2 | 3 | 4 |

ARITHMETIC - - - - - - - - - - - - | D | D | D | F |

Knows number facts - - - - - - - | 3 | 3 | 3 | 3 |
Reasons well in solving problems- | 3 | 3 | 3 | 3 |
Shows accuracy in number work - - | 3 | 3 | 3 | 3 |

READING - - - - - - - - - - - - - | D | D | D | D |
Uses phonics and other skills to
work out new words - - - - - - - | 3 | 3 | 3 | 3 |
Reads with understanding- - - - - | 3 | 3 | 3 | 3 |
Reads well orally - - - - - - - - | 3 | 3 | 3 | 3 |

LANGUAGE ARTS - - - - - - - - - - | D | D | D | D |
Uses words correctly in oral and
written work - - - - - - - - - | 2 | 2 | 2 | 2 |
Expresses thoughts well- - - - - - | 3 | 3 | 3 | 3 |
Speaks plainly - - - - - - - - - - | 2 | 2 | 2 | 2 |
Listens attentively- - - - - - - - | 3 | 3 | 3 | 3 |
Masters assigned spelling words- - | 3 | 3 | 3 | 3 |
Spells correctly in written work - | 3 | 3 | 3 | 3 |
Writes legibly and neatly - - - - | 3 | 3 | 3 | 3 |

SOCIAL STUDIES - - - - - - - - - - | D | D | D | D |

SCIENCE AND HEALTH - - - - - - - - | D | D | D | D |

MUSIC - - - - - - - - - - - - - - | 2 | 2 | 2 | 2 |

ART - - - - - - - - - - - - - - - | 2 | 2 | 2 | 2 |

PHYSICAL EDUCATION - - - - - - - | 2 | 2 | 2 | 2 |

My third-grade report card at Lincoln Public School—all Ds and an F!

My mother, frustrated with the school's inability to get me interested, and worried about the stigma I'd face watching my friends move ahead while I stayed behind, had an idea. She enrolled me at Immanuel Lutheran Grade School, where I repeated third grade with a different set of kids.

The introductory meeting at the Lutheran school left a new, shocking and lasting impression on me. Sitting in the principal's office between my parents, my mind was blank. While I had no prior interactions with Norm Ruthenbeck, my experience with school principals had not been positive. I was on my guard, highly suspicious of the man, watching and listening carefully for clues about his intent.

My prejudiced assessment of the role played by school principals was later summarized in the 1986 documentary film, *Ferris Bueller's Day Off*. In the movie, the principal (Mr. Rooney, Dean of Students), was the archenemy of every kid.

With shock, I heard my father tell principal Ruthenbeck, "If he gets out of line, I want you to know you have my permission to give him a beating. And it's okay to use a strap. And if you do, let me know, as he'll get another one when he gets home." I was stunned. Whose side were my parents on? And then it dawned on me how things were. It was adults vs. kids. I was a kid. They were adults—they were the enemy. Little happened in my four years at this new school that changed this core truth.

But something did happen in the summer between my first and second attempts at third grade. I learned to read. New kids had moved onto our street who had comic books, which weren't allowed in our Christian home. I was blown away by Richie Rich, Superman, Donald Duck and Batman. Comics supplied the incentive I needed to learn what was in those bubbles above the heads of the various characters. By the end of the summer, I was reading everything I could put my hands on. This drive to devour books, not just comics, has lasted my entire life.

While I gained a love of reading, I still wasn't very interested in what my teachers were talking about. At school I lived for recess. Outside, playing ball or tag with other kids, or even riding my bike to and from school, was my idea of fun. Understanding my need for activity, my parents let me join the organized fun of the Cub Scouts and 4-H. I read the Cub Scouts magazine cover-to-cover every month, always looking forward to the important tips for young boys on the very last page.

One of the coolest skills I learned from that back page was how to whistle with authority, and I've never forgotten how. I remember practicing the technique outlined in the magazine for days, with very little effect. Then one day, during morning recess, my fingers finally began to find the right spot, or at least close to it. Sounds, only slightly identifiable as a whistle, emanated from my mouth as I forced air between my fingers and lower lip. I didn't quite have it and then—recess was over. Dang!

Back in class, I immediately asked to go to the restroom. "Why didn't you go during recess?" asked the exasperated teacher, who excused me and told me to hurry back. I rushed to the basement bathroom, got into a stall, and began practicing my whistle. And sure enough, after just a few minutes I nailed it. Loud, long, sharp screeches flowed. I was thrilled, repeating it over and over, as I didn't want to forget the precise location of my fingers for maximum volume.

What I failed to realize was that the heating ducts running up from the basement broadcast my triumphant whistling to the entire school. Just as I was hitting my stride, Principal Ruthenbeck flung open the stall door, pulled me off the toilet and subjected me to an old-fashioned, firmly applied spanking—with a strap.

Despite the physical punishment and being forced to do things I wasn't interested in, the parochial school had several redeeming qualities. Discovering historic novels in the library was one of them. I drove my teachers absolutely nuts, as I would regularly hide a book behind or under what I was supposed to be paying attention to and transport myself to a world of pirates or explorers discovering America or Jack London's *Call of the Wild* or *White Fang*.

At home, my mother bent the house rules and began buying me Classics Illustrated comics, such as *Robinson Crusoe*, *The Last of the Mohicans*, *Treasure Island*, *A Tale of Two Cities*, *Frankenstein* and many more. I still have them.

* * * * *

Playing in the small sandlot during recess or after school was—for the six boys attending Immanuel Lutheran—all about baseball. Gary Seifert was a skillful player. Not so the rest of us, but we sure tried. When you only have six players, rosters and rules needed to change. A successful pitch was one that was hit, preferably somewhere between 1st and 3rd base, or at least close.

Given our player shortage, when it wasn't your turn to bat you played outfield for the opposing team. We had no catcher. If you swung at a pitch and missed, you retrieved the ball yourself and threw it back to the pitcher. You got three swings to hit the ball. If you didn't swing, nothing mattered or was counted. I assumed all baseball games were officiated in this way.

My parents signed me up to play Little League, with uniforms that had genuine sponsors' names on the back. Each team had a proper coach, and we played on a regulation baseball diamond, flanked by a few rows of bleachers for the dozen or so parents who showed up at the games. I loved my uniform and wore it nearly the whole day before my first game.

When it was my first time up to bat, I stared down the pitcher. He threw a ball over the plate faster than I'd ever seen at our small sandlot.

"Strike!" the umpire called.

"What?" I thought to myself, "I hadn't swung the bat. How could it be a strike?" I also wondered how he expected me to hit a ball that was going so fast.

I resolved to hold my bat rigid on my shoulder for the next pitch so the umpire would be able to clearly see that it had not moved. "Strike!" he called again.

I was totally perplexed when the third throw was also called a strike and the umpire said, "You're out!"

Back in the area serving as a dugout, the father managing our team suggested I sit out for a few innings, which turned out to be the rest of the game. On the way home, finding some dirt at the side of the road, I got off my bike and slid in it, so my parents would think I played when I got home.

I never went back to organized baseball.

The complete Larsen family—Paul and Ruth holding Jurene, with Leif, Naomi and me in the front row.

The most significant obstacle on the path from our house to school was the gauntlet Leif and I ran nearly every day.

First, our route forced us to pass the residence of the feared Johnson brothers. If we somehow made it past them unscathed, we then had to contend with the equally feared Slater brothers, led by Stanley, the oldest. The Johnson and Slater boys delighted in threatening and scaring the bejesus out of Leif and me, although things rarely escalated beyond a few good shoves to the ground.

But damn, those bullies scared us silly.

35

FROM GOLDEN GLOVES TO GHOSTLY ENCOUNTERS

WHEN I WAS IN JUNIOR HIGH, my father, concerned about our fearful stories of walking to school, enrolled my brother Leif and me in the Golden Gloves, an amateur boxing club at the VFW hall. While Leif eventually gravitated toward wrestling in high school, I fell in love with boxing immediately. It was the first sport I'd encountered that didn't depend on teamwork for success.

Under Coach Gene Trembly's guidance, we began with footwork fundamentals, crucial for generating power from the legs. We learned to jab, cross, hook and uppercut, practicing relentlessly on heavy bags. Sparring nights matched us with partners of similar age and size, though occasionally we'd face more experienced fighters. One memorable match pitted me against a 24-year-old army boxer who was home on leave.

Kids could work with Coach Trembly until they were 26, as long as they never boxed or fought anyone outside the gym. "If you're caught street fighting, you're banned from the Golden Gloves forever," Coach Trembly told us.

On two occasions, I nearly broke this rule. The first instance involved John Reilly, a bus ride bully who constantly harassed me. Fed up, I took two sets of boxing gloves over to John's house one day after school. His parents weren't home from work, and he was surprised to see me. I told him I was in Golden Gloves and we couldn't fight, but we could spar in his driveway if he was up for it.

The encounter was far from a movie-style showdown where the bully gets taught a lesson in the playground, but it quickly became apparent that I could hit him at will while he struggled to land a punch. Our "fight" evolved into an impromptu boxing lesson, with me teaching John basic footwork and defensive stances. After about 15 minutes, I took my gloves and rode home, with no idea what the result would be.

The next morning, when the bus dropped me off at school, there was John Reilly in a circle of his cronies. He waved me over. As I cautiously approached, I heard him explaining to his pals how the previous day I'd given him a pounding he'd never forget. To my amazement he exaggerated our encounter substantially, making me sound like some sort of ninja boxing expert. All the teasing stopped, and I didn't get in trouble at the gym.

The second close call came when I was pushed into a fight with a kid named Bill Snyder. By then I was in high school, and I'd been boxing at the gym for a couple of years and had even entered some tournaments. Bill's slow, telegraphed punches were a stark contrast to those of the disciplined fighters I was used to. All he could come up with were some easy-to-dodge, wild haymakers he probably saw cowboys do on TV. The fight ended abruptly when a lucky uppercut of mine collided with his rushing jaw, pushing his tooth through his lip.

Although I never became a club champion, I loved traveling to tournaments. I consistently survived three one-minute rounds, often losing on points but never by knockout. My defensive skills and decent footwork kept me from serious hits.

Curiously, on two occasions, the pre-fight doctor examination disqualified me without explanation. It wasn't until later, during my fateful football physical, that Dr. Kramer discovered my heart problem through multiple blood pressure readings.

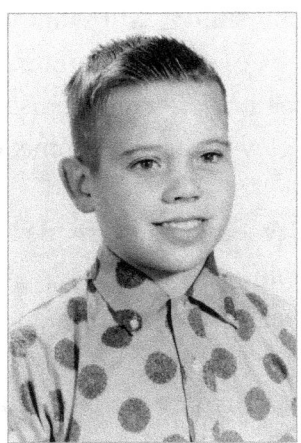

A school photo from around the time I joined the Golden Gloves.

My parents always struggled to put food on the table for their four growing kids. We stocked our garage freezer with sale-priced meats and vegetables, supplemented by my father's hunting. Most years, he got a deer. At one point, he began raising rabbits, big fluffy New Zealand white ones with pink eyes. They were popular for meat as they grew quickly and reproduced like, well, rabbits.

Our one rabbit cage soon expanded to three or four, and cleaning rabbit poop became one of our least favorite chores. But my siblings and I loved the rabbits, especially the baby bunnies. My sisters couldn't resist sneaking them into the house, even though it was against the rules. Invariably, the bunnies would get away and crawl behind a piano or other furniture, coming out only at night. Occasionally, if we couldn't capture them, they'd die in the house, creating foul smells and angry parents.

Somehow, we kids didn't seem to catch on that all the chicken stew we were eating may have been augmented with rabbit meat. We were never around when the bunnies were slaughtered. At some point, Dad got fed up with his sketchy helpers and the nuisance of feeding the rabbits and cleaning their cages. One day, we helped him load the cages, full of bunnies, into the car. Dad drove us all down Lucia Avenue, made a left at Memorial Park Drive, and took us all the way out to Fairview Memorial Park Cemetery. There, we let the rabbits go.

Years later, after I learned how to drive and was looking for a quiet location to park with a female companion, I pulled into the cemetery, turned off the lights and turned the radio up. When we were ready to go back home, I started the car and turned on the headlights to reveal a surreal scene: a vast, manicured lawn dotted with gravestones and hundreds of white rabbits, their pink eyes reflecting the light back at us.

My date squealed with surprise and delight, wondering out loud, "How in the world did so many white rabbits adopt this spot as home?"

I knew the answer, but my lips were sealed.

36

CAMPAIGN MISCHIEF: ADVENTURES OF YOUNG POLITICAL OPERATIVES

IN 1960, AT THE TENDER age of 10, I unwittingly found myself sliding from righteous intent into political chicanery. That year's presidential election marked a significant shift in my family's political allegiance. My father, traditionally a staunch Democrat like his brother Elvin, unexpectedly sided with the Republicans when John F. Kennedy secured the Democratic nomination. Our church held the belief that a Catholic president would effectively put the Pope in charge of the United States, a prospect that deeply troubled my father and our congregation. While my uncle retained his Democratic loyalty, my dad—anxious about Kennedy's chances—threw his support behind the Republicans.

As Election Day drew near, my father brought my brother Leif and me to a Nixon get-out-the-vote event at a local elementary school gymnasium. Quickly bored by the adults' strategic discussions, Leif and I wandered into the cloakroom and discovered a treasure trove of campaign materials—literature, political trinkets and, most enticingly, boxes upon boxes of bumper stickers. When we inquired about taking a few, one of the party faithful enthusiastically encouraged us to take as many as we wanted, assuring us that with the election so near, they had more than they could ever use. Unaware that the box we grabbed contained around 10,000 stickers, we set off into the November night, informing our dad we'd be walking home.

Our first stop was the school parking lot, where we adorned every car with at least two new "Nixon Now" bumper stickers. In the dark, making our way home along N. North Avenue, east of George

Lake, we plastered every parked car we passed with bumper stickers, regardless of whether it was on the street or in a driveway.

About a third of the way home, we realized that unless we prodigiously upped our rate of sticker application we'd arrive home with a mostly full box. Although only junior operatives, we instinctively understood that stickers in boxes wouldn't help the cause, so we got to work.

Stop signs soon had four or five Nixon stickers on them. We covered the boat landing sign and put about 100 stickers on a billboard advertising lakeside lots for sale. We crawled up street signs at every crossing and placed stickers over the street names. A block or two from home, it occurred to us that the mailboxes should also get stickers, and from that point on we decorated both sides of every mailbox on both sides of the street. Even with all that hard work and creativity, we still arrived home with nearly half a box of stickers left.

Our father's reaction upon returning home was less than enthusiastic. The highly reflective stickers had illuminated his entire drive. He explained that we shouldn't have placed the stickers on public property, or on people's cars and mailboxes without their permission. Though he acted displeased, I suspect he might have been secretly amused, knowing that no one could trace our handiwork back to us.

He confiscated our remaining stickers and told us to remove the ones we'd applied the next day. While this was the right thing to do, the exceptionally strong glue used on those stickers proved resilient. Remnants of the stickers remained well into the following summer, long after the election was over.

Years later, my brother Leif said he remembered how much fun we had placing those bumper stickers wherever we wanted, "because they stuck on everything!" Weeks after the election, Leif was still finding more uses for the stickers, like wrapping the handlebars, seat, fenders and tires of his old Schwinn bike.

While I don't recall voting for many Republican candidates, being a Nixon volunteer operative was definitely an exhilarating experience!

37
SUMMER CAMP CHRONICLES

MY FIRST SUMMER CAMP EXPERIENCE, hosted by the YMCA or a similar organization, is a blur of fond memories. While many details have faded, I vividly recall learning to sail a small Sunfish sailboat, participating in an exhilarating game of capture the flag and engaging in various crafts. This secular camp was pure fun, free from religious overtones.

Capture the flag was a definite highlight for me, the game's simple rules belying the excitement it generated. Divided into two teams, we'd infiltrate the opposing side's territory, dodging and weaving to avoid capture while searching for their flag. A "capture" occurred when an opponent snagged the cloth flag tucked into your pants, forcing you to freeze until a teammate freed you. The first team to steal the other's flag won. Playing with nearly 100 kids across the expansive campgrounds—including woods, cabins and the main building—was exciting beyond words.

The camp that left the most lasting impression on me, however, was a Lutheran retreat in northern Minnesota, near Hillcrest Academy in Fergus Falls. My cousin John Gravley, a year older than me, attended Hillcrest and would visit the camp with his friends. My sister Naomi, four years younger, also attended Hillcrest later and credits it with significantly impacting her life. And Jim Roller, a successful business owner from South Dakota, would always show up at the camp in his Dodge Charger, a muscle car with great sounding pipes. I thought Jim was the coolest guy. He was the only person who ever sent me a telegram, when I was in the hospital for my open-heart surgery at age 15.

Summer camps, both religious and secular, were a cornerstone of city kids' experiences, and they're a tradition that continues today. My wife Maggie was also part of that tradition, attending both church and Girl Scout camps as a child. Her mother even served as a counselor at some of the church camps, ensuring that Maggie never missed an evening service.

It's remarkable how many parallel experiences Maggie and I had as children: minister fathers, church camps, school plays and bicycling adventures around town. One notable difference was that Maggie's mother composed a chant for her campers' skit night, something my mother would never have done:

> Root-i-toot-toot! Root-i-toot-toot!
> We're in the leadership institute.
> We don't smoke and we don't chew
> And we don't hold with kids who do!
> Our class won the B-i-i-i-ble!

My Lutheran camp, while enjoyable, placed a heavy emphasis on religious instruction. We attended nightly religious services. Bible quiz contests were frequent, as were competitions to memorize Bible verses. I discovered early on that I had a knack for memorization, excelling in these contests. This skill would later prove invaluable when learning lines for plays.

38

'SLOW' TO CEO: UNRAVELING MULTIPLE INTELLIGENCES

DURING MY EARLY SCHOOL YEARS, from first through 10th grade, I was consistently labeled as "slow" by my teachers. None of them ever pointed to an IQ test or anything, they just sent regular messages to my mother that I wasn't very smart. My mother, ever supportive, never believed these assessments, but she endured years of my disinterest in school, failing grades and lectures about Steve's "failure to apply himself." Looking back, undiagnosed ADHD may have contributed to my inability to focus and my ambivalence toward formal education.

It wasn't until adulthood that I discovered that intelligence isn't a one-dimensional concept. Through Daniel Goleman's groundbreaking 1995 book, *Emotional Intelligence: Why It Can Matter More Than IQ*, and Howard Gardner's research on the eight variations of human intelligence, I learned that our cognitive abilities are far more complex than traditional IQ tests suggest.

The traditional intelligence quotient (IQ), which focuses on logic, reasoning, planning, problem-solving and test-taking, was where I struggled in school. Both my daughters excel in this area, but only with some specific adjustments. Ginger, for example, saw significant improvement in her grades when given extra time for tests. I've noticed similar aptitudes in some of my grandchildren and other family members, who thrive on intellectual challenges.

However, a high IQ doesn't guarantee success. In one of my early leadership positions at a large company, I encountered a team member who exemplified the limitations of relying solely on IQ as a measure of intelligence. This individual was undeniably brilliant—he held a Ph.D., spoke several languages fluently and had authored three books. On paper, he was the epitome of intellectual prowess. When he was first assigned to my team, I remember feeling intimidated, wailing to Maggie, "How can I avoid looking like a dunce next to this guy?"

But as we worked together, a different picture emerged. Despite his impressive credentials, this team member struggled in ways that puzzled me. He had difficulty knowing when to speak up and when to remain quiet in meetings. He couldn't seem to direct his efforts effectively or maintain focus on priority tasks. It turned out that this was his fourth transfer in as many years—previous managers had been unable to extract value from his vast knowledge and skills.

This experience was a pivotal moment in my understanding of intelligence and professional success. It demonstrated that excelling in traditional academic measures—having a high IQ, advanced degrees and impressive accomplishments—doesn't automatically translate to effectiveness in a dynamic work environment. I began to really appreciate how other forms of intelligence contribute to success in both personal and professional realms.

One of these is emotional intelligence (EQ), which plays a crucial role in understanding oneself and others. Both my daughters are off the charts in this area. I always thought I was good at reading a room, but Ginger is even better. She goes beyond seeing what's happening with an individual or group, intuitively knowing what buttons to push to get the results she wants. It makes her a killer negotiator. She's a good team leader and superb at influencing people. She understands which things require attention and which do not, seeing between the lines to things that others miss.

I suspect my oldest daughter Christie is much the same, although I didn't have the same opportunity to watch her develop and don't have as many examples of her in action. One story comes to mind from a trip she and some friends made to Hawaii. The girls were searching for a thermal pool that was mentioned on Trip Advisor but wasn't published in any of the guidebooks. When Christie asked some Hawaiian natives about it, she got a feeling from them that made her choose her words very carefully. In retelling the story, it was clear that her emotional intelligence led to a successful interaction and a subsequent visit to a secret spa, a spot few tourists ever find.

My experience with Steven Snyder, one of my co-founders at Net Perceptions, further highlighted the importance of EQ to me. Steven's background and Ph.D. in psychology made our performance reviews more like therapy sessions, with detailed assessments of what was working and what needed improvement for each of his direct reports.

Before our first performance evaluation meeting, I completed my own assessment, recording my thoughts as if he had written them, using the same form I knew he would use. I went through every section, noting where I was doing well and where I thought I could improve.

Steven's one-on-one meetings began with a discussion of the top priorities of the company, then moved gradually to how each individual was contributing to our forward progress. Steven would verbally step through the assessment form but would also offer several opportunities for dialog and discussion. Finally, Steven would remove his written assessment from a folder and slide it across his desk to be signed.

When we reached this point in my first performance appraisal meeting with him, I pulled out the assessment I'd done and gave it to him. He was surprised. He was reading my form as I signed his and left the room. Later he would tell me, "I don't think I've met a more self-aware person in my life." For the rest of my time at Net Perceptions, Steven had me do my own performance assessments — written in the third person, of course, which he would sign and drop into the file.

Besides self-awareness, those with a high EQ are typically good at self-regulation and self-motivation. They're also empathic, sensing what people around them are thinking and feeling. For instance, I can't help crying at movies and I'm moved when hearing stories of others' experiences. It's hard for me not to put myself into another person's situation and understand what they feel.

Developing EQ starts with being curious about other people. Whenever possible, I engage in conversation with the people around me, even if we're just waiting in line for a coffee or sharing a plane ride, trying to gauge what they're thinking about and what makes them tick. It's also important to listen without judgment, a skill I've been developing through years of helping the MISS Foundation in its efforts with people grieving the death of a child. While I could do better, this may be partly why I get along well with people on all sides of the political spectrum, as well as those with a diversity of religious beliefs and experiences.

Another form of intelligence, the social quotient (SQ), revolves around building and maintaining social networks. This ability really helped me advance in my career, allowing me to become co-founder and CEO at several early-stage technology companies. When venture capital firms found an investment opportunity they liked and needed to set up a real company around a brilliant idea, they called me. My skill, as one VC put it, was that "Steve gets the right people on the bus, the wrong people off and then gets it pointed and moving in the right direction."

My SQ also paid dividends when I assembled a group of car experts to rebuild my Lotus Elan in 2013–2014, an effort touched on in these pages and chronicled in detail in my book *A Mistress in the Garage*. The same type of intelligence also helps create successful, multi-day group motorcycle rides and keeps me surrounded by more than one wonderful group of close friends.

Finally, the adversity quotient (AQ) measures perseverance and resilience—how determined you are to push through plateaus, and how quickly you bounce back after going through a rough patch. People with a high AQ spend little time dwelling on setbacks. Instead, they learn from their failures and quickly plan how they'll do better next time.

I witnessed a high level of AQ in my granddaughter Parker when she was playing with a remote-control rock crawling truck. She created a track behind our house and timed herself, over and over, dropping her times lower and lower, until soon she had the best time, beating everyone else who circled the track. She never let a bad run get her down—she simply lined the truck back up at the starting gate and tried again.

Another way to illustrate AQ is to think of your favorite sports team and the times when the players came from behind against all odds to pull out a victory. People with low AQ tend to choke, while people with high AQ can get beyond even the most boneheaded play or missed opportunity.

Advanced resiliency can be used to turn a negative experience into a helping one, rather than something that holds you back. My own AQ was put to the ultimate test when we lost our son, Eric, in 1992. This devastating experience, while initially seeming like an insurmountable tragedy, eventually became a source of unexpected strength. It gave me a new perspective on life's difficulties, making subsequent challenges seem more manageable in comparison.

During one period, my boss at Prodigy was a weak VP without a backbone, a sycophant living in constant fear that upper management would discover his incompetence. He had four strong-willed and highly competent general managers reporting to him: We each ran major divisions of the company and were all very good at what we did.

When a new performance appraisal system required managers to force-rank their employees, he froze. I was the last of the four of us to be reviewed, and it soon became clear to me that the other three GMs had pushed him into high rankings for themselves. He sniveled, coughed and informed me he was going to have to rank me as "meets expectations." This was the only time I'd ever failed to achieve the highest possible ranking in a performance review.

As I watched him squirm and snivel, it occurred to me, "He thinks he's hurting me. He believes this will make me feel bad." And in one way, he was right. If this had happened years earlier, I may have been devastated. But not now!

Struggling to keep from laughing, I thought, "My god, does he not know how ridiculous this is? I've already been so deeply hurt in my life that nothing else, for as long as I live, will ever be able to touch me. I'm invulnerable! Nothing anyone can ever do or say to me will make me feel bad. The worst has already happened, and I made it through. Everything from here on out is a piece of cake. Thanks, Eric."

Less than a week after my pathetic boss gave me my first less-than-stellar review, I found myself alone in an elevator with Ross Glatzer, Prodigy's CEO. He grinned sheepishly and said, "You know that performance appraisal ranking is bullshit, don't you?"

I just smiled and nodded.

* * * * *

If I could say just one thing to my grandkids, nieces and nephews—and any young person or parent of young children, for that matter—it's this: Don't limit yourself by thinking what schools traditionally measure is the only valuable quality.

While IQ is important, it's just one piece of the puzzle. The emotional, social and adversity quotients are equally necessary for success and fulfillment in life. These skills might not be taught in classrooms, but they can be developed through experiences, relationships and self-reflection.

As you figure out what you're good at and the things you want to do more of, understand that true intelligence is multifaceted. It's not just about acing tests; it's about understanding yourself and others, building strong connections and bouncing back from adversity.

39

NEW HORIZONS: TRANSFORMATIVE DAYS AT FAIRMONT HIGH

THE TRANSITION FROM JUNIOR HIGH to high school often marks a significant change in a teenager's life. For me, it was nothing short of revolutionary. As I stepped through the doors of Fairmont Senior High School for the first time, I had no idea that I was about to embark on a journey of self-discovery that would reshape my entire worldview.

For years, I had been the kid who couldn't catch a break. Poor grades, social awkwardness and a general sense of not fitting in had been my constant companions. But entering 10th grade, the winds of change began to blow, bringing with them opportunities I never knew existed.

The catalyst for this transformation came in the form of a driver's license. Having repeated third grade, I was older than most of my classmates, which meant I could legally drive before they could. This simple fact opened up a world of possibilities and gave me a sense of freedom and responsibility I found intoxicating. In fact, few things motivated me more than being able to drive. From the first time my father pulled me onto his lap and let me steer the car on the bumpy gravel road to the town dump on Saturday mornings, I was hooked.

After excelling in driver's ed, driving became my passion, my motivation and my ticket to social acceptance. Soon, I found myself with my first real friends, Brian Gulla and Ted Hasse, bonded by our shared love of cars and the open road.

My newfound mobility enabled me to expand my horizons beyond Fairmont. I traveled to a national Youth for Christ rally in Indiana, where I was exposed to inspiring speakers like Nicky Cruz and David Wilkerson, the Pentecostal pastor who ministered to New York gang members and wrote the book *The Cross and the Switchblade*. Their messages of hope, coupled with the frenzied energy of the crowd, ignited something within me.

While my parents had Billy Graham, my friends and I had Bill Bright and a cadre of young speakers. Tom Skinner, an African American evangelist, offered not only the classic Christian message of salvation through Christ, but also talked about pulling yourself up by your bootstraps and making something of your life.

Armed with an old RCA reel-to-reel tape recorder, I captured many of these transformative speeches, often convincing the sound engineers at the events to let me plug directly into their boards for the best audio. Back home, I'd replay these tapes obsessively, absorbing not just the religious messages but also the underlying themes of self-improvement and positive thinking.

This led me down a path of personal development I attacked with the same fervor I had once reserved for avoiding schoolwork. I devoured books by Norman Vincent Peale, W. Clement Stone, Maxwell Maltz, Earl Nightingale and Napoleon Hill. Their words of encouragement and self-belief began to counteract years of negative messaging about my abilities.

Mine was not a casual affair with these authors and speakers. I'd listen to the tapes and read and re-read the books. Following my father's example when he read the Bible, I underlined key passages, wrote notes in the margins and memorized important points. I even created 3X5 index cards with my favorite sayings from the books I read, carrying them in the back pocket of my jeans for quick reference. A pivotal moment came for me in 10th grade, when my homeroom teacher, Roy Dobie, noticed potential in my writing that I hadn't seen myself.

On the first day of school, he asked us to write a one-page paper on what we did on our summer vacation. The next day, as I left for my first period class, he stopped me and said that he really liked what I wrote. He even asked me if I'd consider joining the journalism club, which produced the school paper and the annual yearbook. I was too surprised to answer, but I visited the journalism group and determined that my English skills were too poor to actually help.

Then Dobie told the debate coach, Ted Hinrichs, that he should consider me for the debate team. That's when I found a real niche for myself—I didn't know they had a sport that rewarded arguing! Very quickly, debate became my academic salvation. It required quick thinking, research skills and persuasive speaking—areas where I found I could excel. During my first year on the team, Mr. Hinrichs helped us prepare arguments for and against this proposition: *Resolved: That the foreign aid program of the United States should be limited to nonmilitary assistance.* We competed very little, but I learned the rules and got a firm foundation in the basics.

The following year, Bill Perron took over the debate team and all speech competitions. The National Forensic League had announced the 1968 debate proposition as *Resolved: That Congress should establish uniform regulations to control criminal investigation procedures* and I had a head start.

Early in the summer, I attended a two-week debate preparation class at Michigan State University's Communication Arts Institute in East Lansing. Driving my parent's red VW to Michigan made me feel so grown up, as did staying in a dorm with 60–80 others enrolled in the program. The boys stayed in the east wing of Mary Mayo Hall, while the girls occupied the west wing. The campus looked exactly the way one would expect a college campus built in the 1930s to look—brick buildings, meandering sidewalks, hedges around the buildings and massive green elm trees.

Back in Fairmont, Bill Perron would drive our debate team—Ted Hasse, Nancy Hagerman, Jim Odens and me—to competitions all over the state in his rear engine, air-cooled Corvair. When the season finished with Ted Hasse and me competing at the state level, another competitive speech event began—non-original oratory.

I memorized and delivered Patrick Henry's *Speech to a Virginia Convention*, the one that ends with "I know not what course others may take; but as for me, give me liberty or give me death!" Delivered on March 23, 1775, it's a wonderful bit of dramatic writing. My performance of it qualified me for state-level competition as well.

* * * * *

While my metamorphosis wasn't quite complete by the end of 11th grade at Fairmont High, the foundation had been laid. I was no longer the not very smart, failing academically, socially isolated and mostly unpopular loser I had once been. I was on my way to becoming someone new, someone with potential and purpose.

My senior year, spent at Mayo High School in Rochester, Minnesota, would be the final chapter in my teenage transformation. As I left Fairmont in the summer for a lifeguard job in Canada, I had no inkling that I'd never return to my old high school or to Fairmont. I wouldn't have been able to find Rochester, Minnesota on a map.

Our home at 809 Memorial Pkwy in Rochester, MN. The red VW that brought me there from Canada is in the driveway.

40

LOST LETTERS AND FOUND FAMILY

WILLOW SPRINGS BIBLE CAMP WAS located an hour north of Toronto (outside of Stouffville), an idyllic spot if there ever was one. The 14 acres included a small, spring-fed lake with shallow and deep swimming areas, a nice dock and a sandy waterfront. Strongly Christian but nondenominational, the camp offered low rates so underprivileged kids from the streets of Toronto could enjoy a week of great food and tons of outdoor activities, like boating, games, fireside chats and worship services.

My role as a camp counselor and lifeguard was to keep these kids from drowning. Fortunately, I succeeded, but the kids didn't make it easy. They often ignored instructions to avoid deep water, and inevitably I'd hear the shouts and screams of someone panicking. This happened so frequently that I used a boat oar to rescue them, to avoid having to jump in the water all the time.

My fellow counselors and staff were friendly and fun, and the time went by quickly. Toward the end of my two-week stint, a guy named Jerry Jeffs showed up and asked me to spend another week as a counselor at Camp Koinonia, an Anglican synod camp near Seguin, Ontario, two and a half hours north of Toronto. Koinonia is a Greek word meaning fellowship, sharing or communion.

I followed Jeffs to his home in Barrie, Ontario, where I met his wife Beryl and three kids—his oldest, Stephanie, who was my age, Clinton (Clint) and Amanda (Mandy). The welcome I received from the whole family was amazing. Nothing in my life had prepared me for this level of acceptance and love. After a warm family dinner getting to know each other, we headed north the following morning.

The landscape outside Barrie is a lot like northern Minnesota, full of lakes and forests. The large, remote camp sat majestically on a steep hill alongside Haines Lake. One couldn't help but get into shape at the place, hustling up and down the trails to partake in various activities.

Upon reaching the camp, I received a remarkable welcome from the entire staff of counselors, cooks and maintenance people, as well as all the campers. I'll never forget it. Everyone received nicknames and mine was "Stripes," because I was from the United States. And because I had Camp Director Jeffs' full and complete endorsement, the word was out that "Stripes is okay."

* * * * *

A mail strike in Canada coincided with my three weeks as a counselor that summer. The Canadian Union of Postal Workers wanted the right to bargain collectively, the right to strike, higher wages and better management. They defied government policies and staged an illegal, country-wide walkout, which meant that none of the letters my parents wrote to me were delivered. The actions of the Canadian postal workers resulted in one of my favorite stories in the Larsen lore.

While I was in Canada, my parents and siblings unexpectedly moved from Fairmont to Rochester. Needless to say, when I got back to Fairmont and found our house completely empty, I was surprised. Panicked and desperate, I approached our next-door neighbors for information. Cagey at first, Lorraine Thomas eventually told me that my family had moved to Rochester. I had to pay her $20 to get the truth out of her. It seems that my dad, always the cheapskate, had only paid her $10 not to tell me.

While things didn't go down exactly that way, I love the story. What is true is that I arrived in Rochester only a few days before

I had to start my senior year in high school. Our house was one I'd never seen, in a town I'd never visited, and where I didn't have a single friend.

Using some of the negotiation skills I learned on the debate team, however, I was able to leverage the "egregious offense" to which my parents subjected me into several perks, including the elimination of my nighttime curfew.

41

REINVENTION AND REVELATION: FROM MAYO HIGH TO MANKATO

MY ARRIVAL AT MAYO HIGH School in Rochester marked the beginning of a journey that would reshape my identity and set the course for my future. The contrast with Fairmont High was stark and immediately apparent. While Fairmont had just under 200 students in the 1969 graduating class and less than 600 in the entire school, Mayo's Class of 1969 boasted over 600 students, with the school's total enrollment exceeding 2,000.

The school itself was a marvel of modern architecture, designed by the award-winning firm of Hammel, Green and Abrahamson. Its unique circular design featured a central area ringed by classrooms on two floors, with the interior housing a gym, lockers, an auditorium, a theater and music practice rooms.

Almost immediately, I grasped that this was an extraordinary opportunity to remake myself. No one knew of my past educational failures, and I could create a new narrative and backstory. The question was: Who did I want to become?

Seizing the opportunity, I visited the school a few days before classes started. I met with the principal, Dr. Ralph Wright, and his staff. I carefully selected my classes and schedule. And I made a point of going around and introducing myself to teachers as they prepared for the school year, presenting myself as an eager new senior student looking forward to their classes.

My experience in debate became a cornerstone of my new identity. I sought out the teacher who organized the debate team and offered to help "coach" her students. While I quickly realized that Mayo's team wasn't quite at the level I was used to in Fairmont, I saw an opportunity to make a significant impact.

The theater department became another arena for reinvention. Dwain Johnson, my Speech III teacher, expressed surprise that Dr. Wright had let me register for his class without his permission. But after I told him about my taking the state title in non-original oratory and my participation in some of Fairmont's plays, he seemed happy to have me.

The tour of Mayo's theater he subsequently gave me left me awestruck. The venue was beyond anything I had experienced before: 500 plush seats, a professional-grade sound system, an orchestra pit and a maze of catwalks high above the stage. When I clapped my hands once at center stage, the perfect acoustics confirmed that this was a place where I could truly shine.

It was in this grand setting that I met Pati Knappe, Mr. Johnson's assistant and a fellow senior. Our shared passion for theater sparked an immediate connection, and soon after landing lead roles in the fall play, we began dating. While Pati has since passed away, the connections I made during this time have endured, including my friendship with her brother Dan and his wife Fairy.

As I drove out of the school parking lot that first day, a sense of limitless possibility washed over me. "Wow," I thought, "This is going to be great!"

As I had hoped, my Speech III classes became a platform for intellectual growth and self-expression. While officially focused on debates about current events and news, our discussions often veered into topics of religion, ethics, morality and drugs. I quickly gained a reputation for taking "God's side" in any debate, which may have led to my being asked to give the Invocation and Benediction at Mayo High School's commencement ceremony.

Since my decision to remake my image was bolstered by the massive jolt of self-confidence I received as a counselor and lifeguard in

Canadian religious summer camps, I embraced the role of religious warrior, arguing that my generation's embrace of weed, booze and left-wing politics was misguided, except for efforts to stop the war in Vietnam. I was fine with that.

My theatrical pursuits also continued to flourish at Mayo High. Winning the lead in the fall play, *The Glass Menagerie*, and performing well was a real coup. Later in the year, when I auditioned for *Of Mice and Men*, the director said she hadn't seen a more perfect George than me. The role of Lennie, George's large and dim-witted companion, was to be played by Mike Bulger, a six-foot-four-inch, thick-browed student everyone called Lurch. Unfortunately, however, I had to turn down the part of George when my mother expressed discomfort with the character's use of swear words on stage.

Cast photo for The Glass Menagerie, Mayo High School. I'm seated in the chair, with an unknown girl on my lap.

Even my academic horizons expanded dramatically thanks to my humanities teacher, Mrs. Claire Van Zant. Her class quickly became my favorite. Much later I learned of her fascinating background, including her service in the Royal Air Force during WWII as a codebreaker and intelligence officer. After the war, she studied in England under C. S. Lewis and J. R. R. Tolkien before arriving in Rochester in 1963.

Mrs. Van Zant's class focused on philosophers—Plato, Aristotle and Socrates—who had captivated me when my confirmation class-mate's older brother, David Selvig, introduced me to them. This class gave me my first "easy A." Noticing my interest, Mrs. Van Zant introduced me to a couple of early modern philosophers, Rene Descartes and Immanuel Kant. These led me to devote a lot of time studying other 19th-century philosophers, including Hegel, Karl Marx, Nietzsche and John Stuart Mill, at the Experimental College in Mankato, Minnesota.

As I approached graduation, the question of college loomed large. My parents, never having attended college themselves, could offer little guidance beyond encouraging me to go. I had no idea where to apply, how to pay for it or what was required. Fortunately, a chance encounter would change the course of my academic future.

One day, Mrs. Van Zant invited Dr. Charles R. Keller to visit our school. Dr. Keller, who had developed a program at Williams College that combined history, literature and philosophy, not only spent time in our humanities class but also spoke at a school assembly. We even-tually became pen pals, and he even wrote a letter to me that he used as a commencement address, titled "Dear Steve."

Dr. Keller's influence extended beyond our correspondence. As a prominent figure in the national educational community, he played a major role in my acceptance into the "Experimental Program" at the University of Minnesota—Mankato. This unique program would shape my college experience in ways I could never have imagined.

During my first year at Mankato, I was one of just 90 students in the Experimental Program. We lived and studied in the Cooper Center, foregoing regular classes for an interdisciplinary approach designed collaboratively by students and faculty. Traditional struc-tures based on courses and credit hours were replaced with thematic learning patterns, emphasizing learning for its own sake rather than for grades. This was the late 1960s/early 1970s, after all, and experimentation was the order of the day.

In this stimulating environment, I delved deeper into philosophy. My roommate, Lloyd Schley, and I became adept at arguing Nietzsche's points late into the night, along with those of Camus and Jean-Paul Sartre. Years later, during my time at Prodigy Services Company, my friend Robert Kost and I would engage in intense discussions about Martin Heidegger during our commutes between Croton-on-Hudson and White Plains, New York.

The offer letter and invitation to join the Experimental Program had eliminated all doubts about my academic future. As I embarked on this new chapter, I couldn't help but marvel at the journey that had brought me here. From a struggling student in Fairmont to a reinvented self at Mayo High, and now to an engaged, intellectually curious college student at Mankato, my transformation was complete.

42

FAST-TRACK LEARNING: AN UNCONVENTIONAL COLLEGE JOURNEY

MY EXCITEMENT PEAKED AS I perused the recommended reading list in my offer letter from the University of Minnesota—Mankato. I had already read or was familiar with most of the texts, including works by Sophocles, Melville, Huxley and others. This familiarity boosted my confidence as I embarked on this new academic adventure.

After settling into a comfortable routine in the first few weeks, I found myself immersed in extensive discussions and debates about the books we were reading. My staunch "pro-God" debate stance from my high school days gradually receded as I devoured ideas from a diverse range of thinkers, including Aristotle, Plato, Marcus Aurelius, Descartes, Bertrand Russell and Will Durant.

My roommate, Lloyd Schley, was particularly intrigued by the German philosopher Friedrich Hegel, and we often debated his ideas late into the night. My approach to reading evolved; instead of seeking debate points, I developed a deeper desire to understand and connect different thoughts into a comprehensive worldview. For the first time, I engaged in serious writing, struggling to articulate complex concepts that seemed just beyond my grasp. As I delved deeper into these philosophical explorations, the religious framework I'd been raised in became less central to my thinking.

* * * * *

Life in the Experimental College was unique. We all lived and took classes in Cooper Center, formerly an all-girls' dorm. Providing one of the few co-ed living arrangements on campus at the time, the arrangement presented some interesting situations. The girls' 11:00 p.m. curfews led to amusing scenarios where we'd help latecomers sneak in through our ground-floor windows. I'll never forget the fun we all had, waving goodnight to their boyfriends who failed to get them back to the dorm in time. They sure didn't like to see their girlfriends crawling into some other guy's room.

My involvement in campus life expanded when I was elected as our dorm's representative to the school senate. Lloyd became my unofficial campaign manager, taking numerous black and white photos with his 35mm camera for posters proclaiming "VOTE LARSEN." The snapshots, which were attached to the posters, had all disappeared by the time we went around to collect the signs after the election—I was considered cute in those days! My looks, Lloyd's advertising skills and debate points I learned from a senior classman in the school government crowd named David Cowen all helped me get elected.

My foray into student government led to another unexpected adventure, including a free trip to Lubbock, Texas for a conference at Texas Tech University. There, I was mesmerized by a student folk singer named Lisa Gates, who performed at a concert on the last night of the event. She really got my attention when she broke a string on her guitar and said, "Ah, Fuck!" right into the microphone.

After the show, I hung around the back of the auditorium and got to meet Lisa and her manager, another woman at the school. They could tell I was infatuated with Lisa and allowed me to buy them a couple of drinks at a local bar and follow them home. They made up a bed for me on their couch. The next morning, Lisa and her manager had to leave for Dallas, Lisa's hometown, where she had a performance the following day. I talked them into taking me with them on the five-hour ride, abandoning the motorcoach that was leaving to drive the student representatives back to Minnesota.

Lisa's mother wasn't as tolerant of me as her manager in Lubbock had been. I was soon deposited on Interstate 35 so I could hitchhike home. How stupid was this? Here I was, a 19-year-old, long-haired kid, wearing an army surplus Airforce jacket with an upside-down American flag sewn on the back, hitchhiking through Texas in 1969. The I-35 artery was a mainstay for over-the-road truckers. One way to stay awake was to talk to someone, and picking up a hitchhiker was an easy way to do that. I made it back in one piece, albeit it by a somewhat circuitous route.

Somewhere between Oklahoma City and Wichita, a Top 40 cover band on a touring bus picked me up. Riding with them was contingent on my helping them with their gear. How hard could that be? The band mainly played at high school proms, and it was great fun to stand at the control board and watch them play tunes from Credence Clearwater Revival, The Guess Who, Three Dog Night, Jay and the Americans, Blood Sweat and Tears, Tommy James and many more.

It wasn't as much fun unloading the bus and hauling their gear into the venue, helping set it up and then, only a few hours later, tearing everything down, packing it all up, hauling it out of the venue and loading it back into the bus. Any aspirations I might have had to become a professional "roadie" soon evaporated.

After a few days with the band, I hitchhiked my way back to a truck stop on I-35 and found a trucker going all the way to Minneapolis. We got along great except he had to keep poking me awake so I could talk to him.

* * * * *

Drugs were everywhere in our dorm in the fall of 1969, which is when I had my first psychedelic trip. While I was told I was given magic mushrooms (Psilocybin), I suspect it was the cheaper LSD. The trip was fun, visually explosive with an amazing soundtrack, courtesy of my roommate's stereo system and record collection.

While briefly trying other popular mood-altering substances (pot, alcohol, speed and hash), the idea of changing my reality never really appealed to me. I felt most comfortable fully in control of my brain. By the end of my 20s, I abandoned nearly all drugs except for a cocktail before dinner or a couple of drinks at a party. This was the extent of my drug and alcohol use until 2016, when I adopted a vegan diet and stopped drinking alcohol altogether in preparation for open-heart surgery.

As I approached the end of my first year at Mankato, I found my-self at a crossroads. While the school kept its promise and gave me passing grades across the core curriculum for my year's work, enter-ing the traditional college the following year didn't sit well with me.

In my travels to anti-war rallies across the Midwest, I encoun-tered my first real "Jesus Freaks" in Minneapolis. At the time, "freak" wasn't a derogatory term, it was just a neutral modifier for a specific area of interest.

This group was proselytizing at the rally I was at, and they in-vited me to visit them in Iowa City where they lived in a commune. After spending a day or two with them at their home base, I decided to stay: I absolutely loved the lifestyle. While certainly Christian, they'd adopted a hippie-like, back-to-the-land, love-and-peace vibe. Not only that, they also promoted a new and far more radical inter-pretation of Jesus' message. The group read and lived by *Good News for Modern Man*, a 1966 translation of the New Testament written in modern English. Since Jesus and his disciples didn't hold established religious entities of their day in much respect, neither did they.

Jesus had said, "Sell what you have and give it to the poor, and come, follow me." We took that to heart, and ridiculed Christians who failed to follow these clear and precise instructions. Of course, this is a far easier command to follow when you're a college dropout with no money, no possessions and no home.

Just short of a year with the group, I backed away and en-rolled at Rochester Junior College, now the University of

Minnesota—Rochester. I loved the classes, joined the theater program and got the lead in an avant-garde play. I graduated with excellent grades and an Associate Arts degree a year later.

When I graduated, the 1965 white Triumph Spitfire I bought
with my cousin John Gravley was all mine. Real life had started. For
the next 10 years my focus was on developing a career and figuring
out how to support myself, which is covered in the business section.

43

OVER THIS LAUNDRY, I THEE WED

I WORKED HARD TO MAKE my marriage proposal to Maggie as fairytale wonderful as possible. My best high school friend, Randy Larson, helped me find the perfect stone. Armed with this gem, I visited a jewelry store in Minnetonka's Ridgedale shopping center and chose an elegant setting for the engagement ring. To ensure the perfect fit, I secretly borrowed one of Maggie's rings and returned it before she noticed it was missing.

Anticipating the ring's completion, I made dinner reservations at Murray's—a famous steakhouse in downtown Minneapolis—for the upcoming Saturday night. I requested a quiet table in a romantic corner, envisioning a scene where witty banter and heartfelt expressions of love would culminate in the big question: "Will you marry me?"

There was one complication: Maggie's mother was visiting from out of town and staying in our condo that week. To maintain appearances, we separated our bedrooms, concealing any evidence of our shared sleeping arrangements.

On Thursday morning, the jeweler called to inform me that the ring was ready for pickup. Excitement coursed through me as I retrieved it during my lunch break. With the ring safely in my pocket, I could barely concentrate on work that afternoon. My resolve to wait until Saturday to pop the question was quickly crumbling.

Arriving home that evening, I found Maggie and her mother preparing dinner. After changing clothes and making small talk, I couldn't contain myself any longer. I asked Maggie if we could speak privately.

Realizing that either bedroom might raise suspicions with her mother, I led Maggie into the laundry room. There, standing atop a pile of dirty clothes, I fumbled the ring box from my pocket, thrust it toward her and blurted out, "Look what I got you!"

Maggie, seeing through my clumsy attempt, smiled and said, "Of course, I'll marry you. I thought you'd never ask." In that moment, surrounded by laundry and filled with joy, I knew I was the luckiest man on Earth. Many years later, I would learn that my future son-in-law would follow a similar approach during his proposal to ask my daughter Ginger for her hand in marriage.

John Gravley, me and Chuk Batko on my wedding day.

Paul Hagen, me, Chuk Batko and John Gravley. Paul had arranged a grand bachelor party at two of the best gay bars in Minneapolis.

Maggie's unwavering support has been a constant throughout our relationship. In early 1982, when I decided to pursue an MBA at the College of St. Thomas to enhance my business skills, she played a critical role.

Lacking a four-year degree, I needed to take the Graduate Management Admission Test (GMAT). What followed was a scheme I'm not proud of, but one in which Maggie reluctantly agreed to participate. As the superior test-taker in our family, Maggie took the GMAT under my name, while I took it under hers. The results speak for themselves: While "her" scores (actually mine) were passable, "my" scores (actually Maggie's) were stellar, securing my place in the program.

Little did we know that Maggie's assistance would extend far beyond the admissions process. My travel schedule often prevented me from attending classes, so Maggie would go in my stead, taking meticulous notes and reviewing them with me before exams.

Throughout our years together, Maggie has been instrumental in honing my academic and professional skills. Just as she did in the laundry room when I fumbled my proposal, Maggie has always had a knack for making me look better than I am. Her ability to smooth out my rough edges, both in life and in work, has been a constant source of strength in our relationship. Whether it's polishing my words or helping me navigate life's challenges, Maggie continues to be the force that elevates everything I do, turning my clumsy efforts into something beautiful—much like she transformed that impromptu laundry room proposal into the beginning of our wonderful life together.

44

UNDERWATER ADVENTURES: CLOSE CALLS IN PENNEKAMP

SEVERAL OF MAGGIE'S AND MY most engaging stories come from our shared SCUBA diving experiences. Many involve Maggie as a bug-eyed newbie, nearly dead from hypothermia, or as my surface-bound companion while I dove fearlessly below. However, one particular trip to Florida stands out, showcasing Maggie as the most fearless diver in our group.

To celebrate our first anniversary in March 1983, we planned a trip to the Florida Keys. As newly certified SCUBA divers, we were eager to explore the legendary John Pennekamp Coral Reef State Park near Key Largo. This underwater marvel, covering more than 175 nautical square miles of coral reefs, seagrass beds and mangrove swamps, is part of the only living coral reef in the continental United States. It's named after John Pennekamp, a Miami newspaper editor who helped establish the Everglades National Park.

After a night in Key Largo, we arrived at the dock early the next morning, joined by two MIT students on spring break. As we loaded our gear and sipped coffee, Maggie took her usual four Dramamine tablets—a precaution that would prove fortuitous.

As we set out, the captain warned us of an approaching weather front that might cut our trip short. As we headed for the dive spot about five miles from shore, we noticed the waves getting bigger as the boat shuddered about. At the dive site, we anchored in about 35 feet of water. Excited to escape the increasingly choppy surface, we descended into the colorful underwater world.

Our first dive was mesmerizing. The coral and vibrant fish were a far cry from what we saw in the lakes back home in Minnesota, and we enjoyed the ability to move freely in any direction in utter peace. Before we knew it, it was time to surface. I could make out the shadow of the boat on the ocean floor 100 yards from us, and we slowly swam in that direction.

We reached the anchor rope about the same time as our MIT companions and motioned for them to go up first. Although not all that deep, we made a slow ascent as we'd been trained to prevent possible nitrogen accumulation, which could cause decompression sickness.

We arrived on the surface near the rear of the boat where the ladder was located. While we were submerged, the wind had picked up a good bit and we noticed we were in three- or four-foot swells. Helping Maggie to the ladder, I watched as she attempted to time her climb into the boat.

It was difficult getting back into a 25-foot, bouncing dive boat. Imagine you're a rodeo cowboy, trying to get on (not off) a bucking bronco dancing around the corral. Oh, and by the way, you're wearing SCUBA gear, including flippers. Possible, yes. Easy? No!

Inside the boat, the two MIT students took turns tossing their lunches over the side. Once things had settled down, the boat captain looked at us and tentatively said, "Well, you all paid for two tanks, and I'll do whatever you want. Does everyone want to go down again, or shall we call it a day?"

The two MIT guys looked at me, their eyes conveying a desire to quit. Before I could say anything, Maggie exclaimed, "Sure, that was fun. I'll go down again," and looked at the three of us with a big smile. In retrospect, swallowing our pride and skipping the second dive would have been the more prudent option. But the gauntlet was thrown: How could three macho guys say no? We had no choice; we were doing another dive.

No sooner had we dropped to the bottom and our two diving friends headed off than I had the overwhelming urge to throw up. Remembering my training, I resisted my other urge to rip my regulator off my face, and just vomited through it, inadvertently creating a feeding frenzy for nearby fish.

When my air gauge showed less than a third of the tank remaining, I signaled to Maggie that we needed to return to the boat. However, we had a problem. The sun was no longer shining, and there were no shadows on the ocean floor. My mental map of the boat's location was seriously messed up. I looked around, hoping to spot an anchor rope. But there was none.

I motioned Maggie to remain on the bottom, and I rose to the surface to look around. Turning 360 degrees, I couldn't spot any boat. Just as I was about to panic, I realized that I needed to wait for a swell to lift me high enough to give me a better view around. Using this technique, I finally spotted the boat.

Submerging back to Maggie, I pointed in the direction we should go and headed that way. After swimming for about five minutes, however, the anchor rope still hadn't come into view. Back to the surface I went.

The boat was a bit closer this time, but it wasn't where I thought it would be because the underwater currents were moving us around. This time, as I descended from the surface, I kept my eyes on the anchor rope. Even though it faded, I had a good idea where it was. After another five minutes, we got there with our air gauges alarmingly low.

At the surface, we repeated the climbing-onto-the-bronco exercise, which was even more difficult than before as the waves were even higher. I don't think I've ever been happier to be in a boat. Maggie and I quickly got into our dry street clothes before we realized the other two guys hadn't come back yet. Fifteen minutes went by, and there was still no sign of our new MIT friends.

I felt panic for them. Where were they? While all this was happening, the Coast Guard radioed a warning about an impending storm heading right for us. Everyone was ordered to shore—Now!

I knew that if the MIT guys had been appropriately trained, they weren't at super high risk. It was just a matter of surfacing, inflating their buoyancy vests and waiting to be found. Even so, I was in shock when the captain suddenly announced, "I've waited long enough. We need to get off the water."

Maggie and I stared at the captain in disbelief. After 10 minutes of hightailing it to shore, the radio crackled out our captain's name and call sign.

"Go ahead," he said.

"You missing a couple of divers, JJ?" we heard a voice say on the radio.

"Yes," said our Captain.

"Don't worry, we've got them. See you at the dock."

Maggie has never hesitated to support my passion du jour, in this case, diving. She never learned to relax during our SCUBA outings, but she gave it a go every single time. On this particular day, she was better at it than the rest of us. But of course, she wasn't handicapped by a male ego!

45

DIAPERS, DISHES AND DADDY'S FIRST WORDS

THOSE COMMITTED TO EQUALITY IN the workplace, and in life, often forget how deeply ingrained our sexist outlook is and how it affects us daily. When I was in the delivery room with Maggie as our daughter Virginia was born, surrounded by female medical professionals, I was struck by the profound realization that my daughter would grow up in a world of possibilities, unhindered by gender constraints.

As Virginia emerged, I thought, "God help anyone trying to stand in the way of my daughter's being anything she'll ever want to be." I believed she'd grow up in a world where people were judged on their abilities, not their gender or skin color. But sadly, we still have a long way to go when it comes to achieving true equality.

In 1984, when Virginia was a baby, my stint as Vice President of Marketing at Open Systems ended. Since I was between jobs and we needed health insurance, Maggie returned to work at Control Data while I took on the role of stay-at-home dad.

Maggie wasn't entirely on board initially, but she warmed to the idea as she saw how eager I was to give it a shot. The movie *Mr. Mom*, starring Michael Keaton, had recently come out, and I thought, "Hell, why not? How hard could taking care of a single child be?"

Soon, Maggie was heading off to work while I took care of Virginia, who we nicknamed Ginny. What a fantastic opportunity for a dad and daughter to bond. She was coming up on her first birthday: She was perfect without exception and life was great.

Before I relate the events that occurred next, let me clarify two points: First, while in my mind this period lasted about a year, it was closer to three months. Second, I had been an involved father from the start, participating in pre-natal classes, the birth and early care. But this was different—I was now in charge, and I had never done all our family's laundry or been solely responsible for all our meal preparation.

My approach to full-time parenting was, shall we say, unique. I tackled it like a corporate reorganization. First, I overhauled Ginny's closet, meticulously washing and organizing every piece of clothing. As a first child, she received many clothing gifts from family members and friends, and we ended up with piles of hand-me-downs on top of all the new stuff. I emptied every drawer, washed and neatly folded every garment and returned it all to the bureau for safekeeping.

This led to an obsession with keeping her outfits clean, resulting in her spending most days in just a diaper and T-shirt. If the T-shirt got dirty, I could turn it inside out before Maggie got home. Thankfully, we were on the disposable diaper kick already.

Next came the kitchen. On one memorable day, I emptied all the cabinets, cleaned them thoroughly and reorganized everything to my exacting standards. The space was perfectly optimized: every plate, fork, bowl, pot and frying pan was precisely where it should be, although not exactly where Maggie thought they should be. But it was my kitchen now, and my exquisite new design was simply impeccable, in my opinion.

To maintain this perfection, I resorted to using paper plates and plastic utensils. I didn't want any dishes or glassware to ever come out again. Mess up my kitchen? Not on your life! In retrospect, this behavior mirrored my approach to business—I excelled at building and organizing, but often grew bored with day-to-day maintenance.

In my 40s, I was figuring out that I liked being a builder. I loved early-stage companies and deciding on their direction, refining their value propositions, constructing profitable models and creating and executing plans. I was very good at that and loved doing it. I once told a job interviewer, "If you want a bridge built, hire me. But once it's built, get someone else to take the tolls, paint it and maintain it."

Ginny and me, during my Mr. Mom phase.

After my key household goals were accomplished, which only took a few days, I focused on my daughter. I made sure I was getting her out for regular walks around the neighborhood, which was filled with other young families. Running into other homemakers was unavoidable, and eventually I was invited to a coffee klatch get-to-gether. Wow, what an eye-opener that was.

Each mother boasted about her child's exceptional achievements. "Lyle is so advanced, his doctor says he's never seen a boy at 10 months who can crawl as far and as fast as he does," one mom said.

Another chimed in, "My precious little Kathie is much more advanced. She was trying to put a dress on one of her dolls, and she's only seven months old."

Not to be outdone, my next-door neighbor added, "Little Buster is so far ahead of the other boys in his daycare, his teacher told me they've never seen a kid drinking from a sippy cup at that age."

I was amazed. Every one of their kids was in the top cohort, the upper 10%, or in some other way the most advanced child ever—longest, heaviest, most hair, earliest tooth, best motor skills, etc.

Eventually, the moms noticed that I hadn't said a word, and they tried to get me to open up. I was reluctant at first, but then I realized you couldn't have a top end of a scale without a bottom. I told them there was no doubt in my mind that Ginny was clearly retarded. "I think she's in the bottom third of everything they measure kids on," I admitted. "But she giggles well. She really is very good at giggling, although it doesn't seem that much different than other kids her age."

Needless to say, I wasn't invited back. But the neighborhood moms got their revenge by squealing on me to Maggie. They snitched and informed on every minor infraction as if it was catastrophically horrible. Jogging with Ginny on my shoulders or bringing her outside without mittens became scandals. Fortunately, Ginny herself became my best defense. Whenever confronted, I'd ask her, "Did Daddy and Ginny have fun?" Her enthusiastic response always cleared my name. We made a great team, and none of the charges ever stuck.

The day I got into real trouble started innocently enough. I had turned a room into an office directly across from the nursery, but the room was too small for the bookcases we had. So, I decided to move the bookcases into the larger family room. It seemed simple enough: Reach in, grab a bunch of books from a shelf, take them into the family room and pile them on the floor. Once the bookcases were empty. I planned to have Maggie help me move them to the family room and reload.

But what to do with Ginny while I was moving the books? I finally decided to set her up in her bouncy chair so she could sit, play and watch me. After a few trips I knew it would take me a long time to get it all done, so I started grabbing larger loads of books.

Soon, I'd emptied the lower shelves in one of the bookcases but I needed a step stool to reach the top shelves. As I was removing a rather large number of books in this position, the load collapsed and fell to the floor with a loud crash. "Oh Shit!" I exclaimed.

Ginny looked up at me, then down at the mess scattered across the floor. "Oh, Shit. Oh Shit, oh shit," she said gleefully, clear as a bell.

Now I was in trouble. How could I get Ginny to unlearn her new vocabulary? I picked up the fallen books and put them in the other room. Sensing Ginny's eyes on me, I got back up on the step stool and pretended to grab another armful of books and let them fall to the floor. I turned back to her and said, "Oh Shoot! Shoot, shoot!" I enunciated perfectly to make sure there was no mistake in understanding, turning my head from side to side in a look of dismay.

Looking up at me with a twinkle in her eye from her bouncy seat, she said, "Shit, shit, shit. Oh, Shit!"

I'm not sure how many days it was before I got nailed, but it wasn't many. Maggie was putting something away in the kitchen and bumped a cup from the counter onto the floor. Ginny, sitting in her highchair, looked at Maggie and triumphantly said, "Oh Shit! Oh shit, oh shit."

I was out on the deck when I heard Maggie call, "Steve, you better get in here right now!"

Yeah, I was toast. There was no witness for my defense this time. I told Maggie the entire story and she reluctantly forgave me, but not before reminding me how impressionable young brains can be.

Despite the mishaps, I loved my three months playing Mr. Mom. Caring for Ginny was important, and I always took it seriously. There was never a point when I put her in any real danger, although I'm sure I did things most first-time mothers might not do. But mostly, I remember the two of us laughing a lot and having fun.

This experience taught me that parenting isn't about perfection—it's about presence, love and the willingness to learn and adapt. While my methods may have raised a few eyebrows, the bond Ginny and I formed during this time has remained strong throughout her life. And perhaps, in its own way, my unconventional approach to fatherhood was a small step toward challenging traditional gender roles, even if I didn't realize it at the time.

46

THE PIRATE FINGER PAYOFF

DURING OUR EIGHT-YEAR STINT IN Pasadena beginning in the mid-1980s, our home became the go-to spot for Thanksgiving, and occasionally Christmas, gatherings for Maggie's sister and the Stickney family. We loved hosting Diana, Joe and their children, and Ginny relished having her Arizona cousins on her own turf. As the "crazy-but-fun uncle," I was always looking for new ways to entertain and amaze the kids.

In 1990, with Robert (10), Maria (8), Ginny (6), and Isaac (4) at the perfect ages, I conceived a prank that I hoped would become an unforgettable memory. They'd already seen all my magic tricks, played with the remote-control truck, gone on wagon rides and watched me perform every imaginable trick with our sweet Rottweiler, Heidi. It was time for something extraordinary.

At the dinner table on Thanksgiving Day, I began sowing the seeds of my elaborate ruse. "Did you know," I asked casually, "that one of my great uncles was a pirate?" I spun tales of buried treasure and walking the plank to capture their young imaginations. The adults' eyes rolled skyward, but they played along.

The kids had lots of questions about pirate life, and I was happy to improvise plausible answers to their eager inquiries. When dessert was served, I gently set the hook. "My uncle gave my dad a memento of his days on the high seas—a finger from a dead pirate," I said nonchalantly. "My dad passed it on to me, but I'm not sure where it is now. Maybe in the garage somewhere. It's a proper sight to behold, a genuine finger from a dead pirate." Then I fell silent, letting their imaginations run wild.

It didn't take long for Robert to take the bait. "Uncle Steve, do you think you could find the dead pirate's finger and show us?" The other children quickly chimed in, pleading for me to search for this macabre relic. I demurred, claiming it was probably long lost, but their persistence grew with each passing minute.

After dinner the children returned to playing, and I could still hear them talking about the dead pirate's finger. Fifteen minutes wouldn't go by before one of them would bring it up again. Soon, they were all after me once more. "Uncle Steve, can you at least look for the finger?"

Little did they know, I had meticulously prepared for this moment. The day before, I'd crafted a convincing prop: an old matchbox filled with discolored cotton balls, dirtied with brown shoe polish. I'd cut a finger-sized hole in the bottom, allowing me to insert my own finger, disguised as the pirate's dead digit.

As the children's excitement peaked, I excused myself to the bathroom, where I coated my middle finger with iodine, giving it a convincingly dead, yellowish-brown appearance. Returning to the eager crowd, I made a show of searching the garage. The kids crowded around me as I opened drawer after drawer but found nothing. I kept up a steady dialog of, "Well, I haven't seen that thing in years. I'm almost certain it's lost."

They persisted, "Keep looking, Uncle Steve. It has to be here somewhere!"

Finally, I opened the bottom drawer of my ancient tool bench where I'd hidden the old matchbox. "Ah, there it is," I said, pointing to it. They all recoiled in horror. I suspect they believed we wouldn't actually find it.

"Who wants to pick it up?" I asked, knowing full well none would volunteer. They all screamed, yelled and jumped around in place, saying, "No, no, you pick it up, Uncle Steve. Show us, you show us the finger!"

I reached down into the drawer, carefully using my body for cover, and inserted my grotesque-looking finger covered in dried iodine into the bottom of the box. "Well, I hope it's still in here," I said, extending the box toward them. The young ones hung back, but Robert and Ginny leaned eagerly forward toward the box, but not too close. As I slowly slid the cover off the box, the kids' reactions upon seeing the grody finger were priceless—a symphony of gasps, screeches and morbid curiosity.

Finally, I said to Robert, "Do you want to touch it?"

At first he screamed, "No, no, no..." but then when his little brother Isaac said he'd do it, Robert decided to go first.

Ginny and Maria were horrified. They wanted nothing to do with this dead pirate's finger, but they couldn't stop staring at it. I held the box out to Robert as the others gathered close around and behind him.

Robert crept slowly forward and carefully reached out with his hand, one quivering finger tentatively extended to make contact. When Robert's finger was just an inch from the finger in the box, and when every kid's eyes were glued to what was happening, I quickly raised my iodine-stained digit—the dead finger had come alive!

You can only imagine the frantic choreography that occurred next. Robert perfectly mimicked a cartoon character jumping up, turning around in mid-air, and frantically spinning his feet while not going anywhere. When Robert's legs finally got traction, he shot out of the garage, screaming at the top of his lungs. His brother, sister and cousin raced out behind him. They tore down the driveway, screaming at the top of their lungs, not stopping until they were nearly out of sight.

As the adults rushed out to investigate the commotion, they found me doubled over with laughter on the front steps, while the children stood halfway down the driveway, pale as ghosts.

Creating experiences that instill memory treasures in the minds of my nieces, nephews, kids and grandkids has always been one of my greatest joys. I hope my nephews remember this little trick and use it appropriately when their sons, daughters, nieces and nephews are old enough.

47

SKI SLOPE HUBRIS: A LESSON IN HUMILITY

IN 1984, WHILE I WAS working for AT&T, I extended a business trip to Colorado for a couple days of skiing. My choice of Hidden Valley Resort, a local favorite just outside Estes Park, led to a perfect storm of bravado, stupidity, chauvinism and hubris, all culminating in one unforgettable day.

Open from 1955 to 1991, Hidden Valley was a modest resort with an impressive, 2,000-foot vertical drop. It offered a mix of beginner, intermediate, expert and what I'd call "insane" trails. The resort's charm lay in its accessibility and affordability, with $10 daily lift tickets attracting skiers looking to avoid the pricier resorts along I-70. Olive green, canvas-covered army trucks (replaced by school buses by the time I visited) transported the more adventure-oriented skiers to the upper valley, where tow ropes took them to the top of the mountain, allowing a downhill rush through pine groves and powder.

Having not skied in several years, I wisely started my day with a lesson. Soon enough, with an excellent instructor and attentive practice, I felt I had regained my "mid-to-pretty-good intermediate" skills and confidently hit the slopes.

After a morning on the green runs and early afternoon perfecting my technique on the blues, I felt invincible. Post-lunch, fueled by a quick bowl of chili and an inflated sense of ability, I spotted a school bus marked "Upper Valley." Without much thought, I stowed my rented skis and hopped aboard. It wasn't until the bus started moving that I noticed the ominous sign above the driver: "This bus goes only to black diamond and double black diamond slopes—Expert skiers ONLY!"

My mind raced during the 15-minute ride. Pride prevented me from backing out in front of the all-male group of other riders. Besides, I reasoned, I'd survived black diamond runs before. While my performance on those advanced runs might not have been graceful, I got down and never once died. How bad could it be?

At the top, our small group disembarked with an unspoken sense of camaraderie. I followed as we traversed a ridge with an increasingly steep drop-off. One by one, skiers peeled off down the slope. I kept following the guy in front of me, hoping for an easier route that never materialized. As hard as it was to comprehend, the further we went along the ridge the steeper the drop-off became.

With just three of us left, we reached the end of the ridge. Any hope of a gentler slope vanished as we faced a T-Bar leading further up into a thick white mist. Running out of options and terrified of the sheer cliff to my right, I followed my remaining companions up to what I later learned was ominously named "Tombstone Ridge."

Arriving at the top, it felt as if we were close to the summit. My two friends quickly disappeared into the thick fog covering the slope below, while the wind picked up. It was late afternoon, and I was wearing skis at the top of a mountain. Everyone was gone. Thoughts of ski resort employees finding me in the spring alternated with my mumbling to myself, "Don't panic. Just take it one step at a time."

Ironically, the poor visibility became my salvation. I couldn't see the terrifying drop, but I could make out a mid-sized pine tree across the slope. I aimed for it, using its wide branches to break my momentum. Miraculously, it worked. More importantly, I saw a similar-looking tree on the other side of the slope from my new vantage point, only a little further down. I proceeded to ski directly into it as before, using the branches to slow my rapidly accelerating pace and break my fall.

I crashed from one evergreen sanctuary to another, getting slightly skinned up in the process. It was exhausting, but I wasn't dying.

While recovering and gathering energy in the embrace of yet another tree, out of the mist came the savior for which I'd secretly been praying. A skier in the distinctive uniform of the Ski Patrol was headed in my direction. "Oh, thank God, I'm saved," I thought.

As the patroller expertly skied up to me, I was struck by another realization: it was a woman. When she asked me if I needed any help, my bruised male ego took over and I heard myself say, "No, I'm fine, just catching a breather." She smiled (or was it a smirk?), adjusted her gloves and skied off, leaving me to confront my own idiocy.

For what felt like hours (but was likely only 15 minutes), I continued my arboreal descent until I reached an ice-covered half-pipe. With no trees to aim for, I resorted to the ultimate surrender of dignity: I sat down, removed my skis and slid down on my backside.

Emerging at the bottom of the trough, I saw a sign showing a list of runs heading off in different directions. The most beautiful sight on that sign was a blue diamond, indicating an intermediate slope, and an arrow pointing to my left. Thirty minutes later I reached the base of the mountain, alive but humbled.

This experience, while not my first or last brush with misguided machismo, served as a potent reminder of the dangers of overconfidence. It highlighted not just my physical limitations but also the unconscious biases that led me to dismiss help based solely on gender.

Today, I view this experience as both a cautionary tale and a source of rueful amusement. It stands as a testament to the learning opportunities that come from our most embarrassing moments, provided we're willing to examine them honestly. As I continue navigating life's slopes, I strive to approach challenges with a better balance of confidence and caution, always mindful of the lessons learned on that misty mountain in Colorado.

48

GINGER TAKES CONTROL

WHEN OUR DAUGHTER GINNY BEGAN first grade in Pasadena, her teacher—the unwitting villain in this story—set in motion a series of events that would forever change our family dynamic. I could have called this chapter "When I Learned I'd Lost and Would Never Win Again—Ever," but that's a bit wordy and pessimistic, even if it's not far from the truth.

Like most parents, Maggie and I agonized over naming our child. We chose not to learn our baby's gender beforehand, maintaining two lists of potential names. For a girl, we considered Virginia Ruth, honoring both Maggie's grandmother Virginia and my mother Ruth. I was particularly fond of the nickname "Ginny," inspired by a beloved high school classmate of mine. Everyone loved her. She was in the choir and the theater and worked on the school yearbook. Bubbly, outgoing and full of energy, I thought Ginny would be a great nickname for my daughter. But first, she had to be born and her gender identified.

Maggie's obstetrician added an element of humor to our anticipation. He had a long-standing habit of confidently predicting each patient's baby's gender at their first appointment, long before it could be accurately determined. Here we were, at week four or five, and he was telling us with authority that Maggie would be having a boy. He even wrote his prediction down in Maggie's chart as he assured us of his 100% accuracy rate. We found it amusing but paid little attention, continuing our naming discussions for both possibilities.

As the weeks and months progressed, Maggie and I got into child prep big time. We took prenatal childbirth classes every Tuesday for several weeks with other expectant parents. I learned how to be a coach, what to expect and how not to freak out in the delivery room. We bought a crib, baby clothes and supplies. Our friend, Chuk Batko, painted the walls of a small bedroom with a truly incredible kid's mural for boys and girls alike.

Right after dinner on March 13, 1984, Maggie said she was feeling odd and rightfully predicted this might be the night. At around 10:00 p.m., as we were getting ready for bed, her water broke. No panic: we were ready even though it was two weeks before her due date. We got to the hospital just before midnight. I won't describe the 12-hour labor process, but I'm sure Maggie remembers every minute. The important thing was that our daughter was born around 1:00 p.m. on March 14. And as soon as we met her, we knew immediately that we'd call her Virginia.

All the anxiety I had over how—or if—I would love this new little human evaporated in an instant. The second I saw her, my heart stopped and I stood agape. The nurse repeated over and over to me, "Dad, Dad, hey Daddy, do you want to hold your daughter?"

Maggie couldn't wait to tell the doctor that he'd been wrong about his gender prediction, perhaps for the first time in his career. She was quick to bring it up as soon as she saw him for her first post-delivery visit. He scratched his head and said, "No, no, that doesn't sound right. I'm sure I said you'd have a girl."

When Maggie protested, he said, "Hold on, no need to argue. I think I wrote it down. Let's check your chart." He flipped back a few pages, and there it was, written clearly and indisputably: Sex = Girl.

"I told you, I'm right 100% of the time," he said.

Perplexed, Maggie paid her bill and the woman at the counter asked her what she was shaking her head about. Maggie explained what had just happened. The office manager said, "Oh, he pulled that on you, too?"

Maggie looked at her quizzically.

"When he predicts the sex of the baby, he always writes the opposite of what he says," the woman continued. "If he guesses correctly, no one ever asks to see the chart. But if he guesses wrong and the chart is checked, it always proves he's right!"

They both had a good laugh over it. Personally, I was delighted at the creativity of the doctor, using the "long game" to create a fun experience for his patients.

Fast forward to the school in Pasadena where Ginny began first grade. It was an old school in a neighborhood of mostly retired people, so the school district hadn't staffed it with their best or most dedicated teachers.

In visits to our daughter's classroom, Maggie found the teacher playing cartoon videos for the kids as she napped at her desk in the back of the room. Maggie's complaints to the principal hadn't endeared her to the teacher, and sometimes the woman took it out on our kid.

Several times, Ginny came home from school complaining that when her teacher was angry at her she would call her Jennifer Larsen. "Get back to your desk and sit down right now, JENNIFER!" the teacher would yell at her.

"Mom," Ginny complained, "She thinks my full name is Jennifer, and I'm Jenny for short. But my name is Virginia, and everyone calls me Ginny. How can I stop her from calling me Jennifer?"

Always attentive and pragmatic, Maggie explained that Virginia has many good nicknames, just like Margaret, Maggie's given name. Besides Ginny, she could be Virgie, Gina, Ginger, Geena or Gigi, among others. She didn't get far past "Ginger" when Ginny said, "Wait, my nickname could be Ginger?"

Maggie said, "Yes," and Ginny beamed. She'd been watching *Gilligan's Island* on TV, and the character Ginger was clearly her favorite. "Okay," she said, "From now on, I want everyone to call me Ginger. That's my new name."

The next several weeks went by with her politely and patiently correcting people who called her Ginny, telling them her name was now Ginger. One night in bed, Maggie mentioned that our daughter had noticed I was still calling her Ginny and had asked her what to do about it.

I explained to Maggie that I liked the nickname Ginny. It was okay if everyone else called her Ginger and I still called her Ginny. "Lots of dads have a pet name for their daughters that aren't shared with everyone else," I reasoned. "It's like a special dad-daughter thing. Sort of nice, don't you think?"

Maggie said, "Maybe, but I think you're just not trying."

I shrugged it off.

The turning point came one evening as I was decompressing after work with a cocktail and the newspaper. Ginny wiggled her way onto my lap, stuck her legs over one of my arms and leaned her shoulders against my other arm. I did my best to continue reading my paper and ignore her. She just lay in this position, looking up at me, not saying a thing. Finally, I looked down into her face and drawled, "Y . . .e . . .s?"

She looked me in the eye and said, "Daddy, by now, everyone else is calling me Ginger, but not you. I really prefer Ginger, Dad." And she stopped, saying nothing more. Her steady, unblinking gaze left no room for argument.

What could I do or say? My mind went blank. I stared at her for a long time, then gulped and said, "Okay, I'll try."

She gave me a big grin and a little squeeze and said, "Thanks, Dad, I love you." Then she hustled off my lap and was gone.

I sat stunned. Of course, she had won. I never even got to drag out any of my arguments for continuing to call her Ginny. And perhaps more importantly, for the first time, something else dawned on me: It was her determination and persistence. Maybe even stubbornness? She was only six and I marveled at her ability to adapt her tactics to get what she wanted—especially from me. It was a pivotal moment in our relationship, one that foretold many future negotiations.

Many years later, one night halfway through dinner, teenage Ginger announced that she was going to be a vegetarian. "I'm not eating meat anymore," she said, pushing a half-eaten piece of meat to the side of her plate.

After Ginger left the table, Maggie asked, "Oh dear, how long do you think this phase will last?"

"I've got some bad news," I replied. "I've heard that voice before. She won't change her mind, so you better get out the vegetarian cookbook."

Thirty years later, she's still a vegetarian and everyone—including me—calls her Ginger.

While I still look back with contempt on "Mrs. What's-Her-Name," the teacher who was too disrespectful to my child to learn her name correctly and who instigated the argument I lost to a six-year-old, the experience taught me that parenting isn't about always being right or maintaining control. Sometimes, it's about listening to our children, respecting their choices and adapting alongside them. Ginger's insistence on her new name wasn't just about a preference; it was her first step in asserting her identity and independence.

I learned that losing an argument to your child isn't always a defeat. Sometimes, it's the beginning of a new, more mature relationship. And while I may playfully grumble about never winning again, the truth is that seeing Ginger grow into a strong, self-assured woman has been the greatest victory of all.

Virginia and me, about the time she became "Ginger."

49

A LIFE TOO BRIEF: A TRIBUTE TO ERIC MCKINLEY LARSEN

OUR SON, ERIC MCKINLEY, WAS born on September 28, 1990. His arrival was a wonderful surprise, at least for me. While the decision to have our first child, Virginia, had been consciously thought about and extensively planned, it seemed that Eric came onto the scene a lot more suddenly.

I'd recently left my job in Los Angeles. It had been an exceptionally demanding time for AT&T, and my role put me under a great deal of stress. This behemoth corporation was trying to transition from an old way of doing business, which it knew a lot about and was good at, to a new way in which it knew very little. I'd inadvertently sabotaged my efforts early on, but this was only part of the problem.

I was inexperienced and naïve enough not to fully understand the duplicitous nature of some senior managers, who worked behind the scenes to undermine efforts that may have upset the status quo. When we had some success, it ultimately cost me my job.

Fortunately for me, IBM came along with a brand-new idea and a need for someone with my skills, right in LA. I was only six months into this new job when Maggie announced she was pregnant. To me, it felt like Eric was born only a few weeks later, just two days before my 40th birthday.

What a neat present! It was so cool and wonderful to welcome a new little guy to our family. We all loved him instantly. But it wasn't more than a week before we learned something wasn't right.

The Hospital Journey

As I left for work one morning, Maggie told me she and Eric would go in for his one-week check. She wasn't happy with how Eric was doing. Babies should thrive at this age, and she felt he was eating too little and sleeping too much.

Early that afternoon, she called me at work and asked me to meet her at Huntington Hospital's pediatric department immediately. They were concerned about Eric. Soon, we were conferring with doctors Edgardo Arcinue and Ricardo Flores, along with pediatric heart specialist William Vincent.

By the time I arrived, Dr. Flores had examined Eric and was concerned. He wanted to admit Eric into the pediatric intensive care unit (ICU) right away. He determined that Eric's heart wasn't functioning correctly, and they needed to get him stabilized and conduct more tests.

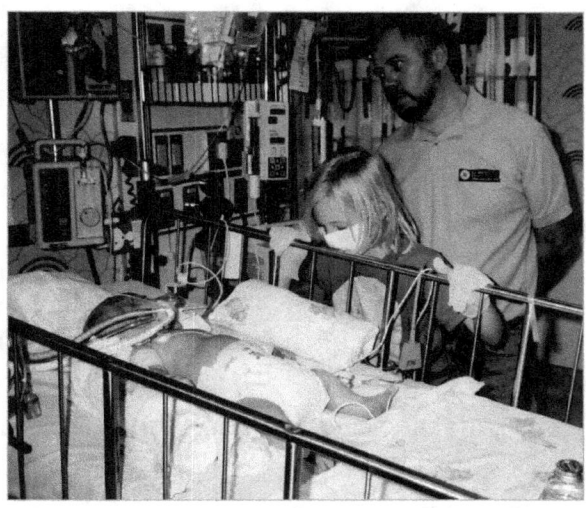

Eric in the ICU, heavily sedated after heart surgery.

By the next day, Dr. Arcinue and Dr. Vincent were intensely involved. Little did we know this ICU would be Eric's home (when he wasn't out having heart surgery) for the next 13 months.

For nearly two years, a day didn't go by without speaking to one of these doctors. Saying this is a long story would be a massive understatement, as Eric's battle to live was epic. The hard copy medical files we keep fill two enormous boxes.

Let me summarize what could be thousands of pages into just a few. Eric would spend days, sometimes even weeks, in a near coma, extremely sick, his life hanging by a thread. Then he would transition to long periods of "getting better," weeks when all the news was upbeat and he eagerly and joyfully interacted with all of us: parents, nurses and staff.

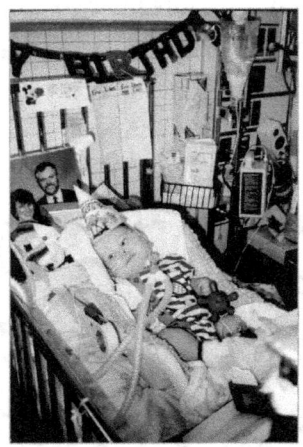

Eric celebrated his first birthday in the ICU at Huntington Hospital.

On his best days, we'd dress him up and he'd tour the hospital and grounds. During one of these periods, he had surgery to repair his heart defects. And then, one day, it happened: he was released to go home with us—with full-time, 24-hour nursing support, of course, as he was still on oxygen. Just over a year in the ICU, and he was alive and coming home!

Coming Home

After a year when Eric had spent 365+ days in pediatric intensive care and survived two "do or die" heart surgeries, he was home and on the road to full recovery. Eric's progress was rapid and remarkable after this incredibly rough start.

In fact, Eric thrived in an almost superhuman way at home. Leaving the hospital at 14 months old, his stunted physical development made him appear much younger. Once home, however, Eric started growing like a weed. He went on wagon rides around the neighborhood and through trails in the mountains, pulled along by his sister, Ginger, or our Rottweiler, Heidi. We took him to a week-long outing to a cabin in Big Bear, California, and he had a ball.

Our memories of Eric revolve primarily around this time at home, seeing him as a happy, bubbly smiling little kid who charmed everyone he saw. It was like he had magic powers. He once wrapped a stoic and hardened group of firefighters around his tiny fingers. He and I would sit at the kitchen counter, reading the Sunday paper. He loved the colorful funnies; however, he was unclear about which part was at the top and which was at the bottom.

Eric loved tours of our Pasadena neighborhood in his wagon, pulled by his sister Ginger or Heidi, the dog.

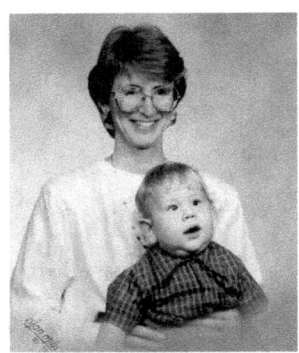

Eric and Maggie, not too long before he died.

His legs weren't developing as fast as some of the other bones in his body, so for several months he wore a brace. The doctor who fitted them at first said Eric might need to wear them for life and, perhaps when fully grown, need the help of a wheelchair to get around.

You can imagine the impression we made on that doctor as we grinned and said, "That's it? That's the downside? He might live his life in a chair? NO BIG DEAL! We can deal with that. Hell, we thought you might have had terrible news for us."

There's no doubt in my mind that this leg diagnosis would have devastated most parents. But we weren't most parents. This doctor didn't know he was talking to parents who'd repeatedly heard statements like, "We don't think he'll make it through the weekend; this is a hazardous procedure." Or "He's failing—do you want us to call someone to perform last rites?" Or "We're worried; you might want to let your daughter say goodbye to her brother."

We heard all this and more, but Eric always came through. His will to live was phenomenal. He repeatedly survived situations where every single one of his caregivers—doctors, nurses, surgeons—had written him off. One time, they even accidentally poisoned him with a 10X overdose of his antibiotic—another near-death experience—but he recovered and thrived.

Maggie and I never gave up hope. Parents don't. We never stopped believing he'd come home and live a normal life. Having him home was a relief, even with supplemental nursing care. Eric found security in his braces; he used them to push himself into a genuine crawl. He looked kind of funny, moving crablike and noisily across the floor. The braces helped him sit upright, and he especially enjoyed doing so in his wagon. The braces caused him to need help getting turned over in his crib, but he rarely complained.

Less than six months into the braces odyssey, Eric had another series of X-rays and the doctor couldn't believe what happened. The X-rays indicated that Eric's legs were coming back into shape, and that the braces could be removed in a few weeks. The doctor saw no reason why Eric wouldn't eventually walk, run and kick a football, just like a normal kid.

Were we thrilled? Of course! What parent wouldn't be overjoyed at this news? While not having to wear braces made Eric and all of us delightfully happy, don't forget the real lesson here. We would have been perfectly happy if he'd been in a wheelchair the rest of his life—and still would be—if only we could have him alive.

Once Eric was home and thriving, he and I loved breakfast with the Sunday funnies. He liked all the colors.

The Final Surgery

At a checkup when he was 20 months old, our doctors recommended elective heart surgery for Eric. It wasn't a requirement. He would be fine for the near term, but if we didn't do it now, he'd likely need the surgery in his mid-teens. Eric's recovery had been so solid, he was so advanced and strong, that the doctors felt he would tolerate the procedure easily. Given that Prodigy wanted me to move to New York, we thought it best to have the surgery done in Los Angeles by doctors who were familiar with his case.

In retrospect, this was a big mistake. Not by us, but by one of Eric's doctors, a cardiologist who shared a practice with Eric's primary cardiologist. He was on the fringes of Eric's host of caregivers from the beginning, and he was absolutely full of himself. Neither Maggie nor I were ever comfortable around him.

We always tried to have another doctor we knew and trusted supervising Eric's care, not this man. Sometimes it couldn't be avoided, and we were always on pins and needles until he was no longer the one in charge. We also made a habit of rigidly making sure this doctor knew what he could and couldn't do, including a prohibition on making any unilateral changes. Early on, under his own volition, he'd changed one of Eric's medications and it had been a disaster.

Eric came through this last surgery with flying colors. The surgeon, visiting with us after the surgery, was so thrilled to operate on a "fully-functioning," strong little boy and not the high-risk baby she'd operated on a year earlier.

They fixed what needed fixing and Eric was doing great. Maggie and I stayed at the hospital until early evening. I left first, but Maggie wouldn't leave Eric's side until he rested peacefully and all was well. She finally came home to a late dinner I prepared.

Even though our least favorite doctor was in charge of the surgical recovery area, we felt it was a low-risk situation. Eric's primary doctors had provided emphatic written and verbal instructions to do nothing. Under no circumstances was he to attempt to extubate Eric (remove his endotracheal tube) or take him off the ventilator. He was to allow Eric to sleep through the night, so they could assess his progress in the morning and determine next steps.

Less than two hours after Maggie left Eric, in the middle of our dinner, a nurse from the hospital called and said we needed to come back to the hospital right away. My heart stopped. I knew even before we began racing down the 110 Freeway to the hospital that they had let him die.

My heart still was dead as we entered the intensive care surgery recovery area. I knew from looking at all the faces and seeing them doing CPR on Eric that it was just for show. He was gone and I nearly died myself right then.

But anger quickly took over, and I attacked the doctor who had decided to extubate Eric. I was genuinely trying to kill him and had to be restrained. This doctor had gone against the written orders in the chart, killing my son through his arrogance. My heart may not have actually stopped that night, but it was broken. And, in so many ways, it's never healed.

Telling Ginger

Driving home, my first thought was how to tell Ginger. She'd always been a huge part of Eric's life. She visited him in the ICU, brought him toys and cried when he wasn't doing well. Once he came home, the two of them were inseparable.

Imagine you're the father of a bright, happy eight-year-old girl who adores her baby brother. She spends every spare minute at home with him on a blanket in the carpeted living room, playing with him. She pushes his brace-girded legs back and forth to strengthen them, so he'll soon be able to walk, run and play. She pulls him all over the neighborhood in a red wagon. If she's awake, she's by his side.

You send your daughter to a Boys & Girls Club camp for the week her brother is scheduled for surgery. With both parents so focused on her brother, her care might be neglected. Her brother is finally strong and healthy enough to fix his heart defect once and for all. Maybe it's best if she spends time in the mountains with a hundred other kids, taking hikes, playing games and having an adventure all her own.

Then imagine the unthinkable, your son dies after the surgery. After a night of screaming and sobbing, you know this event, this horrible blow to the family, must be faced together. You get in the car with your heartbroken wife and drive the two hours to the camp in the mountains to find your daughter and tell her that her brother is dead.

What is going through your head as you park your car in the camp parking lot, two days before the camp is scheduled to end? Are you as numb thinking about this as we were when we walked to the small office and told the camp director we had to take Ginger home early due to a family emergency?

Then you're walking with your wife to a large play area filled with happy children. You spot your daughter, and she quickly sees you. She comes running, confused at why you're there, but still happy anyway. Until, of course, you tell her why you're there early to pick her up.

You thought your crying over the last 12 hours had used up all your tears, but no. Not when you're in a group of three devastated people, holding each other in a circle, desperate for the horrible pain to go away, to somehow get a re-do.

We got home, somehow, and family began arriving the next day. Funeral arrangements were hastily made. The three of us sleep-walked through the memorial service, and it would be years before our happy, outgoing, secure little girl would make her way back to us.

Living with Loss

Our morose and grief-stricken family made our scheduled move to New York. In a way it was a blessing, because being in Pasadena was just too painful. To this day it's hard for us to drive through that area of Los Angeles when visiting friends.

As a family, we were shell-shocked for several years. Ginger had lost her only sibling (at time) and had a huge part of her life stolen from her. Maggie and I eventually began to stabilize, individually finding our footing as we emerged from a long, dark tunnel of anguish.

But it became more and more difficult for Ginger. All the standard resentments she felt about a new child in the family, a sick child who harvested 100% of our attention, had come down on her after his passing like a heavy, impenetrable cloud.

We finally found help for her from a marvelous therapist, Dr. Colette Geary, who brought Ginger slowly and beautifully back—not only from talk of suicide but back to us. Like a tiny miracle, each slowly emerging glimmer of light allowed us to begin to heal. Joy and laughter found a place alongside our loss and loneliness.

In September 1994, on what would have been Eric's fourth birthday, Maggie gave Ginger and me a beautiful card with an image of a bird painted by artist Marvin Oliver, with a poem she had written inscribed on the inside:

On This Day
On this day, four years ago,
Our family grew from three to four.
For one, a brother, for two, a son—
For each, a someone to adore.

At first, he looked like Ginger,
Red-tinted hair and ten small toes.
His "baby blues" were much the same
And, like her, he had Steve's nose.

Unlike Ginger, though, his heart
Was born not trouble-free.
It changed us, each in different ways
But we're still a family.

When Eric died a star went out
The sky is dimmer now
Though many stars still twinkle bright
It's not the same, somehow.

> *Precious is each child born*
> *Winning mothers with their charms*
> *And blessing fathers warm and kind*
> *Who comfort children in their arms.*

It was signed: "For Steve and Ginger, September 28, 1994, Margaret L. Larsen."

Then, in September 1997, Ginger wrote a letter to Eric for an English assignment:

September 25, 1997 - Wednesday

Dear Eric McKinley Larsen,

I'm writing this letter to you for an English assignment. Oh, and by the way, we don't live in New York anymore. About a month ago, we moved to Eden Prairie, MN. It's nice here. There are lots of bike paths. As you probably know, your birthday is coming up in 3 days. You're going to be 7.

Now, back to my assignment. For this assignment I'm supposed to tell you three things. The first thing is about a story my class read. It's called "Von." It's about a boy who escaped from Vietnam with his father to the U.S. When they got here, so many things changed for Von and his dad. Neither of them knew how to speak English, so it was very hard for them to communicate. They managed by speaking French and they had a French/English translator. Von had to start school here. It was very hard for Von, but he picked up on the English language quickly. After practice (and time) they fit right in. I don't believe Von ever saw his mom or siblings again.

Eric, you are one of the biggest influences on my life. You have helped me to become caring, sensitive, and loving. You've helped me learn how to share. Before you were born, I was a selfish, spoiled little brat. You came into the world with a smile. Sure, you had some heart, lungs and limb problems, but that didn't stop you. You were determined to show us (Mom, Dad and me) we could be happy if we tried.

We can make it through anything, as you did. When you left us, we were devastated. How could we ever live life without you?

You gave us so much. I realize now your last gift is the best of all. You proved to my family and me we really could live through whatever is thrown our way, not just operations, but loss. And all we have to do is stay together. You are on earth with us no more, but I know you are still here.

Eric, Thank you. Thank you for all you have taught me, all you have done for me. I know that there is no way I'll ever be able to repay you for that. I just want you to know how much I appreciate all you have given me.

Thanks again.

Love,
Ginger Larsen

P.S. Happy 7th Birthday!

Lessons and Legacy

Losing Eric was a tragedy impossible to describe. But every tragedy has silver linings. In May 2012, I was standing in line at a Starbucks on the corner of 7th Street and Thunderbird in Phoenix. There was a woman in line ahead of me. I didn't know who she was, but I couldn't stop staring at the tattooed lettering across her back. Was it from a movie, a poem or a song lyric? I couldn't tell. But I knew there was a story there.

As we waited for our drinks, I got enough courage to say, "Wow! That's some interesting artwork on your back."

She turned toward me and I watched her size me up, making an assessment and deciding how to respond. She looked directly into my eyes and said, "It's from a poem from St. John called *The Dark Night of the Soul*. It was applied with ink, mixed with the ashes of my dead daughter."

I paused, stunned, and as we stared at each other I teared up and mumbled, "Oh, I know something about what you feel. I'm so sorry for you. I lost my son."

Neither of us said anything more. I tried to talk but couldn't. My emotions overwhelmed me, and I couldn't say anything else. They called her name; she got her coffee and left the shop.

Later, she would write about this connection on Facebook. Someone saw it, thought it sounded like me and pointed me to it. Finding the Facebook posting, I learned her name was Joanne Cacciatore, and she and I ended up corresponding. We soon became friends. After our chance meeting, Cacciatore completed her doctoral thesis on the heartbreak experienced by parents who've lost a child and the best methods for dealing with this level of grief.

She started a non-profit organization called the MISS Foundation, of which I'm now on the board. Others do so much more than I do to help, but I love these people and what they do. If there are angels on Earth, they are here in this organization. In 2022, Joanne published a best-selling book called *Bearing the Unbearable: Love, Loss, and the Heartbreaking Path of Grief.*

A month after joining the MISS Foundation board, and three minutes into my first video conference with executive director Kelli Montgomery, I was startled. A four-year-old blonde child in a bright red sun dress clambered on the chair behind her mother. She thrust a ribbon into her mother's hair with all the skill of the average toddler. She sent fleeting glances toward the computer screen, which projected my voice and image.

Before our call, Alaina had played quietly in another area of the house. Realizing that her mother was on the phone and may no longer be immediately accessible to her every whim, however, she sprang into action.

Unable to ignore her, I soon asked Kelli if she'd introduce me to this beautiful young princess. After the introduction and a few minutes of conversation, including me holding our less-than-enthusiastic kitty, Gilda, up to the camera, we returned to our discussion. Alaina continued to make occasional benign efforts to intrude, but mostly settled down and played quietly in an overstuffed chair behind her mother.

Not until the next day did it sink in. I'd recently seen this same behavior—parents responding to the demands of a child in a way I hadn't expected and didn't seem customary. Kelli, typical of many who work with the MISS Foundation, had lost a child. Losing Madeleine, her firstborn daughter, affects how she interacts with Alaina, her living child.

I remember watching children and parents at my first MISS Foundation conference in Tempe, Arizona. The children didn't behave any differently from children anywhere else, but their parents sure did. I didn't observe a single frustrated parental outburst directed at rambunctious children. Parents seemed to drop to their knees automatically, look into the eyes of wayward or misbehaving children and mindfully listen to find the cause of the child's frustration.

Perhaps bereaved parents, those who've had their children die, view their living children differently. Do standards of behavior change? Are they now more forgiving? Do new expectations for their living children develop? Are they more likely to think, "You don't need to be on the winning soccer team anymore, or get the best grade in the class, or score the winning home run or get into the best college: you just need to live." I believe so.

When Eric died, our daughter Ginger lost her only brother and had a huge part of her life stolen from her. And, in retrospect, I saw that my sometimes overly critical approach to a lot of what she did fizzled out like a defective firecracker. It wasn't long before I altered my interactions with her.

As Ginger entered her pre-teen and teen years, when everyone expects children, especially girls, to become major problems, I was okay with most everything. At 14, when she became a vegetarian, I never tried to talk her out of it. Vegetarian? Hell, I thought, she could be a Presbyterian for all I care.

After college and in her 20s, Ginger told me, "None of my friends' parents are as supportive as you. I can't recall anything I've ever wanted to do that you didn't accommodate. Sure, when I told you I wanted to major in sexuality studies you weren't overly enthusiastic, but you kept sending me articles that applied to my research."

I'm now convinced that parents who lose a child change the way they relate to their living children. Research in this space is inadequate, and I've found no reputable studies on the topic. I've heard speculation that sometimes parents who lose a child make the mistake of either withdrawing from their remaining children or holding them too close.

The third option, loving their living children with intensity and passion and with total acceptance and appreciation, is not a mistake. It may be a way to become more effective as parents, and even those who've never lost a child can learn from it.

Parents expressing visible disappointment when a child's Little League team loses a game is common. Some parents lead their kids to believe that their love and approval is tied to an SAT score or their performance at a swim meet. I've heard parents berate kids for not getting the best score, earning the top grade or winning the highest achievement award.

As a parent who's lost a child, trust me, I'll gladly take the runner-up, the second best, the guys or girls who are eliminated in the hockey tournament in the first round. Hell, give me my son back and put him in last place; I'll take that in a heartbeat. I'd hold him and never let him go. Give me my son back and I promise not to let a day go by without telling him I love him.

Mandy Patinkin, in his role as Inigo Montoya in one of my favorite movies, *The Princess Bride*, approaches his climactic confrontation with the six-fingered villain, Count Rugen, by repeating the line,

"Hello. My name is Inigo Montoya. You killed my father. Prepare to die."

Once he has the upper hand, he commands Rugen to "Offer me money," then "Power, too. Promise me that," and finally, "Offer me everything I ask for!" Rugen repeatedly agrees and finally, desperately responds with, "Yes, anything you want."

Inigo runs his sword into Rugen's stomach and says, "I want my father back, you son of a bitch." I can't watch this delightful movie without tearing up at this scene, as the feeling Patinkin conveys is one that I know far too well.

Later in *The Princess Bride*, after Rugen is dead and Montoya has fulfilled his longest-held ambition, he confesses: "I have been in the revenge business so long, now that it's over, I do not know what to do with the rest of my life."

My anger at the doctor who went against specifically written and emphatic verbal instructions from Eric's heart doctor, his surgeon and his mother not to start a post-surgery procedure on our son has never left me. This arrogant doctor took it upon himself to do the procedure anyway, in the middle of the night on an unconscious and defenseless two-year-old boy, causing his death.

Most parents who've lost children struggle to find reasons to continue living, and not all of them do. A study, *Increased Mortality in Parents Bereaved in the First Year of Their Child's Life*, by Mairi Harper at the University of York in the UK[*], revealed that parents are twice as likely to die in the first 15 years following their child's death as parents who haven't lost a child.

Among bereaved mothers in England and Wales, the risk of premature demise was four times higher than that of non-bereaved parents. But if they make it through, and most do, they may very well address parenting differently.

---

[*]*Increased Mortality in Parents Bereaved in the First Year of Their Child's Life*: statistical points and extensions. BMJ Support Palliat Care 2012;2:1 7

Thirty years after Eric's death, my perception of how the loss of a child affects family members has expanded considerably. For instance, working with the MISS Foundation taught me that a family losing an unborn child can experience grief as intense and lasting as those who got to know their little one.

This is part of why I got so choked up working to put together the story of Eric, my son, for Christie, the daughter I discovered later in life. She is the dear and wonderful sister who never knew Eric, and her amazing daughters are the nieces he never met. They're affected by this loss just as those of us who knew him are.

In anticipation of my first visit with Christie and her family, I did all the straightforward stuff, scanning our photos of Eric, digitizing his videos and his memorial service and compiling everything into a series of folders. Cutting it all down to somehow convey the story's significance, without making it so long that it would take days to get through, was a heavy task.

When COVID concerns led to the postponement of our planned January 2021 get together, a part of me felt relieved—I had more time to direct energy to this project. It would be unfair to point Christie to the folders and say, "Have at it."

Would it be possible to bring her along a path and explain what I think she'd want to know and in what order? I felt the first step would be to acknowledge the potential anger and feeling of being horribly cheated Christie may feel.

There's nothing I could say to help Christie deal with this unfairness. While I could murmur positive aphorisms, I wouldn't have believed them. Eric would have been 30 years old at the time of Christie's visit, and I still think about him daily. Nothing fixes something this tragic.

If your children are alive, be happy. Feel lucky! Don't worry so much about how they measure up to a mass of artificial standards that mean next to nothing. Do you really need to be the one to push your children farther and faster than they're ready to go? Most likely, they'll push themselves when the time is right, when they find the thing that ignites a fire inside. And when they do, they'll succeed, because deep down they really will have something to push off from—their parents' unconditional love and support.

Dr. Joanne Cacciatore. No individual has done more to help families who have lost children than she.

50

A $183 MIRACLE: TWELVE KIDS RESTORE FAITH

IN THE PICTURESQUE TOWN OF Croton-on-Hudson, New York, where history and artistry intertwine, a simple act of honesty by our daughter Ginger would lead to an unexpected miracle that reconfirmed my faith in human nature. This community, nestled along the banks of the Hudson River, is as unique as the story that unfolded within it.

Croton-on-Hudson is perhaps best known for its dam, which holds back a reservoir providing New York City with some of the world's best-tasting drinking water. But the town's character runs deeper than its infrastructure. Over the decades, its population evolved from Quakers to Greenwich Village artists and writers, even housing the American Communist Party nearby at one point. In the 1990s, when our story takes place, the town still exuded an artistic community feel, a remnant of its vibrant 1980s culture.

One Friday, our young daughter Ginger came bounding home from school, her eyes alight with excitement. In her mittened hand, she clutched a $50 bill she had found in the snow on the playground of the Carrie E. Tompkins Elementary School. To a child in 1994, this was a fortune, the equivalent of about $90 today. As she walked home, Ginger's mind raced with at least a dozen ways she could spend her newfound wealth.

"I can keep it, can't I, Mom?" she asked, hope brimming in her voice.

That evening at dinner, we had a family discussion about the money. We asked Ginger how she would feel if she had lost that much money and someone else had found it. What would she want them to do? Slowly, she realized that turning the money in was the right thing to do, with the understanding that if no one claimed it she'd get the money back.

The following Monday, Ginger took the $50 bill to the school office and gave it to the principal. All week, she waited with bated breath, hoping no one would claim the money. As days passed with no one coming forward, she could barely contain her excitement at the thought of soon having $50 in her pocket.

On Friday morning, the principal got a call from a parent asking if anyone had found and turned any money in at the school.

"Yes, we did have some money turned in," the principal replied. "How much are you missing?"

The parent then shared this story. The previous week, their older daughter had celebrated her Bat Mitzvah. Overcome with jealousy at the attention her sister was receiving, their younger daughter snuck into her sister's room and took the gift money received from friends and relatives. For a week, despite questioning and her sister's tears, the younger girl denied knowing anything about the missing money.

Finally, unable to bear the guilt any longer, she confessed. Through tears, she admitted taking the money from her sister's dresser drawer, putting it in her coat pocket and bringing it to school. Her plan had been to show it off to her friends and then return it, but she had forgotten it was there. When she went to retrieve the money from her coat after school, it was gone.

The principal listened intently, then asked, "I understand. But can you tell me exactly how much money is missing?"

"We know the precise amount," the parent replied. "I wrote the amount on each card to help with thank-you notes later. From the mail and the people who came to our house, the total was $183."

At this, the principal glanced down at the envelope where she'd been keeping all the money turned in over the past week. Not just by Ginger, but by 11 other children as well. Each student's name and the amount they turned in was carefully recorded. The total stared back at her: $183. Not $175, not $180, but exactly one hundred and eighty-three dollars.

The precise match astounded us when we heard about it. It felt like more than mere coincidence—a small miracle born from the combined integrity of 12 children.

Years later, when we talked with Ginger about this event, she vividly remembered her excitement at finding the $50 bill in the snow—something she'd never seen before. But what stood out most in her memory was the good feeling she had about turning the money in, and the sense of responsibility she felt while it was in her possession.

51

FROM SPEED DEMON TO BARBIE BOAT

WHILE LIVING IN NEW YORK in the early 1990s, I caught a clip on television about a new radical boat from Bombardier's Sea-Doo division called the "Speedster." This jet boat, weighing less than 1,500 lbs., generated over 170 horsepower from twin Rotax marine rotary engines. The footage showed the boat launching from ramp-like waves and flying over the water. With its lightweight power, agility and 55 mph top speed, it reminded me of my beloved Lotus Elan, but for the water. And like the Elan, it was yellow—at least in a few places.

A bit of research led me to a dealer in Mt. Kisco, New York. He had three Bombardier jet boats in stock, but only one with the twin engines. It cost more, but the dealer's sales pitch was irresistible: The twin-engine model was so fast that Bombardier might withdraw it for safety reasons. Maybe it was too fast and dangerous? Either he was a superb salesperson who pegged me perfectly, or I was the biggest sucker born. Regardless, within hours, I was towing my new boat home.

The "Barbie boat" was a blast in the Hudson River. While it could be scary fast, it also was easy to drive. As a jet boat with no prop, it was safe to be around in the water.

Having this boat on the Hudson River, north of New York City, was a hoot. Among the larger vessels, my little "rocket ship for the water" was a blast to drive. When stationary or trolling slowly, it resembled a floating hot tub, but its performance was anything but relaxing. We often made the 35-mile trip to Manhattan, weaving among enormous cruise ships, powerful tugboats and high-speed cigarette boats. One afternoon, while cruising along NYC's west side, I got into a race with a hotshot captain of a 40-foot racing boat.

I pointed to the end of a pier about a quarter mile down the shore, and suggested we see who could get there first. With several people in his boat egging him on and a host of onlookers, he was eager to shut me up.

We lined up and pointed our respective craft toward the pier, about five football fields away. Someone on his boat yelled, "Go!"

We were off! As his engines roared to life, his props began wild and noisy cavitations. In contrast, my two internal engine impellers promptly launched my lightweight little boat out of the water and toward the pier. We must have been 100 yards beyond the bigger boat before it got onto a plane.

His boat weighed at least 10,000 lbs. empty, and he had half a dozen people in it. It was no contest, given the short distance. When I reached the goal-line pier, I did another thing my little Speedster was great at—turning on a dime and stopping. We calmly sat in the water for almost 10 seconds, waiting for the larger boat to come screaming by.

After he'd finally turned around and pulled his boat close to mine, the chagrinned captain and his amused passengers were intrigued. They had many questions about my little boat and passed us a few beers from their onboard refrigerator.

* * * * *

I loved my little boat. In my mind, it was much like my Lotus Elan, far faster and better performing than anyone realized. Captaining the diminutive craft, I fancied myself a Mario Andretti of the water, capable of flat-out putting other boats to shame.

But one day, as Ginger and I were loading the boat onto its trailer at Croton-on-Hudson's Senasqua Park, my perception changed dramatically. A young girl's excited squeal pierced the air: "Mommy, Mommy, look, look, there's a Barbie boat!"

I was shocked. What could she possibly mean? This was a macho, high-performance jet boat! What was wrong with this kid?

As I got out of the car to strap the boat to the trailer, I began to see things with fresh eyes. Okay, its color scheme 'sort of' looked like it 'could' have come from a collection of Barbie accessories, and the boat was rather small . . .

Ginger, ever the diplomat, guided the little girl around the boat and, with her mother's blessing, helped her up so she could sit inside it. She was beyond thrilled. The child's delight was infectious, and I found myself laughing along. From that moment on, our powerful Speedster lost its dangerous mystique and became affectionately known as "the Barbie boat."

* * * * *

Our move to Minnesota a few years later breathed new life into the Barbie boat. You may not have heard this, but Minnesota has an above-average collection of lakes, as does nearby Wisconsin. The Barbie boat became the ideal cabin accessory for my daughter, her cousins and my in-laws.

They all learned to drive it, and parents learned to relax as they realized it had no dangerous propellers. The kids had so much fun pulling each other around on water skies or aquatic inflatables. The boat was also a hit at the annual Net Perceptions family picnic, even though I could never get our CEO, Steven Snyder, to ride in it.

The boat journeyed with us from New York to Minnesota.
We were quickly reminded of the state's 10,000 lakes.
Sadly, we were unable to explore them all.

The boat made the trek to Arizona with us, too. Pulling it along behind our SUV I saw a spot near Moab, Utah where we could drop the boat into the Colorado River. It was a beautiful, fun afternoon, although Maggie was nervous about what laws we might be breaking.

We enjoyed our Sea-Doo for a few years on the man-made lakes in Arizona, zipping in and out of the water-flooded canyons. Our friend Dan Michael became the boat's primary user and enjoyed many lake days with it, including one in which he towed a stranded craft to shore.

When the time came to let the boat go, Dan prepped it for sale with his usual attention to detail and it sold quickly. While it had transformed from a "rocket ship" to "the Barbie boat" in my mind many years ago, it's always nice to see nautical websites refer to the Speedster as one of the greatest boats ever made.

52

SHEEP, STEAK AND SINGLE MALTS

IN 1994, BEFORE AIRBNB OR VRBO existed, we discovered the International Home Exchange. This postal-based system had perfected the art of temporary home swaps over the course of 25 years. The process was simple: pay a $125 fee, submit details about your home and receive a booklet of available exchanges worldwide.

The booklet contained several hundred pages of homes available for exchange each year. Every home got a single page, featuring one photo and limited details, such as the number of bedrooms, square footage, unique features and exciting sights that could be easily visited in the area. The homes were arranged by region, with sections for Europe, the United States, Asia, Africa, etc. After perusing the listings, members were encouraged to send letters to the owners of a half-dozen homes that appeared to be a good fit. A tornado of letters crossed in the mail, and soon mailboxes filled with home exchange requests.

The "pitch letters" had no restrictions and were aimed at enticing people who had a home where you wished to stay to swap for a stay in yours. The letters we sent out included gorgeous photos of our New York home, with descriptions of its attributes and conveniences, such as the modern clothes washer and dryer, microwave oven, dishwasher and televisions. We also included train schedules into New York City and described the many attractions there.

One of the first letters we got was from a dentist, who, with his wife and two teenage daughters, wanted to exchange their home on the outskirts of Edinburgh, Scotland with our home in Croton-on-Hudson.

Before saying yes, we spent a long time agonizing over another beautiful letter we received from a couple in South Africa. After including highly illustrative photos of their beautiful estate and describing many exciting activities, they admitted they had none of our highly automated appliances.

Besides, there was another real downside they felt was only fair to disclose. They wrote: "Unfortunately, when we go on vacation, we also take that opportunity to give our staff on the estate that time off as well. So, we will leave you with a bare-bones staff comprising a cook, one housekeeper, two drivers and a yardman. Everyone else will have the time off." While that place sounded like it could have been super fun, we finally decided to exchange homes with the family from Scotland.

When our son Eric had been so sick, Ginger had grown accustomed to staying with her cousins in Phoenix. Knowing how she and our nephew Robert played so well together, we invited him to come to Scotland with us.

Then, of course, we worried that all Maggie and I would be doing was babysitting, so we invited Ginger's favorite babysitter in the world, Melinda Wood from Los Angeles, to join us as well. The house had a plethora of bedrooms and lots of places to play outside, so we weren't worried.

We learned that most Home Exchange people coordinated travel so they crossed in the air and never actually met each other face to face. Since we were new at this and a little nervous about turning our home over to strangers, we arranged to pick up our visitors from Scotland at the airport the day before we left. We took them out to dinner and had a nice time, and we didn't expect any problems after meeting them. However, our suspicions that the liquor cabinet might be depleted when we returned were spot on.

The dentist's home in Scotland was clean and friendly. While older, it was quaint and cozy, precisely the sort of house you'd expect. The family put vases of cut flowers throughout the home to welcome us, and flower gardens surrounded the house, walking paths and patios.

Besides the house, there was a separate garage and a stable and corral for a horse. A young man who worked as a gardener on the property was quick to introduce himself, explaining he would be around every third day to mow, weed and manage other yard-related activities. Besides everything in the home, the homeowner had left keys to the family's late model Volvo station wagon and instructions for using it, such as filling it with diesel fuel, not gasoline.

Soon, our days were filled with everything tourists do in Scotland. As I suspected, visiting the Edinburgh Castle only encouraged Maggie's desire to see more. There were so many of them near where we were staying—Stirling, Craigmillar, Lauriston, Balmoral, Glamis, Dundas, Dirleton, Eilean Donan, Dunnottar, Midhope, Cawdor, Tantallon, Culzean, Inveraray, Urquhart, Dunrobin, Duart— and I feared we'd have to see them all.

Fortunately, our ground rules called for visits to scotch distilleries, as well as castles and churches. My first target was the Glenkinchie Distillery, right near Edinburgh, which turned out to be a fortunate place to start on a quest to find the best-tasting scotch in Scotland.

When it comes to scotch, the taste is very different depending on where each distillery is located across five distinct geographic regions. The Lowland scotch distilleries are the closest to Edinburgh, and Glenkinchie is one of the most famous. Lowland scotches are known for being gentle malts with notes of grass, ginger, apple, cinnamon and toffee, with an occasional citrus edge. They're light, breezy and easy to drink, so this was a terrific place to begin my education on single malts. The tour was great, and I loved the 12-year-old bottle of Glenkinchie I brought back to the house.

Although I was only at the beginning of my scotch quest, I knew I needed some help. I stopped at a liquor store in Edinburgh, filled the proprietor in on my task to discover the very best scotch in Scotland, and left with three half-bottles of presumably great scotches to try.

Late that afternoon, I ended up having a conversation with the gardener at the house. As we sat on the patio after he finished his yard duties, we had a "wee dram" and I learned more about his life.

My Scandinavian aunties would have described him as a "strapping young lad." He was medium height, wiry and strong with deep blue eyes and curly, dishwater blond hair down to his shoulders. His life, as best I could make out through his thick accent, involved maintaining the gardens of a half-dozen homes in the area, playing "football" with his mates, going to the pub to "lift a pint" once or twice a week and staying on good terms with several of the "fair lasses" along his gardening route. I came to believe that not all those women were single, if I understood his nods and winks correctly.

Before our conversation ended and we'd finished our third glass of scotch, I outlined my mission to find the best scotch and tested his willingness and qualifications to join me in my quest. He'd need to commit to spending several evenings during the next couple of weeks with me, sampling the spirits I would bring back to the house and helping me select the most delicious scotch of them all. Perhaps unremarkable in hindsight, I found I needed to expend very little persuasive energy to gain his agreement.

Our first family overnight excursion from Edinburgh was to Inverness. The kids wanted to see the Loch Ness monster, and Maggie had a list of fabric shops, castles and churches she wanted to visit along our route. Our trip would take us through the Highlands and into the heart of the famous Speyside distilleries, makers of The Glenlivet, Glenfiddich, Macallan and Glenmorangie.

I wasn't sure if we'd have time to see them all, but we visited all four and even stopped quickly at Aberfeldy in the Highlands on the way up. We didn't go on tours of all of them, but we visited each gift shop and came away with a bottle, half-bottle, or special "cask strength" bottle from each distillery.

These whiskies, east of Inverness along the River Spey, are full of fruity and nutty flavors. They're less peaty than some scotches, making them suitable for beginners. They're distinctive, with a classic, rich oaky flavor that becomes almost creamy with almonds and spice on the palate after you swallow.

While I was unable to visit where the island scotches such as those from Islay were made, I did buy sample bottles to try them. Islay, an island off the coast in the south, is land pounded by the elements all year long. Whiskeys from that area can be medicinally smoky and heavy with peat flavors. Brands like Laphroaig, Ardbeg, Bowmore and Bruichladdich are the ones you hear about most. While I could appreciate their complexity, I didn't like them as much as the Speyside and Highland scotches.

The northern island scotches, like ones from Skye, Jura and Highland Park, also had an intense smoky flavor that didn't instantly appeal to me. The salinity of the sea brings out the minerals in the peat, which leave the palate feeling of warm spices, orange peel, heather and honey. Each scotch from this area is unique, as each island produces an unmistakable flavor.

Only three bottles from the islands entered my unscientific final testing group. If I had continued to drink scotch beyond the 10 years after our trip, I'm confident I would have come to enjoy these more complex, peaty or smoky scotches. I've found that to be true of most dedicated, single malt drinkers. Once one of these scotches gets a hold of your palate, not much will satisfy you other than that one scotch.

Once we got back to our place near Edinburgh, I lined up my bottles on a long bar with a stack of 3X5 note cards. Pouring a shot or two from one of the bottles into a glass, I'd head out to the patio, sip the scotch, watch the kids climb the large tree in the back and record my tasting impressions, slipping each card under the appropriate bottle.

Every few days, my new gardener friend would join me, and we'd sit together, tasting and testing, debating and arguing, admiring and ranking, often late into the night. Can you imagine a better time?

Most nights we ate at home, enjoying meals Maggie prepared. Occasionally, we'd go out for a pub meal (ever tried haggis?), but we worked hard to keep our expenses low. Our budget only allowed one super-nice, fancy dinner on the trip.

After getting recommendations from the locals, we headed 20 miles into the countryside to find a restaurant within a castle. The dining room was nearly the size of a large barn, with exceptionally high ceilings. We were seated on one of the raised platforms that ringed the dining area and had a magnificent view of the castle's interior.

After being given ample time to examine the menu, our server came to take our order. The kids ordered first, and then Maggie ordered the rack of lamb. I said I'd have the pepper steak and instantly felt a kick under the table. Maggie leaned into me and whispered, "Order one of the lamb dishes."

I raised my finger, signaling our server to wait, but I couldn't find a lamb-based offering that appealed to me. I stuck with the steak. Maggie leaned over and whispered, "Okay, but I'm not giving you any of mine."

When our meals came, I found that my steak hadn't come from a slaughtered steer; rather it had been acquired by taking the bottom of someone's old boot, covering it with thick sauce, and coating it with black pepper.

Maggie eventually relented and extended her fork with a generous bite of lamb for me to taste. It was exquisite, melting in my mouth with an incredible burst of flavor. After tasting it, my mouth watered. But all I had was the bottom of someone's boot.

On the way home, as I mentally kicked myself, Maggie gently explained that beef just wasn't a big thing in Scotland. They were much better at lamb. How had I missed this? The kids listened in the back as she explained that so far on our trip, there was ample evidence of sheep everywhere, but hardly any cows.

The next day, on our way to Inverness, we had barely gone a half hour when Ginger called from the back seat, "Hey, Dad, what are those puffs of white up on the hills?" Then she added mischievously, "Are those little, tiny clouds? Oh, no, wait, I know what they are, Dad. They're sheep!" Everyone in the car laughed hilariously except me, remembering my shoe leather from the night before.

Less than an hour later, approaching a small town, we passed a sign urging us to slow down for a sheep crossing. "Did you see that, Uncle Steve? A sheep crossing sign!" Robert teased. "Not a cow crossing, it's a sign to slow down for sheep!" Again, the car erupted with laughter at my expense.

Eventually, the day of final scotch reckoning came. The day before we left to go back to the U.S., we packed our things and got the house in perfect order for the owners. But I still hadn't picked a winner. Fortunately, my assistant was scheduled to show up that night and I knew he was committed to working with me until the early morning hours, if necessary.

The champion emerged sometime after 2:00 a.m. We were both bleary-eyed, never having considered spitting between tastes. By midnight, we had narrowed down my list from 10 candidates to just three scotches. We agreed that any of the three could easily justify a claim to the title, but the rules clearly stated we needed to arrive at a single winner.

We went back and forth for another hour over the three finalists, comparing notes of this and that. No clear standout. Just as a well-reasoned and articulate argument was made to crown one the best, an equal number of good points would be made for one of the others.

And then my young Scottish friend held up a glass, looked at it through bloodshot eyes, smiled warmly and said in his deep accent, "Don't cha know, if it were my best girl, naked, right out of the bath or a bottle of the Macallan, I'd have to go with the Macallan." He took a sip and looked at me, and I knew. We were done. I'd found, for my taste, the very best scotch in Scotland. I had a great story—and a better understanding of a true Scotsman.

Some years later, my good friend Ann Winblad gave me a bottle of 30-year-old Macallan Single Malt for my 50th birthday. I guarded that gift carefully, perhaps drinking it all myself.

53

A FATHER-DAUGHTER STAGE LEGACY

THE TWO-FACED MASK OF COMEDY and tragedy is an ancient symbol of theater. But for me, it will always represent an important lesson I learned from my Speech III teacher in high school, Dwain L. Johnson. It was a lesson that not only improved my performances, but years later allowed me to connect with my daughter Ginger in a meaningful way. It serves as a reminder that in both theater and in life, our most powerful emotions—laughter and tears, love and hate—are more closely linked than we often realize. And sometimes, the most profound connections happen when we're willing to embrace both extremes.

Mr. Johnson, who directed most Mayo High School plays, cast me as Tom Wingfield, the lead character in *The Glass Menagerie* by Tennessee Williams. The role is critical to the play, because Tom is both the narrator and the protagonist. Many famous actors have given the iconic stage role a go, including Kirk Douglas, Sam Waterston, John Malkovich and Christian Slater. While my performance was never in the league of a professional actor's, I like to think they may have wrestled with some of the same issues I had with the part.

The play is heartbreaking. Any actor worth his salt should have the audience in tears during Tom's last soliloquy. In these last lines, Tom says farewell to his mother and his sister. He's left home and will never return, and asks his sister, Laura, to blow out the candles.

Our rehearsals went well. We all knew our lines and the production crew, headed by stage manager Joe Tashjian and assistant director Pati Knappe, was ready. Into dress rehearsal we went. After weeks of closed rehearsals, here was our chance to perform in front of an audience for the first time. Mr. Johnson cautioned us to work with the audience, pausing when they reacted or laughed. I heard him, but I didn't absorb the message.

In the middle of the first act, people started laughing at some of my lines. I was furious. This play wasn't a comedy, it was serious and tragic. I began pushing my lines forward when I felt them beginning to laugh, to keep them quiet. During intermission, Mr. Johnson got us together for a brief pep talk. To me, he said, "Steve, you've got to understand that comedy and tragedy are very closely linked. If you want them to cry during your final soliloquy, you need them to laugh with you first."

I wasn't sure what he was saying, but I knew he understood more about it than I did. I took his advice and began working with the audience, allowing them to laugh and even enjoying it when they did. My soliloquy went fine.

In a pep talk on opening night, Mr. Johnson again elaborated on our experiences in dress rehearsal. He explained, no doubt for my benefit, that when looking at the expansive line of human feelings most people see one end anchored by hilarious, joyous laughter and the other end in tragic weeping. "But it's *not* like that at all," he said. "The fact is that when you look at the range of human emotions, laughing and weeping are together at one end of the spectrum. It's indifference that's far on the other end. So, if you want to get the audience to cry, get them to laugh first. Moving them from laughter to tears is a short distance, and it's easy."

Those words stayed with me ever since, so when Ginger had a similar issue when she played Baroness Elsa Schräder in *The Sound of Music* in high school, I knew exactly what to tell her. This was a fun experience because, as everyone knows, high school daughters rarely think their fathers know anything.

The Baroness, fiancée to Captain von Trapp, is not a likeable character. After she sees how much Von Trapp's children are attached to Maria, and suspects that the Captain may harbor feelings for their nanny as well, the Baroness deviously maneuvers to get Maria out of the way and finally orders her back to the convent.

"Dad, I can really feel the audience when I'm doing this and they don't like me at all—so I'm trying to do my lines right but I'm also trying to be nice and it's just not working," she confessed to me after her dress rehearsal. She went on, "The audience doesn't know it yet, but in the next act I make everything okay because I tell Maria that the Captain really loves her, not me, and then I leave."

Oh, what a perfect set up! Not just by the playwright, but perfect for this dad/daughter moment. I explained what I knew about the comedy-tragedy spectrum, but painted it in love-hate terms. I told her that love and hate were very close together, with indifference at the other end. If she sincerely wanted the audience to love her in the second act, she needed them to really, really hate her in the first.

The solution to her problem wasn't to get the audience to take it easy on her in the first act, it was to throw herself into the part and get the audience to completely despise her. The degree to which the audience would come to love her in the second act was in direct proportion to how much they hated her in the first.

Just like I trusted Mr. Johnson, Ginger trusted me. She nodded and said, "I'll try that."

At the performance that evening, I watched in awe as Ginger threw herself into making the audience dislike her character. And boy, did she nail it. Near the end of the first act, when the Baroness banishes Maria back to the convent, I heard the woman seated next to me involuntarily hiss in hatred toward the stage. The distaste the audience was feeling toward this character was palpable, and I was thrilled.

During the second act, the scene came where Baroness Schräder bows out with dignity and caring, telling Maria that Captain von

Trapp truly loves her. I didn't have to look over at the seat next to me to know that the woman was in tears!

Ginger's part in the production wasn't over. After her ending scene as the Baroness, she went backstage, ripped off her wig and zipped off the fancy dress the Baroness wore, and speedily donned a new costume—a funny wig with large yellow pigtails. She was instantly Frau Schmidt, the woman who refused to leave the festival stage after her act was finished, generating gales of laughter and round after round of ovations so the von Trapp family could slip away. This character generated tons of laughs, no doubt a relief for Ginger.

The best part for me came at the end of the play. When the curtain came up, Ginger received applause for her role as the festival performer, an audience pleaser even though it was a non-speaking part. But then, when she removed the silly pigtail wig and revealed herself to be the actress who had also played Baroness Elsa Schräder, the amount of applause for her went through the roof.

Ginger, with her Aunt Gwen, after her performance in her high school's production of The Sound of Music.

54

A FATHER'S SUPPORT: FROM FISH TANKS TO LAB RATS

WHEN GINGER WAS IN 10TH grade, she approached me with an unusual request. She wanted me to build 11 fish tanks of varying sizes for a science fair experiment. Recognizing my limited handyman skills, I enlisted my cousin Ron Herem to help. As we constructed the tanks, Ron and I exchanged knowing glances, acknowledging the seemingly outlandish nature of the project. But I had made a promise: whatever Ginger needed, I would be there for her.

The following year, Ginger's ambitions grew even larger. She proposed an experiment involving 40 white rats. However, her private school, the International School of Minnesota, couldn't accommodate such a project. And we learned that conducting the experiment at home would disqualify her from the science fair competition.

Undeterred, Ginger took matters into her own hands. She discovered that a nearby public high school had better facilities, including a lab that could house her rats. There was just one catch: only students enrolled in the school could use the lab. Without hesitation, Ginger announced her decision to transfer schools. Maggie and I watched in amazement as our daughter navigated this transition with minimal assistance from us.

Five months later, having completed her experiment, Ginger returned to her private school. I often wondered: What kind of high school student goes to such lengths for a science project? And what kind of parents allow this? The answer to the latter was simple: Parents who are grateful every day that their child is alive.

Both of Ginger's science experiments were resounding successes. Her innovative approach earned her numerous awards, and the rat experiment even took her to the International Science Fair competition in Palo Alto, California. This achievement played a significant role in her receiving invitations and scholarships from several prestigious universities.

Reflecting on these experiences, I realized that my unconditional support had allowed Ginger to pursue her passions fearlessly. Whether it was constructing fish tanks or facilitating a school transfer for the sake of scientific inquiry, I had learned to embrace her determination and creativity. These projects were more than just science experiments; they were testaments to Ginger's resilience and our family's bond, strengthened by the challenges we had faced together.

55

DAD WOKE UP DEAD

DURING CHRISTMAS AND NEW YEAR'S in the late 1990s, we regularly went to Phoenix to see Maggie's sister Diana and her family. We always spent a day or two looking at real estate and fantasizing about getting a second home in Arizona.

When we first saw the house at 802 W. Dahlia, we knew it would be perfect for us. We made an offer, and it was accepted the same day. Engaging in a bit of a white lie, we asked my parents, Paul and Ruth Larsen, to come to Arizona and check out the house. We explained that we couldn't use it for a good part of the year and asked them to consider living in it and taking care of it for us when we weren't there.

This bit of subterfuge came about because my parents had taken to spending the winter months away from their Rochester, Minnesota home, traveling around to warmer locales in a small RV. Maggie and I worried about them, especially since my father's response to his failing eyesight was to get a bigger RV with more horsepower.

We explained our plans to use the house from April through October, with the hopes that they'd take care of it between November and May. Dad thought this might work, although he suspected our motivation. "You're not getting me out of my RV," he said. "I still have lots of places I want to go." But he finally agreed, after seeing the property's RV gate and the spot where his rig would fit perfectly.

They lived happily at 802 W. Dahlia with the RV parked in the back. Although it wasn't what my dad had intended, once parked it never moved. Mom assured us, however, that Dad would top up the fluids, carefully shield the tires from the sun's rays and check the tires' air pressure. Occasionally, he'd even shower and sleep in it.

For two years, my parents lived in the Phoenix house and enjoyed it immensely. Dad's congestive heart failure diagnosis (the same disease that ended his brothers' lives), didn't slow him much. He'd had quadruple bypass surgery to address his coronary artery disease 10 years earlier. The operation took a bit of a toll, but he preferred standing to sitting and walking to being stationary.

Dad loved walking and hiking on Arizona's trails, especially with a six-foot, gnarly wooden staff. Looking like an Old Testament desert prophet, he'd walk the trails between Shaw Butte and North Mountain, near where our house was located. Both North Valley landmarks are over 2,000 feet high.

* * * * *

On Tuesday morning, March 20, 2001, Dad woke up dead. He'd complained the prior week of cold symptoms and rested more than usual over the weekend. But he felt better on Monday. Then, on Tuesday morning, Mom got out of bed to make breakfast. Dad told her he was feeling a lot better and would just lie back down and grab another half hour of sleep while she made something to eat. When he didn't respond to her calls that breakfast was ready, she went in and found that he'd passed. It was the classic "died peacefully in his sleep" scenario, although no doubt a surprise to him.

My father was a devout Christian and loved nothing more than pouring through the more prophetic books of the Bible, including Revelations, the last book of the New Testament. He also spent hours in the Old Testament books of Isaiah, Daniel, Ezekiel and Zechariah. Dad knew with absolute certainty that he would never die, as Jesus would return to rapture all believers, catching them up in the clouds. Paul was looking forward to that trip, thinking it would be fun.

My mother organized his memorial service and grieved for my father for the rest of her life, although she didn't let it hold her back. In fact, with my father gone, my mother blossomed in a way she never allowed herself to do as a "Christian woman who stays in the shadow of her husband."

For 10 years after he was gone and before her own health began to fail, she was a fireball, traveling, going to events and meetings, visiting relatives all over the country and even flying overseas to see her ancestral home in Norway. She did several trips with Maggie and me, and her presence made them more meaningful and fun. Mom would live another 13 years, passing away when she was 91. Dad was 83 when he died.

* * * * *

A few months after my father passed away, with me working in San Francisco and Ginger off at college, Maggie decided she was tired of living in a big house on a golf course in Eden Prairie, Minnesota all by herself. She was going to move to Arizona full-time to be closer to her sister Diana and her family. Hey, it would cut my commute by more than an hour, so I was in.

The call to my mother went smoothly, as she'd already been eyeing a retirement community in Glendale, Arizona called Glencroft, where Maggie's parents had moved. The movers arrived in Eden Prairie and cleaned out the house. The following morning, Maggie, our two kitties and I left in an Acura MDX pulling my fiberglass jet boat.

As we drove out of the Twin Cities, the two cats began to meow and wail. "MEOW, meow, we're going to the vet. Oh no, we hate the vet. MEOW, meow."

After about 30 minutes of this, Tikki, the older of the two cats, looked out the window and commented to Gilda, "You know, this doesn't look like the way to the vet."

Gilda stopped meowing, looked around and seemed to say, "You might be right. Lots more trees." Eventually, they settled down and mostly slept as the miles piled up.

At our first overnight, we pulled into a hotel and, after checking in, snuck the cats into the room. They immediately assumed we'd arrived at their new forever home and spent the entire night exploring every inch and every smell. The following morning, our first 30 minutes of driving was spent listening to a repeat of the prior day's "We're going to the vet" chorus.

The contract to sell our home in Eden Prairie fell through when the house failed inspection. Apparently, the manufacturer of the windows (and doors) in this relatively new home had developed new materials that dramatically improved the house's efficiency. However, the unique installation steps that were required had somehow not been followed, and the result was a home with a severe case of mold.

Consequently, before we could sell the house we had to remove and replace every door and window. The same fate befell about a dozen other homes in our neighborhood. It would take a year for the construction work and then another year to sort out in court who would pay for everything.

In the end, the builder paid a third, the window manufacturer paid a third and we were stuck with the final third. If it hadn't been for my cousin Ron Herem's regular inspections and documentation, this would have been far worse for us. We owe Ron big time.

Looking back at our various real estate purchases, Maggie and I realized that we made money about half the time and lost money about half the time. Overall, though, we think we're ahead, especially if you include happiness in the calculations. We loved the house in Eden Prairie, even though the repairs cost so much. And we enjoyed our years in the West Aster house, even though we sold it at break-even during the housing crisis. We lost money on the Silverbell Road condo, the Stewart Drive duplex and the Rochester rental properties, but it's just water under the bridge.

We're thinking about buying one more home and living happily in it until we wake up dead after a lovely night's sleep.

56

UNEXPECTED CONNECTIONS: A DAUGHTER DISCOVERED

"HEY CUZ! YOU SITTING DOWN?" was the first thing my cousin, Roger Larsen, said when he called me on a Sunday morning in January 2019.

"I can be," I replied.

Once I found a comfortable chair, he blurted out, "You have a daughter!"

"I know," I said. "She lives in California, name of Ginger—did you forget?"

"No, no, not that one. You've got another one," Roger insisted. "I just got an email from her, and she sounds really nice. She lives in Minnesota."

Before I could say anything, he continued, "I just forwarded you the email she sent me about herself. I'm going to hang up now, but you should read it. And I know you Cuz, you'll do the right thing."

My wife Maggie, who'd come out on the deck as I'd taken the call, saw the stunned look on my face. "What was that all about?"

After a brief explanation, we opened my computer and found the email Christina Will had sent to my cousin. In a touching message, she communicated how she learned that her birth father was "unknown" when her mother tragically passed away when she was just a little girl. It left her longing for answers.

As she grew up, she wondered about her birth father and if he knew of her. Did she have a family somewhere in the world? If she found them, what would they be like? Would they look like her? Have similar values? She had so many, many questions.

In November of 2018, after years of fruitless searching and with the expectation of finding an aunt, uncle or distant cousin who might provide clues to her birth father, Christina, aka Christie, got a 23andMe DNA kit, swabbed her cheek and sent it in. Her small support posse of friends who'd coalesced on a mission to help her find her birth father had recommended this move.

On Christmas morning in 2018, Christie got a notice from 23andMe saying she had a father—with a name—Paul Stephen Larsen. I always went by Steve because it was confusing when I was younger to have two Paul Larsens in one house. After a few months of investigating, she found and contacted my cousin Roger Larsen's daughter, Lori Bolanos, online and asked for guidance: "Did her dad know his cousin Steve well? Did he think Steve would want to hear from her? Maybe meet his grandchildren? Would his daughter, Ginger, want to know she had a sister? How would they deal with a potentially giant disruption to their lives?"

Lori encouraged her to write a letter to her dad, Roger, with those questions. Christie's letter to Roger included these key points:

- "I'm not sure if I would want to meet him or if I would want him to meet his grandchildren. The best-case scenario in my mind would be that he would tell me about his life and about his family."
- "I would hope for him to tell his family about me. I know he lost a son and has an adult daughter."
- "Would you guide me here? Lori said that you and Steve are fairly close and talk often. I'm sure you want to look out for your family's best interest, too."
- "My mother, Louann Fitzgerald, kept her pregnancy with me a secret and never talked about Steve. All I know is that they most likely met in 1978 at the mall in Rochester, MN, where she was a server in a restaurant and he was a manager at an electronics store."

To say this was a shock to me would be the understatement of the decade. Maggie and I talked, then quickly called Ginger in San

Francisco. She burst into tears, asked for time to process it all and said she'd call us back. Maggie and I talked some more. Then I replied to Christie's email. In part, I said the following:

> "Christie, wow! As you have no doubt surmised, this is quite a surprise. I remember your mother but was unaware she was pregnant or had you. Our relationship was not a long one. Perhaps I had moved to the Twin Cities by the time you were born and was difficult to locate. Emails and text messages were non-existent in those days.

> "With only a few hours to process, let me tell you my initial feelings: I am thrilled you reached out to me and would love to meet you, your daughters and your husband if you want that. The fact you thought of Ginger and her being your half-sister, and having two nieces she has never met, shows me you are a pretty wonderful and thoughtful woman. In fact, your entire letter was so expressive and beautifully written I can't imagine any man not being thrilled by the idea he might be related to you."

I explained a bit more about our lives in Arizona and then flooded her with questions about her and her family.

A few weeks later, Maggie, Ginger and I made plans to travel to Minneapolis and meet Christie in April 2019. It was a tearful and wonderful meeting I will never forget. Arriving in Minneapolis, we spent the night with my cousin Ron Herem and his wife Gwen in their home in Apple Valley. Of my nearly three dozen cousins, Ron Herem (my mom's brother's son) and John Gravley are the ones I've remained closest to. When we thought of a location for our first face-to-face meeting with our new family, Ron and Gwen's home came to mind immediately.

My heart pounded wildly in my chest as we awaited their arrival. As I watched them come up the walk, it stopped completely. As they came through the front door into the small dining room, nothing could stop the tears and hugs. Just as nothing had prepared me for what I would feel in the delivery room when Ginger was born, I was instantly overwhelmed with love for this person and her children.

Looking back, I had a similar fear and trepidation as Ginger's due date approached. "How long would it take for me to learn to love this new little person?" Every father knows this is dumb, but as a new prospective father it was a worry I genuinely held. Of course, it disappeared the second the nurse handed me the little bundle and said, "Congratulations, dad, meet your daughter."

On the day we saw Christie, I was having those same fears about meeting her for the first time. What if she didn't like me? What if I didn't like her? Would this be just a "one-and-done" kind of thing?

No doubt, Christie had similar fears, which, like mine, evaporated like wet footprints around an Arizona pool in the middle of the hot, dry summer. We became a family in an instant. No, we didn't have the shared memories that traditional families have, but we all seemed committed to do what we could to make up for those years apart.

Over the next several hours, nervous conversations evolved to normalcy. We were a family united, and it felt so very right. The kids played board games; one fell asleep. We ate, laughed, told stories and cried.

When Christie's pastor heard the news, he invited Christie to speak in their church on Father's Day, June 16, 2019, and tell her story. I booked flights to Minnesota so I could attend. How could I not? We secretly invited Christie's new sister, Ginger, to fly to Minnesota for the service too, and we had a fun surprise for Christie when Ginger appeared at our dinner table in a restaurant near Christie's home the night before, dressed like one of the wait staff, pretending to take a drink order.

Christie's 14-minute "sermon" the next morning at the Holy Trinity Lutheran Church in New Prague was touching and eloquent. She told her story of discovering that her birth father wasn't who she thought he was. She talked about wondering why that birth father had abandoned her and her mother. She covered details about her search and about our being ultimately united after 39 years. Here's the text of her talk, only slightly shortened:

"I have always been in a jealous admiration of the relationship my good friend Nikki has with her father, Kendall. I've watched longingly at this beautiful father and daughter relationship, their simple FaceTime sessions as she cooks dinner, or his chaperoning his granddaughter's field trips, or his random phone calls just to say that he loves her. Kendall's constant and unquestionable love and acceptance of his daughter always reminded me of something I desperately wanted but could only sit by and observe.

You see, I grew up having never met my birth father. In fact, I never even knew his name. It wasn't until I was 10 years old, sitting in the middle of a courtroom with my mother dying of cancer next to me, when I learned that my biological father whose name had been withheld, had been previously contacted by my mother, and he denied paternity. He denied me. The records were sealed; the case was closed. My birth father didn't want me.

That was my story, the one that shaped me as a person; disapproval, rejection and abandonment. My mother never told anyone anything regarding my father before she passed away. No name, no address, nothing. She literally took her secret to the grave. So, 30 years of unanswered questions and one heck of a Black Friday deal got the better of me, and I bought a DNA kit.

I waited the five agonizing weeks, obsessively checking daily, sometimes hourly for the progress on the results. But I woke up Christmas morning to a text message alerting me that my results were in. So, with my children downstairs begging to open their presents from Santa, I closed my eyes, took a deep breath, not sure of what I was hoping for, said a prayer without words, and I opened the app.

"Merry Christmas, Christie. You have a father." It took nearly a month of incessant internet stalking by my team of sleuthing family members to learn more about this stranger, this Steve Larsen who lived in Arizona, this man who collects yellow sports cars, who has two sisters and a brother, who grew up in Minnesota, who has a lovely home on the other side of the country.

He'd recently retired from a career that I can't quite figure out. He has had addresses in New York City and California, a wife whom he married a few years after I was born, a daughter named Virginia Ruth only a few years younger than me, and a son named Eric who died when he was only two, leaving his sister behind, grief-stricken and without a sibling. But in fact she has a sister and a brother-in-law, and two nieces, one of whom looks exactly like her when they were the same age.

He has a family that he held together through the most tragic of circumstances. Clearly, this man has overcome heartache and tragedy and has made a wonderful life for himself, a life which does not include me. And what could I possibly offer him?

So there in the back of the church with Pastor Ben, chipping away at my carefully constructed wall, holding my best friend's hand, I sat near paralyzed on this precipice of this idea, this completely terrifying idea. An entire month had passed, leaving me to wonder if Steve Larsen saw the same DNA results I had. Why was there no response? Did he not log onto the app? Is it possible he still doesn't know about me? Is he waiting for me to reach out to him? Is he just ignoring the results? Would I log on tomorrow and find all of his information had been taken off the site?

And what about Ginger? Does she deserve to know that I exist? Would she want me in her life? Would any of them? My view of this impending disruption to his family's life and what I could only imagine as another set of disapproval, rejection, and abandonment had me unable to reach out to my father. That anticipatory feeling of rejection had been palpable and crippling.

But after Pastor Ben spoke that day, I went home, and I drafted one of the hardest letters I've ever had to write. I was too afraid to email my father directly, so I introduced myself to a mutual cousin and connected with her via text, and she gave me her father's email address saying that our fathers were still rather close. With my sliver of newfound courage, I wrote him an email explaining who I was and why I was contacting him instead of my father and asking him for advice on what to do next. He, however, never emailed me back.

His daughter sent me a text informing me that her dad had received my email and there was an email from my father waiting for me. And I still carry that email with me today:

> 'Christie, wow, as you have no doubt surmised, this is quite a surprise. I remember your mother, but was unaware she was pregnant or had you. With only a few hours to process this, let me tell you my initial feelings. First, I am thrilled that you reached out to me and would love to meet you, your daughters, and your husband if you would want that. That you thought of Ginger and her being your half-sister and having two nieces she never met indicates to me you are a pretty wonderful and thoughtful woman. In fact, your entire letter was so expressive and beautifully written, I can't imagine any man not being thrilled by the idea that he might be related to you.'

It was everything I didn't know I needed to hear. And from that moment on, my entire life drastically changed.

Within days, his entire side of the family found out about me and I was surrounded by family from across the country who were eager to accept the idea of me into their lives. I also learned from my mother's side of the family that Steve was most likely the man who had *not been contacted when I was born, that my mother was young, and well, it was the '70s.*

The very thing that had internally shaped the person I am today was based on something that hadn't even been true. My father had not abandoned me. He was merely unaware of my existence. But I had let this thing, this initial sense of rejection, define and sometimes cripple me. As much as I was and am still trying, all of this fear of my brokenness still holds me down. His daughter, my new sister, is beautiful, driven, successful, sweet, soft-spoken, adventurous, and so very thoughtful.

My dad sends me texts just to say hello. He makes plans to celebrate my children's birthdays, which are months away. He arranges for me to meet a family who's still living here in Minnesota. He plots out calendars of when we can be together. He cancels trips in order to spend over two months in Minnesota just in case we can get together to be closer to his new daughter, his son-in-law and his granddaughters.

And he even flies to Minnesota as a surprise to spend our first Father's Day together, to listen to his daughter speak in church. With each of these gestures, my father says to those fears inside of me, 'Look at me, I am here. Take my hand.' And I find myself placing my hand in his, rising up and standing next to my father, as hand in hand, we walk towards something beautiful."

It's been several years now, and we've gotten to know and love Christie, her family and several additional relatives. We visit them frequently in Minnesota and we travel together. They come and stay at our home in Arizona at least twice a year and, like all grandparents, we constantly lobby for more visits.

"Bio-Dad" is how Christie refers to me to her friends and her kids, Emmy and Parker. After all, the father who raised her is still in the picture. When she talks to me, she just calls me "Dad." Emmy and Parker just call me Grandpa and Maggie, Grandma.

Sisters Ginger and Christie have bonded and seem to always be trying to make up for all the time they spent apart. We never seem to tire of the remarkable similarities between Ginger and Christie, as well as the physical resemblance between Christie's daughter, Parker, and Ginger when she was the same age.

The now-united sisters, Christie and Ginger.

For our first visit to the Will residence in Elko New Market, Minnesota, Maggie had brought a stack of snapshots of Ginger between the ages of two and 10 years old. We'd gotten a kick out of her resemblance to Parker and left the stack on the kitchen counter.

A bit later, Christie's husband Jeff came into the house. He picked up the stack of photos as he waited to speak with Christie, who was preparing dinner in the kitchen. I watched from the corner of my eye as he thumbed through the stack, then turned to Christie and asked, "Christie, where did these pictures of Parker come from? I've never seen them before. Where were they taken?"

Christie turned around to see him holding the photos of Ginger and calmly explained, "That's not your daughter, honey. That's Ginger when she was Parker's age."

We all burst out laughing. The resemblance was so close it had fooled her father. Later, I posed Parker to match the way Ginger sat on the rear of my Lotus Elan in a photo from a car show the two of us had attended in New York. Then, using Photoshop, I made a new picture, but this one with Parker's image leaning on the Lotus trunk, wearing similar clothing. Framed side by side, the two photos hang in our hallway. Seeing the picture, people often ask, "Why do you have two of the same photo in this frame?" They're unable to pick out the subtle difference that it's two different girls until we point it out.

Ginger's taken her role of Aunt Ginger very seriously and dotes on her nieces. When she heard Emmy was considering a summer camp, she insisted that she attend Concordia Language Villages in northern Minnesota. While they offer a variety of experiences for campers, Ginger made sure Emmy enrolled in the same immersive French language Voyageurs experience that she'd gone to when she was that age.

Just like Ginger, Emmy tried to back out as the date got close. But she went, and upon her return she sang the praises of her experience and vowed to go the following year—which she did, this time bringing one of her newfound cousins, Katya Stickney from Tucson, along with her.

During the summer of 2023, Maggie, Ginger and I attended a Fitzgerald family gathering they call Christmas in July, with Christie's mom's side of the family. I got to meet Louann's mother, Evelyn. She told me that her daughter, the woman I fathered Christie with, had never told her (or anyone else as far as she knew) the name of the father. Later, Louann's sister, Christie's Aunt Arlene, and I would have dinner. She told me a lot more about Louann's life and her untimely death when Christie was still a child.

In 2024, we took a family cruise to Alaska on the Holland America ship, the Eurodam. We had four cabins next to each other with good-sized connecting balconies, and had a ball watching whales, viewing glaciers, wandering through the cool Alaskan cities and eating dinner together at a massively large round table. Our friends, Ed and Linda Deutsch, joined us, and it was fun having them meet everyone.

Our new full family: Fiancé Chris Hawkins, Ginger, me,
Maggie, Christie, Jeff and Parker and Emmy.

As I reflect on this unexpected journey of discovery and connection, I'm struck by the profound impact it has had on all our lives. What began as a shocking revelation has blossomed into a beautiful expansion of our family, filled with love, laughter and new memories.

The bond that Christie, Ginger and their families have formed is a testament to the power of openness and acceptance. Our shared experiences—from family gatherings to summer camps, from quiet dinners to Alaskan cruises—have woven a tapestry of relationships that feels as if it has always been there.

While we can't reclaim the years lost, we've embraced the opportunity to create a future together. Christie's courage in reaching out, and our family's willingness to open our hearts, have led to a richness in our lives that we never could have anticipated.

This chapter of our family's story reminds us that it's never too late for new beginnings, that family can be both born and chosen, and that love has an incredible capacity to grow and adapt. As we continue to build our relationships and create new memories, I'm filled with gratitude for this unexpected gift—a daughter discovered, a family expanded and a future brightened by the promise of shared love and understanding.

MOTORCYCLES

TWO WHEELS, ENDLESS HORIZONS

MY EXPERIENCE WITH TWO-WHEELED ADVENTURES began long before I could legally ride on the open road. As kids in Fairmont, my brother Leif and I dreamed of owning a motorcycle or scooter.

Leif, the innovator, decided we could build one. Taking an old bicycle, he ingeniously modified it to hold a lawn mower motor below the crossbar. With some clever engineering involving a welded second rim and a long belt system, he somehow put together a working contraption that Rube Goldberg would be proud of.

From that first jerry-rigged motorized bicycle, my obsession with motorcycles has been constant. I've ridden through the twisting roads of New Zealand's South Island, braved the grueling Dakar

Rally in South America and even attempted the precise art of trials riding. I've experienced the thrill of high-speed track days and the meditative peace of long-distance touring. Each ride, each bike, each adventure has added a thrilling new chapter to my life story.

In this section, you'll ride along as I recount some of my most memorable motorcycling experiences. We'll explore the challenges and joys of riding in different parts of the world, from the sunbaked roads of Brazil to the alpine passes of Europe, to remote villages in northern Turkey.

We'll examine the machines themselves—the roar of a Ducati Monster in Italy, the nimble handling of a BMW GS in the Arizona desert and getting a trials bike stuck in a tree. You'll get a taste of the camaraderie among riders, the Zen-like focus required for long journeys and the exhilaration of man and machine in perfect harmony.

But it's not only about the rides. It's about life lessons learned on two wheels, the personal growth gained from pushing your limits and the unique perspective of the world from the saddle of a motorcycle. Motorcycling has shaped my worldview, influenced my business decisions and even affected my relationships.

This is my story of my life on two wheels.

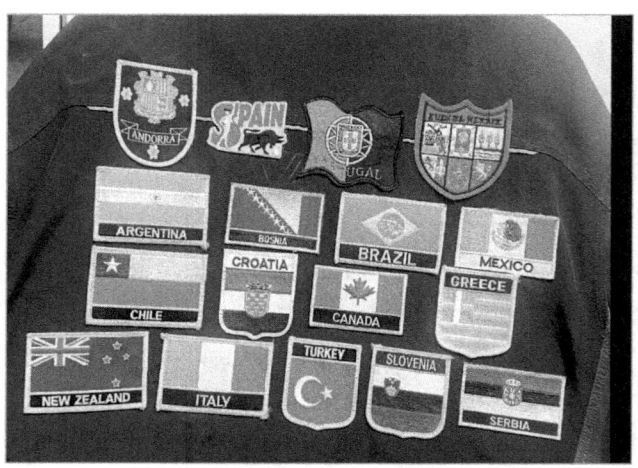

I put a patch from each country I've ridden through on my motorcycle jacket.

57
RIDING A LEIF ORIGINAL

WHEN I WAS ABOUT 12 years old, a tenant of my father's agreed to sell his non-working, home-made scooter to my brother Leif and me for $10. His alternative proposition was to have our dad knock $10 off his rent. Our parents wouldn't hear of buying the scooter for us, so we went on a neighborhood work project to raise the required funds. Leif and I mowed grass, ran errands and did odd jobs. Lacking the ability to stay focused, however, we didn't even come close to getting the amount we needed: $10 was a lot of money back then and the scooter was out of reach.

But then Leif got the idea that we could build one ourselves. He took an old bicycle and changed it to hold an old lawn mower motor below the crossbar. He talked a welder into welding a second rim to the one on the back, next to the rear tire. He ran a long belt from around the rear rim through a pulley that acted as a clutch and pulled the belt tight to the spinning lawn mower motor shaft. It was a brilliant implementation from a young engineer: I pretty much just sat and watched him work his magic.

Somehow, the makeshift motorcycle worked, and I rode it constantly, sometimes even giving Leif a chance. The machine didn't have any brakes, so my heart frequently pounded erratically as I had to drag my feet and skid sideways to a stop.

While we never measured the contraption's speed, I guess it could have reached 30 mph or faster. Did we wear helmets? No. How about protective gear? No. Good sturdy riding boots? No! We had "tenner" shoes and I wore the soles off of them, using them as brakes.

While the Fairmont police couldn't be bothered to chase us down and pull us over, Rochester had different rules. When we moved there and the police pulled Leif over, we retired this homemade motor bicycle for good.

It was likely all for the best, but a fire for two-wheeled, motorized vehicles was lit deep inside me and has never been extinguished.

58

YOUTHFUL BRAVADO
AND A FACE PLANT

WHEN I RETURNED TO ROCHESTER after living with the Jesus Freaks in Iowa City, I came to believe that I could race motocross in my spare time. I was reminded of this time in my life when I recently visited my friend John Binder in Arizona. He was one of the "Old Phartz" in Frank Del Monte's orbit of British bike aficionados, and he had a whole display of photos of himself racing motocross on Catalina Island in the mid-1950s.

Photos of my early motorcycle racing attempts pale in comparison to John's. My efforts weren't sanctioned or sponsored by anyone, and the huge jumps we built on our homemade course that were so vivid in my memory look like little piles of dirt, maybe five or six feet high.

My first efforts at motocross racing–dirt hills in Minnesota.
At least I learned to wear protective gear.

In my mind, those early racing attempts had my friends and I flying over modern, stadium-style motocross courses. More cringe-worthy than the lack of height we achieved, however, was the poor quality protective equipment we had—crappy helmets, cheap boots and poorly padded jackets. My suspicion is that we all can recount moments during our invulnerable youths that, in retrospect, we're a bit surprised we survived.

Most of my friends and I believed racing motorcycles on our quarter-mile track, with its large mounds of black dirt, would translate into us getting girls. One Friday night, while talking to a young woman at the Outrigger bar in Rochester, I had the idea that the sight of me flying high on my motorcycle would impress her immensely, melting her heart. So, I invited her to where we practiced, drawing a map on a cocktail napkin.

At the track the following day I kept looking down the road leading to the farm, hoping to see a car appear with her in it. And eventually, it did. Timing my moves carefully, I rode the track slowly until the young woman and her friend parked their car and were walking close to the track.

Then I gave it my all. I hit each jump to ensure maximum altitude. In my head, I most certainly must have cleared 15 or 20 feet in the air. I slid around the last corner with the back wheel spinning furiously, sending a stream of dirt flying. Pretending to notice them for the first time, I rode the bike over to where they were standing. I locked the rear brake as I slid to a stop close to them, letting the tall bike with its 36-inch-high seat lean over so I could get a leg down.

Dismounting, I pushed the bike back straight onto its side stand, removed my helmet and flashed my most winning smile. She and her girlfriend rushed up to me, giggled and said, "Wow, that's amazing. You look just like those pony riding monkeys in the circus when you go over those jumps."

This wasn't the effect I was going for, but I had to admit, on very tall bikes like these with the suspension set to provide maximum cushion for a soft landing, my short legs didn't come close to reaching the ground. Monkey on a pony? Maybe.

* * * * *

Like a lot of motorcycle riders, I went through a track-day phase. Mine occurred when I was living in California. While attempting to channel the best MotoGP racers I felt like Kenny Roberts, the first American to win a Grand Prix motorcycling world championship. But seeing photos of myself on the track made me realize I looked more like Kenny Rogers, the country-western singer.

The tricks our minds play on us are odd. The first time I noticed this time-affected disorientation was when I revisited a favorite family picnic spot from my youth. Then in our 20s, my brother Leif and I joined our family at this park along the St. Croix River near Taylors Falls, Minnesota.

The picnic area provides easy access to the river for swimming, and hiking trails lead to the high cliffs rising above the river. Reminding my brother that, as youngsters, we launched ourselves into the river from these cliffs, I said, "Maybe we can find the spot where we jumped." After about 10 minutes of climbing the trail through the trees, we were a good way up the cliff. Seeing a clearing, we cautiously approached the edge. I got on my knees, crawled closer and looked over.

Leif was braver than I was, slowly striding to the edge as we peered down at the churning water below. Then we retreated about six feet back from the edge to confer. "This couldn't be where we jumped, could it?" We both concluded this was far too high above the river. One could get seriously hurt hitting the water from this height. One more peek over the ledge and we both agreed that we would never have jumped from there.

As we were about to leave, we heard youthful voices rushing up the trail. These kids were running, approaching rapidly, yelling and carrying on. Not knowing how many there were or how fast they were going, we stepped back out of the way to let them pass. The first skinny kid of about 10 years old glanced to the right and noticed us, but he didn't miss a step as he ran toward the edge and launched himself into the river, arms flailing.

In just another second or two another flash passed, making the same jump, followed by three more. Whoosh . . . Whoosh . . . Whoosh! Leif and I slowly approached the ledge again, looking down at the five young kids in the water, laughing and splashing as they swam toward the shore. After a moment of silence, I mumbled, "Well, maybe we did jump from here. We must have been nuts!"

* * * * *

While I may be older and wiser now, I must confess that some old motocross dreams still haunted me into my late 40s and early 50s. We were living in a cozy, four-bedroom multiplex that Maggie always refers to as "that little house I bought without you" after we moved to Eden Prairie. Unlike every other home purchase which we agreed on together, I bought this temporary house for us to live on my own until we could find something we both loved.

As spring was starting to warm things in Minnesota, I succumbed to the idea that my Suzuki DR350S, which had made the trip with us from New York in the moving van, needed some riding. I was soon cruising the neighborhood streets, getting it warmed up and its fluids flowing. Then I saw a construction site with a deserted gravel and mud road leading into it and piles of cement blocks, forklifts and several flatbed trailers.

While riding slowly through the construction area, standing on my pegs, I spotted a mud path heading toward a grove of trees. That looked interesting. Spinning my knobby rear tire in prime motocross fashion, I took off, flying down the mud path and splashing dirty water in every direction.

God, this was fun, I thought as I upped my speed. But then I crossed a puddle that cleverly disguised a deep hole. The front wheel of the bike dropped in and immediately stopped. The rest of the bike, noting the action of the front wheel, decided to do the same. I, however, continued over the front handlebars and through the air, attempting to gauge where on the road ahead of me I might land.

I didn't have to wait long for an answer. I hit the muddy road, spread eagle and face first, sliding a good 10 feet before coming to a stop. Examining my parts and finding no damage other than muddy riding gear and a bruised ego, I took the filthy bike and far dirtier rider back home. Some people never learn.

My first new motorcycle, a Suzuki 125. Riding and jumping would have been smarter with a helmet and full gear. Young and dumb ... And lucky.

59
RIDING CAMARADERIE

THERE ARE PARALLELS BETWEEN PEOPLE riding motorcycles together and going through military boot camp. Jokes and constant ribbing abound. When it's all men, few things are out-of-bounds for criticism: your choice of bike, inadequate gear, lack of preparation, lousy physical shape, awful hair, general ugliness and of course, ridiculously poor riding skills. Oh, and flatulence.

Staying on that teasing edge, without hurting anyone's feelings, is very macho and fun, but something else grows as the days go by, namely a deep concern for others in the group. This is evidenced by the speed at which everyone rushes to the aid of a fellow biker who's gone down, which can happen when you're riding off road on challenging terrain.

While you're riding, your head is encased in a helmet and you're not talking with your fellow riders. My friend Rich Marin has a whole philosophy about how riding is really a solitary endeavor with nothing to restrain you. You live in your helmet with your thoughts.

However, at every breakfast, lunch stop and dinner, you're together with your group. At every gas stop or rest break, you're together—every single day of the trip. You talk, get to know each other and learn what others do, what they're working on, what they care about and who's important in their lives. Groups learn about each member's business problems, health issues, political ideologies, families and much more.

Once, during a ride in Mexico's Copper Canyon, guided by the incredible Skip Mascorro and his crew, we overheard a few cellphone calls that our riding buddy, Roger Hansen, was having. We learned he was helping his daughter, Jennifer, with the homes she founded to assist recovering alcoholics and drug addicts. We also learned that Jennifer Hansen had emerged from a drug habit of her own that had nearly ended her life. She was now taking on a cause and a struggle she knew all too well.

At her Serenity Houses, Jennifer expects all residents to work full-time, go to school or volunteer. Roger agonized over how and why the State of New Jersey, rather than helping these efforts, worked to stop these homes and attempted to shut them down. At one dinner, Roger pulled out his phone and showed us all a video the residents had helped put together, eloquently expressing how these homes had saved their lives. We all felt more connected to Roger and his family.

On tours like the one we were on at that time, which are organized and guided by a tour operator, it's customary for members of the group to gather tip money for the guides on the last day. Typically, the money is pooled, and riders who are perceived to have given too little are cajoled into giving more.

One person holds the money and watches for an opportunity to present it to the tour operator, along with the thanks of the group. This typically occurs on the final night's dinner, when beverages and glasses are available for toasts.

One doesn't go into the business of offering guided motorcycle tours to become wealthy. A tour operator's motivation is to make some semblance of a living while doing what they love most—showing remarkable parts of the world to like-minded individuals, who value exciting adventures and cultural experiences. I've known several tour operators who I genuinely admire, especially Skip Mascorro, and it's always been my honor to tip generously and keep riding with them in years to come.

During the final night's dinner on our Copper Canyon trip, my good friend Mark Dilly took the leadership role and pulled all the money together. Mark was an effective fundraiser, so following his very nice speech thanking Skip and his crew, the pile of cash he pushed into Skip's hands was definitely better than average.

Tradition then calls for the recipient of the tip to thank his crew, pledge to share a portion with them and tell the participants that they're indeed the absolute best group he's ever had the pleasure of leading.

As Skip Mascorro began his speech, one he'd given countless times before, we could see him hesitating, losing his train of thought. His words and direction changed. Of course, he said all the nice things about his crew and how great it was to ride with us and how he'd love to do it again sometime.

But then, he took the ball cap full of tip money and pushed it in front of Roger Hansen. "If it's okay with all of you guys," he began, "I'd like to give this money to Roger Hansen's foundation to help his daughter and her Serenity Houses."

Roger Hansen is a tough guy, but he couldn't keep the tears from rolling down his face. Nor could the rest of us. Rider fellowship runs deep.

Me, between brother Leif Larsen (L) and Roger Hansen at Mexico's Copper Canyon.

60
MARIN'S FAITHFUL FLYERS

EARLY IN 2000, MY FRIEND Arthur Einstein sent me an intriguing email. Would I be interested in riding with a group of his friends called the American Flyers Motorcycle Club (AFMC)? While I loved owning and riding motorcycles, and always had at least one in the garage, I was out of practice at the time and thought this club would be a great way to get back into it.

So, despite some initial reservations, I enthusiastically replied yes and a few weeks later I was off to Las Vegas to meet Arthur's friends in the AFMC. I rented a Honda Valkyrie, on a lark, only realizing later that Rich Marin, the club's founder—and permanent President, CEO, COO and CFO—was rather fond of Valkyries. With Arthur's blessing and Rich's instantaneous acceptance, the rest of the group welcomed me immediately.

In 2020, Rich published a book that I edited, *The Ride Is All*, chronicling 25 years of American Flyers Motorcycle Club adventures. By then the group had made 58 rides, 44 domestic and 15 international, and I'm proud to say that I was on a great many of them.

Rich is a big guy. When he was eight, they thought he was 12. At 14, an orthopedist told him not to play tennis until his tendons caught up with his size. At 16, he stopped fitting into off-the-rack clothes. He started college at 310 pounds and was recruited to join the football team. As an adult, while not as large as he once was, he still confronts issues that are impossible for those of normal size to imagine.

Rich came to motorcycles as a youngster in Italy. On scooters and small cc motorcycles, he learned to thread his way through the narrow streets and back roads of Rome. Motorcycles gave him freedom.

Marin's leadership of the AFMC has never been questioned, and it goes far deeper than his willingness to do the hard and thankless tasks of planning trips and making sure everyone has a good time. Rich inspires confidence in others because he has so much of it himself. Rich's self-confidence is not the "big ego" sort of confidence, but the organic, home-grown confidence of someone who's done it before, whatever that may be.

On my first ride with the Flyers, out of Las Vegas into northern Arizona, we rode through winds so strong we had to lean our bikes far over to keep moving straight. Not once did I worry that we might not reach our destination. Rich said we'd be fine, and that was all we needed to hear. Only later did I learn that trucks exiting the freeway that afternoon weren't allowed back on.

A lot of Flyers like to ride close behind Rich, although few keep pace with him for long. My theory is that they trust the clarity of Rich's vision on where we're going, more than anyone else in the group. Rich's sense of not only what a single day's ride represents— but also an entire trip—is a unique part of his intellect and no doubt a key part of what led to his highly successful business career. He spent 23 years at Bankers Trust and was a member of the Management Committee. In 2003, he was hired by Bear Stearns as chairman and CEO of Bear Stearns Asset Management. He went on to be chairman and CEO of AFI (USA), a $3 billion distressed commercial real estate company, and president and CEO of New York Wheel LLC. Now, in quasi-retirement, he's a Director at SEDA Experts LLC, a consulting firm providing elite expert witness services for financial services organizations.

I suspect that planning and executing long rides allows Rich to exercise and play with the part of his brain that's so particularly well-suited to getting from A to B. He may not be aware that most people don't have his talent for creating a completely mapped-out vision in the mind, with every stop notated, every hotel and restaurant pictured and the time and distances to be covered.

Once he's traversed an area, it's fixed in his mind forever. He knows that the Moki Dugway is three miles long, has six switchbacks and drops 1,200 feet from the top of Cedar Mesa to the valley floor below. He knows the number of view pull-offs on the Burr Trail to Bullfrog, and how long it takes to get down and back alone versus going with five riders. Very few people can do this, and no one I've ever met is better at it than Rich.

Another notable attribute of Rich's leadership is the unwavering support and loyalty he gives to his inner circle of family and friends. No one is closer to him than his fellow riders in the American Flyers Motorcycle Club. Some years back, Rich invested in one of my startup companies. Soon after he invested, the board changed direction and asked me to step down as CEO.

Rich called the chairperson of the board and read him the riot act, demanding his money back. It turns out he hadn't invested in the company, he was investing in me. Without me in the picture, he wanted nothing to do with them.

The impact Rich has had on my riding life is immense. To this day, emails arrive twice a year with a subject line that says something like, "How about we do Nova Scotia?"

I hope they never stop coming.

L to R: AFMC riders Kim & Rich Marin, Bruce Rauner, Jeanne Dilly, me, Jim Revenaugh, Maggie, Rob & Urch St. John and Mark Dilly.

61

SCENIC OVERLOAD IN KIWI-LAND

RIDING MOTORCYCLES IN FOREIGN COUNTRIES has contributed remarkably to my understanding of the world. Seeing any place on two wheels is so very different from seeing it from inside a car or a tour bus. Motorcycle riding has much more in common with hiking or bicycling through a country than it does with driving.

During my first international ride with the AFMC, I went to Italy without Maggie. On a rented Ducati Monster, I visited some of the most fabulous landmarks the country had to offer. Each night I'd write up our day's adventures and send an email home to Maggie, describing where we'd been and what I'd seen. Back home, at the end of the trip, I combined all my emails into one, along with some photos, removed all the "Honey, I miss you," sections and sent it to everyone who'd been on the ride.

On this ride, tour operator Burt Richmond of Lotus Tours had invited David Searle, the editor of a premier motorcycling magazine, *Motorcycle Consumer News* (MCN). I loved meeting David and his brother Donny, who accompanied him. After receiving my email with all the trip notes, David called and said he had just started writing his article on the trip when he realized he could save himself some time and just publish mine. Would I be okay with that? I was quite flattered by the offer and said, "Of course."

A month later, our issue of MCN arrived with my article in it, and a day later I received a check for $2,500. Wow! That's cool, I thought. Then I called my accountant, asking him if I needed to declare it as income. He said I certainly would, but then added, "You can deduct any expenses that went into creating the article, like your motorcycle rental, airfare to and from Italy, hotels, meals and any attractions you saw and wrote about." It took me about two minutes to decide I was going to become a motorcycle journalist.

The AFMC's next international trip was to New Zealand, an event so momentous it provided powerful motivation for me to see more countries this way. If Mother Teresa had been a motorcyclist when she died, she would have chosen the South Island of New Zealand for eternity. The size of Colorado, this island has majestic, snow-capped mountains, scrub-dotted savannahs, endless sandy beaches, breathtaking waterfalls, towering fjords, volcanoes, turquoise lakes, thermal pools, tumultuous river rapids and enormous glaciers.

Upon this pristine and fascinating landscape, insert twisty roads containing every type of corner you can imagine. Pave the roads with a lava-based material that provides almost unbelievable adhesion. Add in a population density so low that it's possible to ride for hours and see only a half dozen other motorists. Few cars mean even fewer highway patrol officers. If that's not motorcycle heaven, I'm not sure what is.

When locating New Zealand on a map, it appears to be on the other side of the world—and it is. Most U.S. flights bound for NZ leave in the evening from Los Angeles. Our flight left LA on a Monday night at 9:10 p.m. We had dinner on the plane, fell asleep, woke to breakfast and landed in Auckland at 7:10 a.m. the following morning, refreshed and ready for a day of exploring.

"Following morning" is a slight misnomer, however, because there's a 24-hour time change when crossing the international dateline. Instead of arriving Tuesday morning, we arrived on Wednesday, but it felt like Tuesday.

I rented a Triumph Tiger 955i, a "sporty adventure-type" bike like the Suzuki V-Strom or the BMW GS, from GoTourNZ, the premier motorcycle touring company in New Zealand. The bike delivers 104 bhp via a fuel-injected, liquid-cooled, 955cc, three-cylinder engine with 67 ft-lbs. of torque. It was flame-colored and painted with tiger stripes. My riding partner, Philip Richter, chose the Honda Pan-European STX-1300ABS (ST1300 in the U.S.). New Zealand roads allow for some aggressive riding, so unless you only plan on leisurely sightseeing a sportier bike pays big dividends in the twisties.

The genuine "adventure" portion of our ride was an optional excursion on Coronet Peak Road, leaving from Queenstown and taking us deep into Skippers' Canyon. The road is all gravel and closed to rental cars. It's pretty benign, but completely heart-stopping for anyone sensitive to heights.

Twelve kilometers into the gorge, we found the spot where Peter Jackson filmed the Ford of Bruinen in the flood, one of the most dramatic scenes from *The Fellowship of the Ring*. Near the end of this road is a fabulous old bridge that gives you chills when you cross it. Throughout New Zealand, we saw many sights from Peter Jackson's "travelogue trilogy" *The Lord of the Rings*. Although, during our three weeks there, I never saw a single hobbit, much less one riding a motorcycle.

John Fitzwater of GoTourNZ was our master planner. He's led more motorcycle adventures in New Zealand than there are chapters in this book. Educated as a geologist, he's able to explain why all the wondrous things you're seeing all fit together in this magic landscape. One of the most incredible sights we saw was the stunning Franz Josef and Fox Glacier. A peaceful walk of about 30 minutes can take you almost to the edge. Or you can take a helicopter that will land on the glacier and allow you to walk on its top. The Homer Tunnel was also unlike anything we've ever seen. A complete black hole, it swallows all light.

A visit to a bird sanctuary only barely prepared us to meet New Zealand's very own parrot, the Kea, a large, olive-green bird that's native to the South Island. It loves anything squishy or soft, especially the rubber around car windows and motorcycle seats. It's a very destructive bird.

As beautiful as New Zealand's natural world is, the manmade parts are just as spectacular. Queenstown, birthplace of bungee jumping and zorbing (rolling downhill inside a transparent, plastic ball), was great fun. And all the historic inns we stayed in throughout the country welcomed us with open arms. In Hokitika, we stayed at the Kapitea Ridge Lodge, a highly stylish, luxury seven-suite B&B with a spectacular view overlooking the Tasman Sea.

What linked all these incredible experiences, of course, were the days of riding along the winding roads that clung to mountainsides and followed twisting rivers of exquisite clarity. I felt in constant danger of scenic overload. Occasionally, the temptation to stop the bike and simply stare at the exceptional, isolated beauty and tranquility of nature was irresistible.

I had to remember to breathe.

A road along New Zealand's South Island coast.

62

EPIC DAKAR

TALK TO ANY SERIOUS OFF-PAVEMENT rider long enough and the Dakar Rally comes up—either the dream of participating or seeing the race as a riding spectator. It's to dirt riders what Rome is to Catholics, what Hollywood is to movie fans and what the Grand Ole Opry is to country music lovers. It's the Daytona 500 superimposed on the World Cup, lasting as long as the Tour de France.

This competition tests professional drivers at the top of their game and in peak physical condition. It's unique in that amateurs (privateers) are allowed to compete on the same level, on the same course and with the same rules (albeit at a gross disadvantage) as the professionals. To reach any respectable finishing position requires the physical conditioning of a triathlete and the endurance of a marathoner—assuming said marathoner could run 13 consecutive races with a single rest day, sometimes at 15,000-foot altitudes. Superb navigational prowess and technical riding skills, sufficient to traverse deep sand, rocky mountain passes, water hazards and mud at high speed, are also required to even have a chance at finishing. Since 1979, nearly 80 people have died attempting this challenge.

While my moto-journalism riding experience was insufficient preparation to ride the Dakar Rally as a competitor, the chance to join an exceptional group of talented adventure riders and follow the 2011 rally through South America was something I couldn't pass up. After the murder of four French citizens in Africa, the 2008 Dakar rally was cancelled. In 2009, the 31st edition moved to Latin America, where it continued for several years.

As difficult as it is for spectators to keep up with the race, it doesn't compare with what the competitors face. After participating in a Dakar rally, cycle legend Malcolm Smith called it the most grueling and brutal ride he'd ever taken—and Smith has won the Baja 500 six times. Charley Boorman, a lifelong rider and the more skilled rider of the McGregor/Boorman team, featured in the *Long Way Round* and *Long Way Down* motorcycle riding documentaries, attempted the Dakar in 2006 after a year of intense training. Boorman managed just five days before crashing and injuring himself to the point of withdrawal. In his book *Race to Dakar*, he warns would-be participants: "However hard you might think it will be, however well you prepare for it, it will never be enough. It is an emotional, physical, and mental rollercoaster that demands total devotion. If you need to ask about it, you probably shouldn't do it."

Before placing this event firmly in the macho-pain-test category, however, you've got to also factor in a route through magnificent scenery so disturbingly beautiful that you wonder if you're still on planet Earth. We also experienced a generous welcome from the Argentinian and Chilean locals. Pulling into gas stations, we found babies being pushed into our arms for photos by thrilled parents. Kids pushed scraps of paper, t-shirts and even their bodies at us to autograph. Streets of every good-sized town were lined with waving and cheering locals as we went by.

Our first real taste of the rally came on our way to Tucuman, about 1,000 miles from the race start in Buenos Aires, where we got our initial up-close view of rally participants at a checkpoint. Unlike other racing events, there are no massive barriers to protect spectators from the trucks, cars and motorcycles that career through these checkpoints. Only a slim yellow ribbon cordons off the actual check-in areas. As a result, fans crowd the paths that the competitors must take to slide to a stop, have their tickets punched and take off, tires spinning and spraying gravel over the crowd.

From there, we pushed on to Purmamarca, a small village at the base of Seven Colors Hill in the Andes. The town's name translates to "Town of the Virgin Land." At just over 7,500 feet, we selected it to help acclimate us for our first Andes crossing the next day.

Following the Dakar as a spectator meant tracking the rally's cross-continent, multi-country route on motorcycle. Each leg of the 6,000-mile journey, which looped through Argentina and Chile in the year I was there, consumed hundreds of miles daily. We averaged 350+ miles a day, mostly on dirt roads, often with speeding race vehicles just inches from our elbows. Crossing the Andes mountain range involved nearly 500 miles per day and included 15,500-foot passes with sections of the course so obscured with dust you'd think you were riding in a North Dakota snow storm. Precise course layouts are unavailable until 12 hours before the next day's race, and hotels and restaurants are frequently scarce in the areas where riders and drivers stop each night.

Half our group, nearly all experienced adventure bikers, couldn't complete the trip due to equipment failures, endurance issues or extreme fatigue. We all rode BMWs, mostly late-model rentals, though some bikes had been shipped from the States. The 1200 GSs held up well; the 650 GS twins and 800 GSs less so.

Drifting off to sleep in Purmamarca, I thought about the fantastic mountain range we'd be traversing the next day, with its 15,000-ft. plateaus and 16,000-ft. passes. Then I remembered that it won't be our only crossing. We had to repeat the climb on the way back, farther south, through the famous Paso de San Francisco. Bone tired, I put the second crossing out of my head and focused on the first. We'd only finished two days, and I decided I had to take this one day at a time to finish all 14.

Choppers awakened us before 6:00 a.m. as they trained their aerial cameras on the front-runners, who were already tearing up the mountain toward the Chilean border. We met a cold rain and began our ascent a mile beyond our starting point. Our riding gear, generously adorned with sponsor logos, looked great and worked perfectly for the entire trip—except this once. Our jackets funneled the frigid water directly into the front of our pants. Within minutes of reaching the top (and an end to the rain), we parked our bikes on a massive salt plateau, jumped off and immediately stripped down to dry off. Note to self: pack only new underwear.

Before leaving the salt flat, we received some coca leaves from the guides. We stuffed the dry, foul-tasting leaves between our cheeks and gums and slowly swallowed the resulting juice. Chewing coca leaves is popular among locals as a mild stimulant, reputedly aiding in the fight against altitude sickness. While the leaves technically contain cocaine alkaloid, chewing them produces none of the euphoric or psychoactive effects that result from purified forms of the drug.

Dealing with customs and immigration at the 15,000-ft. border crossing lasted several hours. We were missing registration paperwork on several bikes, and the Chilean and Argentinian border authorities didn't appear to like each other very much. Chile never supported Argentina during its dispute with Britain over the Falkland Islands, and rumor has it that Chile had shared intelligence with the United Kingdom. Suffering from the altitude and language limitations, we had difficulty expediting the process as officials pointed fingers at each other and passed blame. The delays devoured precious daylight, and it was nearly dark when we crossed into Chile, aiming for our hotel in Calama.

The temperature dropped like a brick off a cliff as the sun disappeared and the wind whipped up across the vast plateau. Pushing our bikes through the intense, biting wind in the inky blackness was a struggle. Even at speeds approaching 70 mph, we spent another four hours riding in the dark. Two people came off their bikes. The wind blew one rider's bike over when we stopped to count heads. Exhausted, frustrated and angry with the decision to stop on an exposed, high-desert highway with no shoulder or shelter from the wind, one rider refused to go on. Leaving her bike by the side of the road, she pushed into the trailing support truck with the guides, immune to all arguments to get back on the bike.

Still at altitude, we encountered the motorcycle of one of our riders who'd ventured off alone from the border before we did, but he was nowhere to be found. We continued to our hotel, put out a missing person report on our absent comrade and sat down to dinner at midnight. My GPS recorded the highest altitude it's ever traveled at 15,749 feet.

The next day, somewhat rested, we were set to cross the Atacama Desert, the driest place on Earth. We'd see the west coast of South America and the Pacific Ocean and—with any luck—find our errant companion.

Leaving Calama, the group went ahead without me. I wanted to tour this desperately dry city before venturing to cross the southern tip of the Atacama Desert alone. While Calama averages just 0.20 inches of rain annually, the nearby desert has had no rainfall in recorded history. There are no plants, animals or insects, not even flies. According to Dr. Tibor Dunai from Edinburgh University, the hyper-arid conditions go back at least 20 million years. Those studying microorganisms in extreme environments have found that the Atacama is the only place on Earth where soil samples taken back to the lab have shown nothing growing.

The dry desolation lasted for several hours, and I marveled at my audacity in taking this leg solo. Finally, the massive piles of sand came to an end at the Pacific Ocean. Unlike glacier calving in Alaska, with the sudden breaking away of mountains of ice hundreds of feet high, the sand has slowly spilled into the water over thousands of years.

Passing through the small fishing village of Tocopilla, I overlooked a scheduled gas stop. Blissfully unaware of my error, I headed north on Highway 1 toward Iquique. Like the dramatic views along California's Highway 1 between San Simeon and Big Sur, the 200 miles between Tocopilla and Iquique provide otherworldly vistas of immense walls of sand, some appearing to be miles high, tumbling into the ocean. Halfway to my destination, my fuel gauge showed a near-empty tank.

A quick search of my maps and GPS revealed no towns, gas stations or fishing villages nearby. Nothing. Still a hundred miles from Iquique, I slowed to 40 mph and waited for a truck. When a large transport vehicle passed, I temporarily prioritized safety behind running out of gas and tucked in behind it, staying close enough for the draft to help conserve my remaining fuel. Ninety anxious minutes later, I pulled into a gas station on the outskirts of Iquique. The BMW 1200 GS has a fuel capacity of 5.283 gallons. The pump put 5.142 gallons into the thirsty tank.

In Iquique, we reunited with our missing rider. After several hours in the frigid wind and a series of increasingly close calls on one of Argentina's most rugged passes, he'd pulled over, dragged his bike to the edge of the highway and waved down the first motor coach that came by. He begged to be taken out of the crippling cold and down from the altitude that was making him so sick. They took him on board and dropped him at the nearest hotel once off the mountain. Although he was more than a hundred miles from us, we connected with him through his daughter in the United States. After a long cab ride, he rejoined the group the next day and our tour guide relegated him to the chase wagon for the rest of the trip.

One of the highlights of Dakar is watching race participants finish the stage that leads them to the bivouac in Iquique. Cars, bikes, quads and enormous trucks stream down the face of a three-quarter-mile high dune, one of the highest in the world. From our vantage point, it looked nearly vertical. Because of the sand's nature and the slope's steepness, racers have little choice but to stay on the power and head straight down. Backing off the gas for something as mundane as steering causes problems, not the least of which is a possible rollover. For spectators, it's one of the most eye-popping sporting spectacles ever. Hundreds of high-performance vehicles, charging at full throttle, barreling straight down a hill of fine, deep sand with no way to stop or steer. Robbie Gordon's orange, 1,000+ HP Hummer made the crowd roar when momentum carried him 100 feet across the sand in the air as he cleared a rise at the bottom of the dune.

In Iquique, we took the next day off and let the rally go north for a loop to Arica and its famous beaches near the Peruvian border and back again. We welcomed this rest day like a six-year-old welcomes Christmas morning. We slept in and spent the day catching up on laundry, body surfing in the ocean, making repairs and just wandering around the idyllic resort town. It was only halfway through the trip, and I already crammed in more than I've ever done on any other motorcycle adventure.

We put Iquique behind us early on the sixth day. Our goal was to reach a desert checkpoint before the race participants. At only 324 miles and just about 12 hours of riding, this relatively short day promised good glimpses of the riders up close.

We arrived at the checkpoint in the center of a vast sand table that reached the horizon in every direction, just as the workers were setting up. One member of our party, fluent in French, enabled us to converse with the event officials before the action started. This stop was so far out into the desert that we were part of only a handful of spectators. The location allowed us to see competitors approach from nearly a mile away and watch them for almost two miles as they left, climbing a multi-level hill toward the mountains.

This was a fuel top-up point for the motorcycles, which meant the riders had a mandatory 15-minute wait. The pause provided a bit of downtime, during which we engaged a few of the competing riders in conversation. Imagine walking along the sidelines during a Super Bowl game and chatting casually with the quarterback and other players. This is what it's like to talk with these athletes mid-race. We were able to converse with Simon Pavey (on one of the few BMWs), Marc Coma (who eventually won the rally on his KTM) and Cyril Despres of France (who took second).

After an hour or two at the checkpoint, we rode through more sand, this time covered by a dry, brittle surface layer. As our wheels broke the crust, we left lines in the desert that could be seen for miles. We ascended a rise directly above the path of the race and watched vehicle after vehicle choose a line, charge up toward the saddle below the hill where we were standing, go over the crest, and drop into a wide berm of deep sand. The ground was so thick and soft that nearly everyone got stuck.

Seeing cars, bikes and trucks struggle through the mess was mesmerizing. Plumes of sand buried the cars. All we saw was a sizeable, sandy-brown ball vibrating with a screaming engine at the center, wriggling to get free. One truck attempted a route with a firmer pack and assailed the top of the hill where we were perched, directly through a group of spectators. People scattered like dry leaves, and surprisingly, no one was hit.

A sculpture of a giant hand rises 30 feet out of the desert floor.

Leaving the checkpoint in the distance, we soon found ourselves on a large, divided highway. We safely pushed the big BMWs over 90 mph, arriving at our hotel in Antofagasta in good time. The following day, we made a leisurely start and headed south. With only an hour under our belts, we stopped at the "Hand of the Desert." This sculpture of a giant hand more than 30 feet high, emerging from the floor of the desert, is an unexpected sight and such an unusual piece of art that it grabbed and held our attention more than we expected. The Chilean sculptor Mario Iarrázabal created the amazing piece, which was unveiled in March 1992.

We spent the rest of the day on good pavement, fighting only the interminable Chilean winds. Even at a brisk 50 mph, we can handle riding in windy conditions. However, when the wind gathers up material from the desert it turns into a sandblaster. We took it with few complaints, though, because our attention was focused on the night's bivouac before heading to our lodging in Copiapo.

The Dakar bivouac is a 2,500-person moving city managed by the Dakar producers, the Amaury Sport Organisation (ASO). ASO specializes in producing large, multi-day sporting events, such as the Tour de France, Tour of Spain and the Dakar Rally. The bivouac is the epicenter from which everything emanates and where each stage begins. It's every rider's destination, a mobile metropolis that includes repair pits, sleeping areas, dining facilities, a tent hospital with a full operating room and a television production facility.

Professional riders with big sponsors have full support teams in the bivouac that tear down and rebuild their race vehicles while they sleep. Because independent drivers must make all their own repairs themselves, the average privateer manages on just three or four hours of sleep per night. Over a 13-day race, this takes quite a toll and contributes to the immeasurable fatigue the riders face in the rally's later stages.

We brought food to Simon Pavey, the 43-year-old Australian who prepared Charley Boorman and Ewan McGregor for their famous adventures. We talked with Pavey as he tore down and serviced his BMW G450X after finishing that day's stage. Privateers like Pavey spend $25,000 on the Dakar entry fee, which includes the ASO transport of two spare wheels and one footlocker-sized trunk containing tools, parts, a tent and a sleeping bag between bivouacs each day.

Michelin sets up an area where they change tires for free. Bikes need a new rear tire every day and a new front tire every other day. Another vendor provides free part fabrication, mostly plastic and fiberglass. And while they make no promises, stories abound of the miracles they make happen overnight. Food, medical help and insurance are also included in the entry fee, as well as the electronics that the organization installs on all the bikes.

ASO provides three devices for motorcycle competitors. The first is a safety GPS, which remains off until it automatically comes on within 984 ft. of a checkpoint. Because race participants must navigate entirely with their road book, turning the GPS on at any other time results in significant time penalties. The road book is a long roll of paper showing the planned route and obstacles, such as ruts, ditches and other cautions. It tells riders where and when to turn. For convenience, the road book is housed directly in the rider's line of vision between the handlebars and can be advanced and reversed by clicking a switch.

The second device is the Sentinel system. Racing motorcycles have no mirrors, so when cars and other race vehicles approach, a proximity sensor switches the device on so it can emit an acoustic blast that gets louder and more intense if the vehicle from behind gets closer. The device is designed to prevent motorcycles from being smashed like bugs by speeding cars or massively powerful trucks.

And lastly, ASO gives riders a beacon that automatically alerts the organizers if a vehicle stops suddenly or is on its side for eight minutes or more and opens up a communication channel. If a rider can't answer and assure the organizers they're healthy and safe, a helicopter is dispatched to check their status.

The hospital crew for the Rally was comprised of 55 doctors, 20 of whom were available at any given time. Ten medical support cars, with two medical staff members in each car, and three medical helicopters were available for dispatch at the first sign of trouble.

Walking through the acres of tents, trailers, corrals and brightly lit repair areas in the bivouac, it was hard to imagine that the entire place had to be torn down, packed up, trucked several hundred miles and rebuilt the next day, often in the middle of a desert.

* * * * *

The return trip to Argentina from Chile took us over Paso de San Francisco, and once again required almost 500 miles of riding for the day, with nearly 200 miles on dirt roads shared with race vehicles at altitudes over 15,000 feet. We were intent to learn from the mistakes we made during our first Andes crossing and have fewer incidents this time.

Committed to an early start, we awoke at 4:00 a.m., grabbed a quick *café con leche* and a cold ham and cheese sandwich, and were on the bikes leaving Copiapo within 30 minutes. A few hours later, we pulled over at the base of the Andes and got our coca leaves out of the back of the truck. Besides helping with the altitude, the chew would also help us stay alert during the next 13 or 14 hours of riding.

At around 14,000 feet on Paso de San Francisco, we met the dust. Silt occluded the air like a cloud, its consistency like sifted flour. Wind that had mercifully kept the powdered dirt moving suddenly stalled. Visibility dropped to near zero as the delicate mixture hovered, getting inside our helmets and goggles, into our eyes and mouths. Coming around a corner as we climbed, my bike dove into a soft, sand-covered trough and stopped, throwing me off.

Groaning, I looked up to see two other riders just in front of me, attempting to drag their bikes to the side after having suffered the same fate. Panic rushed into my head as I thought of the bikes just seconds behind mine and, even more dangerous, the five-ton trucks coming up the hill only a minute or two behind them. With our hearts thumping manically, the three of us frantically pulled our bikes from the path of the oncoming vehicles while others ran down the hill, waving their hands, attempting to direct the arriving riders and trucks around the dangerous trap that lay ahead. Miraculously, no one was injured but we were all shaken up.

Each of us was forced to develop our own way of coping with the dust, which caused near-total blindness for 20 or 30 seconds after a truck or car passed. When my vision cleared after one such passing, I found myself a second away from slamming into a tree jutting into the road. I soon adopted a more conservative approach of stopping just before a vehicle passed, unless I could see several hundred feet ahead and feel confident about keeping my heading for a quarter mile while riding blind. We plowed ahead.

Several riders in our group crashed that day, and one damaged his bike beyond repair. Others fainted from the altitude. A BMW support vehicle stopped to help, providing oxygen and a lift to the border for anyone who needed it. The brutal route took its toll on our support truck, too. Several suspension bolts sheared off, forcing the vehicle to slow to 10 miles an hour or less. A few miles later, the air bags holding the truck suspension gave out. The truck was now limited to a top speed of four to five miles per hour until it could reach a paved surface. Our group was struggling on all fronts, and the leader asked if anyone could take over the truck. I've driven school buses, motor coaches, skip loaders and farm equipment, so I volunteered to take on the task.

Just when it seemed we were trapped in an endless nightmare of dirt and danger, we emerged over a rise to find salvation: a dreamy turquoise lake stretched before us, deep and clear, surrounded by oddly alien rocks and boulders. The stark landscape held no plants, no birds, no animals—just pristine water reflecting the harsh beauty of our surroundings.

Our exhausted group began to fragment during the descent. The fastest riders reached our scheduled camping site in Chilecito around 9:00 p.m., but an hour later, the second group, including our crippled support truck, could make it only as far as a gas station—still 100 miles short of camp. Too exhausted to continue, we found a local mechanic who promised to fix the truck overnight. The decision was unanimous: we'd stay put. The distant camp site was beyond our depleted energy reserves.

It was after 10:00 p.m., but the local tourist bureau found a resident, with a large and extended family, willing to vacate two adjacent homes to provide beds for us. The faster part of our group backtracked to meet us, and we all had a late dinner before retiring to the homes so generously rented to us on short notice. We were asleep in seconds.

Reviewing photos taken after the dust cleared over Paso de San Francisco (26° 52' 35" S, 68° 18' 5" W), I was awed by the incredible colors and unique character of the terrain. There was a dramatic contrast between the vast emptiness of the desert plateau and the mountain scenes, created by powerful volcanoes and earthquakes.

The next morning, our guides commandeered the homeowner's kitchen and prepared a breakfast of eggs, tortillas and tomatoes. Curious children shyly crept back into the houses after spending the night with friends and relatives. Only slightly easing the "rich gringo takes child's bed" headline in my mind, I was told that our modest fee and generous tips to the home's owner well exceeded a month's income for the family. And, with only a few days left in our adventure, several riders opted to abandon their sleeping bags, tents and clothing to lighten their load, much to the delight of the kids.

Leaving rested and with full stomachs, we pulled into Chilecito just in time for lunch. With only 300 more miles to go to make it to San Juan, we took off. If not for a couple of bikes giving out, it would have been an uneventful day. Roads, pace, heat and distance wear out equipment and humans both. The crankcase on one 800GS completely ruptured during a hard landing on a rock.

The last leg of our journey was a long sprint from San Juan to Cordoba. The group split up again, with one pod taking a longer but safer route. Two riders took an even longer and more adventurous path, which included some significant "water hazards." My riding partner and I began with the safe route, but then decided to try a back way into Cordoba despite warnings of nonnegotiable sections. "We've got a good GPS unit," we thought. "How hard can it be, especially given what we've already been through?"

The warnings proved unwarranted. We encountered a few high narrow roads without guard rails, but that was about it. Some areas turned into foot paths between backyards and farmyards and, at one point, through a monastery.

The GPS worked flawlessly, and we arrived at our starting hotel in Cordoba a half hour ahead of the next set of riders. Others trickled in over the late afternoon, and everyone made it back for our last official night in Argentina, where we had dinner at the largest rodeo in South America. Watching real cowboys attempt to cling to the backs of bucking wild horses seemed all too familiar to us.

Most of my fellow riders concluded that this was the most dangerous, craziest and humbling experience they've ever had. Some said, "Never again," while a few others already started planning for the next year.

With its proximity to the race participants and nearly half the participants unable to finish, the rally itself is unlike anything else I've ever experienced. As a rider with enough skills to appreciate genuine expert riders, I know the difference between amateurs and those who do this for a living. Coming so close to competitors at this level was an indescribable thrill.

The wonders of South American topography, the warmth and enthusiasm of the Argentinean and Chilean people and an amazing ride put the Dakar Rally in the "must-do-before-you-die" category for a true off-pavement riding enthusiast. It rewards you with months of excited anticipation, a dozen-plus days of genuine adventure and thrills and rich memories that will remain with you forever.

* * * * *

Back in Arizona, I had an epiphany. At age 60, it might be time to stop dirt bike riding from occupying so much of my free time. This was not a happy thought, but one I knew to be true.

One rather important aspect of riding off road across sand and rocks is maintaining the right speed. Going too slow leads to accidents, as does going too fast. Crashing and being thrown off a fast-moving motorcycle invariably results in damage to oneself, despite the best riding gear, and I wasn't healing as fast as I used to.

Over the next few months, I sold my off-road motorcycles, keeping only my big BMW 1200GS (and its off-road, Woodies Wheels, of course). To avoid an argument, we won't discuss exactly how many motorcycles that was. What matters most is that it was enough to purchase a new Polaris RZR 800S.

While I would go on rides into Mexico's Copper Canyon and make trips to Moab for off-road adventures, the Dakar was my last great epic dirt bike adventure, and what an adventure it had been.

Crossing the Atacama Desert during the Dakar Rally.

63

SPEED IS RELATIVE: ADVENTURES IN A POLARIS RZR

NOTHING TEACHES HUMILITY QUITE LIKE your first high-speed run in a Polaris RZR. I learned this lesson in Arizona at The Boulders, an Off-Highway Vehicle (OHV) park west of Lake Pleasant, where 60 square miles of trails and the Picacho Wash create an off-road playground. There I was in my new Polaris 800S, determined to test its claimed top speed of 65 mph—or maybe even 70, given all my aftermarket modifications.

Pointing my RZR 800S down the middle of the wide, sandy wash, I floored it. The vehicle leapt forward eagerly, bouncing over ruts and rocks as the air tore at my face, pulling my cheeks back into what I'm sure was a grotesque smile. Certain I was approaching highway speeds, I finally gathered the nerve to glance at the speedometer. A quick double-take confirmed the unbelievable reading: just over 35 mph, heading for 40.

I slowed down, enjoying the rest of the afternoon at a more leisurely pace. Driving home later with the RZR on the trailer behind me, I had another epiphany. My garage was full of vehicles that made 80 mph feel like 40—maybe it was time to appreciate one that made 40 feel like 80.

That appreciation only grew when I upgraded to a four-seat 2015 RZR 1000S XP4. With this more powerful machine, I could go farther and faster and share Arizona's magnificent public spaces with friends and family. Few realize that only 18% of Arizona's land is privately owned. The rest belongs to all of us citizens, managed by various federal agencies but primarily the Bureau of Land Management.

Their charter keeps these vast spaces open and available to the public, creating an off-road paradise without fences or "No Trespassing" signs. Friends from the Midwest, Texas and other states, where most of the land has been fenced off, marvel at the wide-open spaces here in Arizona.

Our regular riding companions were our neighbors, Ralph and Koena Tapscott, who owned a highly modified two-seat RZR. While I enjoyed taking friends on leisurely tours of Arizona's wilderness, Ralph and Koena viewed the terrain as their personal racetrack. Koena especially drove with such enthusiasm that keeping up with her became a thrilling challenge.

My wife Maggie, however, ranked RZR riding somewhere below watching paint dry on her list of preferred activities. But she'd agree to come along with me on occasion if I promised pretty views and reasonable speeds, especially when she liked our traveling companions. So, when Ralph and Koena invited us to participate in a RZR rally at Puerto Peñasco (aka Rocky Point), Mexico, where they owned a home, Maggie surprised me with an "Okay, sure, maybe we could go. It might be fun." Rocky Point is a short three-and-a-half-hour drive south of Phoenix. On the Sea of Cortez, it's often called "Arizona Beach."

I could hardly wait. Two months out, I dedicated almost all my time to prepping the RZR and purchasing new accessories. In Mexico, on the morning of race day, after checking in at a local hotel to get our rally T-shirts and goody bags, we went to the staging spot just north of Puerto Peñasco. At the top of the hour, someone raised a pistol into the air and fired it. About 45 RZR-type vehicles took off in a line across the desert, going as fast as they could.

It was clear from the start that this would not be the ideal ride for Maggie. We were about a dozen vehicles back from the front and the dust was overwhelming. It was almost impossible to see or breathe. Fortunately, we brought good goggles and masks to cover our mouths and noses.

Blasting down the roads, occasionally launching into the air, we were certainly exceeding 40 mph. In fact, I'd guess we were going closer to 60—which felt at least like 100.

After about an hour, we reached our first rest stop, somewhere out in the middle of the desert where everyone pulled into a rough circle. We found ourselves in a group of heavily tattooed and pierced young people, happily drinking beer at 9 a.m., while hip-hop music blasted from souped-up sound systems. What had we gotten ourselves into?

Yet something magical happened as the day wore on. The oppressive heat, massive dust clouds and jarring terrain became normal. We found ourselves admiring tattoos, comparing vehicle modifications and sharing stories and scenic vistas over lunch. Maggie, bless her heart, gripped the handholds tightly but never complained, even managing to be friendly with our colorful fellow riders. In return, I did my best to stay at the front of the pack to avoid as much dust as possible.

That afternoon, coming into town, we joined the other participants at an outdoor Mexican restaurant for beers and burgers before heading back to the Tapscott's at dusk, exhausted and happy. After showers, Advil and sunset margaritas with our hosts, I turned to Maggie in bed. "Honey, you were such a fantastic sport today. You didn't complain once, didn't scream at me to slow down, didn't beg me to go home. You were awesome, and I really appreciate it."

I paused before continuing, "I want to repay you and so, I've been thinking—when we get home, one day I'm going to spend the entire day in your art studio with you, just to show equal support for your hobby."

In the darkness, I heard a low groan and two words dripping with insincerity: "Oh, great."

We both giggled, then burst into full-on laughter that we couldn't stop. When we finally caught our breath, I added, "You know, I could watch over your shoulder and say things like, 'I think you could use a little more blue over here.'"

That set us off again, and I realized that my favorite RZR memory would be one where we weren't even in the vehicle at all.

Though I eventually sold the RZR in 2020, the story has a happy ending. The buyer, Butch Milbrandt, keeps it at his airplane hangar at Sky Ranch Airport and lets me borrow it whenever I like. It's a fitting arrangement for a vehicle that taught me that sometimes the best adventures aren't about how fast you're actually going, but about who you're sharing the ride with—even if they'd rather be watching paint dry.

My pal Mark Dilly and brother-in-law John Woychick, with the 4-passenger Polaris RZR in the Arizona Sand Dunes near Yuma.

64

BATMAN MEETS SANTA

WHILE WE'RE ON THE SUBJECT of Polaris vehicles, only a few of my fellow motorcyclists know that I own a Polaris Slingshot, and even fewer understand how or why. Let's address the obvious question first: No, it's not a motorcycle. While it may be classified as one for legal purposes, in nearly every aspect it drives and handles like a car, albeit one that seems to have escaped from a superhero movie set.

I first encountered this unique machine in 2014, when Polaris Industries invited me to a highly confidential press event in the Twin Cities. They'd imposed an embargo on the announcement of the new Slingshot, which meant the magazine I represented, *Motorcycle Consumer News*, couldn't publish anything about it until they received permission without losing access to future news forever. I wasn't supposed to talk about it, either.

Polaris had already established itself as a master of knowing what toy lovers want before they even realize it. This $4.6 billion, power-sports manufacturer gives its designers free rein to create vehicles that capture the imagination of outdoor adventure seekers between the ages of 18 and 80. Have you ever seen that T-shirt that says, "Grandpas Are Just Antique Little Boys"?

Besides dominating the snowmobile and watercraft markets, Polaris revolutionized off-road vehicles with their innovative RZR and RANGER side-by-sides. Their Victory motorcycles offered cruiser riders a genuine alternative to Harley Davidson, and their revival of the Indian motorcycle brand masterfully blended historical authenticity with cutting-edge technology.

But the Slingshot was something entirely different. Picture this: a 173-horsepower front-mounted engine, a single rear wheel connected to the transmission by belt drive and ultra-wide-stance front wheels, all arranged in a three-point geometry that puts you mere inches above the pavement. From the front, its supercar angularity suggests something the Caped Crusader might drive. From behind, it looks more like a chairlift with a tire attached. With its 105-inch wheelbase and 70-inch track it's impressively wide, and at just under 1,700 pounds it launches from a standstill like a rocket.

When people question the stability of a three-wheeled vehicle, I point them to the humble restaurant table. How often have you struggled with a wobbly four-legged table, shoving napkins and matchbooks under one leg? But a three-legged table? They never wobble. It's simple physics.

What I love about the Slingshot is that it strips away every barrier between you and the road. No roof. No doors. No air conditioning. You enter by swinging your leg over the frame and lowering yourself into a race car-style seat, surrounded by rust-proof polymer body panels. The proximity to the pavement completely transforms your perception of speed—when your backside hovers just inches above the asphalt, 50 mph feels like 90. Even at modest speeds, you can't help grinning while your passengers throw their arms up as if they're on a rollercoaster.

When my Slingshot arrived—one of the first two or three in Arizona—every drive became an event. At each stoplight, surrounding cars' windows would roll down as people shouted questions, snapped photos and stared in amazement. But the real magic happened when we discovered its potential as a holiday attraction.

I wired in a 12V-to-110V inverter and covered the vehicle with strings of red LED lights. Cruising around town in this glowing "one-horse open sleigh," blasting Christmas carols through the speakers while wearing Santa hats, we created memories and moments of pure joy for everyone we passed.

The Slingshot perfectly demonstrates why convertibles, motor-cycles and ATVs hold such appeal—there's something fundamentally human about wanting to feel the sun on your face and wind in your hair while experiencing the world firsthand.

But taking this three-wheeled wonder out on a dark winter night, glowing like a mobile Christmas display, elevates that open-air ex-perience to an entirely new level. It transforms an already extraor-dinary vehicle into something magical—a reminder that sometimes the best toys are the ones that let us share our joy with others.

The Polaris Slingshot is a ball, especially when covered with holiday lights at Xmas time.

65

BETWEEN THE EARTH AND THE SKY

LIKE MANY MOTORCYCLISTS, I'VE ALWAYS been drawn to the freedom of movement. As a kid, I dreamed of flying like a bird, racing up dirt mounds with my mother's kitchen towel tied around my neck like a cape and launching myself into the air at the top, hoping to soar off like Superman. My brother and I built makeshift ramps, riding them like miniature Evel Knievels. That same desire for liberation and excitement would eventually lead me to motorcycles, but not before I explored every possible way to get airborne.

The journey taught me something that would later prove invaluable in my motorcycle adventures: the Dunning-Kruger Effect. Discovered in 1999, this cognitive bias occurs when people don't have enough knowledge to know they don't have enough knowledge. It's a critical overestimation that's present in all humans, and it operates on a scale: the worse you are or the less you know about something, the higher you rate your understanding or abilities. The Dunning-Kruger Effect can be dangerous, whether you're thousands of feet up or carving through mountain curves on two wheels.

My first brush with this reality came through Cessna's pilot training program, an inexpensive course heavily subsidized by Cessna using its 172 training plane. Young and confident, I dove in without understanding the depth of knowledge required. Just as many new riders think mastering a motorcycle means learning to operate the controls, I assumed flying would be pretty straightforward. The program cleverly ended shortly after your first solo flight, just as you began to grasp how much you didn't know. Like a rider graduating from a basic safety course, I had only scratched the surface.

I got my Student Pilot Certificate, allowing me to fly solo under specific conditions without passengers, but if I wanted to keep going and get a Sport Pilot License, the fees increased dramatically.

So I stopped. Not really because of the bait and switch, but because the airplanes were noisy and mechanical, unlike the "bird in flight soaring" experiences I had in my dreams. Another reason I stopped was because I realized I'd need massive amounts of learning and practice to achieve any level of competence and safety.

This pattern repeated itself with hang gliding. A friend's equipment and a few hours of instruction seemed sufficient—until I discovered the vast gulf between imagining flight and actually controlling it. I ran most of the way down a short hill (there are few mountains in Minnesota) before lifting off, climbing to an altitude of at best 10 feet for less than a minute. On landing, I had to run like hell to keep from falling.

Parachuting followed, which promised moments of transcendent beauty and complete silence that reminded me of perfect early morning motorcycle rides. But just as I would later learn that track days weren't my style of motorcycling, I discovered that free-falling didn't match my soaring dreams. One Friday, I went through jump school, learning everything I needed to know and do. The next afternoon was my first jump—a static line jump—where you jump from an airplane's open door with a line on the plane attached to your chute, making it open automatically seconds after you leave the plane.

Nothing prepares you for the heart-stopping, paralyzing fear you experience when stepping out of a perfectly good airplane and dropping like a rock. But once on the ground, I realized it was fun. On my way down to Earth, after my chute opened and the plane was out of earshot, I experienced total silence for the first time ever. It was surreal: Sounds from the ground don't reach past six thousand feet.

Another first for me during that jump was seeing the most beautiful thing ever—a large, perfectly formed parachute canopy above my head after I pulled the ripcord. Nothing compares, not even the Grand Canyon at dusk. The feeling was only rivaled by the magnificent gratitude I felt as I touched the ground safely and my chute collapsed all around me. I wanted to kiss the ground, and I probably did.

Gliding came next, through a club near Northfield. John Kaplan, a customer at Schaak Electronics where I worked in Rochester, Minnesota, was building a fixed-wing glider in his basement in the summer of 1973. Fascinated by what he was doing, I started taking lessons and flying the club's two German-made Schempp-Hirth gliders.

This fourth flight method was great fun but still noisy—not from an engine but from air rushing over the glider's surface area. But I fulfilled one dream: I gave my father a glider ride, which he loved. When the club learned I had my student pilot's license, they were keen to get me certified to fly the tow plane, a tail dragger that was modified and optimized for pulling gliders into the air. One weekend, when I wasn't at the club, an accident killed a glider pilot, damaging the tow plane and destroying one glider. I never returned.

Paragliding, my fifth flirtation with flight, ended up being my favorite. I had my first paragliding experience in Los Angeles, and it was the closest to the bird-like flight I imagined as a kid. The group I joined frequently launched from Soboba Mountain, southeast of Riverside. On July 3, 1991, the *LA Times* even featured me on the front page of their sports page.

My nephew once asked me if I'd ever bungee jumped. I was about to say no, but then I remembered my dozen bungee jumps, all in one day. Arriving at my paraglider instructor's home for our regular Saturday morning class, he slapped his forehead and said, "Oh Steve, I'm so sorry. I canceled class today and I forgot to call you."

He explained that he'd taken a contract to help test a CO_2 firing reserve parachute system. The product, if produced, would automatically be deployed at the push of a button, should a jumper or paraglider have an issue with their main chute. It was a backup parachute, of sorts.

He and his more experienced paragliding pals were heading to a bungee launching spot. There they'd have their ankles attached to bungee cords, inflate their gliders on the platform, fly off, collapse the chute and fire the CO_2 cartridge as they plummeted to the Earth, engaging the reserve chute and floating gently to the ground. At least that was the theory—hence the test. Did I want to come along? I could watch or help.

At the bungee launch site, things went exactly as planned and I was quickly enlisted to assist. It was mostly safe because, if anything failed, our ankles were attached to the bungee cords, which would catch us a dozen feet before we hit the ground. The first time was scary, but after that it was just repetitive work. The reserve chutes worked about half the time, so I suspect it was back to the drawing board for the company that was developing them. I wasn't that impressed with the technology, but I saw my flight instructor grab a few unfired reserve chutes and stick them into his backpack before we left.

I loved paragliding and was getting better at it, too: Just good enough to get cocky. One day, while waiting at the top of the mountain for a group of students to launch, I quickly and repeatedly inflated and collapsed my wing, showing off. On one inflation, a gust of wind picked me up and I was soon being pulled backward toward the other side of the mountain, where a drop would have likely killed me. Thinking fast, I collapsed my chute from about 20 feet, dropping like a rock into some desert bushes. I sprained an ankle and scratched my arms and face, but I wasn't dead. Still, after a few days of thinking about it, I quit paragliding.

I have many friends who fly recreationally, and some who fly as part of their jobs, and I've had repeated opportunities to get back in the air over the years. Dave Waks, my boss when Prodigy first transferred me to New York in 1993, allowed me to briefly pilot his Cessna. Math genius Alan Baratz, who retired from Cisco and Sun and then took on a small company that Steve Pittendrigh and I had invested in called Amber Alert, took me along on a trip to Utah and California in his Pilatus PC-12 turboprop, allowing me to slip behind the controls for a few minutes.

Modern flying is so far from what I did when I was young. Today's pilots study and learn so much, and they have the mindset to fly safely and be prepared for emergencies. My pilot friends meticulously go through pre-flight checklists, paying attention to everything.

It took little effort to recall the shortcuts and abbreviated checks I made on my gear and mental preparation before flying. Describing me as "an accident waiting to happen" is not altogether wrong. When my pilot friends are together and start talking about flying, I know to keep my mouth shut and avoid being an example of the Dunning-Kruger effect.

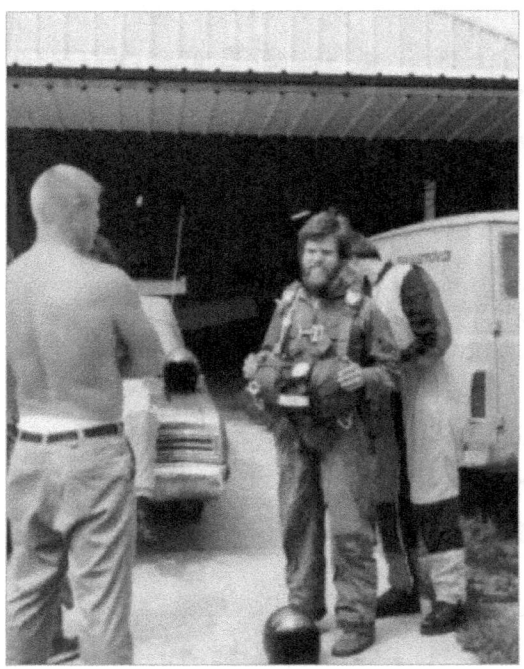

Parachute jumping and paragliding were my favorite ways to fly.

66

PURPLE RIDER IN DEATH VALLEY

I'LL NEVER FORGET STEPPING ONTO the wooden porch of the Crowbar Café and Saloon in Shoshone, California that April morning. The sound reached us first—a highly tuned engine pulling hard near redline, a quick upshift, then another. As the sound mellowed into top gear, a purple VFR appeared at the top of the hill, arcing through the long sweeper toward the T-intersection, where the bike could only go north or south.

We were glad to see it turn north toward us and the dozen buildings that make up Shoshone. The rider's full black leather suit came into focus as the bike pulled onto the gravel. Then came the reveal: long, purple-painted nails emerged from the gloves, red hair tumbled from the helmet. Who was she? What was she doing alone in the middle of Death Valley at 9:00 a.m., 150 miles from anywhere? Why was she riding a purple VFR with pristine white wheels, and who did that incredible paint job?

The more immediate question was, which one of us would dare to approach and talk to her?

Our mystery rider turned out to be named Diane Smith. She was taking one of her first long solo rides from her home in Pahrump, Nevada, after being in an accident six months earlier. She told us that her '04 Hayabusa had developed a high-speed wobble as she entered a left-hand sweeper. "I came off the throttle too quick and the bike just stood up," she said. "It's not something you want happening at 120 mph."

Ending up in a drainage ditch full of boulders, she'd broken 12 bones, including both ankles, her collarbone, right femur, left shoulder, bones in both hands and a couple ribs. "Although I was close to dead when I was air-lifted out, the funny thing was, not one of my fingernails had broken," she laughed.

After three days in the hospital and surgeries to get various pieces replaced and reinforced with titanium, she spent 30 days in rehab. Then she was sent home in a wheelchair to a hospital bed set up in her room, where she continued her recovery. "Even though it was months before my doctors would certify me to go back to work, I rode a bike six weeks after the accident," she says.

Diane Smith dismounting a purple Honda VFR with white rims.

While she was healing, a friend found a '98 VFR advertised in the paper. She had it stripped down and painted purple and added the powder-coated white wheels. Getting up early and taking a 150-mile solo run in the desert was one of her favorite things, she told us. She also said that she replaced her '04 Hayabusa with an '06 model and longed for another Ducati.

After a few more minutes of chatting, she turned around for her ride back to Pahrump and we headed toward Zabriskie Point. As her purple VFR disappeared into the desert morning, I marveled at how motorcycle journeys always seem to deliver these unexpected encounters.

While living in the Bay Area, I discovered it was a motorcyclist's paradise. The weather was perfect for riding, and while San Francisco itself was awful for motorcycles, heading north, south or inland offered hundreds of great roads and scenic destinations. This particular Death Valley trip, organized by my venture capitalist friend David Ezequelle and our friend Andrew Eisner, had become an annual tradition with its perfect mix of challenging roads, dramatic landscapes and chance meetings with riders like Diane.

When we started out on our ride from the parking lot of Buck's Restaurant in Woodside days before, no one expected it would include a vivacious redhead on a purple VFR. Buck's is the famous launching pad for hundreds of startup companies. It's where PayPal got its first money and where hundreds of anxious entrepreneurs outline plans for the next Google to jaded venture capitalists. But on this early Monday morning, no one was pitching plans. All the napkins remained free of diagrams. Instead, entrepreneurs and investors inspected bikes.

Back in Death Valley, before heading toward our hotel, we spent some photo time on the nine-mile Artist's Drive. This spectacular loop is 15 miles south of Furnace Creek on Highway 178. When the sun strikes the rocks, the minerals reveal yellows, oranges, deep reds and greens. Not far away is an overlook providing a view of the Devil's Golf Course, 200 square miles of salt residue from Death Valley's last significant lake, which evaporated 2,000 years ago. Even the off-road tires of the 1200GS would do poorly amongst the gnarly salt clumps and spires, if it were allowed to traverse the terrain.

When we began our ride, our first stop had been San Luis Obispo. Watching countless commuters clog the highways leading into the former fruit groves of Silicon Valley, we headed in the opposite direction. It felt as if we were playing hooky.

Our plan was to be in San Luis Obispo by nightfall, so, of course, we headed in nearly the opposite direction to Patterson through Mt. Hamilton, with a stop at the observatory perched on top. Highway

130 from San Jose to Mt. Hamilton is a fabulous road filled with tight technical corners, offering ample opportunity to slide off the seat and push a knee toward the pavement. The narrow road hugs the contour of the land with so many switchbacks and direction changes, the compass indicator on the GPS never stops spinning.

After a bio break at the observatory, we followed Highway 130 down the backside as it becomes Del Puerto Canyon Road. This 100-mile section offers compressed, non-stop twisties. With endless sets of banked and off-camber turns, it's easily as interesting as the more popular westward routes from Silicon Valley up to Skyline Drive and down to the coast. But this road always has far less traffic, and on this Monday morning we had it all to ourselves.

Next up was Ft. Hunter Liggett. Our documentation (driver's license, proof of insurance and bike registration) was inspected carefully by the officers at the gates of this military base before we were allowed in. At 165,000 acres, Ft. Hunter Liggett is the largest U.S. Army Reserve post. What makes it even more interesting is that it contains the Junipero Serra Peak and the headwaters of the Nacimiento River.

We only passed through a small portion of the base, because the real reason we were there was to take Ft. Hunter Liggett Road, which winds 35 miles over the mountains to US 1. Made of gravel, it's one of the most under-used and incredibly beautiful roads in the United States.

After settling into San Luis Obispo, we had dinner at the Tsurugi Japanese restaurant on Higuera Street. This annual ritual is one we highly anticipate. Two of our group members like to order for everyone, filling the table with incredible sushi and sashimi. Everything was delicious on the tongue and beautiful to the eye. As others raved about the Uni (sea urchin), I favored the nigiri and kohada sushi.

In the morning, we rode to Buttonwillow for breakfast, taking a short jaunt north on Highway 101 before veering off for the beautiful ride on Highway 58 (California Canyon Highway), over the mountains and the north edge of the Los Padres National Forest. After breakfast, we cruised through Bakersfield and down into Mojave, where we left Highway 58 for Highway 14 north to Death Valley.

Furnace Creek, Death Valley, California, is appropriately named. It is hot. Everyone knows that. But what's hard to appreciate is how hot. Furnace Creek recorded the second-highest temperature in the world, 134°F, in 1913. Only the magnificent Sahara Desert topped it, and only once, in 1922, by two degrees.

But the air temperature is only half the story. The ground temperature can be much warmer—by as much as 80°F. The highest ground temperature ever recorded was 201°F, which means you don't want to be walking to the pool barefoot! Thankfully, it was April when we were there, and the ground was still less than 95°F.

Why is Death Valley so hot? It's a long, narrow basin about 280 feet below sea level and walled by steep mountain ranges. With clear, dry air and virtually no plant cover, sunlight heats the surface of the desert relentlessly. The heat radiates and becomes trapped in the valley's depth. While the hot air rises, the high valley walls trap it inside the basin.

The result is far from boring. The landscape in Death Valley is spectacular, with some of the most surreal topography on the globe: sand dunes that go on for hundreds of miles, white salt flats that are blinding, even behind extra-dark sunglasses, sculptured hills and badlands laced with rushing water and multi-hued canyon walls.

Our bikes in the otherworldly topography of Death Valley.

On our first day, we sought the healing waters of the hot springs in Tecopa. Half of the group stayed for a long soak, while the rest of us headed to the date farm at China Ranch. Reaching the farm was a bit of a challenge. Heading south from the hot springs, you stay left (east) on the unmarked Old Spanish Trail Highway for about two miles. As Spanish Trail Highway heads off to the left, you have to remember to stay right on Furnace Creek Road until you see the sign for China Ranch.

What amazes first-time visitors to the date farm is how lush it is. It literally is an oasis in the desert, and the contrast is truly amazing. Open and welcoming to visitors, they have a gift shop with local art, honey and, of course, dates. You can get date bread, date cookies, date shakes, date bars and date cakes. This is a working date farm, dating back to the early 1920s. Half the trees are male and produce only pollen, with the female date trees producing 100 to 300 pounds of dates each season. Even without the delicious date shakes made fresh to order with thick vanilla ice cream, China Ranch is worth a visit.

Our next stop was Three Rivers, Sequoia National Park, because there's no better way to conclude a trip to Death Valley than to experience the extreme opposite of hot and flat—snow and high peaks. We left early and stopped for breakfast in Ridgecrest, then headed over to Walker Pass and up to Isabella Lake for a bit of coffee. A variety of winding mountain roads brought us to our stop for the night in Three Rivers, about 10 miles below the park entrance.

In the morning, we began our last day's ride into the park on Highway 198. We climbed more than 6,500 feet and saw snow on distant peaks. Stopping for lunch at Waksachi Lodge, we got pictures of the bikes against the snow in the parking lot and threw snowballs at each other.

Giving a mother black bear and her cub a wide berth, we pointed the bikes down to Squaw Valley. Skirting south of Fresno to avoid the traffic, we crossed the Central Valley. In Hollister, we made a caffeine stop and were safely back to the Bay Area and home in a couple of hours. All-in-all, it was a great way to spend a week.

In the 1960s, Honda launched their motorcycles in the U.S. with an advertising campaign that said, "You meet the nicest people on a Honda." I doubt the company's executives envisioned a redhead with a matching purple motorcycle, helmet and fingernails bombing through Death Valley at dawn. But, after I met Diane, I always have.

67

CLIMBING TREES ON TWO WHEELS

ONE OF THE MOST HUMBLING experiences of my motorcycle riding career was attempting trials riding. Trials bikes are purpose-built motorcycles designed for a specific type of riding competition called "mototrials" or "observed trials." The sport is prominent in Europe, South America and other parts of the world, with a more limited following in the United States.

If you've never seen a trials bike ridden well, find some YouTube videos and watch them. You'll quickly see what a skilled trials rider can do. The sport requires highly precise and rigorous riding, focused on balance and control at very low speeds.

I have a healthy respect for riders who master a trials bike, especially those who compete. I became good friends with former Moto-Trials champion Gary LaPlante during my riding and writing career. I rode with Gary and went on several trips with him. I wrote about him and his riding school, MotoVentures, for different motorcycle magazines. Gary passed away in 2022, and his sons are carrying on his legacy and training complex.

Gary LaPlante demonstrates a good wheelie.

I also had the good fortune of meeting mototrials rider Geoff Aaron and doing some publicity photos for him. Sponsored by Red Bull, Geoff is an exceptional rider who's made a career out of giving mototrials riding demonstrations at Red Bull events.

My trials training was given to me by Griff Wigley, one of the best teachers on the planet. Griff can teach just about anything to anyone. He's patient, kind and observant, and he knows precisely the right thing to say at the right time. Griff is very civic-oriented and spends most of his time with non-profit organizations, helping them build their communities, online and otherwise. There are few people I admire more for their commitment to the greater good.

When I was living in the Twin Cities area, Griff volunteered to loan me one of his trials bikes and teach me some basics. Thus, one Saturday morning, I found myself some miles out of Northfield, Minnesota at a park with many trails.

Griff unloaded the bikes from the trailer, explaining their nature and operation to me. Trials bikes have super grippy tires running five to eight lbs. of pressure. Tanks hold less than a gallon of gas, so each bike's range is only about 50 miles.

Trials bikes have no seats, so no one uses them for transportation. The top speed is less than 40 mph, and most riding is done at speeds of 10 mph or less. The bikes only weigh about 150 lbs., making them part of a rare breed of motorsport vehicles that usually weigh less than their riders. The bikes have six gears, with the first four being super short with high torque.

What these bikes can do and where they can go is mind-boggling. A trials bike can climb to the roof of a house. I've even seen one ridden up the side of a semi-truck trailer to its top. I was excited to see what I could do with a little coaching from Griff.

After a morning working on the basics, Griff finally allowed me to begin the afternoon on my own, working on the exercises he'd shown me: jumping over logs, balancing along a railroad tie and riding over some large rocks.

At one point, Griff took off on a jeep trail that wound around and up to the top of a small mountain/large hill, through some beautiful pine trees. I followed him but I couldn't keep up, and soon he was far ahead of me. About halfway up the mountain, I saw a good-sized log on the trail. I slowed, recalling Griff's instructions on approaching the log slowly and blipping the throttle while pulling up on the handlebars to raise the front wheel.

I grabbed more throttle than intended, and the bike reared like the Lone Ranger's horse. As the motorcycle began getting away from me, I gripped the handlebars, twisting the throttle wide open. The bike took off on its rear wheel without me, over the steep drop-off at the road's edge. After checking myself for damage and finding none, I tiptoed to the side of the road and looked down for the bike. There it was, hanging from a tree limb about six feet above the ground.

Further down the hillside, I spied a bit of the road. This was a good sign. I slid down the steep 10-foot drop to the tree's base and looked up. Sure enough, there was the bike, stuck about six feet up. Scooting another few feet to the roadway below, I waited for Griff.

When he eventually rode up and stopped, he instantly realized I'd crashed and began looking for the bike. I just stood there. Griff, who was always calm and never flustered, finally said, "Okay, I give up. Where's the bike?" I took him to the side of the road and pointed up into the tree.

Griff looked at it for a while, then laughed and laughed. "I wonder how many points you'd earn for losing your bike that far up in a tree," he said.

To understand Griff's statement, you have to know how scoring in trials competition works. Each contestant starts with zero points and points are added for errors. Dabbing a foot down adds one point, five points are added for going out-of-bounds or going backwards, etc. Like golf, the person with the lowest score is the winner. Getting a zero would be a perfect run. Griff didn't know how many points I'd "earned" for getting a trials bike caught over six feet up in a pine tree, but we both knew it was a lot.

We were covered in pine tar when we finally lowered the bike to the ground. The motorcycle was unhurt, but my riding prowess had taken a considerable blow. The next day, I woke up with every muscle in my body complaining. I could barely move. It eventually dawned on me that the skill, balance and physical conditioning required to ride a trials bike competitively vastly surpassed other sorts of motorcycle riding. I still believe that to this day.

Me on Griff's Beta Evo Trials bike, Wigley on his Montesa.

After I got into teaching precision riding, I often told students that learning to ride correctly at slow speeds was critical for success. Unskilled riders frequently use speed to hide poor technique. Top riders know that executing maneuvers perfectly at slow speeds means you'll always be able to do it right when the speed increases.

My outing with Griff wasn't my only experience with "tree riding." I should be more embarrassed than I am at the lack of judgment this story exposes, but on the positive side it says something about my willingness to try new things.

One spring day, my brother Leif and I took our dirt bikes to explore the bottomland around the Zumbro River. Leif was on his Honda 175, a street bike he'd stripped. I had my Suzuki 125 and a friend of Leif's was riding an old beater.

Trails along the Zumbro are fun, especially when they're not too muddy. Several times that day, we passed a massive tree that had fallen over earlier in the spring. Its trunk ran a modest 20 degrees into the air as it rested on the upper branches. The second time I passed it, I thought, dang, that trunk is flat. I bet I could ride right up it.

The next time we headed toward this area, I allowed Leif and his friend to get ahead of me. When we passed the tree this time, I turned my wheel and rode right up the trunk, sticking my feet out on some upper branches to keep the bike from tipping as I rolled to a stop. Wow! I'd done it. It worked just as I imagined. I couldn't wait for them to come circling back and looking for me. They'd never guess where I was.

As I waited for them to return, I pulled my helmet off and dropped it about eight feet to the ground. The reality of my situation slowly sank in. There was no going forward. There was no backing up. In fact, I had to keep at least one foot on a branch to keep the bike perpendicular.

My brother and his friend were impressed when they eventually returned to find me in this peculiar spot. Then they began laughing as they realized they could ride off and leave me without any recourse. I was stuck.

Luckily, they stayed to help. Eventually, we each removed our belts and hooked them together. Attaching the improvised belt rope to the front wheel, I pushed the bike's rear off the trunk and swung it free, dangling from the belts. Lowering it the rest of the way was a simple task and our riding day resumed.

All this has two clear takeaways. The first is to develop balancing skills on two wheels, even at slow speeds, and be as comfortable riding standing up as you are sitting down. The second is to think through the consequences of an action before jumping in with both feet.

68

ROAD RULES IN BRAZIL

I FELT THE BRISK, SPRING mountain air as I gazed at the chalet rooftops dotting the hillside behind the Serra de Estrela hotel, with its traditional Swiss clapboard style. And, while strolling along cobblestone streets after a full day of mastering twisties and enjoying drafts of German dark beer served in traditional mugs in this Alpine-style village, I couldn't help but let out a sigh of wonder, "Ah, European splendor!"

But wait, it's late May and it's fall, not spring, and this isn't Switzerland, but Brazil. Campos do Jordão, to be specific, a popular Swiss village high in the mountains of São Paulo State, where May brings shorter days and cooler air.

This isn't the first surprise on my motorcycle ride through this amazing country. Another is learning that Brazil is nearly as large as the entire United States and larger than Australia. All that size delivers some of the most incredible motorcycle roads on the planet; I couldn't stay away.

The road surfaces rival most two-lane blacktop roads in the United States, with a level of quality just slightly below the impeccable highways in New Zealand and sparsely populated states like Arizona, New Mexico, Utah and parts of Colorado.

But what truly sets Brazil apart is the behavior of those sharing the road, which always has a big impact on how much fun you'll have on a ride. Brazil scores lots of points in this regard, at least outside the major cities. Most car and truck drivers conduct themselves in ways that a motorcyclist can only dream about.

Imagine exiting a small town and seeing 14 or 15 cars ahead of you, all stacked behind a slow-moving water truck as it begins its laborious ascent up a mountain. You know the roads are double yellow all the way to the top, and in most places you'd resign yourself to a long, slow climb. But in Brazil, something remarkable happens.

As you approach the tail of this slow-moving snake, the end car suddenly pulls to the right. The car in front does the same, making way for you to squeeze by without crossing the center line. One by one, other cars follow suit, and within minutes you're right behind the truck. Then the truck driver flips on his right turning signal—not to turn, but to let you know that even though you can't see around him, it's safe to pass.

This really happens in Brazil. All the time, cars see you approaching in their mirrors and pull right, often driving on the shoulder, so you can pass. There's an implicit contract in place, where all participants work together to keep everyone moving. This courtesy extends to oncoming traffic—if someone pulls into "your" lane to pass, they trust you to move over slightly or briefly use the shoulder to accommodate them. It's not as nerve-wracking as it sounds; these maneuvers are always executed with plenty of time and space for everyone to adjust safely.

The Brazilian approach to traffic laws differs markedly from the American system. While they drive on the same side of the road as we do, speed limits are treated more as suggestions than strict rules. Police seem most concerned with safety in urban areas, where the risk to pedestrians and vehicles is highest. Instead of radar traps, cities employ "busters da suspensão"—suspension busters, or speed bumps. These traffic calming devices are well-marked with bright yellow signs and stripes, often with countdown markers at 500, 200 and 100 meters. The result? Everyone naturally slows down through the towns.

Once beyond city limits, drivers are more or less free to proceed at whatever pace suits their vehicle's capabilities, road conditions and comfort level. There's a widespread understanding that motorcycles will typically move faster, and the prevailing attitude seems to be, "let's help and not hinder the natural order of things."

Brazil's natural beauty provides a stunning backdrop for motorcycle adventures. Verdant forests, towering mountains and awe-inspiring beaches stretch across this vast country. Excellent hotels and resorts dot the landscape, each with its own unique character. One of the most attractive aspects of riding in Brazil is the reversed seasons—my late May/early June ride coincided with the Brazilian fall, bringing sunshine-filled days, crisp air and turning leaves. In eight days of riding, we encountered only an hour of light rain.

While Brazil's politics have gone off the rails a bit since my ride, I still recommend it as an ideal destination when winter grips the northern hemisphere. Book a ride in Brazil, and you'll discover a motorcycling paradise where the roads are good, the scenery is spectacular and most importantly, sharing the road is elevated to an art form.

69

ADMIRING THE ADRIATIC

IN MOSTAR, A CITY IN southern Bosnia and Herzegovina, I stood before a steeply arched walking bridge. Large stones covered its surface like steps, while the frigid Neretva River rushed below. I shivered, recalling the famous photos of young men diving from the top of the bridge. Then I saw a large poster showing this exact spot from the air in 1993, and I froze: the beautiful bridge had been destroyed—bombed to nothing—down to the stone supports. Nearby walls remained scarred with bullet holes and mortar blasts, the surrounding town in rubble.

Americans know the countries of old Yugoslavia for their human tragedy. Yet the eastern coast of the Adriatic Sea and the Dalmatian Coast to the south has become one of Europe's hottest vacation spots, boasting spectacular scenery, historic landmarks, old-world charm and people filled with an indomitable spirit.

In 2013, I had the chance to experience this remarkable region firsthand. My journey began at the Ducati factory in Bologna, where I borrowed a new touring bike for the trip. Before joining my group in Venice, I stopped at the Ducati dealer in Padua to inquire about cruise control for the long stretches ahead.

The representative's response was telling: with snake-like hand movements, he explained, "Ah, you are from America, you don't understand! Ducati only go righta, then lefta, then righta, then lefta... no straighta. No, no straighta." While cruise control is standard in the U.S. with its vast distances of flat, straight highways, it was unheard of in Italy with its network of curvy roads.

When our group converged in Venice, the city's policy prohibiting motor vehicles forced us to leave our bikes in a garage in the outskirts of town. The prohibition is a logical one, as the streets are too narrow for cars to drive on, much less park. And while motorcycles or scooters may be small enough, the density of pedestrians in Venice limit anything greater than walking speeds.

But we were soon on our bikes and pointed north, following roads every bit as thrilling as a state fair rollercoaster. With our mounts rapidly oscillating from side to side, we climbed into Italy's dramatic rooftop, the Dolomites.

At 7,336 feet, the Passo Giau is one of the highest passes in this glorious mountain range. Cool, thin air greeted us as we looked eastward and admired the majesty of steep rock faces, favorites of skilled climbers from around the world. A large parking lot, crowded with motorcycles of all kinds, classic touring cars, SUVs and a few dozen bicycles had room for a few more, so we headed to lunch at a restaurant marked by a bicycle on top of a pole, doing dual duty as sign and weathervane.

After Croque Monsieurs (ham and cheese sandwiches) and cups of hot chocolate, we headed east into Slovenia and the Hotel Cubo in Ljubljana. The English-speaking staff made us feel wanted, tucking our wet bikes into a hidden, vine-covered courtyard in the back of the hotel and serving us hot chocolate so thick it felt like Hershey bars in a cup.

Ljubljana, the capital of Slovenia, is a pristine and picturesque home to 300,000 friendly, upbeat people. Once you learn how to pronounce the name of their city (lube-blee-anna), you find you want to say it over and over. The Ljubljanica River drifts slowly through the center of town at the base of a hill. It was a natural moat in ages past for the castle at the top.

On our way to dinner in Ljubljana's historic old town, we walked across the Triple Bridge and admired architecture influenced by both Germanic and Latin cultures. Musicians, dancers and painters added atmosphere to the streets, where no one seemed to be in a hurry.

The next day, on our way to Opatija in Croatia, we stopped at the Park of Military History in Pivka. The region around Pivka, also known as the Gate of Italy, was one of the most important strategic territories in Europe during World War II. If you like tanks and military vehicles, this is the place for you.

My borrowed Ducati in Pivka, Slovenia. Exhibits are from the timeframe of the former Socialist Federal Republic of Yugoslavia.

As we reached coastal Opatija, the fact that we entered a resort area was obvious. Miles of luxury hotels and massive villas clung to the picturesque banks of the Gulf of Kvarner on the Adriatic Sea.

After checking into the Hotel Milenij, we wandered a boardwalk past the establishments found in every beach town in the world: ice cream shops, T-shirt vendors, more jewelry stores than you can count, souvenir stands, art boutiques and, of course, restaurants with every food imaginable. Opatija is a less expensive version of towns on the French and Italian Rivieras.

Unlike our dinner in Ljubljana, a traditional Slavic feast with lots of meats, stews and wiener schnitzel flavored with black pepper, paprika and garlic, here on the coast the influences are more Greek and Roman with modern Mediterranean cuisine mixed in. This means seafood, pasta and vegetables, flavored with olive oil, rosemary, bay leaf, oregano, cinnamon, clove and nutmeg.

The next morning's ride from Opatija to Zadar along the luminous waters of the Adriatic was pure heaven. We were late enough in the season that the traffic was sparse. Roads hugged the coastline, twisting thousands of feet up the cliffs to reveal panoramic overlooks. Then they plunged down again into the banks of the sea, through turn after turn after turn.

As we entered the Zadar region, the northernmost part of Dalmatia, the topography changed. Contrasting colors of vivid blue skies with deep greens of pine and olive trees grabbed our attention until we finally saw the bright white Dalmatian stone. The Dalmatian breed of dog does indeed get its name from this region, where they were used as guard dogs and sentinels. In areas of the ground where the Dalmatian stone pokes through in slabs or boulders, it's easy to see the similarity between the stone and the dog breed's characteristic white coat with black spots.

After an overnight in Zadar, a sea organ built into the cliff serenaded us as the lapping waves created harmonic tones through natural pipes of stone. We continued down the coast to the ancient city of Split. Before dinner, we headed off to explore Diocletian's Palace, built by the Roman Emperor at the turn of the fourth century AD. He built it as his retirement home. The place is massive, today filled with shops and restaurants and even a church.

Parts of the ornately carved fascia seemed familiar to me. Could I be the reincarnated spirit of an ancient Dalmatian? I dismissed that idea when I learned that scenes from the fourth season of HBO's *Game of Thrones* were filmed there.

In the morning, we rode south along the sea to Dubrovnik. A simple route, we just headed south and took every road that went to the right. We got rain, however, and learned that taking a detour on a ferry out to an island, riding across the island and then catching another ferry does not keep you any drier. However, Maggie reminded me of a very fine cheese shop we were planning to visit, which would perhaps make it all worthwhile.

The splendor of Dubrovnik dissipated any disappointment I felt about the weather. Wow! No wonder it's called "The Pearl of the Adriatic." This is one of the most picturesque medieval walled cities in the world. Small, glass-bottomed boats offered harbor tours. While the view of the bottom was ho-hum, the views of the city from the bay were sublime. I imagined it was hundreds of years ago, and I was on a merchant ship full of goods, entering this bay for the first time and seeing the stone fortress of Dubrovnik spread out in front of me. What a thrill that would have been!

The thoroughly modern and ultra-deluxe Croatia Rixos hotel in Dubrovnik is a remarkable engineering feat. You enter on the top floor with amazing views of the Adriatic, then take elevators down to your guest room. Later, we wandered the city's polished stone streets and peeked into a couple of ancient churches. Assumption Cathedral was packed with frescos, statues and ornate altars. We enjoyed the evening crowd, and eventually found the wonderful cheese shop we were looking for.

Departing the next day, we paused at an overlook and said goodbye to the Adriatic as we headed inland. On the way to Sarajevo, we stopped for lunch in Mostar and came across the Old Mostar Bridge. The Neretva River divides the city of just over 100,000 inhabitants, thriving communities of Bosnians and Croats, with the bridge connecting each part. Designed by Ottoman architect Mimar Hayruddin, the bridge took nine years to build and was completed in 1566. A magnificent structure, it stood for 429 years without fail, until 1993.

When Yugoslavia broke up in 1991, ethnic tensions escalated as Muslim Bosnians, Orthodox Serbs and Catholic Croats fought for independence and territory. Bitter fighting characterized the war: indiscriminate shelling of cities and towns, destruction of mosques and churches, ethnic cleansing and mass rape. Mostar was under siege for 18 months. After more than 60 shells hit the bridge, it finally collapsed on November 9, 1993.

The bridge had no strategic importance, so its bombing was deliberate cultural destruction. The bridge had always been a symbol of how ethnic groups could get along and live in peace, which they did for hundreds of years. This act deliberately destroyed evidence of a shared cultural heritage and peaceful co-existence, known as "killing memory."

Because the bridge was one of Bosnia and Herzegovina's most recognizable landmarks, not to mention one of the most exemplary pieces of Islamic architecture in the world, the Mostar people, with collaboration and support from UNESCO and the World Bank, reconstructed the bridge and reopened it in July 2004. Citizens on both sides continue to work at rebuilding, not just infrastructure, but also the trust they once shared. The bridge is so symbolic that it now enjoys status as a UN World Heritage Site.

The Hotel Central in Sarajevo is a massive structure. Clearly built many years ago, it recently underwent a total redesign and update. The makeover, however, was not "encumbered" by any overarching design theme. Some areas are hip, while other areas exude old-world charm. The exercise room is remarkably artsy, while the front neon lighting has a Vegas-strip feel. But it's a fun place to stay, and our room was huge and the service was attentive. Sarajevo is a great walking city, with interesting buildings and parks, excellent restaurants and at least one genuine Irish pub.

Our last leg was a ride to Zagreb and the Esplanade Hotel. We took back roads for most of the trip, winding through mountains and valleys with small to mid-size towns. Finally, we entered historic Zagreb, with its nearly one million people. As the capital of Croatia, government buildings and artifacts (parks, statues and memorials) abound.

The next morning, I got an early start for my long and lonely ride from Zagreb to Bologna. Given that I had to travel 350 miles and get my bike to Ducati before they closed for the weekend, the only practical route was the Autostrada—Europe's equivalent of an interstate highway.

Unfortunately for me, the A1 and A4 are "All straighta—no righta, no lefta, no righta, no lefta—only straighta."

* * * * *

I was already on the road to Bologna when one of our group experienced a medical emergency, probably a stroke. EMTs were called and our dear friend Andy Forrester got expert care, finally making a full recovery back in the United States.

I mention this because it's the only time (that I can recall) anyone I traveled with had to use the Medjet Insurance we all carried. The insurance truly delivered, with an emergency medical evacuation to a home hospital as soon as he was stable.

70
FAST TRACK TO HUMILITY

WHEN MY INSTRUCTOR TURNED AROUND to look at me, riding one-handed and backwards through Willow Springs' famous bowl turn at full racing speed, just to give me a thumbs up, I had an epiphany about assumptions. But I'm getting ahead of myself.

One of my "beats" when writing for *Motorcycle Consumer News* was training schools. I loved going to them. I ate up learning new riding techniques and enjoyed writing about them. Things I'd always considered impossible on a motorcycle, at least for me, turned out to be doable with expert instruction, patience, practice and a building block approach to gaining the new skill. Willingness to listen to instructors and executing what they say can dramatically improve one's odds of success.

My riding life has included attendance at many of the highest-ranked motorcycle riding schools. Some were focused on off-road skills, others on racing and track proficiency, and still others on slick track riding/drifting, advanced adventure-riding/survival techniques, motocross, trials riding and even wheelies. On top of these, I'm the only civilian to take and pass both multi-week police moto-officer training programs conducted by the Arizona Highway Patrol and the Phoenix Police Department.

While motorcycle riding schools help beginners get their tires dirty, formal training is a superb way for experienced riders to eliminate bad habits and polish their skills. Not to mention the fact that self-taught riders comprise one of the highest risk categories for fatal motorcycle accidents.

One of the best programs I've ever attended was the one provided by Keith Code's California Superbike School, one of the longest-running and most respected track schools around. Code trained champions like Wayne Rainey and James Toseland; his students have won more than 60 world and national racing championships.

If you wish to go fast around a racetrack on a motorcycle, Keith Code is the gold standard for perfecting this set of skills. Code's class, and his books, deliver a proven way to take a motorcycle through a corner quickly.

The most valuable lessons I took from his class were the observational skills necessary to critique my personal riding so I could get better. Code's class provides a template for converting every future ride into a class on better riding, with you as your own instructor.

Code begins the class by dividing people into three groups based on riding and track experience. The first group typically includes the macho, confident types, nearly all young males with some track-racing experience. A second group is made up of riders with a suitable set of basic skills and a desire to get a knee down and go faster around a track. And the third group consists of people with much less time on a motorcycle—I sort of wondered what they were even doing there. As this was my first Code class experience, I ended up in the middle group.

The biggest surprise came at the end of the class, when we found out that the fastest riders were spread across all three groups. Some of the guys in the "fast" group had to unlearn bad habits and poor technique before they could start learning the correct way. And the fastest riders who emerged from the third group had fewer poor practices to unlearn and paid closer attention to the instructors, doing precisely what they were told to do without thinking.

Every lap was timed and videoed through a camera on the back of the bike. After a run, which included a warm-up lap and three timed speed laps, each rider made a quick trip to the video room to watch and critique the replay. Watching with an instructor who pointed out what I was doing correctly and where I needed to improve really helped me. My lap times steadily decreased as I gained confidence and integrated new techniques and instructor feedback.

Toward the end of the second day, my times had plateaued. My instructor rode over to me and said, "Hey, Keith said you wanted to do a hot lap through the bowl at race speeds. You're not sketchy at all, so if you want to do it, we could go now."

Oh, my God—I couldn't believe this was happening. First, some background: The Streets of Willow Springs is a 1.6-mile track, featuring 13 turns. Turn 8 is a big "bowl," a "sweeper-type" turn with a 20% camber. The track, by itself, is one of the fastest in the world, but turn 8 is one of the fastest turns on any track.

Experienced racers dream about riding the Streets of Willow Springs and giving this turn a go, which can be taken pretty much as fast as you want. When signing up for the class months before, I'd written to Code, asking if it might be possible to get a hot lap through the bowl. But I'd completely forgotten it until that moment.

"Hell, yes!" I replied.

The instructor reminded me of what we'd done before. This would be just like all our other laps, just a lot faster. We'd first do a warm-up lap, then the hot lap—a single additional lap, not three—at full race speed. Admonition echoed in my head to stick directly behind the tail of my instructor's bike. We were riding the same type of bike, and if the instructor's bike was safe on a particular line at a specific speed, mine would be, too.

I also consoled myself by thinking, "How unlikely would it be for them to kill a moto-journalist at one of their classes?"

With no more prep than that, off we went. The warm-up lap was no problem, just me loosening up and working the butterflies out of my stomach. Then we crossed the timing line and went into the tight rabbit's ear corner. Things immediately got different, and this is where you need to pay attention, boys and girls.

Heading north, after turn 4, the track goes uphill into a gentle turn 5 before heading more steeply uphill to turn 6. Every other time

I slowed down at this spot, as it was impossible to see over the hill and what lay beyond. I like the idea of seeing where I'm going. But this is the part of the track where one begins to set up for the bowl. This time we didn't slow down—quite the opposite. Following my instructor, who was speeding up, I came over the crest of the hill.

While not actually getting air, the bike certainly got light, very light. Wow, that was scary! Before I could think too much about it, we were heading into the dramatic wide radius of the bowl, absolutely flat out. As I leaned the bike over and slid off the right side of the bike to drag my knee puck, I matched my instructor's bike like an image in a mirror.

I could feel my rear tire bite and tear at the tarmac, but it held. My mind screamed at me, "You're doing it! You're riding the famous bowl full out! You're going through here as fast as anyone ever has— This is exactly what true professional racers feel!"

At this moment of maximum exhilaration and triumph, I saw my instructor turn her head around, look back at me, reach her hand out and give me a thumbs up. And in that instant, it occurred to me, "Well, maybe this wasn't the fastest ever through the bowl, because she's doing it one-handed and looking backwards. And she's a girl!"

I'd been taking instruction from this young woman for the past two days, so I was familiar with her easy and fluid command of her bike and the knowledge she exhibited when critiquing my riding. My comment about her being a girl is aimed at any vestigial sexism you, dear reader, might have. Might I ask, did the first mention of my instructor as "her" in this story surprise you? Just a little? If it did, there's the evidence—you've got work to do on some of those latent sexist attitudes of yours.

Finishing a hot lap through the bowl left me with the same feeling I suspect climbers feel after returning from a successful trek to a famous mountain summit they'd only dreamed about. Happy, relieved and fulfilled.

As in my other efforts to get beyond just being good, I reached a point where the path ahead got very clear. Coming out of the experience in the bowl, what I needed to do to reach the next level of track riding competence snapped into focus. Sometimes, when I see what's required, I think, "I'm okay. I'll stop here. This is good enough." While my results for these few days of riding and competing at Willow Springs put me right in the middle of the pack, my greatest reward was the gratification in feeling much more confident, especially when leaning the bike over at speed.

Although this training made me far more comfortable at track days with a group of ex-racer friends, I never moved much beyond the middle of the pack in those races, either. I'd seen the requirements to get a whole lot better and decided I didn't have that much time. With 30 riders, I was happy to finish in the top 10 and thrilled to get into the top five, which sometimes happened. (Okay, it happened once because two guys in front of me bumped each other and rode off the track.)

When a top-notch high school or college basketball player watches the pros play, they see a different game than the one seen by casual fans who've never played at an advanced level. Professionals play a very different game, and these skill development classes reveal this secret to me every time.

Late in the afternoon of the second day of Code's school, as most of the riders were taking a break, I heard murmuring near the track starting line. Several guys I'd just been speaking with walked over to see what the commotion was about, and I followed.

Then we heard it: "Keith's going to ride. Code's taking one of the bikes around the track."

We heard rumors that occasionally Keith would get on a bike and do a lap. Seeing this legend ride the track on which we just spent two days would be exciting. We all imagined the thrill of seeing him burn up the straights and dive into the corners at unbelievable angles.

As we got closer, sure enough it was the man himself zipping into a leather riding suit. Keith rode back into the paddock area for a bit, pushing the bike from side to side at a slow speed. He then aimed the bike toward the starting line and was off.

We watched as he entered the first tight turns. He didn't seem to be going very fast. One guy standing next to me said, "This must be his warm-up lap." But everyone kept watching.

Code showed very little stress as he circled the track. After crossing the finish line, Code disappointed many of us by choosing not to continue into a hot lap. "Ah dang, we wanted to see him go really, really fast."

As we grumbled, one student pointed to the timing clock high on a pole near the starting line. It was Code's time. He'd just circled the track four seconds faster than the best time anyone had recorded over the past two days.

We all looked up at that timing clock a hundred times over the weekend and always knew the top of the listed times was the current best time. We all noticed when someone beat it, usually by only a few hundredths of a second. No one had shaved a full second from the clock since the early laps on the first day, and now there it was—Four...Full...Seconds.

So, this was a big lesson: genuine professionals make what they do look easy. It's only when trying to replicate it that one appreciates the level of training, skill and experience they bring. Code looked positively leisurely circling the track, when, in fact, he was exceeding everyone's best time by a wide margin.

* * * * *

Years later, I was watching and reporting on MotoGP racing from the Circuit of the Americas track in Austin, Texas. I witnessed the fastest, most powerful racing motorcycles on the planet, piloted by athletes of tremendous mental and physical aptitude. I got to see and interview riders like Valentino Rossi, Casey Stoner, Marc Márquez, Mick Doohan, Mike Hailwood and Eddie Lawson.

Watching the race from beside the track, or on the gigantic screens in the press tent, I realized I was seeing something different from what surrounding fans were watching. That's perhaps the greatest gift from the Keith Code experience: the ability to truly appreciate the profound skill of professional riders, who, like Code himself that day at Willow Springs, make the extraordinary look effortless.

Watching MotoGP racing at the Circuit of the Americas track in Austin, Texas.

71

WHEELIES: BETWEEN PHYSICS AND FEAR

WHAT IS IT ABOUT MOTORCYCLE wheelies?

For me, it may have been watching Saturday TV programs as a kid and seeing the Lone Ranger doing a 'wheelie' with his horse Silver at the beginning and end of each show. Silver rises on his rear legs while the Lone Ranger cries, "Hi-ho Silver, away!"

Or perhaps it was watching YouTube videos of hooligan sport-bike riders doing wheelies on the street. I've been loftily unimpressed for years, of course, and of the firm belief that this behavior was not only immature, but dangerous. Yet, at some level, I wanted the satisfaction of knowing I could do it, too.

So, I took a class. Within 45 minutes of the 8:00 a.m. start time, all five Wheelie School students had made it up and down the track, front wheel lifted off the pavement. Although most of the time our "lifts" were only a few inches high, it was more than we expected.

"I thought we'd spend half the day doing classroom stuff and then practicing in the afternoon," said one of the other students aloud, echoing what we were all thinking. Before 4:30 p.m., that same student—and the rest of us—had traversed 1,000 feet between cones with the front wheels of our Triumph Speed Triples waving in the air.

"Wheelies are like sex," another class member explained. "They have their time and place." The main street on a Saturday afternoon may not be appropriate for either activity, but on deserted back country roads anything goes.

"Like most men, I want to keep it up longer," said another class-mate to much laughter.

The Wheelie School had us all feeling like stallions again. We owed it all to Keith Code, who added the wheelie bike to his long list of motorcycle training inventions, which also includes the No B.S. Bike, the Brake Rig and the Lean/Slide Machine. Code's wheelie bike is a standard, totally stock Triumph Speed Triple with an anti-flip device, or "wheelie bar," attached to its swing arm.

The wheelie bar keeps the bike from flipping over backwards in two ways. First, as the front wheel gets higher, the wheelie bar turns a plastic disk with a switch in it that cuts out one of the Triumph's coils. This eliminates the spark to one of the spark plugs, substantially reducing power. Second, the bar applies the rear brake as certain heights are met. With the wheelie bar in place, students can push the bike hard, without fear of flipping over.

The wheelie bar has five settings. We all started on the first one, and, throughout the day, progressed all the way up to number five. On setting one, the rear brake and ignition cut off much earlier than the higher settings, while the advanced settings provide more freedom to get the front wheel higher in the air. As we got more confident and showed our instructors we were in control, they increased the setting. The goal of the course was to have us find the balance point, or "sweet spot," where we could keep the front wheel in the air while maintaining control of the bike in motion.

We each spent seven minutes making passes up and down the course, with our instructors providing feedback and tips. We went in the same order with no pauses. Seven minutes for one student, then the next, and so on. What that meant for us was seven minutes on with a 28-minute break to watch the other students, think about what we did right or wrong and prepare for our next turn on the bike. During the 28 minutes of waiting, an instructor was always available to talk us through any issues or questions we had.

By noon, we were all on setting two or three and received coaching on throttle management, stability and proper approach speed. The key to getting it right was to keep the bike as stable as possible, so we could relax and focus on what we needed to do with the throttle.

Like many aspects of riding a motorcycle with control and confidence, it ultimately comes down to precise throttle control. We learned that following one's natural inclination to quickly reduce the throttle as the front wheel comes up results in an abrupt return to the ground, shocking the arms and causing a rapid slide into the gas tank.

"Gee, I sure know I'm a boy!" one student sang in a shrill, high voice as he got off the bike when this happened to him.

It was also critical to set the bike's speed at precisely 21 mph and bring the front wheel up in a smooth, steady motion to really feel that balance point. We definitely didn't want to jerk the front wheel up quickly.

Note the wheelie bar on the back, protecting
me from flipping over when learning.

What made a big difference for me was learning to keep my visual attention way out in front of the bike, using a reference point in the distance for orientation. This helped my balance and brought more consistency and predictability to my results.

In the months following the class, I was pulling the front wheel of my own bikes up regularly, even when riding on the street. I told myself it was to cement my skills and stay in practice, but in truth I enjoyed showing off a bit.

But the novelty soon wore off. The safety side of my brain reminded me that two wheels provide more traction and control than one, and that spills for motorcyclists "of a certain age" bear high costs. I eventually stopped doing wheelies, but I still show people the cool pictures of me doing them.

72

BEHIND THE BADGE: MAKING A MOTOR OFFICER

WINDING DOWN THE GRACEFUL MOUNTAIN curves, I relaxed. A glance in my mirror, however, revealed flashing red and blue lights on the motorcycle behind me, and I immediately tensed up again. A quick look at the speedometer said I was doing 70 mph. Lots of questions raced through my mind: What was the speed limit? Should I try to make a run for it? How fast is the bike behind me? Do I stand a chance of getting away? What's the cop going to be like when they catch me?

Nearly all motorcycle riders share this curiosity about highway patrol motor officers. Who becomes one? What bike handling skills are required? How are those skills taught and tested? What does someone go through before getting in uniform and riding a Highway Patrol dress bike? Do they love motorcycles and riding as much as we do?

While I've completed the Phoenix Police Motor Officer's three-week training classes, this story is about the even more intense training done for Highway Patrol Officers in Arizona. With help from *RIDER Magazine* editor Mark Tuttle, I talked my way into attending their motor officer training school to find answers.

The program unfolds in three demanding phases. Phase I begins with seven days at Phoenix International Raceway (PIR). Phase II comprises four days of structured street riding, plus a final day of pursuit tests at Firebird Racetrack. Phase III involves four weeks of on-the-job training. Sergeant Larry L. Kenyon led our class, assisted by seven experienced motorcycle officers/instructors working with 11 recruits and me.

We all started with retired Kawasaki KZ1000 police motorcycles, stripped of their fairings, saddlebags, radios, lights and sirens. Though road-weary, these workhorses seemed willing to take even more abuse in the weeks ahead.

To even try to become a Department of Public Safety (DPS) motor officer, candidates must meet a series of strict requirements: at least two years as a Highway Patrol Officer, a clean record, a referral from a department head and active duty in metro Phoenix for the previous six months or more.

"We look for someone who wants to be part of a pretty elite squad with a strong desire to ride," Kenyon told me, describing his ideal candidate. "We like to see some prior motorcycle experience. Good dirt riders seem to do best in the class. Experienced street riders sometimes have bad habits that must be unlearned."

Our first day began with bike orientation, learning basic controls and the idiosyncrasies of each bike. Although they run on 20-year-old technology, KZ1000s have good clearance and a fairly short wheelbase for a big bike, allowing excellent maneuverability. We also learned important maintenance techniques, such as how to lube the chain, check the oil and adjust the clutch and brake. From then on, it was up to each of us to care for our bikes for the duration of the class. Another skill we were taught early on was how to pick up a bike correctly after it's been pushed over—you'd be surprised how frequently motor officers are called upon to do this.

The real challenge began with exercises teaching us what the bikes could do and how to control them. Critical to nearly every maneuver was mastering what instructors called the "gray zone," or what I knew from an experience with the Arizona Precision Motorcycle Drill Team as the "friction zone." This involves the precise coordination of throttle, brake and clutch inputs, combined with handlebar control and body position to execute smooth maneuvers.

Each exercise started with detailed instructions and demonstrations that made impossible-looking tasks seem effortless. We mounted up and did our best, but our first attempts often ended with crashes and scattered cones. "Low speed is where officers learn to control and master the motorcycle," Kenyon explained. "Very little skill is required to ride fast. Speed often masks poor riding skills or faulty technique. Placing students into extremely small spaces where they must go slow forces them to learn the right way to do things. There aren't multiple ways to get through most of these exercises; there's only one." It made perfect sense, as the most capable motorcyclists I've ever seen are trials riders who rarely exceed five mph when competing.

As I watched other students crashing here and there, Kenyon remarked that he didn't care what happened to the bikes. "This is all about officer safety," he said. "They fall down here, going slow on these trainers, so they won't fall down later, in the street on full dress police bikes at higher speeds. The fastest way to learn a bike's limits is to go slightly beyond them, and then back off."

The attrition began early. One student injured his ankle on day one and dropped out. Another withdrew after the weekend, admitting, "This isn't for me. I'm not getting it and if I keep going, I'll get hurt." As one instructor noted, "The minute we reach consensus that a particular student cannot complete the class because of an inability to deal with either the physical or mental requirements, we get them out to avoid endangering themselves or other students." Five days in, we were down to eight from the original 12.

One of the released students, although not happy, accepted the decision. The other was pissed off. "He thought he was doing fine, and he wasn't, which is a good sign we made the right decision to let him go," Kenyon told me. This echoed the feeling of the instructors, who felt this student never really knew why something had or hadn't worked in an exercise.

Plus, he was sketchy, meaning he'd do something well once or twice and then completely blow it the next time, mowing down cones. "When we move to controlled aggression exercises, we may lose a couple more," Kenyon remarked. "The judgment part we won't know until after they complete all the proficiency tests and spend four weeks with their Field Motor Training Officer (FMTO). We may lose someone even at that late point, although it's unlikely."

The training followed a carefully crafted progression, with each exercise building skills needed for the next. High-stress drills alternated with competitive challenges, like relay races or dirt rides through the terrain that surrounded our practice track. The pace was relentless—just 15-minute breaks in the morning and afternoon, 30 minutes for lunch, and otherwise constant riding, coaching or absorbing instructions.

What impressed me most wasn't just the instructors' phenomenal bike control, visible in everything from formal demonstrations to casual movements between exercises. It was their fierce dedication to developing competent motor officers. On the practice field and on the track, they threw themselves into coaching every student, using a perfect blend of encouragement, humor and exaggerated exasperation to draw out peak performance. During breaks and side conversations with each other, they meticulously analyzed each trainee's progress.

By Wednesday of Phase I, things were getting more intense. Starting at 6:00 a.m. with bike inspections and warm-ups, the group tackled increasingly challenging exercises. The first was out on the high-banked PIR track, where the group worked on pullouts. This was the first exercise Kenyon asked me to observe, without participating. Officers lined their bikes up three feet apart along the inclined track, facing the wall toward the stands, which were five or six feet from the barrier.

The exercise involved riding forward about three feet, executing a sharp, 90-degree turn and then riding between the row of bikes and the walled barrier. If you turn too soon, the back of your bike hits the motorcycle parked next to you. If you go too far and can't make the 90-degree turn, you hit the barrier, fall over and land on the bikes beside you. And don't forget, you're on a steep incline, which makes it even harder.

Critical to success in this exercise is being able to coordinate the throttle, clutch and rear brake, while leaning the bike and turning. This exercise was tough. Every time a trainee goofed up, the other bikes went down like dominoes. Everyone had to pick up their bike and brace for the next attempt. Everyone was under powerful peer pressure to get it right next time, and few of the officers failed more than once.

If you mess up this exercise, all the bikes fall down and you become quite unpopular with the other trainees.

Next, we returned to the asphalt outside the track area for the Brake & Evade (B&E) exercise. Nothing was driven home harder through words and repeated practice than the importance of proficient, hard braking. I rode the first few times with the group, before Kenyon had me stop as the speeds increased.

We began the exercise about 500 feet down the track, accelerating to the specified 35 or 40 mph before crossing between two marker cones. We had to bring our bikes to nearly a complete stop before hitting a line of cones set 70 feet in front of the markers. Once stopped (or sufficiently slowed) we had to make a 90-degree turn for a graceful exit.

A radar gun ensured that we were at the specified speed as we passed through the first two marker cones. Students were dinged for going too fast or too slow, for braking too early (a common problem), locking up either brake or running through the cone barrier wall.

Our next exercise took place within a circle of cones, 18 feet in diameter, with an entrance on one side. The aim was to enter the circle, ride the interior circumference without running any cones over, and exit

Once we reached a level of proficiency, two students rode into the circle at the same time. After that, three bikes entered, and finally, the set of students who were doing very well were challenged to ride the circle with four bikes. If this doesn't sound challenging, remember that each bike is six feet long. Lined up, four bikes are 24 feet and the circumference of the circle is only 56 feet, leaving little room for error. I decided I needed to take pictures when it got to four bikes.

Once most of the students mastered this exercise, we moved to a cone setup that featured two circles side by side. We had to execute a figure eight in both directions. Once again, more bikes were added into the circles at the same time as our proficiency increased.

After these three exercises, we reached what equated to a full day's effort in any other training program. We were exhausted, but our day wasn't nearly over.

Next up were 140-degree pullouts. This involved placing the bike's rear tire against a board, lined up at a 140-degree angle to a cement barrier. Students were then required, from a stop, to exit in the opposite direction from the way they were facing, without hitting the barrier. After 30 minutes of this, we rode back to the high banked track of PIR to repeat the exercise against the wall on the steep incline. With a shorter angle, about 90 degrees instead of 140, it's much harder to do. Again, I sat this exercise out.

After the pullouts, we shut off our engines, started at the top of the inclined, banked track and coasted toward the infield in a series of S-Turns. As we reached the bottom and ran out of incline, we had to bump-start our bikes and ride back to the top to repeat. This exercise teaches control of the bike when you don't have the motor to rely on. Just as the exercise started getting fun, it was back to the very difficult, frustrating and intimidating pullouts close to PIR's high wall.

Leaving the track and heading back to the asphalt practice area, we began the last new exercise of the day, the single cone Bump & Go. Although the exercise is easy to explain and demonstrate, it's very hard to do well. You ride up to a single cone and bring the bike to a stop as you gently bump the cone. Then, immediately as the bike begins to fall left or right—while keeping your feet on the pegs—you apply throttle to straighten the bike and turn and ride to the next cone. The secret to mastering this exercise is keeping your head and eyes up while looking where you want to go. Our instructors weren't happy until we came to a near full stop and our bikes began to fall just before we applied power.

Sergeant Kenyon was strict about which exercises I could do with the group. He didn't want me messing anything up or getting one of his guys hurt. Plus, the primary focus was on the trainees and helping them reach their objectives. But given all of that, I was surprised by how many exercises he allowed me to work on with the team. He often complemented me on my skills, which I really appreciated.

The day ended with another 45 minutes on the critical B&E exercise. This exercise was pass/fail. All the students' results were recorded on all the different runs. Their speed was noted, as was whether they braked too early, locked up either brake, hit any cones or put a foot down. Students wash out of the course faster by making mistakes in this maneuver than any other.

Midway through this phase of the training, we were introduced to Accelerated U-Turns. Two cones were set up 200 feet apart (later moved to 225 and 250 feet). Fifteen feet to either side of each cone was a line of four cones. We began the exercise by following an instructor as they rounded one cone and then used maximum acceleration to head toward the cone at the other end.

Applying maximum braking, the instructor did a 180-degree turn around the center cone, avoiding the four cones on either side, then accelerated again toward the cone at the other end. Back and forth we went, with the instructors quickly pulling ahead of us. Before four laps were completed, the instructor was almost always coming up on the back of the last student rider. The instructor then slowed down, waited for everyone to catch up behind him, and took off again. The order of the students was shuffled, so faster students were put closer to the instructors as those going more slowly moved farther back.

Accelerated U-Turns not only bring together everything the students learn in the course, but they also replicate a maneuver that motor officers do nearly every day: chase down speeders. As an instructor told me, "If I'm stopped at the side of the road running radar and someone comes by me going 80, 85 or more, how much faster do you think I need to go to catch him or her? And once they decide to pull over, how fast do I need to stop? This exercise gives students the skills and practice to do this safely. You must do this aggressively and be able to do it safely if you're going to be a motor officer."

"To be a motor officer, you must have the right amount of aggression," Kenyon added. "Too little and you won't be effective, too much and you'll ride over your head and get someone killed. We have to assess where each student is on this scale and make sure they're going to end up at the right point. The competition of the Accelerated U-Turns exercise exposes the aggressiveness of the students to us."

"Face it, these folks are all competitive," another instructor chimed in. "The guy in front of this pack hates that the instructor is faster than him. The second guy back thinks he should be first and right on down the line."

"It's easy to spot those with too little aggression, those who are 'driving Miss Daisy,'" said another instructor. "They're not accelerating hard enough, they upshift too soon, they brake too soon and don't really get aggressive in the corners. Spotting those riding too hard is simple, too. They knock down cones at the least and crash at the worst."

Friday, the seventh and last day of Phase I, comprised a short practice and a timed test. A half-mile course was laid out, which included all the different exercises the students had been practicing in the following order:

1. A 140-degree pull out
2. A ride through a four-quadrant intersection
3. Aggressive acceleration across the parking lot, followed by a quick deceleration into two sets of cone weaves
4. Brake & Evade
5. More cone weaves down the straight to the other end of the course
6. Maneuvering through a complex cone setup known as the In & Out House.
7. A high-speed section with a long sweeping turn
8. A snowman of three circles, 19, 18 and 17 feet, respectively

While the instructors allowed me to ride the course a couple of times, they didn't bother to time me. Students must complete the course in less than six and a half minutes. Five seconds are added for every cone knocked over and every foot touched down, and only five faults are allowed before the run is scratched. Dropping the bike or riding out of an exercise disqualifies a run. Students are allowed six runs to get it right.

The remaining students, the ones who've made it to this point, all pass. One student made it with only a couple of seconds to spare and had two completely unacceptable runs. He was what instructors call "on the bubble." He could go either way. Another student, also on the bubble, only completed two successful runs in his first five attempts, and they were both over time. It all came down to his last run. As he crossed the last set of cones, the timing officer hits the stopwatch at six minutes and 11 seconds. However, his cone-hitting penalties gave him an adjusted time of 6:31, one second over.

Instructors huddled in the trailer, focusing on the two students who were on the bubble. After much discussion, including an evaluation of each student's entire effort in the first seven days, the instructors decide not to hold the one student back for being only one second over time, particularly as the trainee had always ridden safely and showed consistent improvement. The student sat down with Kenyon, who told him, "You made it to Phase II, but only by the skin of your teeth. We'll be observing you to ensure you continue getting better."

Later, I asked Kenyon about bending the rules. "Well, we didn't, really," he said. "The 6:30 time limit is set by having four or five instructors run the qualification course as fast as they can. The guidelines then say we are to add 20–25% to that time. So here, based on the time the instructors ran it, the time could have been set anywhere from 6:22 to 6:45. So really, 6:31 was in the allotted range."

A new phase of training began the following Monday. At the Knutson Station, full dress police bikes were issued to all the students, used Kawasaki KZ-1000s handed down from more experienced officers. Assuming they graduate, these are the bikes they'll ride on patrol. I rode along on my big yellow Goldwing, obvious to everyone that I wasn't one of the cops.

The students spent three hours cleaning and detailing their bikes. After a shower, a quick lunch and a change into uniforms, we all sat for a two-hour lecture on street riding from instructors Tom Simon and Mitch Lanoue.

Instructor Simon began by explaining that a police motorcycle is a very busy place. So many details require attention that the skills learned the previous week must now be done automatically. With dispatcher instructions coming through the headset, watching for traffic violators, avoiding road hazards and managing all their unique equipment, a motor officer has no time to think about correct throttle application, clutching or braking. These activities have to be as natural as breathing. The bike must become an extension of the body.

Most of the lecture focused on safety basics and riding techniques you might hear in an advanced Motorcycle Saftey Foundation (MSF) course, with a few unique twists. Bullet-proof vests make good body armor if you go down. Helmets keep you cooler, even in the Phoenix summer heat, than going bare headed. The lecture included sections on lane selection, surface appraisal and how and why officers ride side by side. Basic procedures for turning, passing, lane splitting and reacting to hazards were also covered.

The afternoon comprised of a ride to the Fire Department Training facility in Tempe, a city just outside Phoenix. Many of the same cone exercises from the previous week were set up again, so the students could run through the maneuvers on full dress bikes with fairings, saddlebags, lights, sirens and radios. They found that many of the exercises were much more difficult to do with a fairing blocking their view and saddlebags sticking out that kept sideswiping the cones.

The trainees spent a lot of time riding over the next two days, in small pods of two students in front with an instructor following, observing and coaching. Tuesday was all city riding, focusing on hazard recognition and the precise action to take in different circumstances. Hazards included balls bouncing in the street, cars poised to turn in front of you and cars approaching too fast from the rear. Trainees were cautioned to always expect the unexpected with the least possible warning.

Civilian training for group rides recommends a staggered formation, with a minimum of two seconds between you and the bike directly in front of you and one second between you and the bike to the side. Most motor officers, when riding together, ride side by side in "deuces." Although considered unsafe for civilians, motor officers have a reason for this practice. First, each officer focuses his or her attention on what's happening on their side of the road, expanding the field of vision.

They also have a system for communicating problems they see on their respective sides of the road, and pre-determined actions to take based on what they see. "It's a very active way of riding and takes a good amount of attention and discipline," instructor Simon explained. "When I'm out riding on my bike with another officer on my day off, we ride staggered. Staggered is more relaxing, easier and safer when we're not doing police work. Riding deuces wears you out."

On Thursday, before our first night ride, we left the station just after noon for a ride through the urban landscape of Phoenix and Tempe. The officers were all on their cop bikes, and I trailed behind on my yellow Goldwing. Then we headed into the mountains to Tortilla Flat. This popular tourist stop comes at the end of 35 miles of winding mountain roads. The students rode in pairs with instructors following behind, observing and critiquing their selected corner entry speeds and lines through the curves.

From Tortilla Flat, we headed back down the mountain to Florence Junction, then east again into the mountains until we got to Globe. In Globe, we had dinner and waited for dark. After sunset, the students rode down the mountain curves, learning a good deal about the limitations of the Kawasaki's headlights in the process.

On Friday of the second week, it was out to Firebird Raceway for live pursuit and final qualifying. One officer played the role of suspect in a white unmarked car, attempting to evade and/or outrun the motor officers around a 3/4-mile course. While the fleeing car went around cone weaves and blew through simulated stop signs, the motor officers had to obey the rules, somewhat leveling the playing field and making it an actual race. Students took turns chasing the "suspect" while two instructors trailed behind, watching to ensure that no cones were knocked down and that proper procedures were followed. All students passed.

After passing the first two phases of training, the group of students I was with were well on their way to becoming full motor officers, but they weren't quite finished. "We teach them how to ride, first at the track and then on the street, but that doesn't mean they can do the job," explained Kenyon. "The third phase of the training, which we do in the field, teaches them how to be motor officers."

Each applicant officer who makes it to this point of the training is assigned a Field Motor Training Officer (FMTO), who they ride with for four weeks. As in each of the other phases of training, specific objectives must be met. One requirement is a minimum of 10 Brake & Evade exercises each day. FMTOs are encouraged to do B&Es later in the day, when fatigue has set in. "It's not always at the beginning of your shift when you're fresh that some truck pulls out in front of you," Kenyon said.

During the first week of this last phase of training, the FMTO and student ride side by side, covering a minimum of 1,000 miles. The focus is on saddle time, not enforcement. FMTOs give the new officers tips on riding safely and doing the job well.

In the second week, the pairs move to lane splitting, riding sidewalks, crossing overpasses and even reverse lane splitting, which means riding into oncoming traffic. Of course, this is done only when traffic is stopped and it's never comfortable, but it's sometimes necessary to reach an accident scene quickly.

"You are no longer a car officer, and you can no longer think like a car officer," Kenyon explained to me. "Motors think differently. They see traffic differently. Everything is different on a motorcycle. There are far fewer restraints on where a motor officer can go and how quickly we can move, but only if you're thinking right."

Enforcement work is the main emphasis of week three. This includes traffic stops, radar work, looking for vehicles and responding to dispatches. The work is done together, with the FMTO providing hints and instructions along the way.

And then, finally, week four is a five-day final exam. Trainees do everything on their own with the FMTO observing. Trainees make all the decisions. Trainees decide how to work, where to work, how to ride and what they respond to. At the end of the week, the FMTO, in consultation with Sergeant Kenyon, decides whether their trainee will graduate or go back to cars.

"Do trainees ever fail this far along?" I asked Kenyon.

"Not frequently, but it happens. It happened twice last year," he said.

Seeing how intensively motor officers train should prompt all motorcyclists to reconsider their own dedication to improving their skills. My first-hand observation of this specialized course convinced me that motor officers possess the most highly developed riding skills on the road. Becoming a motor officer requires a great deal of desire, persistence and commitment. And, if successful, after graduation these officers become part of one of the most elite teams within law enforcement.

What advice do these motor officers and instructors have for civilian riders? In a word, practice. Sergeant Kenyon stressed to me that "Civilian riders should all know how to be in control of their motorcycles. It's not about going fast, but about how proficient and safely you can ride."

Spending three weeks with these guys was an amazing experience. While I'm not exactly part of their fraternity, we found a level of friendship only experienced when people go through an extended period of high stress and effort together. For a year after the training,

I found myself showing up regularly at my cohort's coffee and lunch haunts, grabbing a chair and hearing the latest gossip and news.

The next time you see a Highway Patrol motor officer (preferably not with lights flashing in your rearview mirror), use it as a reminder to enroll in another skill enhancement course. Hazards are everywhere!

Receiving my course certificate from Don Nochta, head of the Phoenix Police moto officers training program.

73

THE "JUST TURN LEFT" RIDING PLAN

MULTI-DAY DOMESTIC MOTORCYCLE RIDES, IN groups of riders with well-matched skills, have been a highlight of my motorcycling life. Many have been with the American Flyer's Motorcycle Club (AFMC) over its 25-plus-year history. On the cover flap for *The Ride is All*, the book by AFMC founder Rich Marin that chronicles the group's rides from 1996 to 2020, Rich wrote:

> *"What could be more whimsical or fickle than seeking to be alone in a group. And yet this is what a motorcycle group ride is about. Motorcycling is a solitary endeavor. There is nothing to restrain you, no one to annoy you. People who need people may be the luckiest people in the world, but motorcyclists who need people form groups."*

One of the most memorable and unplanned group rides I've ever been on occurred after I participated, as a member of the Arizona Precision Motorcycle Drill Team, in an international competition at the Gaylord Opryland Hotel in Nashville. Our team took second place out of 15 teams from the United States and Canada. We practiced four or five nights a week for nearly a year, under the meticulous eye of Jim Graybeal, the team's founder. We worked hard to hone our routines to impress the judges and the crowd, and our dedication showed.

By focusing so myopically on the competition and winning, however, we neglected to thoroughly plan for our return trip to Arizona. We split into two groups. One group decided to take a more direct route back to Phoenix, mainly using interstate highways. But Dennis

Brink, Charly Seeburger and I decided that a more epic adventure was in order.

Our first stop was the Tail of the Dragon, 200 miles east of Nashville. While I'd ridden this 11-mile section of road when it was known as Deal's Gap, my companions had never experienced it and were eager to give it a go. My two friends, in peak shape after a year of daily riding practices, were disappointed by the number of slow bikes on the road and the road's short duration.

"This doesn't hold a candle to the Devil's Highway (Highway 191, old route 666) in Arizona, with 650 corners, 120 miles and 5,000 feet of elevation change," Charly said. "What's the big deal?"

With rumors of an incoming hurricane, we followed 50 miles of the Great Smoky Mountains Parkway to a hotel in Knoxville. As the heart of the storm was reported to be moving at roughly 25 miles per hour, we planned to outrun it the next day, momentarily forgetting that hurricanes don't usually stop to sleep at night.

This miscalculation meant that we spent an extra day in Knoxville, waiting for the storm to pass, and rejected our original plan of riding north to Cleveland (Rock & Roll Hall of Fame), then through Michigan into Canada, then to Winnipeg, then south to Arizona, perhaps along the Mississippi River.

Suddenly, Seeburger had an idea—one I've always tried to claim credit for. "Since the storm is heading north, why don't we go south?" he reasoned. "We could go straight south until we hit Florida and the Gulf of Mexico. Then we turn right (west) toward Arizona and take every road going to the left we come across. We won't even need a map! We'll bounce along the Gulf, eating great seafood and staying in cheap hotels." No one had a better plan, so that's what we did.

Somewhere between Panama City and Miramar Beach, we found Route 98. What a great road! This idea of bouncing along the Gulf Coast was paying off. Route 98 eventually led us across a long bridge into Pensacola.

One result of our "take any road to the left" gambit was entering Louisiana and making a left onto Route 329. This highway dead-ended at Avery Island, home of the factory that makes Tabasco. Beyond the museum, garden, and factory tours, visitors can explore a country store offering an astounding array of Tabasco hot sauce varieties and sizes. We discovered exactly how many mini Tabasco bottles will fit into a motorcycle top case.

Avery Island produces over two million tons of salt each year, from three large salt mines operated by Cargill. McIlhenny Company owns the Tabasco brand and the mines. Most of the salt is used to de-ice roads and, of course, to make more hot sauce.

Me with Dennis Brink and Charly Seeburger on Avery Island.

As we rode along under-used, flat two-lane roads, an occasional wild hair would emerge and I'd hurtle forward at substantial speeds. I felt immune from expensive tickets because of Dennis Brink, the Phoenix police detective who was riding with us. I assumed he'd rescue me if I got pulled over—he was my personal "get-out-of-jail-free" card.

Outside a small hotel one night, however, Dennis set me straight. "I would never ride at the speeds you're going through another officer's territory," he said. "NEVER! Disrespecting a fellow officer is not cool! And just so you know, if I saw you pulled over, I'd be hard-pressed to stop and help you out. I might, but trust me, I would be embarrassed to admit to riding with such a disrespectful jerk. And just so we're clear, if you keep riding like this, you're on your own."

This wasn't the first time a riding compatriot told me I rode too fast, pointing to the raft of tickets and traffic stops I'd accumulated as evidence—the ones I humorously referred to as my "Velocity Awards." After extensive training and riding on closed courses, whether racetracks or parking lots, I know how to push the limits. I've tested those limits, occasionally crashing, but always with minor damage to myself and my ride. My talk with Dennis did change my attitude toward speeding, although it was several years before my interactions with highway cops and speed cameras began receding.

Closed-course racing and training eliminate the variables of other vehicles and inattentive drivers. Everyone is going in the same direction on a racetrack, and tracks are cleared of debris, sand and rocks. There are no unexpected obstacles. Trained first responders are frequently nearby, and sometimes even an ambulance.

A year after my Nashville experience, I completed the Phoenix Police Motor Officer and the Arizona Highway Patrol Motor Officer training programs. I improved not only my riding skills but also my attitude: Several "ride-along" opportunities allowed me to see traffic stops from an officer's perspective.

A smarter individual with better judgment would have used his experience and skill never to get pulled over again. While getting a good bit of the way there, I occasionally got stopped. I was usually able to talk my way out of a ticket—carrying a motor officer challenge coin and having low-key but visible police decals on my bike certainly didn't hurt. I also learned that unless you're doing something idiotic, most officers are open to letting you off with a warning if you don't lie or present a bad attitude.

* * * * *

Entering Texas, our group stayed with our "Go West—Take Each Left" plan. It continued to work in principle, but it got complicated near Port Arthur, when swamps pushed us away from the water and back onto Route 73 until we got to Winnie. Then we took Route 124 south through Stowell and back down to the water, before finally returning to the familiar Highway 87. We followed this along the coast, expecting to reach Galveston. Instead, the road stopped at Port Bolivar, and we were forced to board a ferry, which turned out to be great. They let us park the bikes in the front and it was free!

Somewhere around Corpus Christi, we realized that sticking with the "follow the Gulf" plan would land us in Mexico. Long out of clean underwear and growing weary of each other, we got on the super slab and headed directly for Phoenix.

We picked up Interstate 10 in San Antonio and began the 1,000-mile ride home, taking two long days. We entered from the north, avoiding Tucson and instead going through Globe and Superior.

It felt great to get home. We'd been gone for three weeks, ridden 5,000 miles, placed second in a motorcycle competition and endured a hurricane, mosquitos, fog, blazing heat, so-so food and some of the worst hotels ever—but no cops.

Life does not get better than this.

Receiving one of my not infrequent Velocity Awards,
while Andy Forrester looks on through his mirror.

74

A SAFETY-OBSESSED OUTLAW'S CONFESSION

MY RIDING STYLE HAS DEVELOPED over the years as I've gained experience from riding with experts. When I'm cruising the open highways, I pay little attention to posted speed limits. Do I occasionally speed? Probably. Do I care? No. When I was younger, did I accumulate more than my share of Velocity Awards? Yes I did. But when riding on streets with automobiles, my focus is on minimizing risk and staying alive. I would prefer a speeding ticket to spending time in a hospital, or worse, if some car runs into me.

At intersections, I prefer to be the first vehicle at a stoplight. When the light turns green, I use the weight and power advantage of the motorcycle to get out in front of other traffic quickly. I want to find pockets between groups of cars, rather than be part of a pack with cars moving at various speeds on either side of me. Cars travel in groups, frequently close together, with large portions of road sparsely occupied. I want to be in those open areas as much as possible.

Once out in front of the other cars, I slow down to stay behind the clump of cars in front of me. This sweet spot, between car crowds, maximizes my view of the road ahead and gives me additional processing time for analyzing various scenarios, based on road and traffic conditions. It also makes me more visible to other drivers.

On the highway, you may see my bike moving through traffic, accelerating around cars and trucks as I seek out these pockets of greater safety. It may appear that I'm riding dangerously, but the opposite is true. Moving five or 10 mph faster than surrounding traffic is far safer than allowing traffic to overtake me from behind. If I'm going faster than someone, they can't hit me. And I'm less vulnerable to being struck from behind by distracted drivers.

While I'm not advocating riding all that much faster than surrounding traffic, I suggest speeds within a rider's ability and comfort. Motorcycles are nimbler and quicker than most cars and trucks. Smart riders use these capabilities to increase their safety. Judicious pulls of the throttle can get me out of a blind spot, away from situations where everyone is braking and putting me at risk of being hit from behind.

Safe riding requires confidence in your command of the clutch, throttle and brakes. It's knowing how far your bike will safely lean over and being comfortable at those angles. It has to become second nature, to the point where you can execute what needs to be done instantly, without a conscious thought.

And that means training and practice. A pianist plays scales on the keyboard, a marksman tunes her skills at an archery range, a runner stretches and warms up before a race. It's just as important for us motorcyclists to remember and refresh what we know and learn what we don't, because there's a lot of dangerous metal out there!

Many riders overstate their riding proficiency. At one training class I attended, the instructor asked us to include the number of years we'd been riding in our introductions. Many were new, reporting their riding experience in months. But some chests puffed with pride as they boasted 25 or even 30 years, as the newer riders glanced at them in awe.

The instructor then got everyone's attention. "Most of you who claim 25 or 30 years of riding experience actually have only one year of riding experience, which you've repeated over and over," he said. "Or worse, you have 25 years of bad habits, which will take time and effort to unlearn."

The instructor proved highly prescient as the lessons began. Many long-term riders were slower to "get it." They required more repetitions before moving to the next stage of training. This is a perfect example of the Dunning-Kruger Effect, the human cognitive bias where people with little expertise or ability assume they have superior expertise and ability.

Readers of my magazine articles about motorcycle riding know that I'm a big believer in training. Using my associations with *RIDER*, *Motorcycle Consumer News*, *RoadRunner* and other biker magazines, I reported on many outstanding training schools, including several courses created for and limited to full-time professional riders.

Countless riding courses have tested my skills, as have some amateur races on big-name tracks. My off-road skills have been exercised in chasing the Dakar Rally and numerous rides in and around Arizona, Utah, Mexico and Colorado. And competing with the Arizona Precision Motorcycle Drill Team required the most intense and lengthy training effort I've ever experienced.

I've been honored to ride with many professional riders over the years, including motorcycle cops, World Superbike and MotoGP competitors, flat-track racers, trials riders and people who teach motorcycle skills for a living. Amateurs practice something until they can do it right. Professionals practice until they can no longer do it wrong. I'm lucky enough, at least in riding, to know the difference.

How do I rate my riding skills? On a scale of 1 to 10 I'm a solid 7, maybe a 7.5 on a good day. Without gloating or exaggeration, my riding skills are better than 95% of the people riding motorcycles on the streets today. I don't care how good you think you are on a motorcycle. Until you've ridden with those who ride many hours every single day of the year, and whose livelihoods depend on the skills required to be safe, aware and nimble, you do not know the width and depth of the gap between your abilities and theirs.

* * * * *

For most of my riding life, I began every year with a new riding skill to learn or training goal to reach. I tried to make them big deals that would actually require a full year's worth of effort. I don't remember missing any of them, although sometimes they took longer than a year to achieve.

Honoring this pledge by attending a motorcycle training event at least once a year, to learn a new skill or hone existing ones, has had substantial payoffs. In 2018, I traveled to Moab, Utah to attend a small group with Bill Dragoo at his Dragoo Adventure Rider Training (DART) school.

Unlike other off-road riding programs, Dragoo focuses on what to do when your plans go awry. This class features the fundamentals of riding motorcycles through challenging terrain, with plenty of time to practice skills and learn what to do when you end up in a situation you don't want to be in.

What do you do if your bike slides out in the mud and you're alone or your buddies have gone ahead? If one bike has a catastrophic failure and won't run, how can you tow it with another bike? What's your next move if you're stopped and stranded close to the top of an immense rocky hill?

I love the way Dragoo addresses all these situations, while sharing methods of creative problem-solving you can use when you're taking your bike off the beaten path—way off. His two intense days of learning new skills, followed by four days of putting them to use off road, results in a tremendous boost in rider confidence.

One of Dragoo's training sessions was at 3 Step Hideaway, a remote ranch near Monticello, Utah that's basically off the grid. Electricity is a precious commodity, provided by solar panels and a couple of backup generators. Forget about cellphone coverage. But the cabins are comfortable, the food is excellent and the team running the place is friendlier and more helpful than you can imagine.

3 Step Hideaway sits right along the Trans-America Trail, and they have a garage full of tires, motorcycle parts and tools to help get people on their way. Riders often ship tires ahead and book a day or

two here before moving on. It's a terrific place, and I highly recommend it.

Some of the other better-known training sessions I've attended include:

- Gary LaPlante Trials Training
- Keith Code's California Superbike School (plus his Wheelie School)
- AZ Highway Patrol Training Class
- Phoenix Police Department Motor Officer Training
- Jim Hyde's RawHyde Adventures
- Larry Grodsky's "Stayin' Safe"
- Reg Pridmore CLASS School
- Lee Parks "Total Control" Classes
- Northwest Motorcycle School—Ride Like A Cop
- Motorcycle Safety Foundation—too many classes to count

75
DESIGN, DEDICATION, DUCATI

IF YOU'VE EVER OWNED OR ridden a Ducati motorcycle, I don't need to explain the appeal of the brand. While Ducati riders don't typically tattoo their bodies with the logo like some Harley Davidson fans do, the passion and affinity for Ducati run just as deep. And, as Catholics go to Rome, Muslims to Mecca and Lotus lovers to Norwich, many Ducati aficionados make a pilgrimage to the Ducati factory and museum just outside of Bologna, Italy.

My non-riding friends and family members may not view a trip to a motorcycle factory—even one with a museum—with the same level of urgency or anticipation as I do, but fortunately northern Italy offers many excellent opportunities for subterfuge. It's easy to justify family trips to Venice, Florence or Milan—all stunning travel destinations. And once you get everyone into any of these areas, slipping away for a few hours to the Ducati factory and museum becomes an easy side trip.

Bologna lies just 100 miles south of the Venice airport, a mere 85 miles south of Florence or 130 miles southeast of Milan in the Po valley. For the culturally inclined, it's the city of towers and home to one of the world's oldest universities, founded in 1088. For us riders, though, it's simply the birthplace of every Ducati motorcycle ever made.

Reservations to see the Ducati factory are a must, with tours available in both English and Italian. I've done and enjoyed both, even with rusty to nearly non-existent Italian speaking skills. The passion for Ducati comes through loud and clear in any language, starting in the museum where the company's remarkable journey unfolds.

Long before the distinctive rumble of Ducati engines echoed through Italian streets, the company began as a manufacturer of radio components, vacuum tubes and condensers in the 1920s and 30s. The factory survived repeated Allied bombings during World War II, but it wasn't until the 1950s that Ducati's true destiny began to take shape. The transformation started in 1944, when Aldo Farinelli developed a small gasoline engine on the other side of town that could be mounted on a bicycle.

These "Cucciolo" engines, named for their puppy-like sound, were initially sold alone, with mounting left to the buyer's ingenuity—something that reminded me of my early mechanical adventures with my brother Leif back in Fairmont, Minnesota. Eventually, companies like Ducati began offering complete motorized bicycles: one of those original Cucciolo motors, along with an early factory-built motorcycle, now holds pride of place in the Ducati museum's first alcove. That little 60-cc bike weighed just 98 pounds and could reach a top speed of 40 miles per hour, while delivering an impressive 200 miles per gallon. Before long, Ducati dropped the Cucciolo name and introduced its own branded bikes, the 55M and 65TL, soon racing them into the history books.

While the museum thoughtfully preserves these humble beginnings, it's Ducati's racing heritage that dominates the space. From Mike Hailwood's Isle of Man winner to the super bikes ridden to victory by Doug Polen, Troy Corser, Neil Hodgson, Troy Bayliss and Raymond Roche—along with a wall of winning MotoGP bikes—the collection is pure nirvana for racing enthusiasts. And yes, there's a gift shop that tests the resolve of even the most frugal visitor.

The real heart of Ducati beats in its 200,000 square-foot factory, where every motorcycle, including Valentino Rossi's MotoGP racing bike, comes to life. As Gabriele Del Torchio, CEO and President, puts it, "We don't just make vehicles here, we make dreams. We make motorcycles that fulfill the dreams of our customers." This philosophy has driven the company to embrace risk and innovation, never more evidently than during recent challenging times.

When the global economic downturn of 2004 and 2005 dramatically reduced worldwide demand for Ducati motorcycles, the company faced intense pressure to scale back and downsize. The sensible path seemed to be cutting spending, lowering projections and reducing R&D expenses until the recession ended. Instead, Ducati chose to innovate its way forward, entering a new market with a revolutionary product: the Multistrada, a motorcycle designed to transform itself for different terrains and circumstances.

The factory itself reflects this commitment to excellence, with more than 1,000 employees spread across two floors. While designers and engineers occupy the top floor, the ground level hosts an impressive series of circular assembly lines surrounded by parts "supermarkets" and testing areas. The process begins with workers collecting components from these markets—everything from cylinders and gears to valves, clutches and pistons—into large trolleys, or carts.

Given the critical nature of the engine, each one is hand-assembled by two skilled craftspeople, one handling the bottom assembly on the first line before passing it to a colleague who completes the top assembly on the second. Unlike traditional factories where workers or machines attach single parts at fixed stations, Ducati's artisans walk alongside their creations, assembling each engine as it moves down the line.

The gamble on the Multistrada proved brilliant. In its first year alone, Ducati sold more than 10,000 units, exceeding their projections and invigorating the entire category of adventure touring bikes. The bike continues to be a strong seller today, with the factory cranking out about 70 new Multistradas each day. This success sparked a renaissance in the segment: Yamaha's Super Tenere and Honda's VFR1200 joined the fray, while established players like

BMW's 1350GS, Triumph's Tiger 1050, and KTM's 1290 Adventure saw renewed interest.

Whether you've owned a Ducati or not, visiting the museum and factory makes it nearly impossible not to fall under the spell of this remarkable company and the passionate individuals who dedicate themselves daily to turning dreams into reality. In every corner of the facility, from the historical displays to the assembly line, you'll find testament to why Ducati continues to capture the hearts of riders worldwide.

One of my visits to the Ducati Factory took place in February of 2012, during a rare cold snap and snow.

76

THE QUEST FOR THE PERFECT MOTORCYCLE

"WHICH MOTORCYCLE IS BEST?" AS someone whose life has been shaped by motorcycles, I hear this question constantly. I've extolled the advantages of the BMW 1200GS (my current bike) and have recommended it to others for years. I urged my good friend Roger Hansen to buy one, and he's ridden it all over the world.

My first long ride on a GS was in the fall of 2005. I picked up a brand-new one in Istanbul, Turkey, before a 12-day circumnavigation of the country led by the famous tour guide, Kazim "Kaz" Uzunoglu. Kaz has his own tour company, but he's frequently hired by other tour operators like MotoDiscovery, Baltic Tours, Road Scholar and others. He's familiar with more than 40 countries and has put in more than 300,000 miles guiding motorcycle tours around the globe.

The proprietor of Turkey's "Camel Hotel" urged me to ride one of the bikes into the courtyard. Later that night, I piloted around tables of amused diners.

BMW had just replaced its venerable R1150GS with this new model, which weighed 66 lbs. less and delivered 100 brake horse-power. The BMW faithful were livid. "It has too much plastic and feels like a Japanese bike," they said, the ultimate put-down from this circle of enthusiasts. I agreed that the R1100GS and R1150GS both had stability and tractability like no other mounts, but after spending two weeks riding the new model, my reaction was quite the opposite.

"They need to get over themselves," I thought of the angry BMW fans. "This is a fantastic motorcycle."

A moto-journalist colleague of mine, Fred Rau, also liked the new GS. He began his print review by saying, "While vastly improved, the big GS remains so ugly bugs won't hit it." I recall Fred getting many complaints about his motorcycle aesthetics. Fred, however, made a brilliant point: "The GS puts performance and ride perfection ahead of appearance."

After returning from the Dakar Rally in South America (also aboard a 1200GS) in 2011, and after a painful pre-trip dismount on my Crown King tune-up ride on the V-Strom, I grudgingly knew it was time to get rid of a bunch of motorcycles. The dirt bikes had to go, and soon they were history. My garage was suddenly down to only two motorcycles: the venerable yellow Honda Goldwing and the Suzuki V-Strom. A Honda Grom was coming my way, but I didn't know it yet.

Loving the extra garage space, I decided it was time to go all the way and merge the Goldwing and V-Strom into one machine. This led to my multi-year, epic quest to find "The One Bike to Rule Them All." Yes, I stole this from J. R. R. Tolkien's "One Ring to Rule Them All," but it's appropriate here.

My moto-journalist experiences made me aware of the ultimate futility of detailed comparisons among motorcycles. As one who's taken part in evaluating and writing motorcycle Shootout stories, most bikes are far more similar than they are different. Readers of motorcycle magazines don't know how difficult it is to find and highlight differences among the top brands in a single category.

Review Shootout trips followed a well-established process. On the first day of the trip/review, bikes are frequently swapped around so all the writers in the group get at least one or two rides on each bike.

We'd desperately try to find any fundamental differences at dinner the first night. The general feeling from everyone was typically, "For this purpose, these are the same. It won't matter which one a reader picks to buy, they'll be delighted with any of them. They're all priced within $500 of each other, weigh within a few lbs., have the same warranty, seating position, handling, acceleration, braking, etc. Let's go home."

Of course, the lead writer of the piece would be panicking at this point. Somehow, an article about five different 650 cc sport bikes that says, "They're all pretty much the same; any of them will do," would never get past the editor-in-chief and wouldn't please the readers or the advertisers.

So, over the next two days, we'd all try to tease out every tiny, superficial, insignificant difference and exaggerate them enough to make a story. Trust me, auto journalists have the same problem.

Scaling down to a single bike for myself was an attitude challenge for me, as well. For years, my answer to "How many motorcycles should one rider have?" was always "One more than they have now." Throughout my entire motorcycling career, I strenuously argued that multiple bike disorder (MBD) was not a disease but, in fact, the only proper way to approach motorcycle ownership.

My garage once reflected this philosophy perfectly. For street riding alone, I maintained three distinct machines: the Honda Goldwing for long-distance touring, a Suzuki V-Strom for shorter trips requiring some luggage capacity, and a Ducati 750 Monster for pure canyon carving. And that barely scratched the surface of what a well-equipped rider might need. I'm still leaving out several important categories, such as weekend cruising, represented most notably by popular Harley and Indian models. I also don't have a pure sport bike on the list, a motorcycle you could respectably take to a track day. So really, to adequately cover the needs of an all-around, street-only rider, you need a minimum of five motorcycles.

Moving to off-road bikes, the choices are even more plentiful depending on terrain, ride length and other factors. To ride off road and go any distance, you need an adventure-oriented machine that can handle luggage, spare parts and maybe even camping gear. If you want to go over jumps and whoops, you need a motocross bike. If you're going desert riding, you need a lighter, single-thumper model. Each serves its distinct purpose—try riding a typical trials course on anything other than a proper trials bike and you'll understand why its first three gears are designed for speeds under 10 mph. Like the fully equipped street rider, a well-rounded off-road rider needs at least five different motorcycles.

At one point, I had nine different motorcycles, and I watched countless friends struggle to find the one magic bike that would do it all. And now here I was, attempting the same impossible task.

After a bit of research, mostly online, I identified nine candidates on my shortlist for "The One Bike to Rule Them All." They were:

1. KTM 1190 (now 1290)
2. BMW 1200GS (now R1300GS)
3. Triumph Tiger
4. Ducati 1200 Multistrada (now 1260-V2)
5. Honda Africa Twin
6. Suzuki V-Strom 1000
7. Honda ST1200
8. Yamaha FJR1300
9. Kawasaki Concours

Although they were all fantastic machines I loved to ride, I quickly eliminated the Yamaha FJR1300, Honda ST1200 and Kawasaki Concours (the "Connie") as too road oriented. It's the same reason why another bike I loved, the BMW RT, never made the list in the first place. The ultimate bike for me had to be up for some off-road duties.

After participating in a press Shootout between the Suzuki V-Strom 650 and the Suzuki V-Strom 1000, I cut the V-Strom 1000 from my list. I had owned the 650 "Wee-Strom" for years, and while I loved the bike, I knew its suspension limitations all too well.

One significant benefit of writing for motorcycle magazines is that it's easy to try out any motorcycle for weeks at a time at no cost. The PR departments for most top brands are happy to find something for you to test. So, I "tested" my remaining five candidates for the next two years. Plus, I read reviews, shoot-outs and other comparisons of these specific models.

Of the five bikes that were still on my list, I had vestigial prejudices toward two of them that needed addressing. On the plus side was the Triumph Tiger, which I'd ridden in New Zealand for two weeks. I was blown away by both its handling on the tarmac and its off-road prowess when venturing into spots like Skipper's Canyon. It was always well-planted, predictable and did everything right.

The BMW 1200GS, on the other hand, triggered some negative feelings in me. While I loved the bike and its capabilities, I was put off by its ubiquity—"You can't swing a dead cat and not hit a 1200GS," I'd often say. I credit much of its popularity to Ewan McGregor and Charley Boorman, who rode it in their TV specials, *Long Way Round* and *Long Way Down*.

I also had problems with Honda's Africa Twin, but not because I was predisposed to it one way or the other. It was just hard to come by in the U.S. back then. I'd seen it several times on foreign trips, and it looked positively brilliant, but I had difficulty acquiring one to test.

Ducati has always been very good to me, and I've become friends with several people in their PR department. They graciously provided me with a 1200 Multistrada Touring model for use on a two-week trip over the top of Italy and down the Dalmatian coast in the fall of 2013. This exquisite trip was in the company of a bevy of BMWs and a KTM 990 EFI (precursor to the 1190), ridden from Turkey by my friend, Kaz Uzunoglu.

Not only did I get long days on the Ducati, but I also swapped with Kaz and some of the other riders to test the KTM and a few BMWs to compare same-day riding impressions. The Ducati went from a starting point in the middle of the pack to now being my first choice after this trip, especially given its performance in the wet—which was simply amazing. The computerized, "sky hook" on-the-fly adjustments to suspension and ABS are nothing short of incredible.

At the beginning of 2015, my list of bikes looked like this, with the top 3 in a statistical dead heat:

1. Ducati 1200 Multistrada (now 1260-V2)
2. KTM 1190 (now 1290)
3. BMW 1200GS (now R1300GS)
4. Triumph Tiger
5. Honda Africa Twin

Two important factors ultimately shaped my decision. First, the Ducati lacked cruise control—a deal-breaker for long-distance touring. Second, both the Ducati and KTM used chain drives. After a lifetime of chain maintenance, I was ready for something different. These considerations pushed the shaft-driven BMW 1200GS to the top, despite my resistance to joining its massive owner community.

While it made total sense analytically, I struggled to want the same bike every other Tom, Dick and Harry owned—and, in my case, every Bob, Jim, Jane, Kevin (he has three) and Roger (he has two). I wanted to be thought of as highly discriminating, and that meant not riding what everyone else was riding.

Two years went by. A friend finally took my V-Strom and I added a Honda Grom to the garage, so I was down to two motorcycles—more accurately one and a half if you don't consider the Grom a full-size motorcycle, which it's not.

Late in 2016, I wandered through GoAZ in Scottsdale, my favorite dealer. They're always well-stocked and represent all major brands, including Aprilia, BMW, Ducati, Husqvarna, Honda, Indian, Kawasaki and Royal Enfield. Don Reiff, the sales manager and an old friend, had a 2017 BMW 1200GS with everything I wanted. Before I knew it, I was trading in my Goldwing and Grom for a new BMW, complete with $4,000 in accessories, which any GS owner will tell you is just the beginning.

The bike has proven itself worthy of my choice. It's sublime. It handles curves like something half its weight yet tackles serious off-road terrain with confidence. Outfitted with Woody's stellar off-road wheels, knobby tires and other accessories for tackling dirt, I've taken it to Moab's challenging trails and down into Mexico's Copper Canyon. I even invested in training with Jim Hyde's RawHyde Adventures and Bill Dragoo's DART sessions, ensuring I could handle this capable machine in any condition.

While the bike's popularity still occasionally irks me, I've made peace with owning a GS by making it uniquely mine. Custom handlebars and foot pegs fit my riding style perfectly. Enhanced lighting improves visibility well beyond stock, and interchangeable wheels and tires let me quickly adapt for different terrain.

After years of resistance, I'm proud to say I've found my "One Bike to Rule Them All"–even if it's the same one everyone else has.

I'm happy with the BMW 1200GS. Ruslan Stickney, my nephew's son, tries it on in December of 2021.

77

TALES FROM THE ROAD: WRITERS WHO RIDE

THE ROOM FELL SILENT AS Annette Birkmann took the stage at the Mountain View BMW/Triumph dealership. It was early 2009, and the Danish rider with piercing blue eyes had just completed a year-long solo journey from Tierra del Fuego to San Francisco on her 2001 BMW F650 Dakar. The audience of 80 riders sat transfixed as she shared her story—one that I would later convey to the readers of *Motorcycle Consumer News* (MCN).

Birkmann's book, *The Road to Getting Yourself Out of the Way: A Journey to Effortless Living*, transcends the typical motorcycle travelogue. Rather than focusing on mechanical preparations or route planning, she explores the profound personal transformations that occur on long-distance rides, where you're forced to come to terms with life's elemental truths. Her descriptions of riding without fear, being completely present in the moment and experiencing time standing still resonate deeply with anyone who's struggled with wrong-headed thinking and the roadblocks that prevent them from feeling the simple joy of just being alive.

Her writing joins a special collection on my bookshelf—works by friends who've found ways to capture the ineffable experience of motorcycling in words. Each brings their unique perspective to the challenge of explaining why we ride and what we discover along the way.

Take Gregory Frazier, my colleague at MCN, whose fantastic books chronicle global adventures with characteristic wit and insight. One of his book titles competes for longest in publishing history—*Down and Out in Patagonia, Kamchatka, and Timbuktu: Greg Frazier's Round and Round and Round the World Motorcycle Journey*—but the length is warranted by the breadth of his experiences.

Mark Barnes, another MCN colleague, approached the subject from a unique angle in *Why We Ride: A Psychologist Explains the Motorcyclist's Mind and the Love Affair Between Rider, Bike and Road.* Like Frazier, he couldn't resist a lengthy title, but the psychological insights justify every word.

The American Flyers Motorcycle Club (AFMC), the group of riders that welcomed me into their fold, has produced its own literary subset. Rich Marin's *The Ride Is All* stands out not just for its physical heft, but because I was fortunate enough to participate in many of the rides it documents. The photographs alone tell stories that words can barely capture.

Another AFMC member, Frank O'Connell, couldn't keep motorcycles out of his ostensible business book, *Jump First, Think Fast*—proving that once riding gets in your blood, it influences everything you do.

Some books earn their keep through pure utility. I've bought at least six copies of Frank Del Monte's *Motorcycle Arizona! A Guide to Touring Arizona by Motorcycle*—not because I keep wearing them out, but because every friend I loan it to seems to "forget" to return it. Its dog-eared pages have guided countless adventures through my adopted state.

Lawrence Grodsky's *Stayin' Safe: The Art and Science of Riding Really Well* combines practical wisdom with philosophical insight. His columns for *RIDER* magazine, alongside my own articles, have earned permanent space on my shelves, too weathered now to part with.

Another friend, Arthur W. Einstein Jr., who introduced me to the AFMC, wrote *Ask the Man Who Owns One: An Illustrated History of Packard Advertising.* While it never mentions motorcycles, Arthur's influence on my riding life has been so profound that any discussion of motorcycle literature would feel incomplete without acknowledging him.

Looking at these books lined up on my shelf, I often thought about adding my own contribution someday. Each author has captured something unique about the motorcycling experience—the freedom, the friendships, the self-discovery that happens on two wheels. As you're reading these words now, I suppose I've finally joined their ranks, sharing my own tales from the road and hoping to inspire others just as these writers have inspired me.

Our stories may differ in the details, but they share a common thread: the profound way motorcycling changes us, and our deep need to share those transformations with others. Whether through epic adventures like Birkmann's, technical expertise like Grodsky's or psychological insights like Barnes's, each writer helps explain why we're drawn to this remarkable pursuit.

Annette Birkmann at the Golden Gate Bridge in San Francisco,
nearing the conclusion of her life-changing trip.

RELIGION

FROM FAITH TO REASON

IN THE TAPESTRY OF HUMAN experience, few threads are as vibrant, complex and contentious as religion. This section of my memoir delves into my intellectual pilgrimage through the realms of faith, doubt and, ultimately, reasoned skepticism.

From my early days as a fervent young believer, memorizing Scripture and winning Bible quizzes, to my current stance as a thoughtful agnostic, my relationship with religion and ethics has been a winding path of discovery, disillusionment and deep reflection. This journey has taken me from the pews of Evangelical churches to the rigors of philosophical inquiry, from the comforting certainties of childhood faith to the nuanced complexities of adult skepticism.

In these pages, I'll share pivotal moments shaping my world-view: the trauma of losing my young son and its impact on my faith, my experiences with various religious communities and my gradual awakening to scientific reasoning. I'll explore the ethical dilemmas I've faced, the hypocrisies I've witnessed and the profound questions I've grappled with about the nature of morality, ethics, community and purpose in a world without divine oversight.

More than anything, this section is an invitation to reflect on the role of religion in our lives and society. We'll confront some challenging questions: Can one be moral without being religious? How do we find meaning and build community in a secular world? What are the societal impacts—both positive and negative—of organized religion? Are the similarities between world religions good or bad?

Through it all, I aim to approach these sensitive topics with honesty, respect and a spirit of open inquiry. Whether you're a devout believer, a confirmed atheist or somewhere in between, I hope this section provokes thought, encourages dialogue and perhaps even challenges some long-held assumptions in a world where the answers are rarely simple and the questions are always worth asking.

78

WHEN IT ALL ENDED

I STOPPED BELIEVING IN GOD in the days and weeks after my son Eric died, just short of his second birthday. A well-meaning clergyman had put his arm around me and said, "It was God's will."

I was seething. Why would God let something like this happen if He were able to prevent it? What had I done to deserve this? If God were omnipotent and cared even a whit about me, He'd have intervened to prevent this horrible thing from happening. But He didn't. Instead, He allowed my son to die, because of a stupid mistake born of petty hubris from a jealous doctor. Eric's death could have been so easily averted.

It made no sense.

My bitter anger at God and what He allowed to happen hit a crescendo, and then slowly dissipated in the weeks that followed my encounter with the clergyman. It wasn't immediate, but my angry internal dialogue went from "If you're going to treat me like this, I'll stop believing in you!" to the gradual realization that I had had serious doubts about the existence of God long before Eric's death. Doubts I'd just pushed away, too fearful to acknowledge them. As the days went by and I lived with this new-found consciousness without fear, waves of peace and calm began to replace my anger and distress.

This revelation was incredibly freeing and deeply profound. And even though it gave me so much peace, I decided to keep it quiet in my heart. It was clear that others around me had not experienced this, but I was finally certain about what I believed. There was no supreme being who was dumping on me. The universe is a big place where random things happen, good and bad, all the time, and God isn't hearing one person's pleas over another's and granting any sort of result or rescue.

I felt so much better. Feelings of calm and tranquility flooded over me, and a tremendous burden of guilt and angst was lifted from my mind. While relieved, however, I wasn't happy yet. I was still suffering terribly from my son's death, but I could see light at the end of the tunnel and had hope for the first time in months.

It was actually more than hope. I finally found the peace, acceptance and love so many Christians talk about after they've been "saved." This was my moment of salvation, although admittedly a unique one. For years, I'd agonized over feelings of inadequacy when I heard church members and fellow Bible school campers stand and testify to the elation they felt when Jesus came into their hearts. The joyous feelings and bliss they described were finally filling me, making me feel whole in a way I never felt before. But it wasn't because I found Jesus; it was because I accepted the idea that he doesn't exist, in me or anywhere else.

But I don't speak about this often. I don't wish to cause disagreements or make anyone uncomfortable or defensive, least of all my family or close friends. I don't want people to try to convince me I'm wrong and shouldn't believe what I do, although I am open to discussion about this topic. It's also clear that for some of the people closest to me, religion, a belief in God and involvement with their church fill a deep need and provide them and their families with significant benefits.

Not believing in God has not made me a bad or immoral person. Most everyone who knows me well would tell you that I'm respectful of others. I don't lie, cheat or steal. I try to be honest and transparent in all that I do, unless it might hurt someone. I work hard to do right by my family and friends, and I treat others the way I wish to be treated.

C. S. Lewis, one of my go-to authors for substantiation arguments in defense of Christianity, lost his faith after the death of his wife, just like I did after the death of my son. Eric's passing was the starting point for me to question and understand my beliefs. Maybe deep grief triggers new thinking, and maybe people can change their beliefs when faced with different realities.

In his final book, *A Grief Observed*, Lewis outlines his loss of faith, wondering if it had been real all along. After a career as a leading Christian apologist, he felt compelled to confess publicly that his faith had been imaginary. It reminds me of a quote often attributed to boxer Mike Tyson: "Everyone has a plan until they get punched in the mouth."

The seeds of my non-belief had begun years earlier. But when was it, exactly? As a teenager, my family, neighbors and fellow church members couldn't help but recognize my religious commitment and passion. Photos of me at nine or 10 years old show a small New Testament sticking out of my front shirt pocket.

Early photos of me often show a New Testament sticking out of my shirt pocket.

While a lackluster student in school, my ability to memorize and recite Scripture was superb and often commended. No other kid in my confirmation class held a candle to my knowledge of the Lutheran catechism. At summer Bible camp, some campers refused to take part in Bible quizzes or other contests if they knew I was competing, as they believed I would inevitably win.

I was active in Campus Crusade for Christ and attended religious conventions and rallies all over the Midwest. My role as a counselor and lifeguard at two religious summer camps in Canada in the summer of 1968 is still recalled by those who were there as an inspiration to their Christian lives. I actively worked to recruit friends and neighbors to God's army. My reputation as an enthusiastic Christian youth also played a defining role in my secular public school, where most saw me as God's debate champion.

In 1969, during my senior year at Mayo High School in Rochester, I maintained a reputation as a staunch, outspoken Christian. I turned down the offer of the lead in my school's production of *Of Mice and Men* because the script included curse words, and I (well, technically more my mother) felt it was inappropriate for a Christian young man to be heard using swear words on a public stage.

I was well known for actively defending my faith and the existence of God during frequent religious and philosophical discussions, particularly in my humanities and speech classes. So well-known were my views, that the principal, Dr. Ralph Wright, asked me to lead our class graduation ceremonies in the Invocation and Benediction. This was the first time in city history that a student, not a prominent clergy member, had received this honor. My classmates voted me most likely to become a minister or priest.

Sharpening my arguments for God and religion was a constant task. Although I grew up on a steady diet of select Bible passages in a conservative Christian church amongst a dedicated, Bible-believing family, I wanted a deeper and more profound understanding to build even more substantial arguments and make sure my prayers would be answered in a less random way.

Looking back, I see two different things going on. The first was easy. I knew what side I was on—the Christian team—and wished to arm myself for battle as best as I could. A favorite hymn, sung frequently in my church, was *Onward Christian Soldiers*:

Onward, Christian soldiers,
Marching as to war,
With the cross of Jesus
Going on before!
Christ, the royal Master,
Leads against the foe;
Forward into battle,
See his banner go!

The second is that I was desperately seeking God. I wanted the deep assurance that my pastor and all the visiting evangelists preaching at our church seemed to have. Why did these rapturous, euphoric, life-changing feelings happen to everyone else but me? Didn't I pray hard enough? Long enough? How could I show God my sincerity and deepest desires? Why didn't I feel *saved*?

If there was a god, wouldn't I have been a prime candidate to recruit? What was the reason for this complete and utter radio silence? There wasn't one specific, concrete message I could latch onto. In my effort to figure things out, I convinced my humanities teacher, Claire Van Zant, to give me class credit for reading the Bible in its entirety, cover to cover, word for word. She agreed, and I planned everything out meticulously.

My game plan featured a desk layout with a fully annotated Bible in front of me—the highly regarded Thompson Chain Reference version, which I still have—a dictionary to my right and *Strong's Concordance of the Bible* on my left. A Bible concordance is a reference in which words from Scripture are arranged alphabetically in a kind of index. I finally had the tools to collect all the evidence that would allow me to easily win every future religious debate—I was so jazzed!

Over the course of three months, I spent hundreds of hours reading, studying, taking notes, underlining passages and doing my best to understand every book, chapter, page and verse. When I finished, thoughts on what I read bounced around in my head for weeks.

I desperately wanted to use this newfound knowledge to win more arguments for God, but it wasn't working out. Frankly, the Bible wasn't very good at strengthening my arguments. I found it to be mostly dull and irrelevant, containing ponderous genealogies and racial purity hang-ups. It promoted fights over real estate and women, arcane rituals, folk medicine and insider politics.

The God of the Bible, in my reading, appeared arbitrary, mean, foolish and morally bankrupt by most modern standards. He was full of human foibles, such as jealousy, anger and hubris, to name a few.

Richard Dawkins, the famous British author, Oxford University professor and scientist, put it bluntly: "The God of the Old Testament is arguably the most unpleasant character in all fiction: jealous and proud of it; a petty, unjust, unforgiving control-freak; a vindictive, bloodthirsty ethnic cleanser; a misogynistic, homophobic, racist, infanticidal, genocidal, filicidal, pestilential, megalomaniacal, sadomasochistic, capriciously malevolent bully." While that may seem bitter, it's difficult to refute after reading the complete Bible.

I found it incredibly challenging to try and justify and explain the Bible's inconsistencies and contradictions. It wasn't unusual for me to flip back to something I'd read before, after finding a passage that was diametrically opposed to it a few chapters or books later on. How could this be? How do I resolve this?

God claimed that He loved everyone but demanded his followers to do downright evil and abhorrent things to other people, such as stoning them for minor infractions and having his disciple Lot send his virgin daughters out to be raped by a crowd to protect visiting angels in his home. Why did angels need protection? Couldn't God take care of them if they couldn't take care of themselves? If Lot were a moral human being, wouldn't he sacrifice himself to stop his daughters from being raped?

And then there was the mass genocide. God didn't like how some people on Earth were behaving, so He wiped out everyone on the planet but one family. In a flood. He drowned nearly everyone, including the animals! Thanos, the ultimate villain created by Marvel Comics, only decimated 50 percent of the human population and is considered the most heinous and evil creature the Marvel writers could come up with. As bad as he was, his deed wasn't as bad as the one done by the God of the Bible.

Years later, a cousin shared an observation that captured my experience in a humorous way: If you buy a Bible and don't read it, you'll be a Catholic. If you buy a Bible and read only the parts you like, you'll be an Evangelical. If you buy a Bible and read it thoroughly and completely, you'll be an atheist.

While I didn't stop believing in God in high school and remained a committed supporter of God's existence during my college years, I stopped using the Bible to support my pro-religion arguments. I never quite got over what I read, or the contradictions caused by being told by my fundamentalist family and our church that the Bible was "the infallible and holy word of God," every bit the absolute authority for judging any subject. The seeds of doubt were planted, but I wasn't ready to acknowledge them yet.

Years later, when that clergyman told me that Eric's death was "God's will," everything crystallized. My son's death wasn't what drove me from faith—it was simply the final thread breaking what had already been unraveling for years. This bitter anger at God peaked, then dissipated in the weeks that followed. As I lived with this newfound consciousness without fear, peace replaced my anger and distress.

As I mentioned earlier, here was that "saved" feeling, a heartfelt acceptance so many Christians talk about after receiving Christ, that I'd been hearing about—and longing for—for years. Those joyous feelings were finally filling me, making me feel whole in a way I never felt before.

What I thought was an ending—the death of my faith along with the death of my son—turned out to be a beginning. Free from the need to justify an interventionist God or reconcile biblical contradictions, I could finally explore what it truly means to be good, to find meaning and to face life's mysteries with honest uncertainty.

Sometimes the bravest thing we can do is let go of the answers we've been given and begin asking new questions.

79

A DEBATE CHAMPION'S GUIDE TO NOT BEING FOOLED

I HEARD AN INTERVIEW ONCE on NPR, where a woman spoke about "her truth." I cringed. There's no such thing as "my truth." There's only one truth, the one based on facts. Everything else is opinion.

In high school, debate was my sport. I loved debating. My competitive nature was well-suited for a team that made it to the state level, and I achieved every honor the American Forensic League awarded.

Anyone in debate knows that arguments require support. And the first step in building support is collecting verifiable facts from trusted sources, such as encyclopedias, newspapers and magazines. One's sources meant something. Judges didn't score facts ripped from the pages of *Reader's Digest* as highly as those from *The Wall Street Journal* or *The New York Times*.

If you lacked factual support for an argument, you then went to the next tier of proof: expert opinion. Sometimes, a quote supporting your position from a well-known, highly educated and credible individual with a trusted position on a subject could be almost as persuasive as a fact. The more authoritative your sources and quotes supporting clear reasoning and logic, the better your chances of winning.

Our Fairmont High School team, especially Ted Hasse and I, accumulated impressive wins that ultimately landed us in competition for the state championship. Debate wins come by collecting points, which are based on the "quality and reasonableness" of an argument and the sources used to back it up. We quickly learned the hierarchy of what was credible and what wasn't—the sources judges respected most and awarded with the most points, and those not worth mentioning, even if they contained good soundbites.

To friends attempting to make sense of what's happening in today's politics, with controversy swarming around climate change, immigration and the economy, it's important to know what sources can be trusted for accuracy, objectivity, lack of bias and transparency in data collection and methods of analysis.

Having authorities with relevant credentials and experience is a major key in winning debates. While my diagnosis of what's wrong with your 1975 Triumph motorcycle might sound good, someone like Frank Del Monte would give a far more comprehensive rundown. Getting health advice from a neighbor who's watched every episode of *House*, *Grey's Anatomy* or *ER* may not be as prudent as consulting a Mayo Clinic doctor.

Sources take many forms, some of which are obviously better than others. Based on my own experience and assessments, here they are, ranked in descending order:

Scholarly, peer-reviewed research papers, by recognized experts from leading institutions, are most likely to be unbiased and present information objectively, without distorting facts to fit a particular agenda. The big plus for peer-reviewed articles is that other scientists or experts in the space have had the chance to read them and discover errors or faulty logic. The downside is that they often take more effort to read, digest and evaluate. Great accuracy doesn't always lend itself to brevity or catchy phrasing.

Legal documents, such as official records of court filings and rulings, also set a high bar for material facts and accurate information. Being wrong in legal documents is rare, as the consequences of errors or misstatements are significant. Judges can throw out a case for even minor flaws. They can fine someone, or even put them in jail, for not being truthful in court filings or testimony. If you seek the truth, pay attention to what's said in court. At the risk of seeming political, my ears perked up when I read that attorney Sidney Powell defended herself in court documents, in a defamation suit brought by Dominion Voting Systems, by arguing that "no reasonable person" would ever believe her claims that the machines were inaccurate.* Got that?

Reputable news outlets, adhering to recognized journalistic standards and fact-checking procedures, are also good sources of information. When debating, we knew that quoting *The New York Times* or *The Washington Post* would score us points, whereas a quote from *The National Enquirer* could prejudice a judge against our arguments.

Government agencies often release reports that can be considered relatively authoritative. They typically base their content on thorough research and data analysis. Of course, this doesn't include publications from political parties aimed at swaying voters.

Books by reputable scholars in their areas of expertise often provide insight and in-depth analysis on specific topics, although they lack the same level of peer review as scholarly articles. Information from well-established and accredited educational institutions is mostly reliable, as they prioritize academic rigor and integrity.

Credible non-governmental organizations (NGOs) that specialize in a particular area can provide valuable data and research findings relevant to social, environmental and humanitarian issues. The ones to avoid are often obvious.

Industry reports and studies, conducted by reputable professional organizations, can also be helpful in debates about economic, business or technological matters, but watch for bias. If the Raisin Growers of America sponsors a study on the health benefits of

---

*Plaintiffs, Dominion Voting Systems, Inc. sued Sidney Powell in the U.S. District Court of the District of Columbia. Her lawyers argued that "no reasonable person" would have believed her claims about election fraud were "truly statements of fact." The judge rejected Powell's argument to dismiss the case, allowing Dominion's $1.3 billion defamation lawsuit to proceed.

raisins, greet it with some skepticism. White papers released by reputable businesses can offer insights and analysis on specific issues, but may also have a similar bias, so watch the sources they cite and especially who funded them.

Opinion pages and editorials can provide alternative perspectives, but it's essential to use them cautiously in formal debates, as they're subjective. Most newspapers draw an obvious line between their reporting—which must be supported by multiple sources and where writers are subject to strict ethical scrutiny—and the editorial page. Editorials are positioned as opinion or entertainment, and, as such, don't have the same controls or fact-checking process as the news.

Opinionated television networks, full of talking heads who espouse a particular line of thought that reflects what their audience wants to hear, are notoriously unreliable. Networks like MSNBC and Fox are primarily concerned with ratings so they can sell more advertising, often at the expense of factual objectivity. While sometimes entertaining, this kind of low-cost content is abysmal as an information source. There's little to no fact-checking, and much of what's covered is sensationalized to maximize entertainment value. Content is shallow, lacking depth, nuance and accuracy. These outlets also lack a diversity of perspectives, only inviting those with similar views to reinforce the echo chambers they've created.

Blogs, personal websites, social media platforms and Internet forums can be highly biased and misleading, as unverified information in these spaces abounds. Neither I nor my debate team colleagues Ted Hasse, Nancy Hagerman, Jim Odens and Paul Irvine would have ever used these sources in our debates if we had access to them. We would have lost instantly.

Sorting fact from fable isn't always an easy task, but you can think of my preceding explanations as a blueprint to streamline the process. If something sounds too good (or bad) to be true, see where the information comes from before you give it too much, or too little, weight.

During a presentation for my friend Rich Marin's graduate class on business ethics, I recommended *The Inventor: Out for Blood in Silicon Valley*, a documentary film about Theranos produced by Oscar-winner Alex Gibney. You don't win Oscars in the documentary category by making stuff up. Gibney is good at revealing his sources and how he found and used them.

My other professional experience in getting things right occurred when I began my freelance writing career. Some magazines publishing my work subjected it to fact checkers. Wow, that was an experience! These professionals walked me through my submissions sentence by sentence, challenging everything I'd written. They wanted to know how I knew the truth of what was on the page. Did I have more than one source? What were the sources?

Dan Gilmore, a reporter for the *San Jose Mercury News* in the early 2000s, exposed me to the efforts newspapers put into making sure their reporting is free of any outside influence. Admiring his stories about other Silicon Valley startups, I contacted him to cover our company.

He agreed to meet me at a coffee shop near our offices. Standing in line to get our coffee, I reached to pay but he pushed a five-dollar bill onto the counter. A bit surprised, I asked him about it after we sat down. He explained that, as a reporter for the *Mercury News*, he couldn't take any form of consideration from an individual or company he was writing about, not even a cup of coffee. "It would get me in trouble with our ethics board," he said with a smile. He wrote about us several times and would call me for background on other stories.

Once, I sat next to him at a conference and during a break he lamented about not having enough American Airlines frequent flyer miles for an upcoming trip. He had tons of United Airlines miles but was short on AA. I said I had tens of thousands of unused AA miles and would happily swap. We went online and quickly traded 50,000 of our respective miles. I didn't give it another thought.

A few months later, reaching out to him about covering an upcoming product launch, he told me he could no longer cover our company. When I asked why, he said, "Because now we're friends—we exchanged miles." Although our miles exchange had equal value, he told me his editor would assign a different reporter to cover us, but he could no longer write about me or any of my companies. And he never did.

No doubt, all top journalistic publications have similar ethics rules. It's too bad that most politicians don't.

80

GETTING A GRIP ON GOD

IN THE SUMMER OF 1968, between my junior and senior years of high school, I was about to leave to work in a Christian summer camp. My attendance at various religious conferences led to an invitation to become a counselor and waterfront director—essentially a lifeguard—at Willow Springs near Stouffville, just outside of Toronto, Ontario. While I was a strong swimmer and had passed the classes necessary to become a lifeguard in Fairmont, I didn't get one of those prized summer jobs at one of its many swimming beaches, so I was off to Canada.

Before I left, on June 24, 1968, two brothers drowned in George Lake, right near our house. I was reading outside on our front steps when I heard shouts and cries for help from the lake. Running down to the water, I saw a pontoon boat with frantic teenagers jumping up and down and pointing to various spots on the water. I slipped off my shoes and shirt, dove into the lake and began swimming toward the pontoon. Before I could reach it, a girl shouted that I should look for a boy who'd gone under and not come back up.

I felt an arm on my second or third dive below the surface, and my heart skipped a beat. Grabbing it, I pulled the boy to the surface, struggling to drag him to a nearby boat. No sooner had we wrestled him into the boat than the panicked kids yelled that there was another boy still under the water. I began swimming around, trying to find the second boy, and eventually did. I was closer to shore this time and started pulling him to the water's edge. The boat followed. A crowd, including my mother, who was a registered nurse, was waiting at the shore, and soon the ambulance arrived and took over our rescue attempt. But it was too late. Both boys were dead.

I didn't know what to feel. A whole list of "if only" thoughts filled my head, but nothing worked to calm my empathy for the family of these poor brothers.

The *Fairmont Sentinel* newspaper covered the incident in a front-page article the following day, June 25, 1968. The clipping of the article remains in my scrapbook—photos showing my involvement in the failed rescue. What a send-off as I began my stint in Canada as, of all things, a lifeguard. I left two days after the drownings.

June 25, 1968 front page of the Fairmont Sentinel. *The top photo shows me pulling a body into the boat. In the second photo, my arm rests on the body of a drowned boy. In the bottom picture, my mother looks on as they perform CPR on one of the brothers.*

When I was just a baby, my father was a pastor in Canada and had attended seminary school. My recollections of our church were vague, except that we were different and separate from "the world." After my family moved back to Fairmont from Canada, I can't recall much about the churches we attended when I was in grade school.

Memories of my religious upbringing and church teachings come into sharper focus once we started doing the 20-mile drive from Fairmont to Blue Earth, Minnesota, home to the small, conservative Faith Lutheran Brethren Church led by the Rev. Morris Vold. He was the pastor there from January 1962 to September 1966. This Evangelical Lutheran church had its headquarters and religious high school in Fergus Falls, where my sister Naomi and cousin John Gravley both went to school.

We made the journey to Blue Earth every Sunday, and I also attended Saturday morning confirmation classes for a year in my early teens. The class included three others my age, including the pastor's daughter, Judy Vold, and my friend, Mike Selvig. We needed to learn the Lutheran Catechism, a 25-page summary of the principles of the Christian religion as practiced by my church.

It was mostly a list of questions and answers, and Pastor Vold narrowed them down for us a few weeks before we had to stand before the congregation for questioning. Using self-taught memorization techniques that would later help me when I got into theater, I memorized every answer and passed with flying colors on confirmation Sunday.

Several times, Pastor Vold kept me after class to find out whether I had asked Jesus into my heart without reservations, and if I sincerely believed what I was studying. I always replied as honestly as I could. I told him, "Yes, I have." But he never seemed convinced.

He'd ask me repeatedly to kneel and pray with him, once again asking Jesus Christ into my heart and life. But he never seemed quite satisfied. Perhaps he sensed something about me, of which I was yet unaware. I questioned if I was sincere, wondering if my conversion had hit the mark and was good enough. I was as earnest as I knew how to be. More than anything, I wanted to be confident in my heart that I was "right with God."

Many church services I attended included an altar call, asking anyone who didn't know Jesus to make a decision. "Make it now," the preacher would urge. "If you die on your way to school tomorrow, do you know where you would go? Where will you spend eternity?"

After a pause, the preacher would say, "If you've already prayed the 'prayer of salvation' and have given your heart to Jesus, are you *really* sure? Maybe you've backslidden!" That was a dreaded situation for those who once were saved but now found themselves living a life of sin.

Our particular faith tradition taught us that we were born with a sinful nature, and that no sin was too small to make God angry. God was pure, holy and righteous, and therefore couldn't tolerate even a tiny bit of dirty sin. Sitting in the pew, I would suddenly remember taking a piece of candy from the dish on the table after being told not to, or pushing dirty clothes under my bed instead of putting them in the hamper in the hall. Would a pair of dirty blue jeans cause me to burn in Hell forever?

My Catechism classmate, Mike Selvig, had an intellectually-oriented older brother, David, who was reading a book on the German theologian and anti-Nazi dissident Dietrich Bonhoeffer. He lent me the book containing Bonhoeffer's letters and papers from prison, a treatise that served as Bonhoeffer's last will and testament. Other books soon followed, including C. S. Lewis' *Mere Christianity*. Finally, I discovered a part of Christianity that engaged my brain cells, and I was hooked.

Mere Christianity was the gateway to other C.S. Lewis books, including *The Screwtape Letters, Miracles, Surprised by Joy* and *The Problem of Pain*. I loved and admired the arguments Lewis made to destroy nonbelievers. I thought Lewis was a genius and would later add his reasoned arguments to my arsenal of weapons for shooting down points against God in high school and college.

81

MY LIFE WITH THE JESUS FREAKS

AFTER FINISHING MY FIRST YEAR at Mankato State University, I headed south to Iowa City, Iowa. At a political protest rally in Minneapolis, I first encountered the Local Church movement and met some people who lived in a commune in the Hawkeye State. They invited me down to check it out.

My year at Mankato had left me with religious concerns and questions about my beliefs. I had a difficult time reconciling my faith given my first-year studies in the Experimental College, which had focused so much on philosophy, humanities and social sciences. My brilliant high school teacher, Claire Van Zant, had introduced me to many of these ideas, but back then I had an easier time deflecting the inconsistencies I came across.

Drawing me to Iowa City was a combination of wishing to find a way around the logical issues in my head and my lingering fear that all those early altar calls and prayers to accept the Lord Jesus into my heart hadn't worked. I never felt the euphoria others seemed to experience and so energetically described. The conflict between what my head was telling me and what the church was saying had become a far bigger issue in my first year of college.

I immediately felt at home in the communal house on Clinton Street in Iowa City. Long hair wasn't an issue for me because I already had it. Dressing like a hippie was fine with me, and smoking pot was okay, too. This was the summer of 1970 and the counterculture of the 1960s was still in full swing. Richard Nixon was navigating the complexities of the Vietnam War. Led Zeppelin, Simon & Garfunkel, The Beatles and Creedence Clearwater Revival filled the airwaves. We read Kurt Vonnegut and Eldridge Cleaver, watched the *Mary Tyler*

Moore Show on television and saw George C. Scott portray General Patton in the movie theater.

While the group I was with took on many elements of the hippie counterculture, their main emphasis was the importance of having a personal relationship with Jesus. While theologically consistent with most of the teachings of the church where I grew up, the group rejected conventional mainstream church practices in favor of street evangelism and communal living.

The movement was modeled after the historic Christian churches in the New Testament. Our go-to sources of inspiration were the Bible and religious writer Witness Lee, a follower of Chinese theologian Watchman Nee. Our spiritual gurus emphasized the subjective experience of Christ versus doctrinal knowledge, advocating against denominations and hierarchies.

Because we were all young and unemployed, or working at low-wage or temp jobs, it was far easier for us to follow the instructions in Mark 10:21 to "Sell everything you have and give to the poor... Then come, follow me."

Among other odd jobs, I repossessed pianos for a music store and helped assemble manufactured homes. One of these homes would later blow apart from a strong wind, and I was called as a witness in a lawsuit on the poor quality and lack of skill showed by the crew that put it together. My cousin, John Gravley, joined me at the commune and got a job at a Mr. Quick hamburger franchise, bringing home a paycheck and as much food as he could.

The students at the University of Iowa, where we would often hang out, referred to us as "Jesus People" or "Jesus Freaks." We handed out tracts on campus, and occasionally mounted a soapbox to preach.

Looking back, I can see now that the group had several cult-like aspects. We had a sign we used to identify each other, a single finger raised in the air that meant "one way." We had our charismatic leaders, and we liked the music of Larry Norman. His 1972 album of straight-ahead rock, *Only Visiting This Planet*, had one of my favorite songs on it—"Why Should the Devil Have All The Good Music."

During the summer, I hitchhiked to Canada to spread this new way of following Christ to the group of Christians I'd met there when I was a camp counselor at Camp Koinonia. I secretly wanted to get feedback from Jerry Jeffs, a man I admired who had spent much of his life in the Anglican church. He said nothing to dissuade me, and even seemed to encourage this new way of thinking.

I returned from Canada with a 20-year-old woman. Her family hoped I could help her find a good drug withdrawal and rehabilitation program in the United States, after the ones in Canada failed her. Once we returned to Iowa City, however, she showed little interest in the church and no interest in giving up drugs. Eventually, she found a boyfriend and wandered off.

Besides my cousin John Gravley, I was joined in Iowa City by my friend Kirby Walton. We met during our senior year in Rochester at Youth for Christ meetings. My brother Leif showed up at Clinton Street on occasion, as well. Leif's friend, Linda Gambill, was enrolled at Cornell College, just 20 miles north in Mount Vernon and she visited frequently, too. My high school girlfriend Patti Knappe came and stayed for a while, but found little in common with the "hippie chicks" at the communal house.

My cousin John was smitten with Linda and used to drive the white 1965 Triumph Spitfire we bought together from Jerry Russell, a member of our church in Iowa City, to visit her in Mount Vernon. They would later marry and produce Sarah, one of my favorite nieces (technically my first cousin, once removed).

When I moved back to Rochester in 1971, many of the people in my church group, including Jerry Russell, moved with me. The plan was to establish a "local church" there, which eventually did happen. After a few months I left the group, but not before dragging my brother Leif, my sister Jurene and my parents into it. Jurene remained with a version of the group in Spokane, Washington, and raised her two children in that faith. While my personal religious issues played a role in my departure, the more significant problem was Jerry Russell, who I came to see as a profoundly manipulative and destructive person. I just didn't want to be around him.

The local church group they built in Rochester grew and became an established part of the community. My parents remained in the movement until they died. Dad had finally found the church home he'd always longed for, and my mother—well, she followed my dad.

My negative feelings about this group of Christians intensified over the years. I was disturbed at their tendency to isolate members from their families. For instance, church retreats were always held over the Thanksgiving holidays. I also watched how many in the Phoenix church group took advantage of my mother after my father's death. Perhaps she noticed it, too. Despite maintaining friendships with several people in the group, my mother gradually pulled herself away from the congregation.

82

PLAYING THE LONG GAME: A FATHER'S IMPORTANT LESSON

A KNOCK ON OUR DOOR one Saturday morning in 1984 changed how I would parent for decades to come. Our daughter, Virginia Ruth, was just a few months old, her nursery still fresh with the mural painted by our friend Chuk Batko, when I opened the door to find a short, roundish man with sparkling eyes and a clerical collar.

"Everyone just calls me Pastor Rod," he said after introducing himself formally.

While my first thought was "Oh dear, I don't have time for this," something about his manner drew me in. His St. Andrew's Lutheran Church lay just a mile away, and he spent his Saturdays inviting neighbors to visit. He listened more than he spoke, and when I confessed my decade-long lapse in church attendance, he just smiled.

"Oh, we know that," he said. "We lose you until you're married, and a child comes along. Then you'll look for someplace to have it baptized and we get you back."

He was right, of course. My parents had been asking about Ginny's baptism for weeks. Before long, we found ourselves part of Pastor Rod's community at St. Andrew's. He and his wife excelled at welcoming new members, focusing more on building connections than religious piety. They organized parents' nights out, with church teenagers babysitting while adults watched movies or joined discussions. Saturdays often found the men gathering to plant trees, build flower beds or even excavate and set forms for new sidewalks.

There I was, having fun, learning some cool skills, eating pizza and helping people out. It felt good to be part of a community. Many years later, I learned that this Eden Prairie church, which was affiliated with the Evangelical Lutheran Church of America synod, would establish a sister church in New Prague, Minnesota. It was the same church where I surprised my other daughter Christie on Father's Day in 2019.

During a young couples' overnight event back in the 1980s, Pastor Rod delivered a lesson that would reshape my approach to fatherhood. After separating the husbands and wives, he faced a room of about a dozen men with a simple question: "How many of you have young daughters?"

More than half the hands went up. Then came his follow-up: "How many of you guys are thinking ahead to the time when your little girl is a teenager and starts dating?" We all looked toward the floor, mumbling audibly.

"What if I could show you something to do right now that would throw a massive monkey wrench into any plans some teenage boy might have for your daughter?" he asked. He had our full attention. "What if I showed you something easy to do, now, which would make your daughter invulnerable to the slick moves any hormone-hyped teenage Lothario determined to seduce her might attempt?"

We were on the edge of our seats, eager to learn this magic trick. But he held back, piquing our interest by asking the same question in various ways for nearly five minutes.

In a near frenzy, we were all desperate to know how we could protect our precious daughters, as he promised. And then he finally whispered the answer to a room of utterly quiet men who had stopped breathing, all perched at the edge of their seats. "It's simple, really," he said. "Love her mother."

There was a pause, some grumbling, a feeling in the room we'd been taken in. But then he went on.

"If your daughter observes your every interaction with her mother as one of love and respect, she'll come to believe that's how a man should treat a woman," he explained. "And when she's older, if any boy or man tries to treat her in any other way, she won't have it. She'll drop the guy like a hot potato, and trust me, you won't have to worry about him."

The discussion that followed led to some practical resolutions, like being more generous with compliments and taking disagreements with our wives out of our daughters' earshot. I immediately put the advice into practice. Whenever Ginny entered the kitchen where Maggie was working, I'd find a reason to stop by and express my love to my wife. At dinner, I listened attentively, asked thoughtful questions and showed my best self. If Maggie and I needed to argue, we did it privately.

At first, Maggie wondered what I was up to, but eventually it became natural. Whenever Ginny was around, Maggie knew she'd see the best of me. It almost became a game. Did it work? You'll have to ask our daughter Virginia about that, but I think it did. I remember overhearing her in high school one time, talking to Maggie about why her girlfriends found certain boys attractive when they seemed like inept bozos to her.

What Pastor Rod had introduced to me and my fellow fathers was the concept of playing the long game, a strategy employed by successful people across all fields. Olympic athletes often begin training in childhood. Warren Buffett's investing approach and China's infrastructure development both exemplify long-term thinking. It works for individuals, too: leaving parties early for proper rest, maintaining healthy habits, investing daily in relationships and living below your means are all examples of the long game in action.

The principle is simple but powerful: just as the accumulation of tiny advantages makes the future easier, the accumulation of tiny disadvantages makes the future far more difficult. In parenting, as in life, the most important victories often come from consistent, thoughtful actions taken years before they bear fruit.

Looking back, that Saturday morning knock on our door brought more than just a church community, it delivered a parenting philosophy that would shape our family for generations. While I've had my share of doubts about organized religion over the years, I remain grateful for those moments when people like Pastor Rod delivered exactly the wisdom I needed when I needed it most.

83

GOING TO HELL
IN A HANDBASKET

WHEN SHE WAS LIVING IN San Francisco, our daughter Ginger had a bumper sticker that said, "Where am I and why am I in this handbasket?" It's a funny way to express a natural feeling that everything has gone wrong, and that just maybe the "good old days" were a little bit better.

No doubt every generation feels this way. Britain's postwar population pined for the Victorians as beacons of moral fortitude. And the Victorians? They looked back to the days before "the Industrial Revolution screwed everything up." Even the ancient Greeks and Romans moaned about changing family values. The writings of Socrates and Hesiod complained about how lazy the youth were and how much better things were when they were young.

I frequently hear complaints about how our country's values are deteriorating. "Things are bad and getting worse," the headlines scream. Is this perception accurate, and if so, to what extent? Perhaps it depends on how one defines moral values. How you think about mass shootings, drug use, racial hatred, homosexuality, abortion, marijuana legalization, cohabitation, social injustice, incivility, fraud or white supremacy will have a big impact on how you view the state of the world today.

Less controversial is what's causing people to think things are getting worse. The most often cited examples include mass media and social media, peer pressure and poor family involvement. How can one not believe everything is going to hell if that's the only message one gets, over and over? No number of facts, statistics or trends can stand up to the onslaught of a narrative so consistently and constantly sold.

But what are these stellar morals of the past that are decaying? Morals are the prevailing standards of behavior that enable people to live cooperatively, providing basic guidelines for civil human interaction. Morality often requires people to sacrifice their own short-term interests for the long-term benefit of society. We're supposed to direct our political behavior around service, for example: "Ask not what your country can do for you—ask what you can do for your country," as John F. Kennedy eloquently asserted in his inaugural address.

Moral, good behavior becomes harder to define as individuals. People often make decisions about what's moral and immoral for themselves, based on their unique circumstances. Agreement on standards of behavior is exceptionally difficult, and I'm not sure if it's even possible. But it's worth thinking and talking about, at the very least. The more people discuss these topics, the greater insights they gain.

Authors like Steven Pinker, Rafaela von Bredow, Ray Kurzweil and Johann Grolle have written extensively about the dramatic improvements human beings have made since the 18th century in the areas of racism, slavery, imperialism and genocide. Kurzweil goes to some length to explain why life on Earth is exponentially better, and continues to get better in just about every area. He believes our progress on the health front is driving humans toward immortality.

Pinker points to extensive data showing how things are getting better across a host of measurable areas. For instance, one's risk of dying a violent death at the hands of another has gone down precipitously. The number of people who die of malnutrition and disease has shrunk, as well.

Pinker addressed critics of his book, *Enlightenment Wars: Some Reflections on 'Enlightenment Now,' One Year Later*, in a long essay that's a much easier read than his book, although I recommend them both.

As a fun thought experiment, Pinker suggests asking yourself, "If you had to choose one moment in history in which you could be born, and you didn't know ahead of time who you were going to be—what nationality, what gender, what race, whether you'd be rich or poor, gay or straight, what faith you'd be born into—you wouldn't likely choose one hundred years ago. You wouldn't choose the 1950s, or the '60s or the '70s. You'd choose right now."

So, what causes our persistent feelings of decline, despite concrete evidence to the contrary? Every year, Gallup asks people two questions: How are things now and how will they be in the future? Every year, respondents insist we're on a downward spiral, yet the proportion who say things are bad right now never increases. In fact, it's remarkably stable and even went down in 2020, which some speculate may be due to an increasing faith in our fellow humans amid the COVID-19 pandemic.

The poll results seem to say that there's a persistent belief that things are going to get worse, alongside evidence from the same people suggesting that, over time, it hasn't. Some pundits argue that the idea of a morally debased youth has been turned on its head with the rise of the "woke" generation, who stand accused of being too righteous. Call them naïve, misguided or sanctimonious, but morally weak? Maybe not so much. School kids today report bullying and harassment from other kids more frequently than when we were young.

While evidence of decline is debated in the areas of murder, crime, health and safety, examples of changing attitudes in other areas are easy to find: same-sex marriage laws in dozens of countries, the first black president of the United States, removing the stigma from mental illness.

Often, our youth are the ones raising moral concerns—even children sometimes, like the climate strikers who pushed environmental issues to the top of the agenda at the World Economic Forum in Davos, Switzerland. It will be up to future historians to decide whether these changes in moral values point to decline or improvement, but I'm optimistic about the future.

My great-grandparents lived in a time when people could own other people. It was fully moral and supported by laws, tradition and the church. But today, most people are glad that aspect of our history is over. Morality is a moving target.

My parents lived in a time when it was against the law for people of different races to marry, facing jail time if they gave into their choices in a mate.

And, for a good part of my life, people of the same sex couldn't get married. They lost jobs and careers and were socially ostracized because of who they loved. Those laws and attitudes have changed, and each year that passes fewer and fewer people will be around saying, "I want those policies and attitudes back."

Morals develop with the culture they serve. History will judge us on the choices we make, how hard we try to get things right and how much work we put into doing the right things.

In a similar way to how morals evolve, science finds truth from building upon and modifying its past. While science isn't truth per se, it changes its opinion based on cumulative discoveries. That doesn't mean that it lied previously. It just learned more. When you hear the word "science," you should think about a rigorous set of steps aimed at building and organizing our knowledge of the natural world. A systematic, scientific study involves careful observation, measurement, experimentation and the development and testing of theories.

My learning about science, another step undermining my religious beliefs, came while helping my daughter Ginger. She cared most about science in high school, due in large part to the inspiration she got from her teacher, Jason McNellis. Her love of science and learning began influencing me as I assisted her with science projects. Her involvement with the International Science and Engineering Fair (ISEF) really drew me in.

The science fair organizers made it a practice to reach out to parents of participating students to act as judges of other children's projects. They taught us the process for evaluating projects and interviewing students, and showed us how to complete the various judging forms. Soon, I became a judge, which introduced me to the process of scientific discovery, its rules and ways of thinking. It blew a door open in my mind.

Science was far from my strongest subject in high school or college. My memories and initial understanding of Charles Darwin and the theory of evolution came from my involvement in our high school's production of *Inherit the Wind*, a fictionalized account of the 1925 Scopes Monkey Trial, which resulted in John T. Scopes' conviction for teaching evolution to a Tennessee science class in violation of state law.

Talking to Ginger and other young science nerds, I finally understood how science worked. I was so hooked that I got a copy of Charles Darwin's *On the Origin of Species* and read it from cover to cover. What an eye-opener! It became the first of many more books I would read about science. My television watching now includes a healthy mix of documentaries on the natural world, and I attend science conferences at least once or twice a year.

I learned to love it all. Many people think science is a group of people or a set of published theories. It is not. While it encapsulates things that have already been discovered and proven, science is a practice and process for acquiring new knowledge and proving whether something is true or not.

84

FROM GENESIS TO GENETICS

DARWIN REALLY DID CHANGE EVERYTHING. From the moment he published his theories on evolution and natural selection, a literal reading of the biblical story of creation became improbable, at best a primitive metaphor to condense a then-unknown process that took billions of years into a simple, seven-day explanation people of the time could understand. The authors of the Book of Genesis didn't have facts, so they invented a legend which some people still think is real. Now that's a mote in thine eye if there ever was one.

In his 1859 book, Darwin hypothesized that all species of organisms arise and develop through the natural selection of small, inherited variations that increase the individual's ability to compete, survive and reproduce. Darwin arrived at this theory using the scientific method, the same one used by the young budding scientists at my daughter's science fairs.

Many Christians were shocked by Darwin's ideas and worked actively to keep the concept from getting out. And believe it or not, this is still happening today. In 2005, the Dover Trial in Harrisburg, Pennsylvania, regarding the teaching of "intelligent design" in schools, generated a transcript so ridiculous and bungling that it would be hilarious if it wasn't so simultaneously sad.

The presiding judge excoriated members of the Dover, Pennsylvania school board, who he said "lied to cover up their religious motives." Using statements such as "breathtaking inanity" and "dragged their community into a legal maelstrom resulting in an utter waste of monetary and personal resources," the judge did not hold back. Judge John E. Jones III, a Republican appointed by President George W. Bush in 2002, concluded that intelligent design was not science. To claim that it is, proponents admit they must change the very definition of science to include supernatural explanations and magic.

If you care about the effectiveness of the medications you take, how food is certified as safe, what makes up the most reliable component in a manufacturing process, which cancer treatments have the greatest likelihood of success and a host of other issues, you should know and understand the scientific method. No matter what alternative methods have been tried, including religious or biblical approaches, the scientific approach always wins. Not 98 percent of the time, but 100 percent.

It wins because it isn't a belief, but a process with concrete steps designed to lead to the truth. The scientific method dictates how experiments must be done. It specifies things like double-blind testing and other processes that eliminate or minimize the influence of bias or prejudice in the experimenter—even bias and influences they don't know they have. The scientific method provides an objective, standardized approach to conducting experiments and, in doing so, improves the accuracy and reliability of the results.

Does science know everything? Of course not, which is why we do it. If we had all the answers, there would be no reason to keep looking. But with each new study, we learn a little bit more. This careful and systematic method for testing ideas determines which ones are grounded in reality and truth and which ones are fiction. Because of science, we know more now than we knew last year and the years before that. The fact that science doesn't know everything is a powerful argument for more science.

One area frequently rife with potentially biased testing is high-end audio equipment. For years, I sold mid- to high-end gear and owned many of the top brands. I wrote several reviews of phono cartridges for hi-fi magazines. And I learned many techniques and tricks to favor one piece of equipment over another.

In our store, we knew where we could place a set of speakers that we wanted to sell to make them sound better than other speakers. Another trick we used was to switch the sound from one set of speakers to another right after prompting a prospect to "listen to how much clearer the vocals sound on these DLKs." The suggestion caused people to hear what we wanted them to hear. By the way, I'm not necessarily proud of this.

A friend and I once went to the home of a high-end audiophile in the hills above Los Angeles for a party hosted by *The Absolute Sound* magazine. Men (isn't it always men at these events?) mingled and drank wine while listening to the newest, over-the-top expensive set of speakers, driven by state-of-the-art and equally expensive amps and pre-amps. I wasn't in the listening room for two minutes before hearing something wrong, but no one else appeared to notice. Tracing the wires connecting the amp and speakers, I quickly spotted the problem. They were wired out of phase, and they sounded like it.

Just as owning a fast car won't make you a skillful driver, spending tens of thousands of dollars on audio equipment won't make you a skillful listener. My friend D. Michael Shields, engineer, acoustician and studio magician, further helped tune my ear by allowing me to spend hours listening to his system. Even now, decades after my time in the music business, my hearing is still sensitive to tonal nuances in recordings, movie scores and live performances.

For the truth about audio equipment, science can be your best ally, even if the elite manufacturers see it as a form of heresy. In the 1980s, audio engineer Floyd Toole, at the National Research Council of Canada, designed bias-free tests to determine what degree listeners could consistently identify high-end audio components from those that were more modestly priced.

The study found that many listeners struggled to consistently identify differences between high-end and mid-range equipment. Factors such as room acoustics and speaker placement had a greater

impact than the components themselves, and the correlation between price and perceived audio quality was weak to nonexistent.

Established scientific theories have withstood hundreds,
and sometimes even thousands, of rigorous tests and scrutiny. I
sometimes hear Christians denigrate evolution as "just a theory."
Technically, in scientific speak, they're correct. But positioned like
this, gravity is also "just a theory." I'm not sure how many people
would wish to throw themselves off a cliff to prove it wrong.

Penicillin was developed as a theory—one that saved millions of
lives. Vaccines have prevented countless deaths and diseases because
someone followed the scientific method to the truth. The development of antiretroviral therapies in the 1990s transformed HIV from
a death sentence to a manageable chronic condition. The scientific
process for in-vitro fertilization has helped millions of people con-
ceive children. Robotic surgery has allowed for minimally invasive
procedures with great precision. Targeted cancer therapies have improved efficacy and reduced side effects. This last one I learned from
my cousin Annie (Larsen) Hackett, who stayed with us in Phoenix as
she went through some of these treatments in the summer of 2024.

Following science has huge payoffs outside of medicine, too. The
historian Simon Winchester captures the explosion of human inven-
tion across a broad swath of disciplines in his book, *The Perfectionists:
How Precision Engineers Created the Modern World.* Winchester uses the
lens of precision to examine the history of the industrial age and
mankind's extraordinary progress. The book covers John Wilkinson's
boring machine for cannon barrels and Henry Maudslay's precision
lathes and screw-cutting techniques in the 19th century. Finally,
Winchester explains the advances required to make the first jet engines in the 20th century, improvements in chip manufacturing and
Moore's Law. Nearly every innovation depended heavily on following the scientific process.

When I embraced the scientific view of Earth's history instead
of the biblical view, the cracks in my religious foundation became

wider and eventually irreparable. I'm not opposed to studying the biblical myth of creation, so long as the proper facts relating to the scientific understanding of our natural world are taught alongside it. No one actually believes in Jack and the Beanstalk, Paul Bunyan and his Blue Ox, or Hansel and Gretel, but they're fun stories that teach valuable lessons, just like God inventing Earth, the universe and everything else in seven days.

85

POLITICS

I RECALL AN EARLY POLITICAL experience during my first year of college in October of 1969, when participating in protests over the Vietnam War. Vice President Spiro Agnew was giving a speech, and we drove up from Mankato to join the protests on the University of Minnesota campus. While thinking of Agnew as a near devil then, I couldn't help but love his famous line putting down the media for their coverage of the war: "In the United States today, we have more than our share of nattering nabobs of negativism. They have formed their own 4-H club—the hopeless, hysterical hypochondriacs of history," he said. Always a sucker for clever, concise, alliterative wordplay, I learned later that William Safire, a speechwriter for the Nixon administration, had written it.

As we rallied around the building where Agnew was to speak, students pushed close to the front, attempting to interfere with his speech. We were packed together like rush-hour commuters, chanting, pushing and jumping up and down. I worked my way toward the front, got within six or eight feet from one door and observed what I can only describe as a farcical snapshot of real-world absurdism at play.

A police officer had positioned himself at an open door. He held a long night stick with both hands, horizontally across the front of the door, wedged there by pressure from the pushing students. He kicked anyone who tried to crawl under, and he punched anyone trying to come over. It was a standoff. Then a protester reached out and took the officer's police hat from his head and began passing it back into the crowd. It hadn't gone over three or four rows of protesters before the young officer cried out, "Hey, give that back. We have to pay for those!"

Suddenly, the hat stopped moving. There were some murmurings, as the nature of the officer's plea made its way back to the protesters with the hat. Slowly, the hat began moving in the other direction. A student in front of the officer held out the hat, but the officer couldn't take it because he was holding the baton and bracing the door. After a few seconds, the officer locked eyes with the student and glanced down at his baton as if to say, "Will you hold this a second?"

The student reached out, took the club, and held it while giving the officer his hat. As the student held the club with both hands, the officer adjusted the hat on his head until it was straight, reached down and hitched up his pants. Feeling everything was in order, he put his hands back on the club, took a deep breath and nodded to the protester in front of him. Then the jumping, shouting and pushing all resumed as if nothing happened.

Two other incidents had a heavier influence on me politically. The first was a lawsuit that reshaped the Internet. *Stratton Oakmont v. Prodigy Services Company* happened on my watch at Prodigy, and had major impacts on the online lives of AOL, CompuServe and Prodigy users. A single message board post ignited a legal firestorm. Repercussions from this lawsuit and subsequent legislation still affects every user of Facebook (Meta), TikTok, YouTube and Twitter (X) today.

Our Prodigy bulletin boards—hundreds of them on just about every subject imaginable—were one of our most popular features. In the financial topics discussion board called Money Talk, a member referred to Long Island-based securities brokerage firm, Stratton Oakmont, as "a bunch of crooks." The Prodigy user said they'd committed fraud. Our bulletin board leader, an outside contractor, didn't remove the post and the brokerage firm sued us.

Upon hearing of the lawsuit, I called a Wall Street friend, asking if he'd heard of Stratton Oakmont. His response left me dumbfounded. Before I could even finish my question, he cut me off with a gruff chuckle, "Stratton Oakmont? Yeah, everyone knows those crooks . . . "*

As head of Prodigy's communications products line of business, I knew we had a problem. Taking the elevator down to see George Perry, our chief legal counsel, I asked him what he thought. After he answered, partially tongue-in-cheek I suggested, "Perhaps we should argue the case on its merits."

Like most lawsuits, this one wasn't unexpected and there was a plan in place. The case proceeded quickly through New York's state court system. Prodigy's loss in the case became the catalyst for political and legislative action from every online entity—CompuServe, AOL and all the rest. Now everyone knew there was a need for clearer legal guidelines regarding online content and platform liability.

The lawsuit brought about the passage of Section 230 of the Communications Decency Act (CDA) in 1996. It established immunity for Internet service providers publishing "information provided by another information content provider especially content from users." With this act, the U.S. House of Representatives explicitly stated that they intended to overturn the result reached in the *Prodigy* case.

I had the chance to lobby for passing this section of the act with Prodigy's head of PR, Brian Ek, along with hired experts. The briefings were in the Washington, D.C. offices of various elected officials. Everyone listened respectfully and asked good questions, and some

---

*Stratton Oakmont was expelled from the NASD and shut down in 1997. They were found to be engaging in practices like pump-and-dump stock sales and money laundering. In effect, they were crooks. Founders Jordan Belfort and Danny Porush were charged. Belfort was convicted and served 22 months in prison. Porush was convicted and sentenced to 39 months. Martin Scorsese directed the film *The Wolf of Wall Street* in 2013, starring Leonardo DiCaprio and Jonah Hill, based on Stratton Oakmont.

even took notes. None of the meetings had a senator or representative attending, however, only staff.

Tired after a full day of meetings and explaining why their vote on the act was so important, a senior staffer pulled me aside and said, "You seem frustrated. Do you want to know why no one is enthused? Your presentation was okay, but you missed the most important piece of information."

I waited.

"You failed to tell us how many votes my representative is going to gain (or lose) in his district if he votes the way you recommend," he concluded.

Listening to the staffer's blunt words made me boil over in frustration. All our careful arguments and hard work came down to pure politics? Not wanting to say something I'd regret, I bit my tongue.

"Hey, I can see what you're thinking, and I know you're angry, but that's Democracy my friend," the staffer told me. "If you don't like it, you should move to another country." Of course, he was right. Democracy is about knowing and following what the most voters want.

My second political lesson came when I got an email from Doug Barry, a general partner at one of the venture firms that invested in BigFix, where I was CEO. Barry invited me to a Sunday morning brunch at his house to meet Gavin Newsom, who was running for mayor of San Francisco. I replied, "Sorry Doug, but I doubt Gavin will have any interest in me. As a registered voter in Arizona, I can't vote for him in California." I assumed I'd won that round and was off the hook.

But Doug quickly replied, "Gavin has no interest in your vote, Steve. He's interested in your money. See you Sunday. Bring your checkbook." Oh my, has that lesson been reinforced over and over again, with a thousand emails and texts from political operatives screaming for money with every pitch imaginable.

Both the political right and the political left raise massive amounts of money by emphasizing differences and fanning the flames of distrust and fear. Combine this with a media bent on exploiting this schism for financial gain (billions of dollars in ad revenue), and there's far more money to be made from discord than from finding common ground.

* * * * *

A few months ago, while on the phone with my motorcycle riding buddy Bruce Rauner, I told him I was including a chapter on politics in this book.

"Why the hell would you want to do that?" he asked.

After I explained my reasons, I suggested he could read the chapter and give me the opinion of an expert, since he was elected governor of Illinois in 2014 and had to deal with a host of complex political issues. If anyone understood politics, it would be him.

"Oh, I wouldn't call me an expert on politics," he laughed.

His instant response perfectly illustrated a fascinating aspect of the Dunning-Kruger effect: while novices often overestimate their abilities, true experts tend to undervalue theirs.

86

WHEN, EXACTLY, IS THE END OF THE WORLD?

A RECENT FACEBOOK POST FROM my cousin caught my eye. She wrote (or perhaps re-posted) about the imminent rapture, microchips, the Mark of the Beast and government control—familiar territory for anyone raised in certain Christian traditions. "I don't know when the rapture will take place," she concluded, "but I believe it could be soon. And I KNOW that I won't be left behind when that trumpet sounds!"

Her certainty reminded me of my father, a devout Christian who believed he would never die. If Christ wasn't returning "this month," Dad was convinced it would be the next, or certainly "very, very soon." He would pore over his Bible, expounding on passages from Revelation and pointing out what he saw as "blatantly obvious clues" about the end times in current events.

This belief in an imminent end isn't new. Early Christians made sense of Jesus' teachings—"Take no thought for the morrow" and "Give all you have to the poor and follow me"—because they believed the second coming would happen within months, perhaps weeks. Two thousand years later, each new generation discovers fresh "evidence" that the end is near.

The predictions I've encountered throughout my life form a recurring pattern. As a teenager, nearly every sermon in my Lutheran Brethren church referenced the approaching rapture. Later, living with the Jesus Freaks in Iowa City, we discussed it constantly. In the 1970s, Hal Lindsey's *The Late Great Planet Earth* convinced many of us that graduating college was pointless since the world would end first. Some of us, me included, dropped out to join Christian communes, prioritizing prayer and worship over worldly pursuits.

Lindsey's ideas still captivate audiences regularly. One Amazon. com reviewer put it this way: "Every three years, Hal Lindsay writes a new book denoting how the world will end in five years. Each subsequent book explains how he WASN'T wrong in the previous book and the world will end in five years ... He has followed this pattern for three decades and is now acknowledged as 'the foremost authority on Biblical prophecy in the world today.'"

Current believers see no irony in buying into the same thing when it's repeatedly proven incorrect. Einstein is widely reported as saying, "Insanity is doing the same thing over and over again and expecting a different result."

Looking back, these predictions follow a fascinating historical tradition. Lutheran scholar Michael Stifel, for example, calculated that the end would come before 1550. "All Martin Luther's work held a sense of urgency as time was short... the world was heading for Armageddon," he wrote. After Luther died in 1546, Lutheran leaders claimed the end was near. In 1584, a Lutheran scholar named Adam Nachenmoser wrote *Prognosticum Theologicum*, predicting, "In 1590, the Gospel will be preached to all nations and a wonderful unity will be achieved. The last days will then be close at hand." He eventually settled on 1635 as the most likely date.

The Anabaptists were certain of a 1533 rapture, but when their prophecy failed to materialize, they became more zealous, not less. Claiming that two witnesses (Enoch and Elijah) had come as Jan Matthys and Jan Bockelson, they set up a New Jerusalem in Münster and began preparing the city for Christ's expected return, turning the place into a frightening dictatorship under Bockelson's control. All Lutherans and Catholics were expelled from the city, dissenters were executed and polygamy was instituted. The Millennial Kingdom never came.

The Presbyterians under Thomas Brightman predicted, "between 1650 and 1695, we will see the conversion of the Jews and a revival of their nation in Palestine . . . the destruction of the Papacy . . . the marriage of the Lamb and his wife."

Scottish cleric Edward Irving wrote a book in 1828 called *Babylon and Infidelity Foredoomed*, in which he wrote "There can be little doubt that as one thousand two hundred sixty days concluded in the year 1792, and the 30 additional days in 1823, we are now entering upon the last days, and the ordinary life of a man will carry many of us to the end of them."

Joseph Smith of the Latter-Day Saints made dozens of prophecies, which are carefully recorded in the sacred texts of the Mormon faith. The prophecies included predictions of the Civil War, the coming of Jesus and more. At least the Mormons are upfront in presenting them all and showing which prophecies came true and which did not.

The Baptists under William Miller predicted the Second Advent of Jesus would occur before March 21, 1844. When this date passed, a new date, April 18, 1844, was predicted.

Jehovah's Witness and first president of the Watch Tower Society, Charles Taze Russell, calculated 1874 as the year of Christ's second coming, followed by the resurrection of the saints in 1875, the rapture of the saints to heaven in 1878 and the end of "the day of wrath" in 1914. A 1917 Watch Tower Society publication predicted that, in 1918, God would destroy churches and millions of their members. When that didn't work out, J.F. Rutherford asserted that the Millennium would begin in 1925 and that Abraham, Isaac, Jacob and David would be resurrected as "princes." Despite their many failed predictions, The Watch Tower Society went so far as to build a house in California for the soon-to-return ancient prophets—a level of commitment I can't help but respect, even while questioning the underlying belief.

During World War I, the Assemblies of God church stated, "We are not yet in the Armageddon struggle proper, but at its commencement, and prophecy clearly shows that Christ will come before the present war closes. Armageddon, it seems, has begun."

Calvary Chapel founder Chuck Smith published *End Times* in 1979. Smith is a well-known Bible scholar and prophecy teacher. He wrote, "As we look at the world scene today, it is clear the coming of the Lord is very, very close. Jesus taught that the generation that sees the 'budding of the fig tree,' the birth of the nation Israel, will be the generation that sees the Lord's return; I believe the generation of 1948 is the last. Since a generation of judgment is 40 years and the tribulation lasts seven years, the Lord will come back for his church any time before the tribulation starts, which means any time before 1981. (1948 + 40 − 7 = 1981)."

So, why does any of this matter? The psychological mechanism behind this phenomenon fascinated me when I discovered *When Prophecy Fails*, a 1956 study of a UFO cult that predicted Earth's destruction by flood. When the flood didn't happen, members didn't abandon their beliefs, they became more committed. This led to the development of cognitive dissonance theory, which explains how people often rationalize their beliefs rather than change them when faced with contradictory evidence. The idea of "maybe we were wrong" rarely enters the picture.

When the most studied, most thoughtful, most sincere and most committed Christian scholars of their day all predict the end times or an imminent rapture—and then all of them are wrong—only one of two conclusions is possible. Maybe the religious scholars didn't do their homework, failed to read the Bible carefully enough or misinterpreted the times in which they were living and misapplied their observations to Scripture. Or, far more likely, the many authors of the Bible made a series of predictions open to a wide variety of interpretations.

With the first being disingenuous and unlikely, I'll go with the latter. It makes sense to me and it's likely why current scholars fail to go back and study the work of earlier scholars and adjust accordingly.

Their egos lead them to believe they possess rare overriding insight, or "divine inspiration," that previous religious scholars didn't have.

Finally, and perhaps most importantly as I look at the professing Christians I know today, most don't appear to really believe any of the fear-mongering. They say they do, and yet they don't appear to be acting or living consistently with this belief.

One lesson I learned from my tenure at Net Perceptions was how you can take input based on what people say or on what they do. When tested, we found actions spoke far more truthfully than words. At the time of our tests, few people reported watching the television program, *Jerry Springer*. And yet, we knew from the ratings that it was a highly popular show, watched by millions.

To test whether someone truly believes in an imminent rapture, consider their life choices:

1. Property and Possessions
   - Have they sold their earthly goods and given the proceeds to the poor?
   - Do they own a home, or do they rent? (True believers should see no point in building equity for a future that won't arrive.)

2. Financial Planning
   - Do they maintain savings accounts, 401(k)s or investment portfolios?
   - Why plan for a retirement that will never come?

3. Next Generation
   - Have they established college savings accounts for their grandchildren?
   - Do they encourage their children to excel academically for future success?
   - If the world is ending soon, why invest in long-term education?

4. Health and Lifestyle
   - For those who might enjoy smoking, why quit?
   - Why worry about cancer when the rapture will come first?

- Why exercise or maintain a healthy diet?
- What's the point of preventing diabetes if earthly existence is temporary?

The reality is stark: most people who proclaim belief in an imminent rapture continue to make long-term plans, invest in their health and prepare for their family's futures. They give lip service to end-times prophecies, while living as if they expect many decades ahead. In the end, actions reveal true beliefs more reliably than words ever could, which is exactly as it should be.

87

BALANCING RELIGION'S PROS AND CONS

DESPITE MY EVENTUAL DEPARTURE FROM faith, I don't view religious people as inherently flawed. Many lead exemplary lives, prioritizing others' needs above their own. Throughout my life, I've encountered countless loving, caring individuals of faith, and only a handful who exhibit questionable moral judgment. While I've found no correlation between religious belief and good behavior, I have, however, observed instances where religious fervor justified or spawned unethical actions.

After years of reading, research and reflection, I've come to agree with Sam Harris' assessment that religion's overall impact tilts slightly negative. But this balance sheet is complex and deserves careful examination.

Let's start with religion's positive contributions:

Family stability stands out first. Religious practice often intertwines with and strengthens family units. Research shows that churchgoers tend to have more stable marriages, higher marital satisfaction and lower divorce rates. Regular church attendance serves as a reliable predictor of marital stability and happiness.

Poverty reduction comes next. Evidence suggests that regular religious practice helps people escape poverty, particularly in inner-city environments. It provides young people with moral frameworks and sound judgment, protecting against various social problems, including suicide, drug abuse, out-of-wedlock births, crime and divorce.

Charitable giving represents another significant benefit. Giving USA consistently reports that religiously affiliated organizations receive the largest share of charitable donations. In the United States, with its limited social safety net, these contributions provide essential support for many people, though recent years have seen declining donations alongside declining religious affiliation.

The mental and physical health benefits of faith are also well-documented. Regular religious practice correlates with reduced depression, improved self-esteem and better recovery from addiction and marital problems. It can also increase longevity and improve outcomes for various illnesses.

On the other hand, religion's negative aspects warrant equally careful consideration. Anti-science positions have historically hindered human progress. From threats against Isaac Newton, Charles Darwin and Socrates, to modern anti-vaccination movements, some religious groups have consistently opposed scientific advancement. Consider these examples:

- The development of antibiotics faced religious opposition, as do vaccines today
- Roman Catholicism long opposed medicine, viewing disease as divine punishment
- Religious beliefs still sometimes prevent life-saving medical treatments
- Some Christian religions insist that dinosaurs and humans walked the Earth simultaneously
- During the Black Death, religious fervor led to the burning of thousands of Jews

Hypocrisy appears within religious communities with disturbing regularity. Televangelists and prosperity-gospel leaders preach modesty, while living lavishly on followers' donations. In 2019, the Mormon Church faced scrutiny over a $100 billion investment fund, which was built from member tithes. Many religious organizations preach love, while practicing discrimination.

Cultural resistance to progress is another consistent issue. Religious groups have historically opposed interracial marriage and supported slavery, and some continue to discriminate against LGBTQ+ individuals. Some churches, including one in my Phoenix neighborhood, celebrate white supremacy and xenophobia.

Most troubling is religion's potential to justify violence. While business competitors and sports rivals rarely resort to killing, religious beliefs have repeatedly provided justification for murder and execution throughout history. From the Crusades to modern terrorism, sincere religious conviction has sparked countless atrocities.

Let me expand on this as it applies to the political arena. Arguments can get cantankerous, with debates often becoming heated. But rhetoric containing the idea that one would consider killing those with opposing political viewpoints seems to recently have come into vogue in the United States. This change corresponds with the period in which those on the political right have been welcoming religious activists who wish to turn the United States into a "Christian nation."

This far-right Christian nationalism threatens religious freedom, promotes anti-Muslim bigotry and antisemitism, threatens LGBTQ+ rights, calls for capital punishment for abortion providers and advocates for government-sponsored religion. Every country that has gone down this path has done so at its own peril.

Turkey, a country with a 95% Muslim population, flourished under Ataturk's secular government from the 1930s on. Then, in the early 2000s, Islamic groups challenged the concept of a secular state under Recep Tayyip Erdogan's Justice and Development Party, moving religion into a more prominent position within the government. Turkey's problems have become significant ever since, and their status in the world has dropped precipitously. Without getting into too much detail, their admission into the EU has stalled, relationships with the U.S. and other countries are strained and press freedoms and human rights have mostly gone away.

To me, the moral certitude and messianic lack of self-doubt that some religious people exhibit, whether they're Christian, Jewish, Muslim or anything else, scares me the most. Sincerely held religious beliefs, for example, spurred the tragic events of 9/11. Oddly enough, some Christians saw these terrorist attacks as "God punishing America for its sins."

History is rife with examples of religion being used to justify a host of killing and wars: the Islamic resistance to French colonialism in West Africa or the Mahdi versus the British in Sudan; Muslim against Hindu in the partition of India; Muslim against Russian in Chechnya; various Christian groups against the Turks in the Balkans. The list gets long quickly, even without mentioning the Crusades or the Inquisition and other atrocities in the name of Christianity, or the sadism and barbarism used in Islamic Jihads. While secular disputes can usually be negotiated through material compromise, religious conflicts often escalate to existential struggles against "infidels" and "unbelievers."

Here in Arizona, we've faced a 30-year saga, in which religious leaders from the Fundamentalist Church of Jesus Christ of Latter-Day Saints (FLDS) have been systematically raping young girls. Girls as young as 12 were among the 482 alleged victims when Warren Jeffs was finally convicted and sent to prison. It took almost 20 years, but the head of this religious group is now behind bars, although he continues to lead a small group of believers from there. To be clear, no Mormon I know would ever condone the actions of Warren Jeffs. What he did is deeply offensive to every one of them.

In early 2002, the *Boston Globe* published a series of articles on their investigation of Roman Catholic priests. Over time, it was proven that priests and lay people in the Catholic Church had sexually abused minors on a massive scale, with accusations reaching into the thousands over several decades. While many cases were reported in the U.S., victims have also come forward in Ireland, Canada, Australia, New Zealand, India and other nations.

Making it worse were the actions of some Catholic bishops who tried to keep these crimes secret by systematically reassigning offending priests to other parishes, where they had unsupervised contact with young people and continued their abuse.

In what secular institution could something like this grow, flourish and spread? Other than the Boy Scouts (renamed Scouting America as of 2025), what secular organization is plagued with this issue? Does this happen in Little League baseball? The Boys & Girls Clubs are primarily secular, and you rarely see these sorts of headlines. How about 4-H, Big Brothers and Big Sisters of America or Campfire Girls? Rarely a scandal.

What is it about bringing religion into the mix that somehow attracts and gives license to some of the most vile and base aspects of humanity? I remain open to evidence that might change my conclusion that religion has a net negative impact on society. Until then, my personal experience and research suggest that while religion offers significant benefits, its potential for harm outweighs its positive contributions.

88

SAINTS AND SCHOLARS: THREE MEN OF FAITH

THREE MEN OF FAITH HAVE profoundly influenced my thinking about religion: my brother-in-law, Deacon Joseph Stickney; my father-in-law, Dr. Robert Kirven; and my father, Paul T. Larsen. Each represents a different way of living with religious conviction, and through them I've seen both the beauty and complexity of faith in practice.

Joe Stickney's path began at Gonzaga University, where he initially pursued the Catholic priesthood. Though marriage to my wife Maggie's sister Diana redirected his journey, his devotion to God and the Catholic Church have never wavered. As a teacher of religion, philosophy and ethics at Brophy College Preparatory in Phoenix, and later as a deacon performing sacraments for Spanish-speaking congregations, Joe has lived his faith through action.

But it wasn't his official religious functions that most influenced my thinking—it was his way of life. The Stickneys are always first to help others in need, providing housing to immigrants fleeing persecution and distributing clothes, food, furniture and money to the less fortunate. Joe's counseling and support have guided thousands of young men toward better life decisions. His impact for good defies calculation.

I once revealed my admiration for Joe during a visit to St. Peter's Cathedral in the Vatican. As I lit a candle and solemnly placed it on an altar, Maggie whispered with amusement, "So, you have a favorite saint now?"

"Only one—St. Joseph," I replied softly. "And I think you know who I mean."

Another religious man I admired was my father-in-law, Robert Kirven, Ph.D., who approached faith through scholarship. A theologian, author, professor and polyglot, he mastered not only English—in which he authored eight books—but also Hebrew, Greek, German and French, with a little bit of Sumerian and Assyrian thrown in for good measure.

Before Dr. Kirven died, the world acknowledged him as the leading authority on the writings of Swedish theologian Emanuel Swedenborg, the 18th-century scientist, philosopher and mystic who was influenced by Newton, Plato, Aristotle and Descartes. My theological discussions with Dr. Kirven were brief; the intellectual gap between us was like an NBA star practicing with a promising high school player. Yet I observed how he used religion and philosophy as a playground for his brilliant mind, dedicating his life to teaching Swedenborg's lessons and publishing his own insights about faith's value.

The third religious pillar in my life, my father, used his strong religious beliefs to govern his daily behavior and life decisions. Religious considerations and faith factored into most everything he did, along with prayer requests to the almighty for wisdom and guidance. While I admire and loved my Dad, it was clear to me that, in the end, he did what he wanted, saying it was "God's will."

He carried his Bible everywhere, finding verses to justify whatever course of action he deemed correct. He used his interpretation of Scripture to tell me that my opposition to the Vietnam War was wrong and would condemn me to Hell. When he wanted my mother to sit down and shut up, there was a verse for that. Dad exemplified what Dietrich Bonhoeffer warned against—reading the Bible to support existing beliefs rather than to challenge them. Bonhoeffer advocated the idea that "we must learn to read the Bible against ourselves, not just for ourselves," being open to Scripture's critique of our assumptions and cultural norms.

My father's opportunistic religious judgments taught me to fight back in the same way, using the same book with similar logic, but this only deepened my skepticism about using the Bible as a practical life guide.

The word "religion" stems from Latin, referring to the bond between humans and gods. My friend Kevin Brown, who holds a doctorate in divinity, traces it to even earlier roots meaning "to bind together," encompassing both individual relationships with God and connections within religious communities. For practical purposes, religion represents a system of beliefs and values about reality and the divine, including rituals, ceremonies and moral frameworks.

My observations suggest that religious people fall into three distinct groups:

1. Those who use religion to enhance their lives and others', taking commandments like the Golden Rule to heart
2. Those who use religion to justify harmful behaviors and beliefs, often expressing anger and political fervor
3. Those who claim belief but rarely practice, likely agnostics or atheists if they bothered to think about it. Kevin Brown is more generous, putting them in the "spiritual but not religious" category

While the first and third groups don't bother me too much, members of the second group can be downright evil. These individuals and organizations, which include modern-day Christian Nationalists, Arab Islamist extremists, the Taliban and Al-Qaeda, promote division and hurt others, which I find unconscionable.

As mentioned earlier, my upbringing was in an Evangelical Christian church, where a strong emotional experience—getting "saved" and entering into "a personal relationship with Jesus"—was a critical step. This strong emotional experience resembles becoming deeply enamored with a fictional character or a movie star, and it can be particularly powerful during the formative teenage years, when hormones subvert level-headed judgment. The dopamine release we get from emotionally charged religious experiences creates a potent addiction, which can be especially attractive to young people starved for attention and love from parents, teachers and peers.

The problem is that this kind of "feel-good" high proves unsustainable. When the "Jesus Loves Me" phase no longer provides adequate satisfaction, some believers escalate into powerful negative emotions, including hatred, reinforcing an "us against the world" mentality and the dangerous notion of divine invincibility.

I don't believe any religion should espouse hate as a tenet. It seems tragic to me that an emotion of "pure love" toward God and other people can be redirected to a love of negative things, such as selfish attitudes toward immigrants, people of other faiths or groups who have different cultural traditions. Yet these diversions are part of some modern church communities, and often become associated with religious conviction.

89

THE PRICE OF BELONGING

THE HARDEST PART ABOUT LEAVING faith isn't losing God, it's losing community. Religious groups excel at providing a sense of belonging, something encoded in our very DNA. This loss cuts deeper than any theological debate or philosophical disagreement ever could.

Beyond the mere fear of spending an eternity in Hell for one's lack of faith, people who leave churches often face the more significant and earthly consequence of living with scorn and rejection from those they love the most. It takes a lot of courage to "come out" about one's agnostic tendencies, and it's no doubt why I've been so quiet about it and slow to reveal my reality.

Our ancestors who found ways to belong to the group survived; those who couldn't, perished. Modern churches understand and masterfully cater to this primal need, creating bonds that make questioning faith feel like questioning family itself. I experienced this firsthand in my youth, in what today would be characterized as an Evangelical church. We never got a break from community. Sundays began with Sunday school, followed by the main service, then "fellowship" in the church basement. You left home in the morning and didn't return until after lunch. Often, there was an evening service too.

The week unfolded like a carefully choreographed dance of belonging: Monday might be free, but Tuesday brought choir practice, Wednesday was prayer meeting, Thursday meant Bible study and Friday was youth night. Saturdays hosted special events— Christmas pageant rehearsals, funerals, guest speakers, missionary presentations. Summers meant Vacation Bible School or Christian camps, complete with nightly sermons and Bible quizzes.

Looking back now, I find myself experiencing a strange envy toward religious communities. As agnostics and atheists, we have no services, sing no hymns, share no sacred texts. We lack the centuries of stories to enchant our children and miss that powerful sense of having a community of friends, ready to support us in times of need.

So why not just sign up and enjoy the good parts? That's kind of what I did at Pastor Rod's church in Eden Prairie. But now, I can no longer reconcile myself with the hypocrisy I see in some religious institutions. This includes:

- The selective application of biblical teachings, condemning homosexuality while ignoring other prohibitions
- The disconnect between Christ's teachings about poverty and the celebration of wealth
- Preachers exploiting the vulnerable while living in luxury
- Grand churches built while parishioners struggle in poverty
- The contradiction between Christ's "open arms" and anti-immigration stances
- The tribalism that turns members of other faiths into enemies
- The political hypocrisy of supporting amoral leaders while preaching godliness
- The colonial mindset of missions while rejecting foreigners at home

The older I get, the more sensitive I become to these contradictions. While I deeply admire religious groups for fostering strong, positive communities, I can't sit in church mumbling hymns, bowing my head in prayer and shaking hands with fellow worshippers without feeling like a hypocrite. And so I stay away, even as I miss what I've lost.

90
WE'RE ALL BELIEVERS—
JUST IN DIFFERENT THINGS

I BELIEVE IN THE RIGHT to believe. If faith in gods or God helps someone be a better human, that's fantastic. However, if faith leads to unkindness toward fellow humans or animals, then that "religion" becomes an abomination. This tension between belief and behavior has shaped my own journey away from traditional faith.

The intellectual split began long before I acknowledged it. Even in 1984, sitting in Pastor Rod's Eden Prairie chapel and enjoying the camaraderie, I found myself mentally shooting down Christian tenets like clay pigeons. My careful reading of scriptures during high school had planted seeds of doubt that grew stronger over time. It became increasingly difficult to stop my brain from generating contrary arguments.

Long before my epiphany in Pasadena, California after Eric's death, the questions kept surfacing. How could all other religions be wrong and this one right? Were devout believers of other faiths really destined for Hell because of where they were born?

When hearing beautiful passages like "Love is patient, love is kind," I couldn't help but wonder how the same book could condone slavery. How can you read from a book with so many horrible things in it, even if an occasional passage offers a nice message?

Even today, certain expressions of faith cause my eyes to roll. Recently on Facebook, I saw a young woman thanking God for helping her find her car keys. "Thank you, Lord! I wasn't late for work," she wrote. I couldn't help but think that a child dies of malaria every

30 seconds, and God is unable or chooses to do nothing about it, but He helps you find your car keys?

Such heretical thoughts often swirled in my head during sermons, but I knew raising these issues with the pastor would be fruitless—believe me, I tried.

Over the years, more than a half-dozen agnostic or atheist family members, suspecting sympathy from me, have reached out and confessed their non-belief. Their conflicts are a lot like mine: While it would be nice to be authentic and reveal this part of themselves, they can't for fear of reprisal from loved ones. They've already witnessed harsh reactions to anyone who dares not to believe: "Those immoral degenerates are going straight to Hell, and I don't care." Even hints that they have questions could cause considerable pain.

What strikes me most is that these secret doubters are often outstandingly kind and non-judgmental, with a desire not to disrupt or make others uncomfortable. They exhibit far more grace and love than the judgmental "Christians" they live amongst.

The culmination of my youthful religious training, my education in philosophy, my experience with the Jesus Freaks and the ensuing years of life and intellectual discourse have led me to more of an atheistic outlook. I don't believe in God—not a god, not "the God," not anybody's god.

I've never seen or read any credible proof that God exists, but if anyone knows of any I'd be happy to see it. No, let me put it more strongly—I would LOVE to see it. I've been looking for it my entire life.

But perhaps the search itself has taught me something more valuable: that what we believe matters far less than how we treat each other. Those secret atheists in my family, keeping quiet to avoid hurting others, may understand this better than most. We're all believers in something—if not in divine power, then in human kindness; if not in sacred texts, then in lived truth; if not in religious doctrine, then in the simple power of treating each other with respect and dignity.

91

ETHICS BEYOND THE PULPIT

A FEW YEARS AGO, MY friend Rich Marin invited me to teach business ethics to his graduate students in San Diego. The assignment forced me to crystallize something I'd long believed—that ethics aren't theoretical concepts confined to classrooms or church pulpits, they're practical tools for navigating daily life from the smallest decisions to the most consequential choices.

For the class, I chose Theranos as my case study. The company's journey from a $9 billion valuation to zero, culminating in its CEO's fraud conviction and 11-year jail sentence in January 2022, offered perfect material for exploring ethical decision-making. The company's charismatic founder, Elizabeth Holmes, had convinced countless investors, journalists, business analysts and even a former U.S. president that a single drop of blood could provide reliable test results, comparable to traditional vein draws.

Her faith in this vision was so compelling that even her employees believed it. Only the dogged investigation of *Wall Street Journal* reporter John Carreyrou finally exposed the truth: tests were faked, negative results dismissed or destroyed and only apparently successful outcomes acknowledged.

Preparing for this class led me to reflect on the ethical challenges I faced in my own business career. Real-world examples often resonate most strongly with students, and my experiences taught me that ethical decisions rarely involve simple choices between clear right and wrong. Every day, we face ethical decisions ranging from small temptations (lying about a child's age to save money) to life-altering choices (deciding to stop a loved one's life support). The more complex and ambiguous the decision, the more important ethical considerations become.

Despite high-profile scandals, business ethics isn't an oxymoron. While fraud at Enron, cheating at Goldman Sachs, illegal foreclosures at Countrywide Financial and Bernie Madoff's Ponzi scheme might suggest otherwise, these are anomalies. Most businesses work hard to operate within the law, and many maintain strict ethical standards. Today, nearly every sizeable company provides ethics training and many employ chief ethics and compliance officers. They've learned that ethical failures can create embarrassing, expensive messes, and that it's better to do things right the first time.

In 2015, Volkswagen got caught for intentionally programming diesel engines to turn on emission controls only when being tested. This allowed the vehicles to meet U.S. standards when, in fact, they emitted up to 40 times more nitrogen oxide. The scandal cost Volkswagen billions of dollars in fines and severely damaged its corporate reputation. The same sort of issue affected Wells Fargo and, more recently, Boeing with its 737 MAX testing shortcuts. The numerous case studies chronicling these ethical shortcomings are fascinating to read.

While researching Theranos for my class, I marveled at how thoroughly the Internet preserves history. I found Holmes' early TED talk, footage of her with Bill Clinton and countless magazine covers—from Roger Parloff's *Fortune* profile ("This CEO is out for Blood") to Ken Auletta's deep dive in *The New Yorker*. Though my Silicon Valley timeline overlapped with Theranos, it wasn't on my radar during its pre-IPO "quiet period." The thorough documentation helped me create such a compelling case study that Rich invited me to present for several subsequent years.

Throughout my career as a CEO and top-level executive, I emphasized ethical behavior and the importance of owning mistakes without fear, making a point of meeting each employee personally to reinforce the values of honesty and integrity.

Now that I'm retired, living ethically and passing these values to my family remains one of my life's most important goals. Just as religion provides moral frameworks for many, I've found that practical ethics, grounded in real-world experience and careful consideration of consequences, offers a rich guide for navigating life's complexities.

Whether in the boardroom or living room, the principles remain the same: be truthful, admit your mistakes and consider how your actions affect others.

92

NAVIGATING LIFE BEYOND BELIEF

MY ATHEISM ISN'T A DENIAL of gods, but rather a lack of belief in them. Comedian Ricky Gervais illustrated this distinction brilliantly in a conversation with television host Stephen Colbert. Gervais pointed out that historians have documented roughly 3,000 gods or deities that people either believe in today or have believed in throughout history. He then said to the deeply Catholic Colbert, "You don't believe in 2,999 gods. I just don't believe in just one more."

I believe this story helps believers better understand nonbelievers. Most Christians are monotheists like Colbert, believing in just one God. If they can imagine not believing in all the other gods, it may make it easier to understand how an atheist just adds one more god to that list. If you want me to believe in your god, you need to provide good evidence proving that he or she exists. I don't need to prove that your god doesn't exist. If that were the case, you'd have to prove that the gods of every other religion don't exist as well.

Another problematic concept for me is the presumed immortality of the human soul. Growing up, this was presented as a somewhat exclusive and core tenet of my religion, and of Christianity in general. Then, in my college history courses, I found remarkably similar beliefs predating Christianity, based on pagan traditions.

These stories existed long before the earliest Christians. Babylonians and Egyptians believed in an immortal soul, life after death and a path to heavenly reward. They believed in the god Osiris, who was killed but resurrected from the dead and brought back to life, offering followers the possibility of a new life after death. Sound familiar?

Egyptians taught that when a person died, their spirit began a journey to a Hall of Judgment, where they would be presented to God. There, one made their case for entry into eternal life. If the scales of justice came out against you, you were instead delivered to the underworld to be torn to pieces by demonic torments. The whole concept of heaven, hell and judgment before a savior were parts of pagan beliefs in Egypt long before they became part of Christianity. Why wasn't this mentioned in my church?

Most religions hold themselves up as the "one true religion" and denigrate the beliefs of millions of others, even though there are many similarities.

Hinduism embraces one supreme reality (Brahman) manifesting in many forms. Several Mother Mary temples in India are dedicated to Jesus' mother. The birth of Krishna parallels Christ's: both born of virgin mothers, both part of a holy trinity, both resurrected from the dead, both performed similar miracles and both had angels looking after them. Their teachings share common ground, too: nonviolence, forgiveness, love and prayer.

Buddhism's similarities to Christianity are equally striking. The devil tempted both Buddha and Christ, disciples traveled with each leader, they both performed miracles and rebelled against the religious elite. Both advocated "The Golden Rule"—treat others as you would wish to be treated. Both promoted peace, love and "right action"—do not kill, steal or slander.

Islam and Christianity also share similar foundations. Both have divine rules for all people and teach that obeying these rules maintains a "right" relationship with God. Both view Satan as evil and believe Jesus will return from heaven. Both support monotheism. The significant difference is that Muslims don't believe Jesus was the Son of God, though they accept everything else in the Bible and feel that nothing in it contradicts the Quran.

Religious people, whether Christians, Muslims or Hindus, often find themselves on the wrong side of critical social issues, although some faith leaders, like Dr. Martin Luther King, have been powerful forces for good. Growing up in the central United States, my observations were primarily shaped by Evangelical Christians, whose pulpits regularly issued strong warnings against movements or beliefs deemed heretical.

The track record of religious organizations is telling: In the 1600s, those believing the Earth was round were imprisoned, ridiculed and shunned. The Bible spoke of the "four corners of the Earth"—how could it have corners if it were round? When Galileo hypothesized that the Earth rotated around the sun, the Catholic Church deemed it "foolish and absurd." Though initially tolerant of Galileo, they later branded his work heretical, forcing him to recant and spend his final years isolated under house arrest.

The pattern continued through American history. Interracial marriage was anathema to most Christians during my childhood. In 1960, when I was 10, I remember it being condemned from the pulpit. Thirty-one states outlawed it, with Virginia making it a felony offense. The judge in Loving v. Virginia argued that "Almighty God" placed people on separate continents, showing he didn't intend races to mix. Jerry Falwell began his career fighting for segregation, claiming desegregation was "offensive to God."

Some Christians were slavery's strongest supporters, using both Old and New Testaments to justify human ownership. Many fought against civil rights—my devoted Christian father would seethe at TV footage of Black protesters, muttering they should "all be shot." When AIDS emerged, too many Christians turned their backs, dismissing it as a "gay" disease deserving of contempt rather than compassion.

Women's suffrage met fierce religious opposition, with certain Christians insisting the Bible relegated women to subordinate roles. When I urged my mother to speak up, her understanding and intelligence often exceeding my father's, she would demur, calling herself "a proper Christian wife." While many Christians have evolved on these issues, the pattern persists with LGBTQ+ rights. Despite 63% of Americans supporting marriage equality, many Evangelical Christians continue fighting against it, though the tide of history clearly signals they're wrong again.

Some Christians today use religion to justify inaction on climate change, arguing that Jesus' imminent return makes environmental stewardship unnecessary. They ignore biblical verses like Numbers 35:33, "You shall not pollute the land in which you live." Their ancestors used similar selective reading to deny women pain relief during childbirth, claiming it would defy God's punishment of Eve.

The pattern extends to inter-religious conflicts. In my youth, our church vilified Catholics as hell-bound idolaters and drunks—prejudice I later learned stemmed more from fear of immigrants than theology. My father, a lifelong Democrat, switched parties rather than vote for Catholic John F. Kennedy.

Through Prohibition, Christians tried forcing their views about abstinence on everyone, despite Jesus being a wine drinker and wine maker. This compulsion to make others follow their worldview represents one of my deepest disagreements with religious thinking. The same pattern appeared in battles over contraception, with religious leaders convincing Congress to ban interstate birth control information until the 1970s—though today, 98% of sexually active women have used contraception.

Steven Weinberg, winner of the 1979 Nobel Prize in Physics, captured this pattern perfectly: "With or without religion, good people can behave well and bad people can do evil; but for good people to do evil—that takes religion."

None of the major religions is free from small lunatic fringe groups that sometimes become militant. Yet typically, these groups represent only a tiny percentage of the whole. Most followers, be they Christians, Muslims or Hindus, strive to live peacefully with their fellow humans.

Ironically, when these groups have gone to war, the most vicious aggression has been aimed at factions within their own religions. The conflict between Sunni and Shia branches of Islam dwarfs any fight between Muslims and Christians or Hindus. While often portrayed as purely religious, this conflict is kept alive by Iran and Saudi Arabia's economic battle over control of the Strait of Hormuz. It's just one example of how governments and business interests manipulate and exploit religious groups for their own ends.

What frightens me most as a student of religion is how the basic human abhorrence of killing can be overcome through religious arguments. Throughout history, religious beliefs have justified slavery and murder. Various interpretations of Christianity, Judaism and Islam have supported these crimes against humanity. In Judaism, slaves received certain protections, but they remained other people's property. Early Christian authors maintained the spiritual equality of slaves and free people, while accepting slavery as an institution. The "curse of Ham," a biblical story, was used to justify enslaving African people.

In the United States, this manipulation of religion for violent ends found expression in the KKK of the 1920s, which built its ideology on Protestant Christianity while targeting Jews, Catholics, minorities and people engaged in "immoral" activities like adultery, gambling and alcohol abuse. Under the auspices of religion and scriptural justification, the KKK was responsible for thousands of lynchings between 1882 and 1968. Though virtually every Christian denomination has now denounced the KKK, this dark chapter in our history demonstrates religion's potential for justifying unconscionable acts.

Of the 3,446 lynchings of Black people between 1882 and 1968, many were in the South and instigated by the various groups operating under the KKK moniker. I was 18 years old in 1968 when these atrocities finally ended, although others have been recorded since.

It took many years for me to arrive at the beliefs now making up my view of myself and the world. I don't believe in any organized religion that claims to be the only path to salvation. I find it hard to believe any doctrine that claims to be the immutable word of God, because the words were all written by humans and humans are fallible. No religion disputes human fallibility, except maybe the Catholics about the Pope, who was human before becoming Pope, right? And I don't believe the Bible because I have read it, cover to cover.

Yet I will fight for the right of anyone to believe what they like. While I would enjoy being part of a church community, like many agnostics and atheists I feel it would be hypocritical to attend a church to take advantage of the "community" while quietly harboring a lack of belief. One thing I've learned about atheists is that they have a low tolerance for hypocrisy—it seems to bug us a lot more than it does others.

93

MORALITY BEYOND RELIGION'S INFLUENCE

SOME OF MY MORE RELIGIOUS family members sincerely worry about what happens to honesty, ethics, morality and good behavior if you pull religion out of the mix. I understand the feeling, but I don't see the issue in the same way. In fact, religions often contribute to much of the hate in the world.

In my lifetime, I've watched Jesus metamorphose from a humble servant of the poor into a symbol for gun rights, prosperity theology, hatred of those who are different, anti-science thinking, a government with little consideration for the destitute and fierce nationalism. This has to be one of the strangest transformations in human history. Religion, to the degree these changes continue, is losing its claim to be the source of good, ethical and moral behavior.

There are far better secular examples to use as a model for a "good life." It's no coincidence that philosophers and ethicists during the Enlightenment would often toss out religious considerations when attempting to create a framework for a moral, just and ethical life. The Enlightenment, which took place in the 17th and 18th centuries mostly in Western Europe, gave us influential thinkers like John Locke, Voltaire, David Hume, Thomas Jefferson, Jean-Jacques Rousseau and Immanuel Kant. They didn't say one couldn't believe in a god or gods, only that such belief was irrelevant to being good and leading a moral and ethically consistent life.

Even the founders of the United States, when attempting to create a perfect framework of government to ensure "life, liberty and justice for all," went to considerable lengths to eliminate religious considerations from government, adamantly insisting they be separate.

Not believing in the existence of God doesn't make me or anyone else a bad or immoral person. I suspect I spend more time reading and thinking about how to live a good life than many of my religious friends.

Michael Schur, the creator of *The Good Place* television series, made some great points about being a better person in his 2022 book, *How to be Perfect: The Correct Answer to Every Moral Question*. If anyone asks me what I believe, or how to have a happy and good life, I generally paraphrase Schur by saying something like this:

> *"We live on a planet with other people, and we owe them certain courtesies. This means living by rules that decent and reasonable people wouldn't reject as unfair. When contemplating whether something is okay to do, ask yourself if your friends and people you respect would come to the same conclusion you have as to what is right. If you feel these smart friends of yours would reject your idea of what to do, maybe you don't do it. Do something else. If it's still not clear, ask yourself if you'd be okay if everyone did this. What would the world be like if every single person did precisely what you planned to do in these circumstances? If the world that would result seems unfair, nonsensical or weird, maybe do something else.*
>
> *While living your life, think about the key attributes on which we judge people: kindness, generosity, loyalty, honesty, courage and determination. Now aim yourself at the exact right amount of those qualities equally, as best you can. Like Goldilocks and the Three Bears, you want to have just the right amounts.*
>
> *Aristotle said you want to strive for the middle, knowing that if you go to either extreme you're not doing things right. Our lives are all about trying to determine right from wrong, assessing how we're doing and vowing to do better next time. You may need to draw the*

line between good and bad repeatedly, but the idea isn't to stop do-
ing it, it's to keep at it.

When I talk to my granddaughters, nieces and nephews about this important subject, I usually expound on two ancient principles: "Know Thyself" and "Nothing in Excess." That's not all of it, but it's a good foundation. Being a good person is hard work, but with effort, it becomes less like a chore and more like an interesting puzzle to solve.

The key is thinking more about others and less about ourselves. We won't always get it right—we'll make mistakes and sometimes cause harm, even with good intentions. But that's okay. Take a deep breath, apologize and keep trying. As my friend Rich Marin's favorite baseball cap warns: "Hold on while I overthink this." Sometimes the simplest answer is the best: just try to do better tomorrow than you did today.

This is the path to happiness. Not the "sitting around watching a movie with friends" sort of happiness, but a deep and lasting one. It's the feeling you get from doing good, acting with honest intentions, abiding by the rules you'd want everyone to follow and causing a minimum of harm to those around you.

Two of my best friends spend their days diagnosing and fixing problems on old British motorcycles. They're exceptionally good at it and their YouTube channel has thousands of subscribers. They've become experts at sensing when something just isn't right with a particular machine, and they use that information as the starting point to finding the root of a problem that needs repair. They've learned to resist the "well, it's close enough," or "it's running pretty good," assessment and listen to that little voice telling them things are not perfect—yet.

Once on a motorcycle ride in New Zealand with Maggie, I made a boneheaded decision to impress her by doing a "stoppie." Soon after my show-off maneuver, she pulled off her helmet and said, "That's the last time I'm ever riding with you." And indeed, it was many years before she rode with me again, perhaps a decade or more.

I learned a lesson from that experience and changed. I became a model for ensuring that the passengers on my motorcycle felt comfortable and safe so they could have a great ride. My article on this topic, *The Art of Two-Upmanship: Ensuring First-time Passengers a Great Ride,* set the record for most requested reprints at the magazine where it was published.

My journey away from religion hasn't been a journey away from morality—if anything, it's brought me closer to the core of what it means to be good. I've learned that ethics isn't about following rules written in ancient texts, but about the daily choice to make the world a little better than we found it.

For those who find community and inspiration in their faith, I offer not criticism but a gentle challenge: Look closely at what your religious community actually does, not just what it says. Does it bring people together or push them apart? Does it expand the circle of human dignity or contract it? Are its doors truly open to all, or just to those who look and think alike? The answers to these questions matter far more than any doctrine or creed.

I may stand outside the walls of organized religion, but I've found that goodness needs no supernatural foundation. It grows naturally from the simple recognition that we share this brief moment in time with other conscious beings, each carrying their own hopes, fears and dignity.

My moral compass points not toward heaven but toward humanity. When faced with difficult choices, I ask not "What would God do?" but "What would make the world more just, more kind, more worthy of the intelligence and empathy we humans are capable of?"

This isn't always easy. Living ethically requires constant attention, like tending a garden that could always use a little more care. But I've found profound meaning in this work—in choosing kindness when it would be easier to be cruel, in standing up for others when it would be simpler to stay silent, in admitting mistakes when pride urges otherwise.

Love, that most celebrated of virtues, means nothing without action. We must do the work that love demands: the daily acts of kindness, the hard conversations, the standing up for those who cannot stand up for themselves. This is my faith now—not in gods or sacred texts, but in our human capacity to grow, to learn and to be better than we were yesterday.

I'm still working on it. We all are. And perhaps that's the most sacred thing of all.

EPILOGUE

AS THE ROAD AHEAD GROWS shorter than the road behind, I find myself reflecting on how the six distinct threads of my life—health challenges, automotive passions, business ventures, family connections, motorcycle adventures and spiritual questioning—have woven together to create something greater than their parts. Like the precision engineering of a fine automobile or the intricate coding of software, each element has played its vital role.

Looking back at these six threads of my life, I'm struck by how they've influenced and enriched each other. My heart condition gave me an even greater appreciation of precision engineering. My business experiences helped me approach my spiritual questions with analytical rigor. My love of motorcycles provided solace during family tragedies. Nothing exists in isolation.

We all have our own threads—the different passions, challenges, relationships and questions that make up who we are. Perhaps you're not into cars or motorcycles, but you might have your own outlet that brings you joy and teaches you about life. Maybe your challenges aren't medical, but you've faced other obstacles that have shaped your character. Your family story might be different from mine, but you've likely experienced both profound connections and painful losses.

The key isn't in which threads make up your life, but in recognizing how they weave together to create something unique and meaningful. Don't be afraid to pursue multiple passions, to question deeply held beliefs, to take calculated risks or to change direction when needed. Let your struggles inform your triumphs. Let your joys temper your sorrows. Every experience, every relationship, every challenge and victory become part of your distinct pattern.

As I look ahead, I know my warranty may be running low, but my enthusiasm for life remains high. There are still roads to explore, startups to mentor, family moments to cherish and perhaps a few more mechanical marvels to add to the garage. While I can't predict what's next, I know my heart will be in it—just as it has been from the start.

INDEX

3 Step Hideaway, 430
4-H Club, 214, 485, 500

A

A Grief Observed, 451
Aaron, Geoff, 382
Accelerated U-Turns, 414
Acura MDX, 313
Acura NSX, 38, 48, 51–60, 62, 63, 65, 68–72
Adriatic Sea, 389, 391
Adversity Quotient (AQ), 229, 231
Agnew, Spiro, 485
Agnostic, 117, 447, 503, 505, 506, 508, 517
Alexandria, Minnesota, 37
Allied Radio Store, 96
Al-Qaeda, 502
Alsop, Stewart, 122
Altos Computer, 121
Amaury Sports Organisation (ASO), 354, 355
Amber Alert, 372
American Forensic League, 458
Amidon, Stephen and Thomas MDs, 27
Anabaptists, 491
Andes (Mountain Range), 347, 348
Andretti, Mario, 295

Anglican church, 236, 469
Apache Mall (Rochester, MN), 86, 94, 96, 99, 107
Apple Computer, 117, 118, 182, 189
Arab Islamist extremists, 503
Arcinue, Edgardo, MD, 273
Aristotle, 242, 244, 502, 519
Arizona Commerce Authority (ACA), 77, 191, 192
Arizona Precision Motorcycle Drill Team, 408, 422
Arizona Sand Dunes, 364
Armageddon, 491–493
Artist's Drive, 376
Assemblies of God Church, 492
AT&T, 5, 76, 126–134, 148, 158, 171, 176, 264, 272
Atacama Desert, 350, 360
Atkinson, Rowan, 62
Auletta, Ken (New Yorker Magazine), 510
Austin Healey, 40
Autostrada, 395
Avery Island, 424
AZ Highway Patrol Training Class, 396, 425

B

Babylon and Infidelity Foredoomed, 492

Babylonians, 512

Baker, Stuart ("Stu"), 119, 123

Banner, Ed MD (Mayo Clinic), 78–84

Banner, Ed, JR - MD, 84

Baptists, 492

Baratz, Alan, 372

Barnes, Mark, 444

Barnett, David, 72

Barrie, Ontario, 236, 237

Barry, Doug, 488

Batko, Chuk, 101, 108, 109, 124, 186, 250, 268, 471

Bergen Church, 204

Better Life Media, 185, 187

Bianchi, Joseph, 192

Bible, 29, 145, 225, 233, 312, 447, 452–455, 468, 490, 493, 502, 503, 505, 506, 513, 514, 517

Bible School, 450, 506

Big Bear, CA, 275

Big Brothers and Big Sisters of America, 500

BigFix, 76, 178, 179, 180, 182, 400

Birkmann, Annette, 443, 445

Bivouac (Dakar Rally), 354, 355

BJ's Brewhouse, 20

Black Death, 497

Blondi, Tom, 192

BMW F650 (MC), 443

BMW G450X (MC), 354

BMW GS's (MC), 328, 343, 360, 435, 436, 439, 440, 441, 442

BMW M5, 53, 54, 56, 57

Bockelson, Jan, 491

Bologna, 389, 394, 395, 432

Bombardier Sea-Doo Speedster, 293, 296

Bonhoeffer, Dietrich, 465, 466, 502

Bonte, John, 119, 120

Boorman, Charley, 347, 354, 440

Borud, Russ, 109

Boston Globe, 499

Bovinette, Zach, 129

Boy Scouts, 500

Boys & Girls Club, 279, 500

Brahman (Hindu God), 513

Brake & Evade (B&E motorcycle exercise), 415, 419, 441

Bright, Bill, 233

Brightman, Thomas, 492

Bristol, England, 49

Brophy College Preparatory, 501

Brown, Kevin, 503

Brown, Wendell, 122, 188

Buchhalter, Francine, 24

Buckland, Brian, 47, 49

Buck's Restaurant (CA), 376

Bulger, Mike (Mayo HS), 241

Bump & Go (Motorcycle exercise), 413

Bungee jumping, 345, 370, 371

Bureau of Land Management (BLM), 361

Burr Trail (UT), 341

Bush, George W. , 480

Buttonwillow (CA), 377

C

Cacciatore, Joanne, PH.D., 284, 289

Calvary Chapel, 493

Camp Koinonia, 236, 469

Campos do Jordão, Brazil, 386

Campus Crusade for Christ, 452

Cannon Falls, MN, 101

Carreyrou, John (WSJ), 509

Carrow, Jack, 97

Castaneda, Aldo MD, 14

Catholic Church, 499, 501, 514

Cessna Pilot Training Program, 368

Chalk Hill Winery, 15

Chamberlain, Troy, 54

Chapman, Colin, 45, 49, 67

Chilecito, 357, 358

China Ranch (Date Farm), 379

Christ, 233, 452, 453, 455, 465, 468, 469, 490, 491, 492, 493, 506, 513

Christians, Christianity, 29, 197, 214, 233, 236, 247, 312, 313, 450–453, 455, 463, 465–470, 480, 483, 490–499, 503, 506–508, 512–516

Circuit of the Americas, 401, 402

CitySearch, 53, 76, 154–157, 161, 162, 175, 176

Clausen, Bob, 86

Cleveland Clinic, 21

Clinton, Bill, 510

Coca leaves, 349, 356

Code, Keith, 396, 397, 401, 402, 404, 431

Colbert, Stephen, 512

College of St. Thomas, MN, 251

Colorado, 46, 48, 61, 83, 89, 90, 132, 264, 266, 343, 386, 429

Colorado River, 296

Coma, Marc, 352

COMDEX, 117, 122

Control Data Corp. (CDC), 5, 76, 118, 119, 176, 181, 120, 121, 123, 124, 256

Conway, Ron, 121

Cooper Center, 242, 245

Copiapo, 354, 356

Copper Canyon, Mexico, 21, 336, 360, 442

Coppola, Francis Ford, 15, 16

Cordell, Bill (Schaak), 107

Cosby, Bill, 14, 17

Cote, Ellen (Schaak), 109

Count Rugen, 286

COVID, 288, 477

Cowen, David, 245

Croatia Rixos, 393

Croton-on-Hudson, NY, 141, 144, 243, 290, 295, 297

Crowbar Café and Saloon, 374

Crusades, 498, 499

Cruz, Nicky, 233

Cub Scouts, 214

Cucciolo (Ducati), 433

D

Dakar Desert Checkpoint, 352

Dakar Rally, 327, 346, 347, 348, 351, 354, 355, 359, 360, 429, 437

Dalmatian Coast, 390, 440

Darwin, Charles, 28, 29, 480, 479, 497

Davis, Peter, 124

Dawkins, Richard, PH.D., 454

Death Valley, CA, 374, 376, 378, 379, 380

Debate, 6, 28, 30, 165, 234, 238, 239, 240, 244, 245, 452, 453, 457–460, 477, 498, 505

Del Monte, Frank, 444, 458, 331

Dennis, Ron, 68

Department of Public Safety (DPS), 408

Descartes, 242, 244, 502

Despres, Cyril, 352

DeValeria, Patrick MD, 19, 20

Devil's Golf Course (CA), 376

Devil's Highway (CA), 423

Digital Den, 76, 116, 118, 151, 165

Dilly, Jeanne, 341

Dilly, Mark, 337, 341, 364

DNA, 210, 316, 319, 320, 505

Dobie, Roy, 233, 234

Dolliff, David, 86, 87

Dominion Voting Systems, 459

Donovan, Greg, 107

Doremus, John (KNXR), 92

Dragoo, Bill, 430, 442

Dubrovnik, 392, 393

Ducati, 342, 375, 389, 391, 432, 438, 439, 440, 441

Ducati Factory, 389, 395, 432–435

Ducati Multistrada , 391, 434, 441

Dunning-Kruger Effect, 368, 372, 429, 489

Dyson, Ester, 122, 142, 144, 158,

E

Edinburgh, Scotland, 297, 299, 300, 301, 350

Egan, Peter, 48

Egyptians, 512, 513

Eiesland, Gary, 94, 95, 97, 110–114

Einstein, Arthur Jr. , 145, 339, 444

Eisner, Andrew, 376

Ek, Brian, 487

Eliquis, 28

Emergence Capital, 76, 177, 178, 181, 182

Emotional Intelligence (EQ), 226, 227, 228

End Times, The, 490, 493

Engel, Brett, 57, 102

Enlightenment, The, 476, 518

Enron, 510

Erdogan, Recep Tayyip, 498

Este, Carl, 95

Ethics board, 461

Eurodam (Holland America), 324

Evangelical Lutheran Church, 465, 472

Evangelicals, 29, 447, 455, 514, 515

Experimental College (U of MN), 242, 243, 245, 467

Ezequelle, David, 376

F

Fairmont High School, 37, 232, 234, 235, 239, 240, 243, 457, 458

Fairmont Sentinel Newspaper, 208, 464

Fairmont, MN, 11, 37, 39, 40, 109, 150, 167, 195, 200, 206–212, 233, 235, 237, 327, 329, 433, 463–465

Faith Lutheran Brethren Church (MN), 461, 465

Falwell, Jerry, 514

Felber, Bub, 39

Felber, Effie, 39, 46

Felber, Tom, 39

Fergus Falls, MN, 224, 465

Field Motor Training Officer (FMTO), 410, 419, 420

Firebird Raceway, 407, 418

Fish Tanks, 309, 310

Fitzgerald, Arlene, 324

Fitzgerald, Evelyn, 324

Fitzwater, John, 344

Fixed-wing gliders, 370

Flathers, Harley, 90, 91, 92

FLDS (Fundamentalist Church of Latter Day Saints), 492, 497, 499

Fletcher, Tom, 109

Flores, Ricardo, MD, 273

Ford of Bruinen, 344

Forrester, Andy, 395, 426

Fox Glacier, 344

Frazier, Gregory, 444

Freeborn, Mark, 107

French Voyaguers Language Camp, 324

Frogner, Dave, 92

Ft. Hunter Liggett, 377

Furnace Creek (Death Valley), 376, 378, 379

Furth, Fred, 15, 16

G

Galileo, 29, 514

Gambill, Linda, 469

Game of Thrones, 392
Gardner, Howard, 226
Gates, Bill, 125, 162, 165
Gates, Lisa, 245
Gaylord Opryland Hotel, 422
Geary, Colette PH.D., 281
George Lake, Fairmont, 211, 212, 463
Gervais Ricky, 512
Gibney, Alex, 461
Gilda, 47, 285, 313
Giles, Ernie, 99
Gilligan's Island, 269
Gilmore, Dan, 461
Ginther, Paul, 108, 109, 125
Glatzer, Ross, 134, 135, 140, 231
Globe, AZ, 418, 426
GoAz (Motorcycle Dealer), 442,
Golden Gloves, 218, 220
Goldman Sachs, 510
Goleman, Daniel, 226
Gonzaga University, 502
Goodwin, Chris, 66
Google, 121, 164, 182–184, 204, 376
Gordon, Kevin, 108
Gordon, Robbie, 352
GoTourNZ, 344
Graham, Billy, 233
Gravley, Charles, 27
Gravley, John, 40–42, 85, 129, 133, 197,
    224, 248, 250, 317, 465, 468, 469
Grodsky, Larry, 431, 444, 445
Grolle, Johann, 476
Gross, Bill, 53
Gulf of Kvarner, 391
Gulla, Brian, 232

H

Haartsen, Jaap, 197
Hagen, Paul, 100, 101, 108, 109, 250,
Hagerman, Nancy, 234, 460
Haines Lake, 237

Hairston, Tanaha, 192
Hall of Judgement, 513
Hall, Corky, 186, 187
Hand of the Desert, 354
Hang gliding, 369
Hansen, Jennifer, 336
Hansen, Roger, 336, 338, 436
Harley Davidson, 151, 152, 153, 182,
    365, 432
Harper, Mairi, 287
Harris, Sam, 497
Hasse, Ted, 232, 234, 235, 457, 460
Hauck, Nikki (Kraft), 319
Heidegger, Martin, 243
Heidi (Rottweiler), 261, 275
Henry, Patrick, 235
Herem, Alma (Gravley), 197
Herem, Bertha, 197
Herem, Gwen, 24
Herem, Jacob Olaus Knutson, 197
Herem, Knut, 197
Herem, Oscar, 197
Herem, Ragnhild Bakka, 197
Herem, Ron, 24, 185, 197, 210, 310,
    314, 317
Hethel, UK, 44
Hidden Valley Resort, 264
Hill, Napoleon, 233
Hindu (Hinduism), 499, 513–516
Hinrichs, Ted, 234
Hisrich, Robert, Dr. , 191, 192
Hobbit, 344
HOGWILD, 152, 153, 182
Hollister, 379
Holmes, Elizabeth, 509
Holy Trinity Lutheran Church, New
    Prague, 318
Homer Tunnel, NZ, 344
Honda Africa Twin, 439, 441
Honda Grom, 437, 441

Honda ST1300, 439

Honda Valkyrie, 339

Honda VFR, 375

Hopf, Pat, 186

Hotel Cubo, 390

How to be Perfect, 519

Hume, David, 518

Hummer Winblad Venture Partners, 125, 161

Hummer, John, 125

Huntington Hospital, Pasadena, 273, 274

Husband, Rick, 43

Huvden, Erve, 209

Hyde, Jim, 431, 442

I

IBM, 5, 76, 78, 122, 130, 131, 134, 140, 142, 144, 146, 147, 149, 155, 158, 159, 181

ICU (Intensive Care Unit), 273, 274, 279

Immanuel Lutheran Grade School, 213, 216

Inherit the Wind, 479

INR, 25

International Home Exchange, 297, 298

International Science & Engineering Fair, 310, 478

Iowa City, IA, 41, 42, 85, 247, 331, 467, 469, 490

IQ Test, 226

Iquique, 350, 351, 352

Irvine, Paul, 460

Irving, Edward, 492

Isaacson, Portia, 122

Islam (Islamic Jihads) , 394, 498, 499, 503, 513, 516

Izguerra, Aristeo (Izzy), 62

J

Jackson, Dave, 121

Jackson, Jess, 15

Jaguar XJ-S, 109, 124, 125

Jaguar XK120, 37

Jay and Ray, 210, 212

Jefferson, Thomas, 518

Jeffs, Amanda, 236

Jeffs, Beryl, 236

Jeffs, Clint, 236

Jeffs, Jerry, 236, 469

Jeffs, Stephanie, 236

Jesus Freaks, 41, 85, 247, 331, 467, 468, 490, 508

Jews, Jewish, Judaism, 98, 492, 497, 499, 516

Johnson, Dwain, 240

Jones, John E. III, 480

Jones, Tom, 90, 93, 94,

K

Kant, Immanuel, 242, 518

Kapitea Ridge Lodge, 345

Kasson, MN, 43, 103, 106–108

Kawasaki KZ1000, 408

Kea (parrot), 344

Keith Code California Superbike School, 396

Keller, Charles R. PH.D., 242

Kennedy, John F. , 222, 476, 515

Kenyon, Larry L. (Sergeant), 407

King Harald III (Bluetooth), 197

King, Martin Luther Dr. , 514

Kirven, Robert PH.D., 502

KKK, 516

Klauser, George, 97

Klein, Mark, 188

Kliewer, Donald L. , 94

Kline, Paul, 54, 55

Knappe, Dan, 107

Knappe, Pati, 240, 306

Knutson Station, 416
KNXR (Rochester), 41, 93, 94, 109
Kost, Rob, 139, 140, 152, 154, 158, 243
Kraft, Kendall (Nikki's Dad), 319
Kramer, MD, 11, 12, 219
Kramer, MD, 11, 12
Krishna, 513
KROC Radio/Television, 79, 90
Krugle, 181, 183, 184, 189
Krugler, Ken, 182
KTM Adventure, 352, 435, 439, 441
Kurzweil, Ray, 476

L

LA Times, 370
Lab Rats, 309
Lanoue, Mitch, 416
LaPlante, Gary, 381, 431
Larsen, Alma, 198, 200
Larsen, Annie (Hackett), 483
Larsen, Carl Gustav, 198, 210
Larsen, Carl Gustav, 198, 210
Larsen, Dennis, 39, 198, 208
Larsen, Donny, 39, 198, 208
Larsen, Effie, 39, 46, 198, 200
Larsen, Elvin, 198-200, 201, 207-210,
    222
Larsen, Eric McKinley, 5, 27, 273-
    279, 281-283, 285, 288, 298, 320,
    449, 451, 455
Larsen, Ginger, 3, 7, 22, 24, 55, 155,
    158, 160, 196, 226, 227, 250, 267,
    269-271, 275, 279-283, 285, 286,
    290-292, 295, 298, 303, 305-310,
    313, 315-318, 320-325, 475, 476,
    478, 479
Larsen, Ginny, 256-261, 263, 267, 269,
    270
Larsen, Gladys (Vogen), 198, 199,
    208, 209
Larsen, Gordon, 198, 199

Larsen, John Walter, 198
Larsen, Jurene (Phaneuf), 196, 201,
    209, 217, 469
Larsen, Kari or Carrie (Thorson), 198
Larsen, Leif, 137, 196, 202-206, 209,
    210, 212, 217, 218, 221, 223, 327, 329,
    330, 333, 334, 338, 384, 385, 433, 469
Larsen, Maggie, 2, 3, 7, 20-22, 24,
    46, 55-57, 76, 109, 120, 121, 124, 129,
    133, 137, 140, 141, 155, 159-161, 170,
    181, 190, 196, 225, 227, 249-257, 259,
    260, 261, 267-273, 276, 278-281,
    296, 298-300, 302, 309, 311,
    313-317, 322-325, 334, 341, 342, 362,
    363, 392, 473, 501, 520
Larsen, Naomi (Woychick), 24, 196,
    201, 217, 224, 465
Larsen, Paul T. , 198, 199, 202, 217, 311,
    312, 316, 501
Larsen, Roger, 89, 137, 198, 208, 212,
    315, 316
Larsen, Ruth (Herem), 124, 195, 197,
    201, 217, 267, 311
Larsen, Steve (Idaho), 1, 2
Larsen, Steve (Triathlete), 2
Larsen, Wilmer, 198, 199
Larson, Randy, 41
Lee, Witness, 468
Leno, Jay, 48, 58, 69
Lewis, C.S., 242, 450, 451, 466
Lewis, John MD, 14, 27
LGBTQ+, 100, 498, 515
Libby Foods, 89
Lindsay, Hal, 491
Lion's Club, 99, 104
Little League, 208, 216, 286, 500
Ljubljana, 390, 391
Lock Ness monster, 300
Locke, Chris, 142, 143, 147-148, 167
Locke, John, 518

London, 44, 45

London, Jack, 215

Long Game, The, 269, 471, 472, 473

Los Angeles (LA), 46, 53, 89, 94, 95, 129, 131, 133–138, 146, 161, 176, 271, 278, 280, 298, 343, 370, 482,

Los Padres National Forest, 377

Lotus Elan, 4, 5, 38, 42–48, 50–52, 55, 57, 59, 64, 67–70, 73, 101, 102, 106, 114, 229, 293, 294, 323

Lutheran Catechism, 452, 465

Lynchings, 516

M

Madeline Island, 110, 113

Madoff, Bernie, 510

Magee, Don, 51

Magee, Kathy (Gravley), 51

Maltz, Maxwell, 233

Mankato, MN, 85, 91, 209, 239, 242–244, 247, 467, 485

Marin, Kim, 341

Marin, Rich, 336, 339, 422, 444, 461, 510, 520

Mark of the Beast, 490

Martin, Keith, 61

Mary Mayo Hall, 234

Mascorro, Skip, 336, 337, 338

Massine, Carrie, 186

Mast, Mark (Rev.), 202, 203

Mathews, Harry, 61

Mayo Clinic, 19, 21, 23, 24, 72, 78, 86, 87, 458

Mayo Clinic, Phoenix, 19, 20

Mayo Clinic, Rochester, MN, 21, 23, 24

Mayo High School, 84, 88, 235, 239, 240, 241, 243, 305, 452, 458

Mayo, Edward (Ned), 87

Mayo, Joanne, 88,

Mayo, Joseph III, (Joe), 88, 89

Mayo, Rita, 87

Mayowood , 86, 87, 89

Mayowood Galleries, 87

Mazda RX-7, 51

MBD (Multiple Bike Disorder), 438

McGregor, Ewan, 354, 440

McLaren, 38, 48, 58, 60–66, 68–70, 72, 73

McNellis, Jason, 478

Mehta, Rajal, MD, 25

Mere Christianity, 466

Michael, Daniel, 296

Michigan State University, 234

Mikesh, Mr. , 86, 87

Milbrandt, Butch, 364

Miller, William, 492

Milwaukee, WI, 46, 96, 98, 130

Minneapolis (Twin Cities), 46, 53, 96, 100, 101, 108, 109, 118, 119, 121, 126, 130, 131, 161, 168, 175, 176, 177, 185, 246, 247, 249, 250, 313, 317, 367

Miracles, 466

MISS Foundation, 229, 284, 285, 288

Moab, UT, 21, 296, 360, 430, 442

Mohn, Stan, 99

Mojave, 378

Moki Dugway, 341

Montgomery, Alaina, 284

Montgomery, Kelli, 284

Montoya, Inigo, 286, 287

Moody, Dwight L. , 29

Moral Compass, 521

Morality, 240, 448, 476, 478, 518, 521

Mostar, 389, 393, 394

Mother Mary, 513

Moto Trials Competition, 381

MotoGP, 333, 401, 402, 429, 433

Motorcycle Consumer News (MCN), 181, 342, 365, 396, 429, 443

Motorcycle Review Shootouts, 437, 440

Motorcycle Safety Foundation (MSF), 431

Motorcycle Wheelies, 396, 403, 404, 406

MotoVentures, 381

Mount Vernon, IA, 41

Mr. Quick, 468

Mrozek, Slawomir, 86

Munger Imports, 42

Munger, Jeff, 42

Murra, Dave, 51

Murray, Gordon, 48, 58, 61, 69, 70, 73

Murray's famous steakhouse, 249

Muslim, 393, 433, 498, 499, 513, 514, 515, 516

N

Nachenmoser, Adam, 491

Nacimiento River, 377

Nagano, Towru (Schaak), 94, 95

National Forensic League, 234

National Research Council of Canada, 482

Nee, Watchman, 468

Nelson, Lori, 186

Neretva River, 389, 393

Net Perceptions, 53, 76, 126, 161–170, 174, 175, 181, 185, 186, 228, 295, 494

New Testament, 451

New York, 46, 47, 53, 58, 86, 134, 138, 139, 141–143, 152, 154, 158, 160, 161, 163, 166, 167, 233, 243, 278, 280, 282, 290, 293, 294, 296, 297, 320, 324, 334, 340, 372, 457, 487

New Zealand, 10, 19, 327, 343, 344, 345, 387, 440, 499, 520

Newsom, Gavin, 488

Newton, Isaac, 497, 502

Nightingale, Earl, 233

Nissan 300ZX, 53

Nixon, Richard M. , 222, 223, 467, 485

Non-governmental Organization (NGO), 459

Norman, Larry, 468

North Branch, Ontario, Canada, 204, 206

Northwest Motorcycle School, 431

O

O'Connell, Frank, 444

Odens, Jim, 234, 460

Of Mice and Men, 241, 452

On the Origin of Species, 479

Onward Christian Soldiers, 453

Opatija, 391, 392

Open Systems, 124, 125, 126, 161, 176, 256

Open-Heart Surgery, 22, 30

Osiris, 512

P

Pahrump, Nevada, 374, 375

Painter, Dan, 89

Parachuting, 369

Paragliding, 370, 371, 373

Parkin, David, 99, 100

Parks, Lee, 431

Parloff, Roger, 510

Paso de San Francisco, 348, 356, 358

Passo Giau, 390

Pastor Ben Hilding, 320

Pastor Rod (Eden Prairie), 471, 472, 473, 474, 506, 507

Patinkin, Mandy, 286

Pavey, Simon, 352, 354

Peale, Norman Vincent, 233

Pennekamp, John, 252

Perron, Bill, 234

Perry, George, 487

Personalization Summit, 126, 167, 176

Phoenix International Raceway (PIR), 407

Phoenix Police Moto Officer Training, 396, 407, 421, 425, 431

Phoenix, AZ, 2, 24, 46, 47, 49, 72

PhoneTell (CallSpark), 122, 188, 189, 191

Pilatus PC-12, 372

Pinker, Steven, 476, 477

Pirate, dead, 261, 262, 263

Pittendrigh, Steve, 372

Pivka, Slovenia, 391

Plato (Ancient Philosopher), 242, 244, 502

PLATO (Control Data) , 119, 120, 121, 151, 242

Pochettino, MD, 23

Polaris RZR, 48, 360, 361

Polaris Slingshot, 48, 356, 366, 367

Popoff, Peter, 26

Powell, Sidney, 459

Precision Motorcycle Riding, 384

Price, Robert M. , 123, 126

Pridmore, Reg, 431

Prodigy Services Co. /IBM, 5, 76, 134–140, 143, 149–154, 157, 158, 165, 176, 230, 231, 243, 278, 371, 486, 487

Prognosticum Theologicum, 491

Puerto Peñasco (Rocky Point, Mexico), 362

Purmamarca, 347, 348

Q

Queen's Theater, London, 45

Quran, 513

R

Rabbits, 212, 220, 221

Radar Gun, 412

Radio Shack, 97

Rainey, Wayne, 397

Rainier, Gil, 126, 127

Rainy River, Ontario, Canada, 202, 203, 204

Rau, Fred, 437

Rauner, Bruce, 115, 341, 489

Redman, Tami, 78, 82, 107

Reiff, Don, 442

Reilly, John, 218, 219

Revenaugh, Jim, 341

Richmond, Burt, 342

Richter, Philip, 15, 48, 60, 344

RIDER Magazine, 181, 407, 444

Ridgedale Mall, Wayzata, MN, 108, 249

RoadRunner, 429

Roberts, Kenny, 333

Roberts, Oral, 26

Robertson, Pat, 26

Rochester State Junior College, 75, 86

Rochester, MN, 21, 23, 24, 41, 50, 52, 75, 78–80, 84–87, 89–93, 95–97, 99–101, 105–109, 115, 125, 235, 237, 239, 242, 247, 248, 311, 314, 316, 329, 331, 332, 370, 452, 469, 470

Rogaland, Norway, 197

Roller, Jim, 37

Rolls Royce, 15

Rousseau, Jean-Jacques, 518

Russell, Charles Taze, 492

Russell, Jerry, 41

Ruthenbeck, Norm, 213, 214, 215

Rutherford, J.F. , 492

RV (Recreational Vehicle), 311

S

Saffell, Clayton, 57, 73

Safire, William, 485

San Diego, 20

San Francisco, 15, 121, 126, 167, 179, 189, 313, 376, 443, 445, 475, 488
San Jose Mercury News, 461
San Luis Obispo, 376, 377
Sarajevo, 393, 394
Satan, 513
Sauda, Norway, 197
Schaak Electronics, 42, 43, 75, 78, 94–99, 101, 107–110, 118, 119, 125, 165, 166, 181, 370
Schaak, Richard, 94, 116, 118
Schley, Lloyd, 243, 244
Schur, Michael, 519
Scopes, John T. , 479
Scotch (MaCallum and others), 299–304
Screwtape Letters, 466
Scripps Memorial Hospital, 20
SCUBA, 253, 255
Searle, David, 342
Searle, Donny, 342
Seifert, Gary, 216
Selvig, David, 242, 466
Selvig, Mike, 465, 466
Senna, Ayrton, 65, 67–69
Sentinel System (Dakar), 355
Serenity Houses, 337, 338
Serra de Estrela, 387
Serup, Jens, 210
Sheep, 297, 303
Shell, Bill, 127
Shia, 516
Shields, D. Michael, 94, 109, 482
Shields, Denny, 125
Shipley, Chris, 188
Ski Patrol, 266
Skiff, Jim (Schaak), 95, 96, 97, 166
Skinner, Tom, 233
Skipper's Canyon, 440
Sky Ranch Airport, 364

Skyline Drive, 377
Slater, Stanley (Fairmont), 217
Slovenia, 390, 391
Smith, Chuck, 493
Smith, Diane, 374, 375
Smith, Joseph, 492
Smith, Malcolm, 347
Smothers Brothers, 14, 15, 17
Smothers, Tommy, 16, 17
Smothers-Remick Ridge Vineyards, 16
Snyder, Bill (Fairmont), 219
Snyder, Steven PH.D., 161, 162, 228, 295
Soboba Mountain, 370
Social Quotient (SQ), 229
Socrates, 242, 475, 497
St. Andrew's Lutheran Church, 471
St. John, Rob, 341
St. John, Urch, 341
St. Paul Bible Institute, 202
St. Paul Venture Capital (SPVC), 76, 162, 174, 175, 177, 182, 185, 186
St. Peter's Cathedral, 501
Stephenson, Frank, 67, 68
Stewartville, MN, 96
Stickney, Diana (Kirven), 261
Stickney, Isaac, 261, 263
Stickney, Joseph (Joe), 501
Stickney, Maria, 261
Stickney, Robert, 261, 262, 263, 298, 303
Stifel, Michael, 491
Stone, W. Clement, 233
Stoppie , 520
Stratton Oakmont, 486, 487
Streets of Willow Springs, 398
Studebaker Avanti, 37
Suk, Bob, 99, 104, 105
Sunday, Billy, 29

Sunni, 516

Surgery, 9–11, 13, 14, 16, 17, 19–24, 25, 27, 34, 224, 247, 273, 274, 277–279, 287, 312, 483

Surprised by Joy, 466

Suzuki 125, 335, 384

Suzuki Hayabusa, 374, 375

Suzuki V-Strom, 343, 437, 438, 439, 440, 441

Swedenborg, Imanuel, 502

T

Tabasco hot sauce, 424

Tail of the Dragon (Deal's Gap), 423

Taliban, 503

Tango, 86

Tapscott, Koena, 362

Tapscott, Ralph, 362, 363

Tasman Sea, 345

Taylors Falls, 333

Texas Tech University, 245

Thanos, 455

The Absolute Sound, 482

The Art of Two-Upmanship, 521

The Dark Night of the Soul, 283

The Fellowship of the Ring, 344

The Glass Menagerie, 241, 305

The Golden Rule, 503, 513

The Good Place, 519

The Inventor: Out for Blood in Silicon Valley, 461

The Perfectionists, 72

The Princess Bride, 286, 287

The Problem of Pain, 466

The Ride is All, 444

The Sound of Music, 306, 308

Theranos, 461, 509, 510

Thomas, Lorraine, 237

Thompson Chain Reference, 453

Thunderbird School of Global Mgmt., 76, 191, 192

Tibirke, Denmark, 198, 210,

Tieden, Mike, 107

Tierra del Fuego, 443

Tikki (the cat), 237, 313

Tocopilla, 350

Tolkien, J.R.R., 242, 437

Tombstone Ridge, 265

Toole, Floyd, 482

Tortilla Flat (AZ), 418

Toseland, James, 397

Traffic law - Brazil, 387

Transient Global Amnesia (TGA), 32,33

Trembly, Gene, 218

Trials Bike (Motorcycle), 381, 382, 384, 439

Triumph Speed Triples, 403, 404

Triumph Spitfire, 41, 43, 85, 248, 469

Triumph Tiger, 343, 439, 440, 441

Trom, Randy, 93

Truth, 28–30, 48, 66, 104, 106, 134, 135, 214, 237, 267, 444, 457–459, 461, 478, 481–483, 494, 508, 509, 511

Tsurugi Japanese Restaurant, 377

Turner, Gary, 49

Tutterow, Sam, 186

Tuttle, Mark, 407

U

UNESCO, 394

United Kingdom, 44

University of Minnesota Heart Hospital, 12, 14, 17, 27

University of MN, 161, 176, 242, 245, 485

Uzunoglu, Kazim (Kaz), 436, 441

V

Vacation Bible School, 506

Van Zant, Claire, 241, 242, 453, 467, 468

Vanzyl, Adrian, 188
Vatican, 501
Velocity Awards, 425, 426, 427
Venice, 432, 389, 390
Victorians, 475
Victory Motorcycles, 366
Vietnam War, 501
Vincent, William, MD, 273
Vold, Judy, 465
Vold, Morris, Rev. , 461, 465
Volkswagen, 510
Voltaire, 518
von Bredow, Rafaela, 476

W

Waksachi Lodge, 379
Wall Street Journal, 148, 457, 509
Walton, Kirby, 85, 469
Wangensteen, Owen MD, 14
Warfarin, 25, 28, 33
Watch Tower Society, 492
Wayne, Miller MD, 27
Weinberg, Steven, 515
Westphal, Lise, 210
When Prophecy Fails, 493
Whistling, 211, 215,
White, Roland (Rev.), 202
Wigley, Griff, 382
Wilkerson, David, 233
Will, Christie, 3, 7, 196, 227, 228, 288, 316–318, 320–325, 472

Will, Emmy, 196, 322, 324, 325
Will, Jeff, 323, 325
Will, Parker, 196, 230, 322, 323, 324, 325
Williams, Tennessee, 305
Willow Springs Bible Camp (CA), 236, 396, 398, 463
Wilson, Myron MD, 86
Winblad, Ann, 53, 124–126, 161, 162, 165, 167, 168, 304
Winchester, Simon, 72, 483
Women's suffrage, 514
Wood, Melinda, 298
Woodfield Mall, Chicago, 98
Woodies Wheels (Spoked), 360
World Superbike, 429
Woychick, John, 87, 364
Wright, Ralph PD.D., 239, 452

Y

YMCA, 224
Youth for Christ, 233, 469

Z

Zabriskie Point, 375
Zadar, 392
Zagreb, 394
Zehnenter, Judy, 108, 109
Zelazny, Roger, 120
Zumbro River, 86, 111, 384, 385